THE XIIITH WORLD CONGRESS OF PROCEDURAL LAW: THE BELGIAN AND DUTCH REPORTS

THE XIIITH WORLD CONGRESS OF PROCEDURAL LAW: THE BELGIAN AND DUTCH REPORTS

A.W. JONGBLOED (ED.)

intersentia

Antwerp – Oxford – Portland

Intersentia Publishers
Groenstraat 31
BE-2640 Mortsel
Belgium
Tel.: +32 3 680 15 50
Fax: +32 3 658 71 21

The XIIIth World Congress of Procedural Law : the Belgian and Dutch Reports
A.W. Jongbloed (ed.)

Antwerp – Oxford – Portland
www.intersentia.com

ISBN 978-90-5095-860-8
D/2008/7849/102
NUR 822

TABLE OF CONTENTS

LIST OF CONTRIBUTORS

B. ALLEMEERSCH, Attorney at Law, Brussels, Associate Professor of Civil Procedure, Faculty of Law, Catholic University of Leuven, Belgium

W.D.H. ASSER, Justice of the Dutch Supreme Court, Professor of Civil Procedure, Faculty of Law, Leiden University, the Netherlands

E. DE BAERE, Attorney at Law, Ghent, Belgium

S. DEDECKER, Researcher in Criminal Law, Faculty of Law, Catholic University of Leuven, Belgium

H.A. GROEN, Professor of Civil Procedure, Faculty of Law, Maastricht University, the Netherlands

M. GROENHUIJSEN, Professor of Criminal Law, Faculty of Law, Tilburg University, the Netherlands

J.-F. HENROTTE, Attorney at Law, Liège, Belgium

A.W. JONGBLOED, Professor of the Law of Enforcement and Seizure, Faculty of Law, Utrecht University, the Netherlands

H.B. KRANS, Professor of Civil Procedure, Faculty of Law, Groningen University, the Netherlands

X.E. KRAMER, Associate Professor of Civil Law, Erasmus University Rotterdam, the Netherlands

C.H. VAN RHEE, Professor of European Legal History, Faculty of Law, University of Maastricht, the Netherlands

M.L.L.V. STORME, Honorary President International Association Procedural Law

B. SUJECKI, Assistant Professor of Civil Procedure, Catholic University Brabant, the Netherlands

P. TAELMAN, Professor of Civil Procedure, Faculty of Law, Ghent University, Belgium

F. VERBRUGGEN, Professor of Criminal Law, Faculty of Law, Catholic University of Leuven, Belgium

INTRODUCTION

A.W. JONGBLOED

From 16 until 21 September 2007 the XIIIth World Congress on procedural law was held in Salvador de Bahia, Brazil. The congress was dedicated to the theme `New Trends in Procedural Law" and was organised by the International Association of Procedural Law and in particular the Instituto Brasileiro de direito processual chaired by Professor Ada Pellegrini Grinover. For a congress like this the organization invites General reporters who, in turn, (sometimes aided by the organization of the congress) try to find national reporters. The Netherlands had a General Reporter for the theme New Trends in Pre-action: the Maastricht Professor Groen (the joint general reporter was his colleague from Oxford, Andrews). Of course, he was in Bahia to deliver a presentation. Furthermore, most national reporters from Belgium and the Netherlands were present in Brazil.

Reports are mostly published after the congress (sometimes there is a delay of some years), but in this case the participants received, at the opening of the congress, a thick book in which speeches and general reports were included.[1] But as the national reports were not made available by the organisers of the congress via the Internet, the idea occurred to publish the Belgian and Dutch national reports together. In this way the law in both countries could be compared and the reports could be given a broader focus.

It soon became clear that Belgian or Dutch reporters had not been requested for all the themes and also that not every report was suitable for publication. Some reports provided only a brief answer to the questions asked in the questionnaire, while the authors did not have the opportunity to edit their contribution for this volume.

It means that no report can be found on the first theme - Specific Procedures[2] - and the fourth theme - New Trends in Insolvency Proceedings.[3]

---

1 A. Pellegrini Grinover and P. Calmon (eds.), Direito Processual Comprado, XIII World Congress of Procedural Law, Editora Forense Rio de Janeiro 2007.

2 Y. Taniguchi, WTO dispute settlement system as seen by a proceduralist, p. 39 ff and U. Haas, Die Streitbeilegung durch Schiedsgerichte in Internationalen Sport, p. 50 ff.

Theme 2 - Information Technology in litigation is addressed in the reports by Henrotte and Jongbloed / Sujecki.[4] Krans wrote the Dutch report for Theme 3 - New Trends in Pre-action, while the general report by Groen is also included.[5] Theme 5 - New Trends in Standing and Res Iudicata in collective suits led to reports written by Taelman / De Baere and Asser.[6] Verbruggen / Dedecker and Groenhuijsen devote attention to theme 6 - New Trends in Illegal Evidence in Criminal Procedure.[7] The last Theme -7 - was reserved for those who wished to raise subjects of their own choice in a workshop. Van Rhee, Allemeersch and Kramer have taken that opportunity and their contributions are included in the Pellegrini bundle. But Van Rhee has raised an issue which is different to that included in the bundle.[8] Allemeersch's text has been adapted to recent developments and Kramer's text was (incorrectly) no more than one page and included a sort of synthesis.[9]

It has been decided that the texts sent to the general reporters would form the basis of this book, unless there are recent developments that render text outdated.

The conference was well organized, there was a pleasant atmosphere and an exchange of views, but it was not as four years earlier in Mexico. The reason for this is the demise of our esteemed colleague and good friend Jean Laenens. His death on August 20, 2007 at the age of 57, caused a shadow to descend on all of us. But we are very happy that Professor Marcel Storme was willing to pay homage to him and that we can dedicate this volume to Jean Laenens. May Jean rest in peace.

---

3 E.F. Ricci wrote the Civil Law general report (p. 267 ff.) and J.L. Westbrook the Common Law report (p. 283 ff), while P. Gottwald wrote the Synthesis Report.

4 The Common Law General Report has been written by J. Walker and G.D. Watson (p. 119 ff) and E. Jeuland wrote Nouvelles technologies et procès civil, rapport général pour les pays de droit civil (p. 152 ff). A.L. Sosa wrote the synthesis report (p. 186 ff).

5 This general report can also be found in the aforementioned bundle on p. 242 ff. The Common Law report by N. Andrews can be found at p. 201 ff and the Relatório de síntese of J.R. the Santos Bedaque P. 257 ff.

6 A. Pellegrini Grinover wrote an English general report for the Civil Law countries (p. 305 ff) and also in Portugese (p. 326 ff). L.S. Mullenix wrote the general report regarding the Common Law countries (p. 500 ff) and K. Watanabe the Relatório de síntese (p. 534 ff).

7 T. Armenta-Deu (p. 543 ff) and W. van Caenegem (p. 546 ff) wrote the general reports regarding Civil Law and Common Law; A.M. Gomes Filho (p. 608 ff) the Relatório de síntese.

8 The development of civil procedural law in twentieth century Europe: a retrospective view, p. 624-635.

9 P. 648/649.

Finally, I would like to thank all the contributors to this volume, Ms Trix Ditvoorst, Ms Ellen Alferink and Ms Helena Skolozdra (Molengraaff Institute for Private Law, Utrecht University) for editing this volume, Mr Peter Morris LL.B. for his linguistic corrections and Mr Kris Moeremans (Intersentia) for publishing this volume.

Utrecht, 21 July, 2008 Anthonie W. Jongbloed

IN MEMORIAM - JEAN LAENENS

M.L.L.V. STORME

It is appropriate to complete this set of reports from the recent World Congress held in San Salvador de Bahia with a tribute to the late Jean Laenens, who passed away on 20/8/2007. This tribute is all the more fitting because, just before it was discovered that he was suffering from a life-threatening disease, he was still able to attend the academic symposium, devoted to the importing and exporting of rules governing court procedure, which took place in September 2006 in Kyoto (Japan). It was on the very day after his return that his doctors made the tragic medical discovery.

As a former Secretary-General and Chairman of the International Association of Procedural Law, I am able to testify that Jean Laenens was a key figure for our association.

Having defended his doctoral thesis, which dealt with jurisdiction agreements, he was appointed as Senior Lecturer in Procedural Law and Evidence at the University of Antwerp, and immediately became part of the lively international community of procedural scholars. He was already present at the first world congres in Ghent in 1977. I well remember the day when I requested him to act as rapporteur at the World Congress which was took place in Utrecht in 1987, and at which he acted as preliminary adviser on the application of the Enforcement Treaty in Belgium.

From this point onwards he contributed ceaselessly towards our activities, in most cases by acting as rapporteur or by chairing workshops at our symposia and congresses. He also rapidly acceded to membership of our international association, which brings together eminent scholars from all over the world who are actively engaged in research on court procedure, and more particularly the comparative and international law of procedure.

Jean Laenens was not only the most amiable of men, but also a scholar who was capable of identifying the relevant issues with considerable precision, as well as setting out ways of solving them. In addition, he displayed an acute awareness of the world of legal practice, which produced a most fortunate combination of theory and practice. For this was the area in which he excelled – removing the various frontiers which exist in all aspects of procedural law, as witness the following examples:

(1) Both as an academic and as a lawyer, he succeeded in bringing down the frontier between theory and practice. His knowledge of the way in which the courts operate enabled him to identify immediately the most important problem areas and to find ways of removing them.

(2) He also succeeded in overcoming the boundaries between national and foreign legal systems. As has been mentioned before, he was for many years an attentive and active participant in the various gatherings which took place in the context of the international association of procedural law. Shortly before he fell victim to the serious illness which ultimately caused his demise, he was still able to participate in the Kyoto symposium which took place in September 2006, and during which the emphasis was very much on finding ways of exchanging systems of procedural law in order to improve national systems of procedural law.

(3) The fact that procedural law was to a large extent inhibited and restricted by formalism was, for him, a reason to seek rules and formulae which would reduce the degree of formalism inherent in procedural law.

(4) In the context of the current trend towards developing alternative dispute resolution techniques, he succeeded in removing the boundaries between judges and mediators through his proposal that the judge should also act as a mediator.

(5) The unacceptable boundary between the weaker and the stronger citizen seeking legal redress was, for him, a reason for coming to the aid of the weaker party. This is why he devoted a good deal of attention to the rights of the consumer in court proceedings.

(6) In the context of Belgian law, he campaigned against the splitting up – and therefore the insulation – of the courts of first instance. He advocated a return to the original, single, *arrondissementsrechtbank* (district court), consisting of a civil, penal, social and commercial division. He countered the artificial demarcation of the areas of jurisdiction allocated to the various courts acting at first instance by proposing the creation of a single Court of First Instance.

There can be no doubt that he incarnated to perfection the vision of justice as formulated by the Royal Prophet Isaiah in the following terms:

> *See, a king will reign in righteousness*
> *and rulers will rule with justice.*
> *Each man will be like a shelter from the wind*
> *and a refuge from the storm,*
> *like streams of water in the desert*
> *and the shadow of a great rock in a thirsty land*
> (Isaiah 32:1-2).

It is not only the Belgian procedural law community, both scholars and practitioners, who have suffered a heavy blow with the death of Jean Laenens. His passing away also means that the international community of proceduralists, and more particularly the international association for procedural law, have lost an irreplaceable exponent.

NEW TRENDS IN STANDING AND RES IUDICATA IN COLLECTIVE SUITS (BELGIUM)

P. TAELMAN and E. DE BAERE

1. BELGIAN PROCEDURAL LAW: A LACK OF COMPREHENSIVE REGULATION

A global remark that has to be made about the Belgian Judicial Code[1] or any national law concerning civil litigation, is that no general rule is in force which allows court protection for collective rights. The traditional rules, as are laid down in the Judicial Code, were originally designed for the classical two (or maximum small party) proceedings. They have to be used in a creative way and have to be interpreted in such a meaning that these regulations can provide techniques that do give standing to multi party claims or to one (specially designated) party for defence of collective rights.[2]

Hereinafter, several of these traditional rules of the Judicial Code will be discussed, highlighting how they can be used for court protection of collective rights.[3] First, the technique of junction of claims will be discussed(1), secondly the matter of a claim in intervention(2), thirdly group or organizational litigation(3) and finally, the technique of party representation(4).
This text will be completed with a short but critical overview of the European Union's statutes on the matter.

---

1 This is *"Gerechtelijk Wetboek/Code judiciaire"* dated 10th of October 1967 (between 1967 and 1970, it gradually came into force. Since 1970, the Judicial Code has seen a great number of changes.

2 Useful reference on the subject: E. DE BAERE, "Procederen in zaken van massaschade: naar een class action in Belgisch recht", *T.P.R.* 2007, 7.

3 These traditional techniques can be used for both plaintiff and defendant class action.

1.1. JUNCTION OF CLAIMS[4]

Junction of claims is a technique foreseen in article 701 Judicial Code. This article stipulates that several claims between two or more parties can be filed together when they are 'coherent' or 'connected'.[5] In other words, this article provides a first possibility to combine a plurality of claims (between two or more parties) and to bring them together in one proceeding.[6]

As article 701 states, this technique can only be used when claims are connected. The Judicial Code defines in article 30 that this condition is fulfilled whenever cases should be tried together in order to prevent judgements that are irreconcilable if they would be tried separately.[7] The downside of this article is, since it is vaguely formulated and since every judge is given the authority to rule on the connection/coherency between claims, that much is left to the discretion of the court. This evidently makes it a very casuistic notion.[8] In brief, study of Belgian jurisprudence reveals a rather strict approach of the notion of connection. A mere junction of individual claims is not enough; similar legal problems or legal questions have to be tight together by a 'higher' interest which exceeds the individual interests.[9]

---

4 Some useful references on this subject: P. TAELMAN, "Cumulatie van vorderingen: pro en contra", (noot onder Beslagr. Rb. Veurne 18 maart 1992 en Kh. Gent 28 maart 1995), *A.J.T.* 1995-96, 12; P. TAELMAN en PH. THION, "Bundeling van vorderingen", *T.P.R.* 2003, 1495 ff.; P. TAELMAN, "Cumulatie van vorderingen. Collectieve dagvaardingen", in STORME, M. en TAELMAN, P., *Het proces in meervoud. Le procès au pluriel*, Antwerpen, Kluwer, 1997, 2 ff; P. DAUW, *Burgerlijke rechtspleging / Het Geding*, in *Artikelsgewijze commentaar Gerechtelijk Recht*, Antwerpen, Kluwer, 2003, artikel 701 Ger. W, 11 ff.

5 Art. 701 Judicial Code states: *"Diverses demandes entre deux ou plusieurs parties peuvent, si elles sont connexes, être introduites par le même acte."*

6 In Belgian doctrine a distinction is made between *"objective junction"* and *"subjective junction"*. The first concept refers to the junction of claims by one party: one claimant (or one defendant) files several claims (counterclaims); the latter refers to the number of parties in one proceeding. The junction as discussed in this article has to be understood in the subjective sense.

7 Art. 30 Judicial Code stipulates: *"Des demandes en justice peuvent être traitées comme connexes lorsqu'elles sont liées entre elles par un rapport si étroit qu'il y a intérêt à les instruire et juger en même temps afin d'éviter des solutions qui seraient susceptibles d'être inconciliables si les causes étaient jugées séparément."*

8 This was affirmed by the Supreme Court *(Hof van Cassatie)* in its decision of 28th of September 1984 (published in *Arr.Cass.* 1984-85, 169 and *Pas.* 1985, 145).

9 See for example: Brussel 4 februari 1994, *J.L.M.B.* 1994, 661; Rb. Brussel 11 oktober 1989, *J.L.M.B.* 1991, 201.

However, reference can be made to one exceptional judgment from a lower court which reveals a new approach to the term of connection of claims.[10] This judge situates the prescription of connection in a larger social context and takes the economical reality (mitigating costs of litigation, administrative and judicial efficiency ...) of multi party claims into consideration for granting the joinder of claims.

The traditional approach of connection of claims, as can be found in the jurisprudence, is still widely supported in Belgian doctrine. However, in a social reality of courts dealing with a maximum of cases on a daily basis, doctrine is already aiming towards an economical appealing litigation and searches for means to decrease costs. It is clear that a more 'liberal' approach of the connexity of claims can be a means to increase access to Justice for multi party claims, without needing any amendment of the Judicial Code. In practice however, it appears that the technique of junction of claims is still a very individualistic model, suitable for only small party claims.

1.2. CLAIM IN INTERVENTION

A second traditional technique which can be used to bring plural party claims to court, is the claim in intervention as is foreseen in articles 15[11] and 16[12] Judicial Code. This technique makes it possible for third parties to get involved in proceedings which are already hanging before a court. A third party, other than the original litigating parties, might intervene in the pending trial. This can either happen voluntarily (in which case the initiative lies with the third party) or coercively (in which case one of the original litigating parties sues the third party to intervene).

Both discussed techniques, junction of claims and claims in intervention, are deficient when it comes to multi party claims or defence of collective rights. In both techniques it is always required for all parties to physically take part in the proceedings. These techniques don't merely make it possible for one

---

10 Court of first instance Veurne (judge of seizures)18th March 1992, *A.J.T.* 1995-96, 10.

11 Art. 15 Judicial Code stipulates: *"L'intervention est une procédure par laquelle un tiers devient partie à la cause. Elle tend, soit à la sauvegarde des intérêts de l'intervenant ou de l'une des parties en cause, soit à faire prononcer une condamnation ou ordonner une garantie."*

12 Art. 16 Judicial Code stipulates: *"L'intervention est volontaire lorsque le tiers se présente afin de défendre ses intérêts. Elle est forcée lorsque le tiers est cité au cours d'une procédure par une ou plusieurs parties."*

person ('the forman') to litigate on behalf of all the plaintiffs and obtain a judgement which can bind (i.e. has *res judicata*) other parties that weren't involved in the proceedings.

1.3. ORGANIZATIONAL LITIGATION

1.3.1. A third model

A third model that can be used for multi party proceedings is the organizational litigation. This technique will appear to be the first model that actually gives standing to a plurality of individuals and brings protection to collective rights.

In a more complex society where aggrieved individuals are confronted with 'powerful' entities (public authorities, national and international corporations...), these individuals often feel the need to unite themselves. The (spontaneously) founded communities can take over the common interests of the members of the group and bring a certain balance of power in relation to the 'powerful' entities. Several individual claims can be combined by an organisation which can file one claim in name of the whole group. In addition, individuals enjoy other (important) advantages when uniting their interests: share of costs, concentration of information and evidence, rule out the possibility of first comes first serves...[13]

During the last decades, organisational litigation has been the subject of a hot debate in Belgian doctrine, mostly focusing on consumer and environmental groupings. The issues which doctrine addresses and which define the model of organisational litigation is the standing of an organisation*(a)* and the interests it can represent*(b)*.

---

13 The latter is a risk that victims of mass exposure accidents are frequently confronted with. A mass exposure accident is characterized by a serial of injuries, spread over a certain amount of time (whereas mass disaster accidents are so called single-event disasters, for example an air plane crash). Victims who can identify their damage in an early stage can get consolidation long before other victims of the same accident are even aware of their injuries. When funds are limited on the side of the person or entity liable for the disaster, an unfavorable system of 'First comes first serves' will be unavoidable. A community or organization defending the victim's interests can (partially) avoid this negative effect by uniting the plurality of claims and divide the resources between the group of victims.

1.3.2. Standing of an Organisation

The Belgian Judicial Code only gives standing to an organisation with legal personality. This principle is based on the adage *'pas d'action sans personnalité'.*[14] This legal personality can only be obtained after fulfilling several administrative formalities. However, in practice, victims of collective torts will group themselves more or less in a spontaneous way (and create and ad hoc organization).[15] The organisation will therefore not fulfil the statutory criteria to obtain standing in proceedings and access to the courtroom will be denied.

For a very limited amount of organisations, bills of law grant standing without needing to fulfil the required prescriptions for legal personality.[16] The legal personality as required by the Judicial Code gets replaced by a sort of statutory personality. However, the organisation which enjoys this statutory exception will only receive standing for the limited issues determined by that bill of law.
The requirement of legal personality is obviously the first obstacle for organisational litigation to become a useful model for protection of collective rights.

1.3.3. Interest

Even though an organisation fulfils the requirements for obtaining legal personality, this organisation will encounter difficulties filing one claim for defence of all the individual interests of the members of the group. Article 17 of the Belgian Judicial Code states that a claim can only be filed by a person who has 'the interest' to do so.[17] This is based on the principle *'pas d'action*

---

14 Cass. 12 november 1935, *Pas.* 1936, I, 49 en Cass. 11 januari 1979, *Pas.* 1979, I, 464.

15 It is often the outside world that qualifies victims of a mass tort as a group and identifies them as such.

16 Reference can be made to the trade unions which are granted standing in article 4 of the Act of 5th of December 1968, without having the necessity of obtaining legal personality.

17Art. 17 Judicial Code stipulates: "L'action ne peut être admise si le demandeur n'a pas qualité et intérêt pour la former". Belgian doctrine has devoted a lot of attention to this article. Useful references on the subject: P. LEMMENS, "Het optreden van verenigingen in rechte ter verdediging van collectieve belangen", R.W. 1983-84, 2004;: P. VANLERSBERGHED, 'Algemene beginselen: Voorwaarden van de rechtsvordering', in Artikelsgewijze commentaar Gerechtelijk Recht, Antwerpen, Kluwer, 2002, artikel 17 Ger. W., 9; J. VERLINDEN, "Het belang als ontvankelijkheidvoorwaarde voor de rechtsvordering (Art. 17 en 18 Gerechtelijk Wetboek)", *Jura Falc.* 1987-88, 20; J. VAN COMPERNOLLE, *Le droit d'action en justice des groupements*, Brussel, Larcier, 1972, 241; P. VAN OMMESLAGHE, "Le droit d'action

sans intérêt'. Although there's no legal definition of the principle of interest, Belgian doctrine and jurisprudence agree that according to this prescription, litigating parties will be denied standing when they have no (material or moral) advantage pursuing their claim.[18] Belgian jurisprudence however, requires the interest to be a 'personal' interest. This non statutory condition descends form a tradition of prohibiting an *'actio popularis'*.[19] Thus, a personal interest requires the existence of a personal subjective right.

The requirement of a personal interest makes it in practice very difficult for an organisation to file a claim. The interest defended by an organisation can take three forms. Firstly, an organisation can file a claim for the personal damages caused to the organisation. The Belgian Supreme Court has ruled that an organisation can file a claim for its personal damage whenever its patrimony, honour or reputation is affected.[20] Secondly, an organisation can defend the general interest, for example the environment. This interest is however not different than any other civilian has concerning the protection of the environment. It then becomes an *'actio popularis'* which is not allowed in Belgian civil procedure. The last interest an organisation can claim to defend is the collective interest of the members of the group.

The organisation representing the individual members interests, will not (easily) obtain standing in Belgian litigation. Belgian jurisprudence reveals that only the individuals obtain standing for their personal interests without having the possibility of delegating this authority to an organisation. A mere sum of personal interests of the individual members of the group, does not create a personal interest for the group itself.[21] In Belgian doctrine, a minority pleads to give standing to an organisation representing the interests of the

en justice des groupements, notamment des groupements tendant à la défense de l'environnement", in BOCKEN, H., *Vorderingsbevoegdheid voor milieuverenigingen*, Brussel, Story-Scientia, 1988, 25 en 30; H. BOCKEN en B. DEMEULENAERE, "The defense of collective interests in the Belgian civil procedure", in STORME, M., *Effectiveness of judicial protection and the constitutional order*, Deventer, Kluwer, 1983, 153.

18 The issue of interest is a preliminary question that has to be raised at the commencement of every proceeding. However, it can not lead to an inquiry of the grounds of the claimed right itself.

19 An actio popularis is a claim defending the general public interest. This is however an exclusive authority for the public prosecutor.

20 Decision of 19th of November 1982 (published in *R.W.* 1983-84, 2032).

21 This interpretation is supported by the Supreme Court (Cass. 9 december 1957, *R.C.J.B.* 1958, 249).

member. This is in fact still a different interest then the general interest or the *actio popularis.*

To remedy this strict interpretation of the required interest and the jurisprudence of the Belgian Supreme Court, the legislator has created the possibility for some organisations to undertake legal actions in order to safeguard the general interest or the interests of its members. When an organisation complies with the prescribed conditions in these specific laws, it will gain a sort of statutory interest which replaces the personal interest as required by the Judicial Code (and the Supreme Court).

These bills of law can mainly be situated in the field of consumer rights. Thus an organisation protecting the interests of consumers can initiate proceedings in order to stop violations of the rules on fair trade,[22] on credit contracts for consumers,[23] on electronic transfer of money,[24] on contracts concerning travelling mediation,[25] on amicable recovery of debts of consumers[26] and proceedings aiming at the cessation of misguiding publicity.

The conditions for these consumer organisations to obtain the above mentioned 'statutory interest' are set out in the law of 14th of July 1991 concerning rules on fair trade, to where the other enumerated laws also refer to. According to this law, an organisation must have legal personality (as discussed supra) and the general interest these organisations is safeguarding must be defined in their statutes.

Besides the statutory interest for consumer organisations, bills of law give standing to certain other organisations: an environmental organisation can initiate an action in order to stop an activity which apparently violates environmental law[27] and an organisation which defends human rights can

---

22 Law of 14th of July 1991 (*Loi sur les pratiques du commerce et sur l'information et la protection du consommateur*).

23 Law of 12th of June 1991 *(Loi relative au crédit à la consommation).*

24 Law of 17th July 2002 *(Loi relative aux opérations effectuées au moyen d'instruments de transfert électronique de fonds).*

25 Law of 16th of February 1994 *(Loi régissant le contrat d'organisation de voyages et le contrat d'intermédiaire de voyages).*

26 Law of 20th December 2002 *(Loi relatif au recouvrement amiable des dettes du consommateur).*

27 Law of 12th January 1993 (*Loi concernant un droit d'action en matière de protection de l'environnement*).

initiate proceedings to stop violation of the non-discrimination rules.[28] These laws both require that the envisaged organisation has legal personality and has obtained it for a certain period of time (respectively 3 years and 5 years) and that the statutes define the general interest they are defending.

How logic the organizational litigation for defence of collective rights might be, it appears that the Belgian Judicial Code creates two main barriers for an organisation to obtain standing. Firstly, an organisation has to take on a legal personality. Secondly, the group which has done the effort to obtain legal personality (and has paid the costs accompanied with that legal personality) can't defend the collective interests of its members. Partial legislative initiatives try to remedy this injustice, however a comprehensive bill of law stays out to date.[29]

1.4. PARTY REPRESENTATION

A final technique which can creatively be used for defence of collective rights or multi party claims is the party representation. This model makes it possible for one person to represent a whole group of individuals if that person has collected from each individual of the group the necessary powers of attorney (by means of authorisation). The early jurisprudence of the Belgian Supreme Court stated that party representation wasn't allowed based on the principle *"Nul ne plaide par procureur"*. This principle was completely overruled by the recent decision of the Belgian Supreme Court dated 25th November 1993.[30]

Of all the above discussed techniques, party representation is the most effective one for defence of collective rights. This model was (is) recently used in the well known Lernout & Hauspie case. Thousands of share holders are represented by the NV DEMINOR[31] which collected the required

---

[28] Law of the 10th of May 2007 *(Loi tendant à lutter contre certaines formes de discrimination.)*

[29] It has to be mentioned that some proposals have been done in Parliament to counter this problem (e.g. a proposal of 16th August 2007 (*Proposition de loi complétant l'article 17 du Code judiciaire et l'article 3 du titre préliminaire du Code d'instruction criminelle en vue d'instaurer au profit des associations une action d'intérêt collectif*, see www.lachambre.be, proposition nr.52-0109/001). See also the proposal of 11th July 2006 concerning group litigation (*Proposition de loi modifiant le code judiciaire en vue d'accorder aux associations le droit d'introduire une action d'intérêt collectif*, proposition 51-2620/001). This proposal is not longer pending in Parliament.

[30] Published in *R.Cass.* 1994, 65.

[31] The NV *(SA, Société Anonyme)* is a Public Limited Company.

individual authorities through their website. The NV DEMINOR collaborated with a famous and reliable consumer group (called Testaankoop). The downside of this technique is obviously the large administration that is involved in preparing the proceedings since every member's consent and authorisation is required. The advantage of this model is the binding decision that the group's represent can obtain for all the individuals who gave their consent. Individuals who didn't give their express consent won't be bound by the ruling of the court. This raises the question of the *res judicata* of Belgian judgements.[32]

Belgian jurisprudence (and doctrine) concentrates the debate of res iudicata on the evidential value of the judgement, not only between the litigating parties but also towards third parties (*i.e.* when a former judgement is invoked by a party during later proceedings vis-à-vis a party who wasn't involved in the proceedings that led to the invoked judgment). The Belgian Supreme Court ruled in several cases that the res iudicata has a legal evidential value towards third parties. Hence, a judgment has a binding evidential value for a party not involved in the proceedings, until that party can proof otherwise (not necessarily by means of third party appeal).

As mentioned, this approach only deals with the question of evidence. Traditionally, Belgian judgements are considered only to generate obligations for the parties involved in the proceedings. This relativity of the res iudicata makes it impossible to introduce a system where a foremen (or a representative) can obtain a judgement which generates obligations for third parties not involved in the proceedings (for example victims of mass damages can't invoke a remedy laid down in a judgement when they weren't involved in the preceding proceedings).

2. EU'S STATUTES ON COLLECTIVE SUITS

So far, no European regulation has been adopted concerning class actions or, more in general, defence of collective rights. The same remark as (mentioned above) concerning Belgian national law, can be said about European regulation: traditional rules and techniques must be used in a creative way to make them applicable to international (i.e. cross border) collective actions. It

32 Useful references on the subject: P. TAELMAN, *Het gezag van het rechterlijk gewijsde – een* begrippenstudie, Antwerpen, Kluwer, 2001, 465 p.; P. TAELMAN, "Werkzaamheid van gerechtelijke uitspraken t.a.v. derden", *R.W.* 1993-94, 1156 ff.

can however be noted that thorough research was done in the field of protection of consumer rights.[33] Under European pressure, most national laws (and the Belgian legislator) have adopted a bill of law, inserting procedural aspects for defence of collective consumer rights. Moreover, the (Belgian) Minister of consumer affaires has recently empanelled a working group to give advice on the subject.

The international dimension given to a case will however generate 'organisational' difficulties (for example the search for all the victims of a mass tort) though will also raise some legal issues. In illustration: the question of the competent judge.

In most cases the Brussels I Convention will determine the competent national judge.[34] The Brussels I Convention doesn't however start from the principle of one exclusive forum but gives the claimant a choice of competent national judges. A tort case can for example be filed before the court where the tort took place *(forum delicti commissi)* but also before the court where the damage appeared.[35] Consequently, the different claims of the victims of mass torts can simultaneously be filed before different competent national judges. A lack of regulation which coordinates these claims enhances the negative consequences that will manifest themselves. Article 28 of the Brussels I Convention states: *"Where related actions are pending in the courts of different Member States, any court other than the court first seized may stay its proceedings".* The national judge before whom the exception of article 28 is raised, has the *possibility* to refer its case to another judge where a related action is pending. The consequences this 'possibility' causes are immense: different judges will rule on the same case and will apply different national legislation. Even more, this lack of international coordination can bring forth a perverse effect and can lead to serious forum shopping.

---

[33] In European context one can refer to a study – dating from February 2007 and made by the University of Leuven for the European Commission – on alternative means of consumer redress other than redress through ordinary judicial proceedings (see http://ec.europa.eu/consumers/redress/reports_studies/index_en.htm).

[34] Council Regulation (EC) No 44/2001 of 22 December 2000 on jurisdiction and the recognition and enforcement of judgments in civil and commercial matters (Official Journal L 012 , 16/01/2001 P. 0001 - 0023).

[35] This is due to the interpretation given by the European Court of Justice to article 5.3 from the Burssels I Convention in the Case "Handelskewekerij Bier / Mines de potasse d'Alsace" dated 30th of November 1971 (Published in *Jur.H.v.J.* 1976, 1735).

Avoiding the subject of expediency of European interference in national procedural law, it is our opinion that issuing European regulation today would be too hasty. Certain countries (Sweden, the Netherlands, Great Britain...) have only recently adopted rules on collective suits or class actions. It is advisable first to make a thorough evaluation of these adapted national rules and to reflect on the used principles, rather then issuing class action rules as soon as possible. These national rules and principles, together with the critics in national doctrine, can be useful guidelines for adaptation of European principles or if necessary, regulation. However, it can't be denied that a serious form of international coordination for cases under the Brussels I Convention has to be adopted.

NEW TRENDS IN STANDING AND RES IUDICATA IN COLLECTIVE SUITS (THE NETHERLANDS)

W.D.H. ASSER

1. INTRODUCTION

The Dutch Civil Code (CC) opens various ways to defend collective rights and interests in court.

The Dutch law, however, does not know a class-action, neither for the plaintiffs nor for the defendants. Some scholares advocate the introduction of the possibility of class actions American style. Others argue that under Article 3:305a CC the legislator should open the possibilty for interest organizations to bring actions for compensation.[1] During the debates on the bill on collective settlement of mass damages (see hereafter) the Government has persistently rejected this idea. It cannot be expected that the law will change to this effect in the near future.

2. COLLECTIVE SUITS

2.1. GENERAL PROVISIONS

The general provisions are found in the Articles 3:305a-305c CC. They entitle a foundation ("stichting"), an association ("vereniging") with full legal

---

1 Compare W.D.H. ASSER, H.A. GROEN, J.B.M. VRANKEN (m.m.v. I.N. TZANKOVA), *Een nieuwe balans*, Interimrapport Fundamentele herbezinning Nederlands burgerlijk procesrecht, Den Haag 2003, p. 173-186; N. FRENK, *Kollektieve akties in het privaatrecht* (diss. Utrecht), Deventer 1994; N. FRENK, Bundeling van vorderingen, *Tijdschrift voor Privaatrecht* 2003, p. 1413-1488; N. FRENK, *Collectieve actie*, in: E.H. HONDIUS en G.J. RIJKEN (eds.), Handboek Consumentenrecht, Zutphen 2006, p. 449-470; C.A. GROENENDIJK, *Bundeling van belangen bij de burgerlijke rechter* (diss. Nijmegen), Deventer 1981; H.U. JESSERUN D'OLIVEIRA, *"Group Actions in Civil Procedure"*, in: E.H. HONDIUS and G.J.W. STEENHOFF (eds.), *Netherlands Reports to the Thirteenth International Congress of Comparative Law*, Montreal 1990, The Hague 1990, p. 135-149; A.W. JONGBLOED in *Vermogensrecht* (looseleaf edition), Deventer, Article 305a; P.H. Lindblom, Group Actions and the Role of Courts - a European Perspective, The Hague 1997; I.N. TZANKOVA, *Toegang tot het recht bij massaschade*, (diss. Tilburg) Deventer 2007 S. VOET, Class actions en aanverwante instrumenten inzake collectief procederen in Europa: een procesrechtelijke status questionis, TMD 2008, p. 49-80.

capacity or a public body to take any legal action in order to defend interests of the same kind of other persons, in so far as this is pursuant to its statute.

These organizations cannot, however, bring an action for compensation for the victims.[2] According to the general law of obligations the individual victims may assign their claims for compensation to such organizations or give them a mandate to manage the claims on their behalf. It means the interest organization may then, on behalf of the victims, settle the individual claims with the defendant or bring actions against him. One would not call this a collective action although the actions on behalf of the individual victims may be brought jointly.

Section 2 of Article 305a requires an organization before taking legal action under this provision to take steps to reach its purpose by negotiations with the defendant.

A judgement given on the basis of Article 3:305a has the force of res iudicata with respect to all persons concerned. However a person, whose interests are protected by that judgement, may object to being bound by it, as a result of which the judgement will have no force of res iudicata in respect of that person.[3]

2.2. GENERAL CONDITIONS IN CONTRACTS

As to the specific subject of general conditions in contracts Article 6:240 CC makes it possible for interest organizations, such as consumer organizations, to have clauses in general conditions tested by the Court of Appeal in The Hague on being "unreasonable onerous" in the sense of Article 6:233 CC. To that purpose it may bring an action against a certain company using such general conditions or against an organization representing the interests of entrepreneurs, if this organization promotes the use of such conditions.

If the Court finds a specific clause in the general conditions unreasonable onerous it will declare so and may ban the company from using it, order it to withdraw such a clause or change it in such a manner that it loses its onerous character.[4]

---

2 Article 3:305a section 3 CC.

3 The possibility to "opt out"; Article 3:305a section 5 CC.

4 Article 6:241 CC.

2.3. COLLECTIVE SETTLEMENT OF MASS DAMAGES

Recently (2005) an alternative for collective actions was introduced in Articles 7:907-910 CC (collective settlement of mass damages). A contract for the compensation of damage caused by an event or by similar events, entered into by an interest organization with one or more other parties, who undertake thereby to compensate this damage, may, upon the joint request of the parties that have entered into the contract, be declared binding by the court upon persons to whom the damage has been caused.

The contract shall in any case include (i.a.):

- a description of the group or groups of persons in whose favour the contract has been entered into, according to the nature and the seriousness of their damage;
- the compensation awarded to these persons;

The court shall reject the application if (i.a.)

- the contract does not comply with the aboven mentioned requirement;
- the amount of the compensation awarded is not reasonable
- insufficient security has been furnished to pay the claims of those in whose favour the contract has been entered into;
- the contract does not provide for an independent determination of the compensation to be paid pursuant to its terms;
- the interests of the persons in whose favour the contract has been entered into are otherwise insufficiently safeguarded;
- the interest organization is not sufficient representative or the group of persons, in whose favour the contract has been concluded, is not large enough to justify a declaration to make the contract binding;
- the legal person who, pursuant to the contract, provides compensation, is not a party to the contract.[5]

As soon as the request to declare the contract binding has been irrevocably granted, the contract shall have, as between the parties and those entitled to compensation, the effects of a contract of settlement ("vaststellingsovereenkomst") to which each of those so entitled shall be deemed to be a party. In a contract of settlement the parties bind themselves towards each other, in order to end or avoid any uncertainty or dispute in respect of what, in law, shall apply between them.[6]

---

5 Article 7:907 CC.

6 Article 7:900 CC.

A person entitled to compensation under a contract that has been declared binding under Article 7:907 CC may opt out by a written statement that he does not wish to be bound.[7]

2.4. COMPANY LAW

In the field of company law shareholders representing at least 10% of the issued share capital and trade unions which has amongst its members persons working for the company, (apart from the public prosecutor and other authorities) can petition the Enterprise Division ("Ondernemingskamer") of the Amsterdam Court of Appeal for the appointment of one or more persons to undertake an inquiry into the policy and conduct of business of a company.[8] The Court shall allow the inquiry only if there appear well-founded reasons to doubt the correctness of the policy. The investigators will report their findings to the Court. If, on the basis of the findings of the investigators, the Court establishes mismanagement ("wanbeleid"), it may, upon the request of the applicants who have filed the original petition, take certain measures, e.g. the dismissal of (members of) the board of directors or supervisors or the annulment of any decision of that board.[9] According to the Supreme Court case law the judgement by which the Court establishes mismanagement has no force of res iudicata in respect of the liability of any director or other executive of the company personally.[10] In that respect separate proceedings should be started against them. The Supreme Court has also ruled that the right to apply for an inquiry is not meant to settle or investigate the background of claims of the applicant against the company.[11]

3. CONCLUSION

In the Supreme Court case law and in the above mentioned provisions of the Civil Code the requirements for standing are formulated. It appears that collective actions based on Article 3:305a may only be brought by interest organizations which have full legal capacity (legal persons) and according to whose statute they promote the interests at stake. Furthermore the interests of the "victims" should be similar. Sometimes it is required that an adequate protection by the law of the interests at stake is furthered by combining the

---

7 Article 7:908 CC.
8 Articles 2:345-347 CC.
9 Article 2:355-356 CC.
10 HR (Supreme Court) 8-4-2005, R04/005, LJN: AS5010, JOR 2005, 119; NJ 2006, 443.
11 HR 18-11-2005, R05/042, LJN: AU2465; JOR 2005, 295, NJ 2006, 173.

interests and that the fact the organization according to its statutes promotes the interest at stake is not sufficient to bring a collective action. One may also find decisions in which it is decided that the interest organization is sufficiently representative.

The doctrine generally follows the statutory provisions and the Supreme Court case law.

There are no signs that the law will be changed in the near future.

4. DESIVE

As far as I am concerned, a harmonisation of the law in this field is desirable in view of crossborder mass damages by accidents, polution etc. The EU should take the lead.

PRE-ACTION PROCEDURES IN THE NETHERLANDS

H.B. KRANS

1. INTRODUCTION

1.1. NON-SYSTEMATIC APPROACH TO THE PRE-ACTION PHASE

This paper focuses on pre-actions, those actions concerned with the phase of civil litigation prior to formal proceedings. The Dutch Code of Civil Procedure (CCP) does not contain a general set of rules on the preliminary phase that precedes the actual proceedings. There is no separate section in this code that covers all aspects of the pre-action conduct of litigation.[1] From a certain point of view this is remarkable. Once civil proceedings have started, the conduct of parties is regulated by various sets of rules, both in the CCP and in other Codes.[2] From that point on, the procedural clash of arms is supervised by the court. However, the conduct of prospective litigants prior to formal commencement of a civil claim can be a decisive factor in the development of a trial. However, thus far, there is no systematic approach to this stage of litigation.

Dutch procedural law nevertheless offers several separate instruments concerning the pre-action conduct of litigation. These instruments mainly concern the acquisition of information (provisional production of evidence, obligation to produce exhibits, right of inquiry, obligations to inform). The acquired information enables parties to assess their judicial position and can pave the way to an out-of-court settlement. A minority of these instruments focus on other topics, such as compulsory measures (provisional attachment). In addition to pre-actions concerning the phase of civil litigation prior to formal proceedings, this paper examines some rules that, although they do

---

1 On Dutch civil procedural law in general, see F.A.M. VAN BREE, T.A. DAVID, J.P. HEERING and M. VAN WISSEN, *European Civil Practice*, Volume 2, Netherlands (chapter 58), 2004, p. 370-400 (in English) and *inter alia* W.H. HEEMSKERK, W. HUGENHOLTZ. *Hoofdlijnen van het Nederlands Burgerlijk Procesrecht,* Den Haag 2006 and H.J. SNIJDERS, C.J.M. KLAASSEN and G.J. MEIJER, *Nederlands burgerlijk procesrecht*, Deventer 2007.

2 Eg. the Judiciary Act (*Wet op de Rechterlijke organisatie*).

not precede formal litigation, can prevent regular full-length proceedings, for example, provisional relief proceedings.

1.2. IDEAS FOR REFORM

In January 2002 a limited but fundamental change to the Dutch CCP, introduced in 1838, came into force. During discussions in Parliament about these changes, the need arose for a complete and radical review of fundamentals, principles and basic assumptions of the law of civil procedure. This led to a fundamental review of the Dutch law of civil procedure, carried out by a small group of researchers. This group produced an interim report (2003) and a final report (2006).[3] In this fundamental review the preliminary phase of proceedings is described as 'forgotten'.

The research group presented many proposals concerning the pre-action phase. The starting point for these proposals is that a dispute between parties creates a relation with standards of behaviour. The behaviour of the parties in the preliminary phase has to be determined on the one hand by the general social principle that they must take one another's interests into account when bringing the dispute to an end and that they must aim to settle out of court, and on the other hand by the obligation to prepare properly for the proceedings.[4] The reports are intended to be the basis for a fundamental review and a general discussion. Judging by the number of reactions to the reports, they do indeed seem to serve as such. The Minister for Justice, judging by his reaction to the fundamental review in January 2007, seems to be receptive to several of the ideas in the reports.[5] In this paper I will consider some ideas for reform, but I do not intend to give a complete overview.

---

3 W.D.H. ASSER, H.A. GROEN, J.B.M. VRANKEN, with the aid of I.N. TZANKOVA, *Een nieuwe balans, Interimrapport fundamentele herbezinning Nederlands burgerlijk procesrecht*, Den Haag 2003 and *Uitgebalanceerd, Eindrapport fundamentele herbezinning Nederlands burgerlijk procesrecht*, Den Haag 2006. These reports will be referred to as interim report (2003) and final report (2006) or, together, as fundamental review.

4 Cf. interim report (2003), p. 97 and final report (2006), supra note 3, p. 62/63.

5 Letter from the Minister for Justice to the Parliament, TK 2006 – 2007, 30 951, no. 1. Chapter 5 deals with the pre-action phase.

2. PROVISIONAL PRODUCTION OF EVIDENCE

2.1. WHY PROVISIONAL PRODUCTION OF EVIDENCE?

The Dutch instruments in the field of pre-action conduct of litigation mainly concern the field of the law of evidence. There are several types of provisional production of evidence. Prior to the formal commencement of a claim, the court, in response to the petition of a party, can appoint a provisional examination of witnesses by a judge (*voorlopig getuigenverhoor*). The court can also order a provisional expert's report (*voorlopig deskundigenbericht*) or a provisional court inspection of the premises (*plaatsopneming* and *bezichtiging*). These three forms of provisional production of evidence are based on the Dutch CCP: Article 186–193 CCP (*voorlopig getuigenverhoor*) and Article 202–207 CCP (*voorlopig deskundigenbericht* and *voorlopige plaatsopneming* and *bezichtiging*).

There can be several reasons for the provisional production of evidence. Firstly, it may prevent evidence being lost. Secondly, it may help the parties concerned to assess their position in advance, i.e. prior to the formal commencement of a civil action. Claimants, defendants and third parties that might have an interest in the claim are offered the opportunity to clarify certain (perhaps not very clear) facts.[6] After hearing witnesses in advance or reading an expert's report prior to a formal action, a claimant can consider whether he will succeed in proving the facts he will have to prove in the main proceedings. Provisional production of evidence can also enable the party involved to see who he will have to file his claim against. In addition, provisional production of evidence may promote the chances of accomplishing a settlement, even without turning to the court. These objectives make it clear that the instruments of provisional production of evidence help to avoid formal proceedings.

2.2. A MISLEADING TERM

The word 'provisional' might, in this context, be misleading. When witnesses are examined by a judge in a provisional hearing, their testimonies are usually not provisional. This is made clear by Article 192 CCP: if all parties were present at the examination, their testimonies have the same evidential value as testimonies made during formal proceedings. This also applies to the

---

6 HR (Dutch Supreme Court) 24-03-1995, *NJ* 1998, 414 (Saueressig/Forbo).

provisional production of expert evidence (*voorlopig deskundigenbericht*) and the provisional court inspection of premises (*voorlopige plaatsopneming and bezichtiging*): by virtue of Article 207 CCP, if all parties were present, the outcomes of these forms of provisional production of evidence have the same probative value as evidence produced in the main proceedings. If all parties were not present, the court may disregard certain elements. But in general, the outcomes of the instruments of provisional production of evidence are far from provisional.

2.3. PROCEDURE

The above-mentioned forms of provisional production of evidence require authorization by the court, for which a petition (*verzoekschrift*) must be filed. The petition has to be directed to the court that will probably have jurisdiction to decide on the formal claim.[7] The petition for the provisional examination of witnesses must contain *inter alia* the names of the intended witnesses.[8] The petition for the provisional production of expert evidence must state the points the expert has to report on.[9] The opposing party has, in principle, the right to be heard on the petition.[10]

Authorization will be granted provided that the petition is relevant and sufficiently concrete. Despite the text of the CCP on this point (Article 186 and Article 202 CCP), judges do not have discretional power. The demands of relevancy and being to the point are not as tight as in full-length proceedings. It has to be made clear which facts are involved. It is not necessary for the petition to describe exactly on which facts the formal claim will be based.[11] The provisional production of evidence is just meant to clarify which claims can be made.

If the request for the provisional expert examination of witnesses is granted, there are no possibilities for appeal.[12] If the request is denied, appeal is

7 Article 187 para 1 and Article 202 para 1 CCP.

8 Article 187 para 3 CCP.

9 Article 203 CCP.

10 Article 187 para 4 and 203 para 3 CCP.

11 HR 19-02-1993, *NJ* 1994, 345 (Van de Ven/Pierik) and HR 13-09-2002, *NJ* 2004, 18 (Uiterlinden/Van Zijp). See B.T.M. van der Wiel, Grenzen aan het recht op voorlopige bewijslevering, *MvV* 2005, p. 67.

12 Article 188 para 2 and Article 204 para 2 CCP.

possible.[13] It is argued that if the request is only partially denied, appeal is also possible.[14]

2.4. PROVISIONAL EXAMINATION OF WITNESSES

It is fair to state that the provisional examination of witnesses plays an important part in the practice of civil litigation. The provisional examination of witnesses takes place in court, in front of a judge. Both parties and the judge can ask the witness questions. A formal written record (*proces-verbaal*) is made of the examination.

Provisional examination of witnesses is only admissible in cases that are brought before a civil court.[15] Once this is established, there is no restriction on the types of civil cases that can use this instrument. Since 1951, when the provisional examination of witnesses (*voorlopig getuigenverhoor*) was introduced, the use of this mechanism has been restricted in divorce cases. When the reform of the Dutch CCP came into force in 2002, this restriction, seen as outdated, lapsed. Since 2002 there have been no restrictions on using this instrument as far as the type of civil case is concerned. Witnesses can be heard by a judge on this 'provisional' basis, for example, for claims involving personal injury and/or for pure economic loss. It is not important whether the loss is caused by professional negligence or, for example, by a consumer.

Nevertheless, there are other restrictions. According to Article 192 CCP the court can only appoint a provisional examination of witnesses if evidence by witnesses is allowed. This is of course obvious: in cases where the CCP does not grant evidence by witnesses, for example cases related to insurance policies and agreements to conciliate, a provisional examination is excluded. This restriction does not apply very often. More important are the remedies for ill-considered petitions (see Section 2.6).

---

13 MvA en Nadere MvA TK, Parlementaire Geschiedenis van de nieuwe regeling van het bewijsrecht in burgerlijke zaken, Deventer 1988, p. 311.

14 Pitlo/Hidma & Rutgers, *Bewijs*, Deventer 2004, no. 101. See HR 22 February 2008, LJN BB 5626, R06/129HR.

15 HR 15-07-1987, *NJ* 1988, 2 (Staat/Koca) and HR 11-02-2000, *NJ* 2001, 137 (A c.s./Staat).

2.5. PROVISIONAL EXPERT EXAMINATION AND PROVISIONAL COURT INSPECTION OF A SITE

In the pre-action phase, evidence can also be produced by a provisional expert examination (*voorlopig deskundigenonderzoek*) or a provisional court inspection of a site (*voorlopige descente*). The provisional expert examination: prior to the formal commencement of a civil action, a party can request the court to consult experts. The provisional court inspection of a site concerns the option of asking the court to inspect the site to see for itself, prior to the formal commencement of an action. These forms of provisional production of evidence can be useful if perishable goods are involved. The statutory rules on provisional expert examination and provisional court inspection of a site (Article 202 – 207 CCP) are linked with the rules on the provisional examination of witnesses.

Article 202 CCP does not contain, in principle, any restrictions on a petition for a provisional expert examination or court inspection of a site. Moreover, the decisions of the courts on this issue do not set high standards for the motivation of these petitions.[16] This is in line with the remarks in Section 2.3 on the provisional examination of witnesses.

2.6. REMEDIES FOR ILL-CONSIDERED PETITIONS

Although a petition for provisional production of evidence does not have to meet very high demands, the provisional examination of witnesses can be requested for the wrong reasons. In fact, not every provisional examination of witnesses turns out to be useful. In some cases the parties use the provisional examination of witnesses as a fishing expedition, even if there is no real chance of a formal action. In some other cases parties choose a provisional examination of witnesses because of the low costs.

Provisional examination of witnesses is an often used and generally accepted instrument. Many formal proceedings have probably been prevented due to a pre-action settlement being reached on the basis of the outcomes of provisional evidence. However, at a certain point dissatisfaction prevailed

---

16 HR 06-02-1988, *NJ* 1999, 478 (M/Amev) and HR 13-09-2002, *NJ* 2004, 18.

among judges with regard to the rising numbers of non-helpful provisional examinations of witnesses.[17]

In the opinion of the Council for the Judiciary (*Raad voor de Rechtspraak*), the structure of the provisional examination of witnesses prohibits an effective and efficacious use of this mechanism. According to the Council, in a relatively large number of provisional examinations of witnesses, parties call up large numbers of witnesses although it is not clear to the judge what the provisional examination is about. This prohibits an efficient examination of witnesses and/or a well-based direction to a pre-trial settlement. In these cases a lot of valuable time is lost. The Council for the Judiciary has for these reasons suggested limiting the possibilities for provisional examination of witnesses.[18]

The Council for the Judiciary has suggested three ways of restricting the provisional examinations of witnesses: limitation of the provisional examination of witnesses to emergency cases, limitation of the provisional examination of witnesses to cases with a prominent financial interest, and raising the court registry fee for petitions for the provisional examination of witnesses. The Council also suggests that the courts should be given more authority to deny calling up some witnesses. Parties could be obliged to motivate their choice for the witnesses they want to hear.

In February 2005 the Supreme Court formulated some grounds for denial of a request for provisional examination of witnesses.[19] A petition that meets the formal demands can be turned down if this mechanism is deemed to be abused, or if it is incompatible with the principles of due process, or because there is some other grave objection to granting the petition. The request can also be turned down on the basis of the general rule that a person has no right of action where he lacks sufficient interest (Article 303 CC).[20] In this decision

---

17 Advice of the Council for the Judiciary to the Minister for Justice on the interim report 2003, Den Haag 29 April 2004 <http://www.rechtspraak.nl/gerechten/rvdr/wetgevingsadvisering/wetgevingsadvies+2004.htm> (consulted on 12 February 2008).

18 Advice of the Council for the Judiciary to the Minister for Justice on the interim report 2003, Den Haag 29 April 2004 <http://www.rechtspraak.nl/gerechten/rvdr/wetgevingsadvisering/wetgevingsadvies+2004.htm> (consulted on 12 February 2008).

19 HR 11-02-2005, *NJ* 2005, 442 (Frog/Floriade).

20 HR 11-02-2005, *NJ* 2005, 442 (*voorlopig getuigenverhoor*) and HR 13-09-2002, *NJ* 2004, 18 and HR 12-09-2003, *NJ* 2005, 441 (Royal & Sun Alliance/K) (*voorlopig deskundigenonder-*

the Supreme Court has made it clear that the grounds for rejection of a request for provisional examination of witnesses are the same as the grounds for rejection of a provisional expert examination.

The options for the court to turn down petitions for the provisional production of evidence have increased already as a result of decisions of the Supreme Court. The court has, based on these decisions, the authority to ask the party that requested the provisional examination of witnesses for information to obtain more clarity on the subject of the provisional production of evidence and on the duration and the proportions of the hearings. The authors of the fundamental review concluded that current case law offers enough space for a policy that, on the one hand, allows provisional production of evidence to play a useful role and, on the other hand, stimulates parties to motivate their requests.[21] They do not see any reason for fundamental change to the rules on the provisional production of evidence.[22]

These authors have also suggested considering written unsworn statements as witness statements, provided that they are made in the presence of all parties.[23] In addition, the party opposed to the one that requested the provisional production of evidence should no longer be free of obligations in this matter. If that party does not participate in the provisional production of evidence, this should have consequences, for example for the topic of the costs of civil litigation.

3. OBLIGATION TO PRODUCE EXHIBITS

3.1. DOCUMENTS IN THE PRE-ACTION PHASE

In general, written documents play an important role in civil proceedings in the Netherlands. Dutch civil procedural law obliges litigants – as a starting point, a litigant who refers to a document in his summons or another document presented to the court – to add a transcript of that document

---

zoek). See Advocate-General Langemeijer, advice to HR 27-01 2006, *RvdW* 2006, 131, sub 2.1.

21 Final report (2006), supra note 3, p. 71.

22 Interim report (2003), supra note 3, p. 124 and final report (2006), supra note 3, p. 69–71.

23 Interim report (2003), supra note 3, p. 124. Cf. rule 23.4 Principles of transnational civil procedure concerning an affidavit (a written unsworn statement about relevant facts of the case) and para 391 of the German ZPO that allows the court to take into account an unsworn witness statement.

presenting the relevant facts of the case (Article 85 CCP). There is a specific regulation on producing exhibits in Article 843a CCP (*exhibitieplicht*). This rule allows a party to order a transcript of certain documents from the other party.

This claim for documents based on Article 843a CCP can occur both during formal proceedings or in the pre-action phase. It can be of great interest for a party to claim documents in the pre-action phase. This makes clear the value of this obligation to produce exhibits in the pre-action phase: by exchanging information prior to formal commencement of a civil action, the claimant can better assess his own judicial position and formal proceedings may be prevented. This obligation to produce exhibits is in keeping with the tendency in civil procedural law in recent years for obligations to disclose information to be broadened.

This claim for documents has to meet certain conditions. The claimant's interest must be justified, and the documents must be related to a legal relationship in which the party requesting the transcript is involved as a party. The party which has the documents at its disposal does not have to fulfil the claim if it has important reasons for not doing so, or if delivery is unnecessary for proper administration of justice (Article 843a para 4 CCP). The stipulations for using this instrument are designed to prevent fishing expeditions.

Legal scholars have concluded that the range of application of this mechanism has increased in recent years. Court decisions and the parliamentary comments on this rule have created the opportunity for such a wide application of the obligation to produce exhibits that the authority of the parties to claim documents prior to formal proceedings is not more limited than the authority of the court to claim documents during proceedings.[24]

There is also a statutory rule concerning documents that are lost. The party that has lost a written form of evidence can, based on Article 843b CCP, claim a copy of it from the party that has documents at its disposal that might serve as evidence for a relevant fact. This rule intends to put the party that lost the document in the position it was before it lost it. To implement the European Directive on the enforcement of IP rights, in May 2007 a specific regulation

[24] J. EKELMANS, De exhibitieplicht in de praktijk, *TCR* 2005/3, p. 59–68.

came into force about demanding evidence in cases relating to intellectual property rights.[25]

3.2. ENFORCEABLE DISCLOSURE OF DOCUMENTS?

The above-mentioned options cannot conceal the fact that a party has few possibilities to force the opposing party to produce relevant facts, either in the pre-trial phase or during proceedings. Legal scholars have raised the question whether Dutch civil procedural law should contain a form of enforceable disclosure of documents.[26] The suggestions on how to model a disclosure in Dutch law are very wide-ranging. The disclosure can be based on a new interpretation of the *exhibitieplicht* of Article 843a CCP.[27] Secondly, the preliminary expert report could be used as an instrument of disclosure.[28] Another option is that the new Dutch disclosure mechanism will be modelled on disclosure in English law.[29] Standard disclosure in English law requires a party to disclose several types of document.[30] This concerns the documents on which it relies, documents that adversely affect its own case, that adversely affect another party's case and that support another party's case. This disclosure in English law is regulated by specific rules and requires judicial intervention. There is also an application permitted for disclosure before proceedings have started. This option allows the applicant to find out without undue delay whether or not he has a case for action.[31]

---

25 Article 1019a CCP.

26 See on disclosure in English law in general N. ANDREWS, *English Civil Procedure. Fundamentals of the New Civil Justice System*, Oxford 2003, chapter 26 and JOHN O'HARE and KEVIN BROWN, *Civil Litigation*, London 2005, chapter 30.

27 J.W. WESTENBERG, Een zoektocht naar de feiten?, in: *Het verzamelen van feiten en bewijs: begrenzing versus verruiming, een kruisbestuiving tussen civiel procesrecht en ondernemingsprocesrecht*, uitgave van Nederlandse Vereniging voor Procesrecht, Den Haag 2006, p. 44–45.

28 R.M. HERMANS, 'Discovery' door middel van deskundigenbericht, in: *Het verzamelen van feiten en bewijs: begrenzing versus verruiming, een kruisbestuiving tussen civiel procesrecht en ondernemingsprocesrecht* (2006), supra note 27, p. 76–79.

29 P.J. VAN DER KORST, Transparantieplicht van procespartijen: de gehele waarheid en niets dan de waarheid, in: *Het verzamelen van feiten en bewijs: begrenzing versus verruiming, een kruisbestuiving tussen civiel procesrecht en ondernemingsprocesrecht* (2006), supra note 27, p. 24–28.

30 Par. 31.6 Civil Procedure Rules.

31 See on pre-action disclosure, Andrews (2003), supra note 26, par. 26.57–26.97.

It is argued that in Dutch law an enforceable pre-trial disclosure of documents should be introduced, supervised by the court.[32] The authors of the fundamental review prefer the suggestions of the working group chaired by professor Storme in 1994. That working group proposed as substantial a disclosure or communication of documents as reasonably possible.[33] Based on his reaction to the fundamental review, it appears that the Minister for Justice has an interest in the topic of 'disclosure'.[34]

4. PROVISIONAL ATTACHMENT

4.1. IMPORTANT COMPULSORY MEASURE

Prior to the formal proceedings, a creditor can take certain compulsory measures. The provisional attachment (*conservatoir beslag*) is the most important of these. The creditor can surprise his debtor with a provisional attachment before the proceedings have begun. A provisional attachment aims to prevent the debtor transferring his assets before the case has come to court, so as to ensure that if the creditor's claim is allowed by the court, he will still be able to recoup his losses from the assets of the debtor.

If the debtor transfers the attached assets to someone else in spite of the injunction, in principle this has no consequences for the person making the attachment. Moreover, the withdrawal of property from an attachment is unlawful. Attachment can be levied against the debtor, but also in some cases by garnishment or even against the creditor. If provisional attachment is imposed prior to proceedings about the claim for which attachment is being imposed, the person making the attachment must initiate the proceedings within a certain period after making the attachment.[35]

---

32 See *inter alia* M. DE TOMBE-GROOTENHUIS, Voorstel voor een Europese disclosure, in: E.H. HONDIUS, A.W. JONGBLOED and R.CH. VERSCHUUR (eds.), *Van Nederlands naar Europees procesrecht. Liber Amicorum Paul Meijknecht*, Deventer 2000, p. 301–313 and EKELMANS (2005), supra note 24.

33 MARCEL STORME (ed.), *Rapprochement du Droit Judiciaire de l' Union européenne/Approximation of Judiciary Law in the European Union*, Dordrecht 1994, p. 97. Cf. their proposal for a European Directive on discovery, (Article 4.1.1. and Article 4.1.2.–4.5.2.). See on disclosure and pre-action protocols Section 10.1.

34 Reaction of the Minister for Justice, supra note 5, par. 44 and 119.

35 Article 700 para 3 CCP.

To implement the Directive on the enforcement of IP right a special regulation was also introduced into the law with provisional measures to protect evidence in cases relating to intellectual property rights.[36]

4.2. PRIOR PERMISSION REQUIRED

Prior permission from the court is required before a provisional attachment can be made. The court grants permission for attachment after 'summary investigation' (Article 700 para 2 CCP). It examines only very marginally whether or not the person making the attachment has a substantial claim. The focus of the investigation is on whether the claimant has furnished the facts required for this attachment rather than on the substance of the claim itself. The court is entitled to hear the other party – the debtor whose assets are to be attached – before granting permission, but in practice this does not often occur. A petition for provisional attachment is usually granted, and usually without the other party being heard. As a result, the threshold for imposing an attachment is relatively low and in practice provisional attachment is carried out frequently. A considerable number of actions are preceded by an attachment. A compulsory measure of this kind tends to cause escalation and thus to reduce the chance of an out-of-court settlement.

4.3. REMEDIES FOR ILL-CONSIDERED ATTACHMENTS

If it later turns out that the attachment was unjustified, in principle the person making the attachment is liable for any damages resulting from the attachment. For this liability (based on tort; art 6:162 CC) to come into effect, the claim on which the attachment was based must be rejected.[37] The judicial permission given for the attachment, based on an extremely cursory investigation, does not safeguard the claimant against liability. The claimant is subject to strict liability, i.e. liability which does not depend on culpability.[38] Even if the claim is only partially sustained the claimant may be liable.[39]

The debtor can counter an attachment which has been made too lightly by initiating provisional relief proceedings (*kort geding*) in order to have the attachment lifted. Article 705 CCP specifies several cases in which the court

---

36 Article 1019b CCP.

37 HR 21-02-1992, *NJ* 1992, 744 (Ontvanger/NMB).

38 HR 13-01-1995, *NJ* 1997, 366 (Ontvanger/Bos), confirmed in HR 08-02-2008, LJN BB6196.

39 See HR 11-04-2003, *NJ* 2003, 440 and HR 5-12-2003, *NJ* 2004, 150.

must lift a provisional attachment: failure to observe certain procedures; prima facie evidence that the claimant's grounds for the measure are insubstantial or that the measure is unnecessary; or if the attachment concerns a claim to money and sufficient security has been given. The legal rules concerning division of the burden of proof do not apply in provisional relief proceedings, but if the court decides that one of these grounds is present, e.g. if it finds prima facie evidence that the attachment is unnecessary, it will lift the attachment. The main reasoning behind this ground for lifting the attachment is that there is no need to fear that in the event of a decision in favour of the claimant attachment will no longer be enforceable.

It has been argued that premature attachment is treated too flexibly. Compulsory measures of this kind might lead to escalation in the preliminary phase. The authors of the fundamental review reports have therefore proposed that a premature provisional attachment should entail an obligation to pay compensation for damages, irrespective of the outcome of the subsequent proceedings.[40] They also suggested that the judicial investigation before granting permission for a provisional attachment should be more substantial. To support these proposals, Article 8 Principles on Provisional and Protective measures could be taken into account: the court ought to have the authority to require security or other conditions from the plaintiff for any injury to the defendant which may result from granting the order.[41] The authors of the fundamental review also suggested that provisional relief proceedings with the goal of having an attachment lifted must be able to succeed even if insufficient attempts have been made to solve the dispute in some other way.[42] In response to these proposals the Minister for Justice has now announced that he sees no reason for a legal restriction of the possibilities of levying prejudgment attachment. As a rule, attachment has a useful function, and any unlawfulness in connection to an ill-timed attachment can be left to the courts.[43]

---

40 Final report (2006), supra note 3, p. 63–64 and p. 75.

41 Article 8 International Law Association's Principles on Provisional and Protective Measures in International Litigation, published in *Rabels Zeitschrift* 1998, p. 128–130.

42 Interim report (2003), supra note 3, p. 123.

43 Reaction of the Minister for Justice, supra note 5, para 40.

5. PRE-ACTION PROTOCOLS

In 2006 a Code of Conduct for the Handling of Personal Injury Claims came into being. This code, developed under the supervision of Prof. J.M. Barendrecht, contains twenty principles. The preamble states that the code contains good practices for dealing with personal injury cases and that it outlines the best possible procedures for settling claims. There are also various other codes of conduct and/or regulations, such as that of the Dutch Association of Insurers.

A systematic approach to an early exchange of information between the parties is the goal of a proposal in the fundamental review. Following the example of English law pre-action protocols and offers to settle should be (further) introduced in Dutch law. Pre-action protocols in English law are codified statements of best practices for certain disputes which should be adopted in the pre-trial phase when dealing with potential claims.[44] The claims underlying the protocols, in addition to the exchange of information, should enable parties to avoid litigation by agreeing a settlement and by supporting efficient management of proceedings. There are several pre-action protocols, *inter alia* for personal injury claims, for construction and engineering disputes and for professional negligence. The development of this kind of protocols could be handled by parties who work in the field of the cases the protocol focuses on.[45] Still following the example of English law, protocols could contain a form of pre-action disclosure of documents.

The Code of Conduct for Handling Personal Injury Claims has been criticized, but also praised.[46] The Minister for Justice has asserted that codes of conduct such as that dealing with personal injury claims can help parties to solve their disputes faster and more efficiently. However, he has doubts as to whether it is helpful to attach cost sanctions to protocols.[47] In the literature,

---

44 For pre-action protocols see Andrews (2003) supra note 26, 1.13–1.18 and O'Hare and Brown (2005), supra note 26, par. 6.016–6.026.

45 See for a comparative study on pre-action settlement of personal injury claims I.N. TZANKOVA, W.C.T. WETERINGS, *Preprocessuele afwikkeling van personenschadeclaims.* Een rechtsvergelijkende studie naar de mogelijkheden tot structurering van het proces van buitengerechtelijke afwikkeling van personenschaeclaims in Nederland aan de hand van procedurele normen en andere instrumenten, Den Haag 2003.

46 In the summer of 2006 the Association of Personal Injury Lawyers distanced themselves from the Code. For the code, see for example M.L.M. RENCKENS, 'Zo zijn onze manieren', *TvP* 2006, no. 3, p. 82–83.

47 Reaction of the Minister for Justice, supra note 5, para 42 and 43.

some experts have also advocated pre-action protocols with regard to proceedings against the media.[48]

6. PARTIAL DISPUTE PROCEDURE

In 2006 the Ministry of Justice prepared a draft proposal for a legal regulation of partial disputes.[49] The goal of the proposal was to promote out-of-court settlement of personal injury and loss of dependency claims. The proposal provides for the possibility of asking the judge to decide on a partial dispute in the out-of-court negotiation phase. In this draft proposal a partial dispute is defined as a dispute relating to part of a dispute between the parties, the settlement of which may contribute to reaching a settlement agreement about the claim.

The draft Explanatory Memorandum makes it clear that positive experiences with pre-action examination of witnesses, pre-action expert opinions and pre-action court inspections of premises were a reason for making the scope of application of the partial dispute procedure quite broad. Unlike the pre-action evidence gathering procedures, this procedure is not limited to specific operations. Moreover, for the partial dispute procedure there is no requirement of urgency as there is for preliminary relief proceedings.[50] Whether the court's decision on the partial dispute can be raised for discussion again in the full-length proceedings depends on the kind of decision involved.[51]

7. PRE-ACTION CONFERENCE

7.1. NO GENERAL PRE-ACTION CONFERENCE

Dutch procedural law has no general provision for a court hearing of the parties to try to reach a settlement before formal proceedings commence. In principle, a hearing at which the judge makes some remarks and then the parties explore the possibilities of a settlement takes place only when the proceedings are already underway and written documents have been

48 See for example L.R. van Harinxma thoe Slooten, 'Snel en goedkoop procederen tegen de media', *NJB* 2005, p. 340–347.

49 The proposal may be found at <www.justitie.nl> (last consulted in March 2008).

50 Draft Explanatory Memorandum (to be consulted at <www.justitie.nl>), para 3.

51 See draft article 1019o Rv.

submitted by the parties (a summons by the claimant and a statement of defence by the defendant).[52] Even though the dispute between the parties may have been going on for a long time, the parties meet under the supervision of a judge only when proceedings have been underway for some time.

However, a pre-action hearing is possible in connection with a provisional examination of witnesses. By virtue of Article 191 CCP, at the request of the parties or ex officio the judge may order the parties to appear at a court hearing after a provisional examination of witnesses. This hearing may serve to attempt to reach a settlement, to provide information or to make procedural arrangements.

7.2. PRE-ACTION CONFERENCE IN APPEAL

An experiment was conducted in 2004 in which in a limited number of civil cases the Arnhem court of appeal ordered a court hearing of the parties which more or less preceded appeal proceedings. Lodging an appeal against the decision of a district court is done by means of a notice of appeal. The notice of appeal does not have to include substantive objections to the district court's decision. During the experiment in a selected group of cases the parties were ordered to appear as soon as the case was brought before the court, in other words before the substantive objections to the district court's decision had been formulated. The main goal was to try to reach a settlement. After all, by this point a decision had been reached by the district court (a disappointment to the loser) and an appeal had been lodged (a disappointment to the winner). This might mean that the parties were ripe for a settlement which had not previously been an option. Secondary goals of the conferences were to gain information, to explore the possibilities of mediation, to discuss possible evidence and to reach procedural agreements. The initial results showed that in 60% of the cases a settlement was reached at the hearing or immediately after it.[53] At present a personal appearance hearing may be held at four of the five Courts of Appeal in the Netherlands after the notice of appeal has been served.

---

52 See Article 131 in conjunction with Article 87 CCP.

53 W.L. VALK, C.G. TER VEER, 'De comparitie na aanbrengen in hoger beroep', *NJB* 2005/38, p. 1985–1987.

7.3. MORE PRE-ACTION CONFERENCES?

It is argued that the court's facilitating role in the preliminary phase should be extended. Each of the parties should be able to request a conference with the judge in the preliminary phase of actions. In this conference the possibilities of a settlement could be examined and procedural arrangements made.[54] However, it has been observed in various quarters that at this point the court would have insufficient information to be of service to the parties.[55] The Minister for Justice recently stated that at present there is no need for a general regulation of pre-action personal appearance hearings.[56]

8. OBLIGATIONS TO INFORM IN THE SUMMONS

There a few obligations to disclose information which precede litigation in a certain sense. An action is initiated by a summons. In this summons the claimant must state what defence the defendant has put forward against the claim and the grounds of this defence. Inasmuch as the defendant has disputed the claim, the claimant must also state how he can prove his allegations.[57] It is usually advisable for the claimant to provide evidence at once. The goal of this obligation to substantiate a claim and provide evidence for it, which came into force as of 1 January 2002, is to make proceedings more efficient and to penetrate quickly to the core of the dispute. However, violation of these obligations does not make the summons void. The court may order missing evidence to be provided. If a party does not comply with this order the court may draw conclusions as it sees fit.

This obligation to provide information and evidence is connected with the summons and in a certain sense has nothing to do with the preliminary phase, since the action commences on the day the summons is issued. However, it does imply that in the pre-action phase a claimant must consider the future defendant's defence and the evidence.

---

54 Interim report (2003), supra note 3, p. 125 and final report (2006), supra note 3, p. 75.

55 See *inter alia* Advice council for the judiciary (2004), supra note 13, nr. 2.

56 Reaction of the Minister for Justice, supra note 5, par. 41.

57 Article 111 para 3 CCP.

9. ALTERNATIVE DISPUTE RESOLUTION

The Netherlands has various other forms of dispute resolution in addition to the administration of justice in the courts. Mediation is one of them. At present mediation is not compulsory according to Dutch law. There is no legal provision obliging the parties to seek mediation before applying to the court.

The question has arisen whether mediation should be made compulsory before the initiation of court proceedings. In 2004 the Minister for Justice stated that mediation could not be made an absolute condition to access to the courts. An absolute obligation of this kind would violate the right to access to an independent judicial authority.[58] The draft proposal a for a guideline about mediation in civil and commercial cases does not include an obligation to seek mediation prior to formal proceedings.[59]

The Ministry of Justice wants to promote the awareness and use of mediation by means of a number of policy measures.[60] In April 2005 a project began with the goal of implementing referrals within the courts. Since then 26 courts of law have implemented facilities for referring people to mediation. In 2007 an interim report was issued about the results of these referrals.[61] The aim is to issue a final report in 2009, after which further decisions can be made.[62]

The question has now arisen among legal scholars as to whether it is desirable for mediation to be made compulsory in certain cases. Opinions on this subject are divided. Those in favour argue that mediation is not about excluding access to the civil courts, but postponing it.[63] Others – and this seems to be the majority view – reject the idea, with reference for example to

---

58 TK 2003–2004, 29 528, no. 2. p. 11. Cf. interim report (2003), supra note 3, p. 123 and p. 58.

59 Proposal for a Directive of the European Parliament and of the Council on certain aspects of mediation in civil and commercial matters, COM (2004) 718 final.

60 See TK 2003–2004, 29 528, no. 1, p. 9.

61 J. REITSMA, M. TURNEWU & M. TER VOERT, *Mediation Monitor* 2007, Tussenrapportage. WODC, Cahier 2007-6.

62 L COMBRINK, 'De doorverwijzing naar mediation binnen de Nederlandse gerechten in cijfers', *TvM* 2007 (11) 4, p. 7.

63 A.F.M. BRENNINKMEIJER et al. (eds.), *Juridische aspecten van mediation*, Den Haag 2005, p. 126–127.

the right to go to court.[64] A more practical objection is that there are no criteria for determining which cases are suited to mediation.[65]

10. PROVISIONAL RELIEF PROCEEDINGS

Strictly speaking provisional relief proceedings (or summary proceedings; *kort geding*) are not part of the pre-action phase. Full-length civil proceedings may take a long time; provisional relief proceedings make it possible to provide temporary relief in the short term in urgent cases.[66] The claimant can request immediate relief at the preliminary injunction court.[67] The most important condition for entitlement to a remedy through provisional relief proceedings is that urgent interests are involved. It must be clear that the claimant cannot wait for a decision in full-length proceedings. There must be grounds for immediate judicial intervention.

In provisional relief proceedings the procedures are different than in full-length proceedings. No written documents are exchanged. After the claimant's summons a hearing takes place in which claimant and defendant put forward their positions orally; sometimes a memorandum of oral pleadings is submitted. The legal rules of evidence do not apply, because they are not compatible with the nature of provisional relief proceedings, focusing as they do on speed. The preliminary injunction court may disregard an offer to produce evidence even though it would be relevant in full-length proceedings.[68] The rules concerning burden of proof and the obligation to furnish facts do not apply in provisional relief proceedings either.[69]

In provisional relief proceedings the court can provide interim relief; it is not competent to take definitive measures. The decision the claimant wants must be a measure which as it were anticipates the judicial decision which would be pronounced in full-length proceedings. Immediately enforceable decisions do not prejudice the principal action in any way.[70] Previous Supreme Court

---

64 A. DE ROO & R. JAGTENBERG, *Europese mediationpraktijken*, den Haag, p. 93.

65 Interim report, p. 57. For an overview of the discussion about compulsory mediation see A.H. SANTING-WUBS, *Mediation in juridisch perspectief*, Deventer 2007, section 7.2 (and for the mediation clause and access to the court section 7.4).

66 Article 254–260 CCP.

67 Article 254 ff. CCP.

68 HR 12-12-1975, *NJ* 1976, 495 (Akaha/Van Roon).

69 HR 2-10-1998, *NJ* 1999, 682 (De Schelde/erven Wijkhuisen).

70 Article 257 CCP.

decisions have shown that the decision of the court in provisional relief proceedings does not in fact have any influence on the decision of the court in full-length proceedings. The fact that the consequences of a provisional remedy may be irreversible is not an obstruction to granting this remedy.[71]

A wide variety of measures are requested in provisional relief proceedings: for example, a prohibition against performing a certain action or an order to perform it or an advance on compensation of damages. Over the course of time, provisional relief proceedings have developed in practice into an important instrument to gain provisional relief in urgent cases. In a large number of cases eventually no full-length proceedings are initiated. This shows not only that provisional relief proceedings are a successful instrument, but also that in practice they prevent full-length proceedings, and in this sense can be regarded as a pre-action instrument.

11. RIGHT OF INQUIRY

11.1. RIGHT OF INQUIRY AND THE PRE-ACTION PHASE

The Dutch Civil Code also includes the possibility of so-called inquiry proceedings.[72] This statutory regulation makes it possible to apply to the court to set up an inquiry into the policy and the operation of a corporate entity. Opinions expressed in the literature on the objective and scope of this regulation are divided, but it seems to be commonly accepted that some of the objectives of the regulation are to promote openness and to restore sound relations, and to ascertain who is responsible for any mismanagement which may come to light.[73]

The regulation specifies precisely who is authorized to file a petition for an inquiry.[74] In practice it is usually shareholders who make use of this instrument. If the petition is to be granted, a condition is that there are good grounds to doubt the soundness of the corporate entity's policy (Article 2:350 CC). When a petition is allowed, certain individuals are appointed to carry out the inquiry. They are given certain powers. Based on their findings, the court may decide that there has been mismanagement. It is also authorized to

71 See HR 11-02-1994, *NJ* 1994, 651 (Van Kooten/Wilmink).

72 Article 2:344–2:359 CC.

73 See on right of inquiry in general P.G.F.A. GEERTS, *Enkele formele aspecten van het enquêterecht*, dissertatie Rijksuniversiteit Groningen 2004.

74 Article 2:346 CC.

take measures. Upon request, for the duration of the action it may also take interim measures.

Inquiry proceedings are relevant to the phase prior to formal litigation in more than one respect. Firstly, the regulation has a preliminary phase of its own. The proceedings cannot be initiated without previous notice. Before those entitled to institute an inquiry file a petition they must notify the executive board and the supervisory board in writing of their objections to the policy and operation of the company and give the company a reasonable period to examine these objections and to take measures to address them.[75] In other words, the company may not be taken by surprise. Secondly, one outcome of the procedure might be that there is no ground for action.

In practice, applications for an inquiry play an important role.[76] It has also been observed in the literature that the enterprise division aims to achieve broader application of the right of inquiry.[77] Over the course of time the right of inquiry has become more important. In practice this right seems to be expanding. It has been observed that the interests of the company are no longer always the prime motive for the proceedings, but that the right of inquiry is frequently used for the personal benefit of the applicant, namely to collect material which might be used to initiate proceedings against interested parties involved in the company.[78] This expansion of the right of inquiry focuses mainly on using the regulation for the purposes of subsequent liability proceedings.[79]

---

75 Article 2:349 CC.

76 Geerts has noticed that the Enterprise section of the Amsterdam Court of Appeal (*ondernemingskamer*) in 2005 has given 69 substanstive decisions and 101 other decisions on the right of inquiry (Kroniek Enquêterecht 2005, in: M. HOLTZER, A.F.J.A. LEIJTEN en D.J. ORANJE (eds.), *Geschriften vanwege de Vereniging Corporate Litigation 2005-2006*, Deventer: Kluwer 2006, p. 9.

77 See J.M.M. MAEIJER, Mr. C. Asser's, Handleiding tot de beoefening van het Nederlands burgerlijk recht. *Vertegenwoordiging en rechtspersoon. De naamloze en de besloten vennootschap*, Deventer 2000, no. 525.

78 Advocate-General Timmerman, advice to HR 18-11-2005, NJ 2006, 173, sub 4.13.

79 E.M. WESSELING-VAN GENT, To Fish or not to Fish, that's the question, in: *Het verzamelen van feiten en bewijs: begrenzing versus verruiming, een kruisbestuiving tussen civiel procesrecht en ondernemingsprocesrecht (2006)*, supra note 27, p. 88.

11.2. RIGHT OF INQUIRY AND PROVISIONAL EXAMINATION OF WITNESSES

Recently, attention has also been paid to the relationship between the right of inquiry and the provisional examination of witnesses as described in Article 186 CCP. The decision of the enterprise division in the Laurus case in 2003 shows that there is no place for provisional examination of witnesses if an inquiry has been ordered. According to the enterprise division it would constitute an unacceptable interference in the right of inquiry system if in addition to the inquiry conducted by the appointed investigators a different sort of investigation were to be conducted into the policy and operation of the corporate entity.[80] In other words, according to the enterprise division inquiry proceedings are a lex specialis which excludes the possibility of holding a provisional examination of witnesses.[81] If an inquiry has not yet been allowed, there is room for a provisional examination of witnesses. Parties entitled to an inquiry can use the findings of this examination in the preliminary phase of the application referred to above. Moreover, by virtue of Article 2:349a CC the enterprise division is authorized to examine witnesses and experts ex officio before making a decision about the petition.

12. MASS CLAIMS

In July 2005 the Collective Settlement of Mass Damages Act came into force.[82] This Act provides specific regulation of the settlement of mass damage claims. The intention of this legislation is for representatives of the injured parties to talk to the parties which caused the damage and to reach an agreement pertaining to a collective settlement of the damages. This agreement will specify which injured parties will receive compensation and on what conditions. Parties to the agreement may then turn to the court and jointly ask this mass claims agreement to be declared universally binding. If the court agrees to their request, in principle the agreement is binding for all injured parties, whether or not they were involved in the negotiations. The consequence is that all injured parties who meet the conditions of the agreement are entitled to compensation, but on the other hand they no

---

80 Enterprise section Amsterdam Court of Appeal 09-01-2004, *Ondernemingsrecht* 2004-5, no. 61.

81 See M.M. Tuitel, Samenloop van voorlopig getuigenverhoor en enquête: lex specialis derogat lex generalis? in: M. HOLTZER, A.F.J.A. LEIJTEN and D.J. ORANJE (eds.), *Geschriften vanwege de Vereniging Corporate Litigation 2005- 2006*, supra note 76, p. 245–262.

82 Article 7:907 – 7:910 CC and Article 1013 – 1018 CCP.

longer have the option of initiating an action themselves with regard to the incident in question. Injured parties who do not wish to be bound by the agreement can opt out within a period to be specified by the court. If they take this opportunity to opt out, they reserve the option of taking legal action against the parties responsible for the damage.

This new legislation is relevant to the phase prior to formal litigation in more than one respect. It has a preliminary phase of its own; it is only after they have reached an agreement between themselves that the parties may apply to the court to have their agreement declared universally binding. Moreover, this regulation may prevent a large number of individual actions being initiated and is therefore more efficient for everyone involved, both the parties and the judiciary. Legal scholars have suggested that the court should be given a role in the pre-action phase of mass claim cases. Court supervision of negotiations regarding mass damages settlement might increase the chances of reaching a collective settlement of the damages.[83] It does not seem likely that this will take place in the short term.

13. FINAL REMARKS

There is no systematic approach in Dutch civil procedural law to procedures prior to the formal commencement of a civil action. There are several instruments available in the pre-action phase – in fact, there are a considerable number of instruments. They cover various aspects of the pre-action phase, ranging from the production of evidence to compulsory measures and provisional relief proceedings.

Legal scholars have developed several innovative proposals for reform. New procedural instruments in the pre-action phase will have their limitations and disadvantages. The frontloading of costs would be one of them. These are costs that would not have been incurred had the pre-action instrument in question been avoided. It is plausible that the introduction of more pre-action instruments might increase the costs of pre-action proceedings, both for potential litigants and for judicial authorities. However, a broader perspective on the pre-action phase may have benefits, such as an increased chance of

---

83 W.L. VALK, Het wetsvoorstel collectieve afwikkeling van massaschade vanuit het perspectief van de rechtspraak, in: *Het wetsvoorstel collectieve afwikkeling van massaschade*, uitgave van Nederlandse Vereniging voor procesrecht, Den Haag 2005, p. 47–53 and H.B. KRANS, Een nieuwe aanpak van massaschade, *NTBR* 2005, 2, p. 2–13.

out-of-court settlements and greater efficiency of proceedings. These two elements seem to be common to proposals relating to the pre-action phase.

NEW TRENDS IN PRE-ACTION: GENERAL REPORT

H.A. GROEN

1. INTRODUCTION

The topic of this report is new trends in Pre-Action.[1]

It is about the recent developments in habits or rules – if any – governing the stage of a dispute between parties before the commencement of a civil procedure by the plaintiff.
It focuses therefore on the preliminary phase.

In particular in common law countries, but also in Scandinavia, the trial is the central element in the civil procedure.

---

1 Based upon the following national reports, for which the author is grateful:
ARGENTINA (Roberto Omar Berizonce, Universidad Nacional de La Plata)
AUSTRIA (Georg Kodek, Vienna)
AUSTRALIA (David Bamford, Flinders University)
BELGIUM (Paul van Orshoven and Benoît Allemeersch, Catholic University of Leuven)
BRAZIL (Paulo Henrique dos Santos Lucon, University of São Paulo Law School)
CANADA (Colleen M Hanycz)
DENMARK (1) (M Gregers Larsen, practitioner, Copenhagen)
DENMARK (2) (Laura Ervo, Universities of Helsinki and Turku)
FINLAND (Laura Ervo, Universities of Helsinki and Turku)
GERMANY (Michael Breyer, Düsseldorf)
GREECE (Constantin Polyzogopoulos, University of Athens)
ICELAND (Laura Ervo, Universities of Helsinki and Turku)
NORWAY (Laura Ervo, Universities of Helsinki and Turku)
PORTUGAL (Miguel Teixeira de Sousa and Paula Costa e Silva, University of Lisbon)
SOUTH AFRICA (Wouter de Vos, Rhodes University)
SPAIN (José Luis Vasques Sotelo, University of Barcelona)
SWEDEN (Laura Ervo, Universities of Helsinki and Turku)
SWITZERLAND (Tanja Domej, University of Zurich)
THE NETHERLANDS (Bart Krans, University of Groningen)
UNITED STATES OF AMERICA (Richard Marcus, Hastings College of the Law, San Francisco).

As many national reports show, there is a tendency, once proceedings have started, to regulate the stage before the actual trial, and see whether the parties cannot reach an agreement without the trial being held.

Pre-action instruments aim at avoiding or at least streamlining the procedure. It therefore seems useful to discuss new trends in pre-trial also in the framework of a discussion about new trends in pre-action.
The reasoning behind the introduction of specific instruments may not be identical, but common themes unquestionably emerge.

As the national reports amply show, much can be said about pre-trial or pre-action, even if in some jurisdictions no attention seems to be paid to a phase before the actual proceedings.[2]
I intend to focus on a few main aspects, in particular on those aspects where, in my opinion, new trends can be discerned. I will do so, by going, as it were, backward from proceedings, to pre-trial to pre-action.

Before doing so, let me say a few words about lawyers conduct and protective measures.

2. LAWYERS CONDUCT

Lawyers often play an important role in disputes between their clients. From time immemorial they have had the habit of introducing their clients' disputes in letters to the other party or the other party's lawyer.

Many national reporters mention, as an aspect of preliminary behaviour, the rules of proper conduct of their national bar association, aimed at compromise and avoiding unnecessary legal disputes.[3]

---

2 PORTUGAL (Miguel Teixeira de Sousa and Paula Costa e Silva, University of Lisbon) commenting: Portugal does not recognise any pre-action rules, in addition writing that they are not aware of any proposals for the implementation of pre-action procedures in Portugal.

3 CANADA (Colleen M Hanycz) citing the C.B.A. Code commenting: "we see similar language to the provincial guidelines noted above. Following the rule around advising clients that mandates the lawyer to be "both honest and candid when advising clients", one of the interpretive commentaries holds:

Compromise or Settlement

Principles of civil law require anyone who wishes to make a claim to first address a formal and reasonable substantiated demand for payment, delivery or performance to the counterparty and act in good faith in an effort to avoid needless litigation and the costs resulting from it.[4]

In order to be able to write a letter, aimed at, and with the effect of, convincing the other party, it will be necessary to collect the facts and put these into a structure, in accordance with the legal provisions concerned. Structuring therefore should start already in an early phase of the disputes.[5]

3. PROTECTIVE MEASURES

Prior to initiating formal proceedings, prospective plaintiffs might feel the need to prevent their prospective respondents from leaving the jurisdiction to have certain assets transferred, or evidence destroyed.

Many reports make reference to protective instruments in this respect.

> The lawyer should advise and encourage the client to compromise or settle a dispute whenever possible on a reasonable basis and should discourage the client from commencing or continuing useless legal proceedings."

DENMARK (1) (M Gregers Larsen, practitioner, Copenhagen) commenting that the Code of Conduct established by the Danish Bar Association imposes on the attorney obligation to seek a solution to the client's problem at the lowest cost possible including whenever appropriate, advise on the advantage of trying to settle the matter out of court and/or the possibility of mediation.

4 The present author remembers a story told to him by a Rotterdam lawyer. In that Dutch harbour-city the court and the lawyers were famous for their practical attitude towards disputes.
If your client received a summons, as a lawyer, you used to make a telephone call with the claimants' lawyer and ask him whether the two of you should have a talk in order to come to a solution. Having that habit in mind, my former colleague was very upset when he once, having sent out a summons on behalf of his client, did not get a call, but received a written response in the court proceedings.

5 UNITED STATES OF AMERICA (Richard Marcus, Hastings College of the Law, San Francisco) commenting on the demand letter tradition, citing an experienced American lawyer (Shapiro) who wrote: Few rituals in litigation seem to be as common and well accepted as the demand letter. It is a time-honored tradition to begin hostilities with a summary of one's beef. It's not just that the demand letter allows a party to get his complaints off his chest. There are many correlative benefits. It communicates seriousness. Well written, it may persuade, leading to a quick resolution. Even if it does not, it sets the terms of the controversy in a manner useful to the eventual plaintiff and defendant alike. And in some sense it seems only fair, before the start of a lawsuit proper; in some quarters, not sending a demand letter at the outset is the equivalent of litigation bad manners.

The most far reaching of these instruments is perhaps the procedure to prevent a debtor from leaving the country by having him arrested in order to "keep him within the jurisdiction of the court until it has given judgement against him".[6]

Less far reaching, but not necessarily less effective, are freezing orders,[7] and leave by the court for provisional attachment,[8] aimed at preventing "prospective defendants from disposing of their assets".
Reference is also made to the possibility of a court order for the preservation of potential evidence.[9]

As to new trends, some reports mention a more critical attitude of the courts with respect to ex-parte petitions for protective measures.[10]
Attention is also being paid to the question whether the frequent use of freezing injunctions in the preliminary phase, necessarily leading to court proceedings, is not diametrically opposed to the idea that the preliminary phase is intended for efforts to avoid such proceedings, if at all possible.[11]

---

6 SOUTH AFRICA (Wouter de Vos, Rhodes University) describing this 'arrest tamquam suspectus de fuga'. 'In order to succeed with this remedy the creditor must show that the debtor is on the verge of departing permanently from South Africa with the intention of evading his debts.'

7 SOUTH AFRICA (Wouter de Vos, Rhodes University) describing these so called Anton Pillar and Mareva orders, also commented for AUSTRALIA (David Barnford, Flinders University)

8 THE NETHERLANDS (Bart Krans, University of Groningen) describing this as the most important compulsory measure.

9 ARGENTINA (Roberto Omar Berizonce, Universidad Nacional de La Plata) commenting that preparatory measures aim "to get the facts and information that are essential to the party for the regular constitution of a future process, when required data cannot be collected without the judicial intervention, or to simplify the later trial developments".
AUSTRIA (Georg Kodek, Vienna) mentioning the "Beweissicherung" , a special procedure to preserve evidence if there is a danger that the evidence may be unavailable at the trial.
THE NETHERLANDS (Bart Krans, University of Groningen) commenting: "The Dutch instruments in the field of pre-action conduct of litigation mainly concern the field of the law of evidence. There are several types of provisional production of evidence. Prior to the formal commencement of a claim, the court, in response to the petition of a party, can appoint a provisional examination of witnesses by a judge (*voorlopig getuigenverhoor*). The court can also order a provisional expert's report (*voorlopig deskundigenbericht*) or a provisional court inspection of the premises (*plaatsopneming* and *bezichtiging*).".

10 AUSTRALIA (David Bamford, Flinders University) commenting: "The interference with and impact upon defendants is such that Australian courts regard them as exceptional remedies".

11 W.D.H. Asser, H.A. Groen, J.B.M. Vranken, and I.N. Tzankova, A new balance, A summary of the Interim report Fundamental review of the Dutch law of civil procedure, ZZPInt 8 (2003), P.358 "In the Netherlands it is very easy for a creditor to pounce upon his debtor

4. STRUCTURING PROCEEDINGS

Strictly speaking, we are dealing with pre-action and not with action itself. But the picture, arising from several reports, shows that at least some (ideas behind) new trends in structuring proceedings reflect themselves in pre-trial procedures and in pre-action.

The revised Dutch code of civil procedure, inspired for example by the German code, and unmistakeably by the recommendations of Lord Woolf, obliges any party that appears in court to present his claim and his defence as completely as possible, in particular with respect to the facts.

The idea is clearly to give as much information as necessary to assist the court in reaching a well-founded decision as quickly as possible[12]

---

with attachments before the proceedings have begun (the so-called *"conservatoire beslagen"*, cf. the English freezing injunctions). Of course permission must be obtained for this from the district court, but that is virtually always given immediately in an ex parte-petition without the other party to that petition being heard. The protection of the latter is found in the very easy and quick way – against provision of security – for obtaining the lifting of such an injunction in the *kort geding*. Such an injunction must however be followed by bringing proceedings, with the result that a great many proceedings in the Netherlands in fact begin with bringing a freezing injunction. This represents a line through the account of a preliminary phase in which every effort is made to prevent proceedings. In order to avoid escalation due to such compulsory measures in the preliminary phase, we propose that a premature freezing injunction should lead to an obligation to pay compensation for the damage suffered as a result of this by the person against whom the injunction is brought, that is irrespective of the outcome of the subsequent proceedings".

12 GERMANY (Michael Breyer, Düsseldorf) commenting: "A system like the German one, which knows fact pleading and a loser-pays rule, creates a special interest in pre-action access to information as distinct from the interest in having access after formal commencement of proceedings. Under German pleading rules, parties have to furnish the detailed factual basis of the legal contentions which justify their claims or affirmative defenses. In addition, parties must identify specific means of proof supporting their specific factual allegations to the extent not admitted by the other party. Plaintiff further has to specify the remedy sought. For money claims this means as a general principle that the amount sought has to be specified. The courts, however, accept that money claims need not be specified in cases in which the amount due may only be determined by judicial estimation. Typically, this is the case for damages for pain and suffering. If the burden of allegation (*Darlegungslast*) or the burden of seeking a specific remedy is not met, the claim or defense is dismissed without the taking of any evidence."

THE NETHERLANDS (Bart Krans, University of Groningen) commenting: "There (are) a few obligations to disclose information which precede litigation in a certain sense. An action is initiated by a summons. In this summons the claimant must state what defence the defendant has put forward against the claim and the grounds of this defence. Inasmuch as the

5. STRUCTURING PRE-TRIAL

Recent developments in Scandinavian countries show a preference for an oral, immediate and concentrated procedure, and the need to create a separate stage in this procedure, in order to become well prepared for such a procedure.

In Finland,[13] part of the preparations for the proper trial, is a preliminary oral session after the written preparation.

---

defendant has disputed the claim, the claimant must also state how he can prove his allegations.[12] It is usually advisable for the claimant to provide evidence at once. The goal of this obligation to substantiate a claim and provide evidence for it, which came into force as of 1 January 2002, is to make proceedings more efficient and to penetrate quickly to the core of the dispute. However, violation of these obligations does not make the summons void. The court may order missing evidence to be provided. If a party does not comply with this order the court may draw conclusions as it sees fit.

This obligation to provide information and evidence is connected with the summons and in a certain sense has nothing to do with the preliminary phase, since the action commences on the day the summons is issued. However, it does imply that in the pre-action phase a claimant must consider the future defendant's defence and the evidence".

13 FINLAND (Laura Ervo, Universities of Helsinki and Turku) commenting: " The reform of 1993 was intended to increase the chances of litigants obtaining a correct, well-founded, judicial decision whilst simultaneously streamling the procedures involved. The lower courts were being equipped to deal with intricate cases more thoroughly than before, and with straightforward cases more quicly than earlier. The underlying values were due process of law on the one hand and the rational disbursement of resources on the other.

The reformed procedural system can be described as a "filter" or "strainer" system. The principal aim of the system is to make it possible to decide the cases immediately when they are clear and ready for deciding. Only complex or unclear cases will have to go through the whole system. This is how the judicial power of the state hopes to dispense its resources in a rational way. The pre-trial stage has, of course, very important role among this "filter" system.

The reformed system requires the whole case to be prepared well beforehand. Under the old system it was possible to lawyers to prepare cases piecemeal, as the proceedings evolved, and to eke out the preparatory work over a substantial period of time. The new powers of the courts will now compel litigants and their lawyers to be far more conscientious when they are preparing their cases for trial. For instance the threat of the preclusion compels the parties and their representatives to prepare the whole case already in the beginning of the case because if the legal fact or the piece of evidence has precluded, there is no possibility to reveal to it later. This is, of course, very effective in one way, but on the other hand it can also make the proceedings expensive and slow when the parties have to take all possible conditions into consideration even beforehand.

The reforms were intended to bring about a situation where there is no possibility of adjourning the case, and where everything will be decided in one session. It was no longer

Pre-trial procedures in Sweden[14] and the other Scandinavian countries are based on the same principles.

Three functions of pre-trial procedures can be discerned: prepare for the trial; by doing so, see whether cases can be decided upon without having a trial; and, last but not least, actively seek conciliation between the parties.
In this last respect, the courts have a specific obligation. In Denmark, such an attempt is made mostly, if not only, by the court at the end of the actual trial. [15] In Norway it is made during preparation for the trial, provided that efforts in the pre-action stage did not succeed.[16]

---

permitted to ledge or to read from written statements at the hearings, and the proceedings are now required to be completely oral".

14 SWEDEN (Laura Ervo, Universities of Helsinki and Turku) commenting: "The Swedish and Finnish pre-trial procedures are almost identical and based on the same main procedural principles namely orality, immediacy and concentration. This is no wonder because the Swedish system has been a model for Finland. Even the historical development has been very closed to each other. Finland has namely started with the same starting points and strict rules in order to respect these principles named above even when Sweden has already ceased to use them as a whole and made some exceptions because of the reasonableness and the practical needs. Later the same need for re-reform with exceptions and rules with more discretion came current also in Finland.
It is typical for the civil proceedings in these both countries that there are two different stages, namely the pre-trial stage and then the main proceedings. In this system, the pre-trial hearing has a very important rule. The function of preparation is to serve the main hearing. The other function is to have a possibility to decide clear and simple cases as soon as they are ready for decision. Therefore there are many possibilities to decide the case finally already during the pre-trial stage and without the main hearing. The trend has been to add these possibilities. Nowadays even the decision based on documentary merits is possible in some situations during the pre-trial stage.
The main difference in general is that in Sweden there is even more discretion in procedural rules covering the pre-trial stage. Especially the principle of orality has been modified more than in Finland in the name of reasonableness. However, the Swedish procedure as a whole is based on the orality which has been seen as a very important and valuable principle also in post-modern proceedings, where the technical possibilities, that is phone and videoconference are increased the possibilities refuse to organize the face to face sessions. In spite of these modern possibilities the oral hearing, where all the parties and the members of the court are at present at the same time, has been seen very important in order to maximize the communication in the proceedings. The best possible communication is important because it serves the effectiveness of the proceedings including both time, costs and legal certainty."

15 DENMARK (Laura Ervo, Universities of Helsinki and Turku) commenting: "The existing legislation in Denmark is very similar to other Scandinavian countries, especially to Sweden and Finland. However, the wide reform on the Danish civil proceedings is in progress. The most important difference between Danish and other Scandinavian pre-trial procedures is that in the most of cases the Danish court will mediate at the end of the main hearing when

In both countries this is on condition, of course, that such an attempt is not considered to be a waste of time. It should be mentioned that, whilst Norwegian courts in the past could always try to mediate the case, this option has changed into a duty, again, provided that possibilities for a successful outcome can be seen.

Although an amicable solution can always be reached in spite of proceedings being underway in court, a recent innovation in Greece introduced expressis verbis the possibility of mediation during the proceedings, directed however not by the court, but by the lawyers to the parties or by a third person, acting as a mediator.
The results so far do not seem – from a point of avoiding further proceedings – very promising.[17]

---

the mediation in other Scandinavian countries should usually happen during the preparatory stage. The Danish mediation is based on the idea that the settlement is achieved with the court´s proposal, which will be based on the imagined judgment."

16 NORWAY (Laura Ervo, Universities of Helsinki and Turku) commenting: "The judicial mediation is not an alternative to the procedure before the Conciliation Board or other compulsory mediation before the suit can be brought into court. The judicial mediation happens later when there already is a case brought before the court. So, the judicial mediation can be the second attempt to make a friendly settlement."

17 GREECE (Constantin Polyzogopoulos, University of Athens) commenting: "Une des innovations les plus importantes des dernières réformes du Cpc par le législateur grec dans son effort d' accélérer le procès devant le tribunal de grande instance, fut l' introduction d' une nouvelle forme de tentative de conciliation ou médiation qui porte le titre: « tentative de solution extra-judiciaire au litige » (art. 214A Cpc).
En vérité il s' agit d' une autre forme de « médiation » pendant le procès (donc pas vraiment extra-judiciaire), mais qui est dirigée non pas par le tribunal mais par les avocats des plaideurs ou par un tiers.
Selon l' art. 214A Cpc, tout acte soumis à la compétence d' attribution du tribunal de grande instance selon les règles de la procédure ordinaire, ne peut pas former l' objet d' une audience devant le tribunal sans une tentative préalable de solution extra-judiciaire au litige! Dans ce cas, la notification de l' acte et de la fixation de l' affaire (citation), contient déjà l' invitation au défendeur à comparaître au cabinet de l' avocat du demandeur ou à l' office du barreau en vue de la tentative de conciliation. Pendant les séances qui auront lieu entre le cinquième jour après la notification de la citation et le trente-cinquième jour avant le jour d' appel de l' affaire, les avocats avec ou sans les parties, parfois assistés par une tierce personne d' approbation mutuelle, vont tenter de trouver une solution au litige sans être liés par des règles du droit matériel ou du Cpc.
Si un accord ne paraît pas possible, ou en défaut de comparution de la partie invitée, les avocats (ou l' avocat du démandeur seul) établissent un procès-verbal qui constate l' échec de la tentative de conciliation et le présentent au tribunal pendant l' audience pour que la cause puisse être appelée. Dans le cas inverse, le procès-verbal, qui contient l' accord des parties, sera présenté au Président du tribunal de grande instance devant lequel la cause est fixée, qui

Based on the Norwegian example, Finland[18] and Sweden[19] recently introduced the possibility for the court to transfer a case to mediation.[20] In Finland and Sweden judges may act as mediator.

6. STRUCTURING PRE-ACTION

As to structuring the pre-action phase, there may be statutory provisions forcing the prospective plaintiff to obtain leave from the court, before starting the actual procedure.[21]

---

procédera à l' homologation nécessaire afin que le procès-verbal obtienne force exécutoire. Dans ce cas, le tribunal est dessaisi à cause de l' extinction immédiate de l' instance (art. 214A §§ 3 ss.). "

18 FINLAND (Laura Ervo, Universities of Helsinki and Turku) commenting: "In the spring of 2003 a committee appointed by the Ministry of Justice proposed that a system of court mediation should be introduced in Finland, based on the Norwegian example. The proposal came into force at the beginning of this year. According to the new system, a district court judge may, with the parties´consent, transfer the case to mediation. At this stage, the civil suit would be suspended. The mediator is another judge. If mediation failed, the trial would continue.[18] The new system is introduced in addition to the earlier system for promoting settlements. So, it is not replacing it".

19 SWEDEN (Laura Ervo, Universities of Helsinki and Turku) commenting: "According to Chapter 42, Section 6 of the Code the court shall investigate if there are possibilities for friendly decision in the case. This rule covers both mandatory and non-mandatory civil cases. However, in non-mandatory civil cases the court has more duties in order to make a friendly settlement in the case. In mandatory cases, the conciliation can mean the discussion on the facts, which would be the best resolution for the child in the custody cases. In non-mandatory cases even the mediation is possible. In such a situation, the court may decide the special mediator will continue the mediation. About 60 % of the cases in district courts will be finish by the friendly settlement.
The mediation is possible in large and complicated cases. The requirement is that the parties agree that the mediation will be the next step in proceedings. The mediator can be even an expert - like engineer or economist - but it must be underlined that it is important that the mediator has judicial knowledge as well. Therefore it is also possible to use many different persons as mediators in the same case.
The "climate" has become friendlier to conciliation in Sweden during after the Code of 1948. The legislator had quite a negative attitude towards conciliation in 1948´s reform. The reason was that the proposal for settlement made by the court would destroy the parties´ trustworthiness towards the court. Nowadays it is quite acceptable to make proposals for settlement. One of the reasons is that the conciliation has been seen more effective and cheaper way of the procedure than the traditional court proceedings would be."

20 In THE NETHERLANDS an experiment is being conducted to have the case, pending before the court, mediated with the parties consent.

21 CANADA (Colleen M Hanycz) commenting: "A common pre-action protocol requires a potential plaintiff to obtain the consent of a judicial or administrative officer prior to commencing an action. Most commonly, this protocol is found in statutory provisions that

Apart from this, a distinction can be made between established, but recently renewed, instruments like the conciliation procedure, and other pre-action procedures like pre-action protocols.

I will briefly discuss conciliation and comparable instruments and also briefly pay attention to some other procedures.
I will say only a few words about pre-action protocols.[22]

In Switzerland a conciliation procedure as a rule, be it with several more or less far reaching exceptions, takes place before a claim is brought to the court.[23]
The procedure, mainly provided for in cantonal legislation, is obligatory in most cantons.[24] The conciliation procedure takes place before special magistrates. The procedure is confidential.

As this procedure – before – the – procedure and the results reached by it, are in general evaluated positively, it is retained in the draft Swiss code of civil procedure.

Three elements in the proposed new code are to be mentioned here.

---

specifically mandate leave of the court prior to an action. (...) While the various statutes mandating prior leave of the court before commencing an action are often silent respecting the consequences of proceeding without leave, the implication being that somehow the action will be stopped once this defect becomes known, there is some case law in Canada declaring an action brought improperly without leave to be a nullity."

22 See the general report by Neil Andrews, (xii) Pre-Action 'Protocols'.

23 SWITZERLAND (Tanja Domej, University of Zurich) commenting: "In Switzerland, the most important "pre-action" stage of litigation is the so-called *Sühnverfahren* (conciliation procedure). (..) The conciliation procedure takes place before the claim is brought before the court. It is initiated by a petition of the claimant. The procedure is oral and informal. The parties are, in principle, obliged to appear personally in the conciliatory hearing. Representation by a counsel is admissible only in exceptional cases, especially where a party is not domiciled in the canton. The conciliation procedure is not limited to specific types of claims."

24 SWITZERLAND (Tanja Domej, University of Zurich) commenting: "Where this is the case, an action is not admissible unless the conciliation attempt has taken place. This means that (as a basic rule) the court will reject a claim that is filed "directly" with the court, i.e. without a prior conciliation attempt. However, there are also cantons where the conciliation procedure is voluntary at least in most cases (..)."

Firstly, the conciliation authority has competence to decide upon the matter if no agreement is reached.
Secondly, this authority can issue a judgement proposal.
Thirdly, mediation may be tried as an alternative to conciliation.
In Norway, according to recent legislation, parties are obliged to attempt to reach an amicable settlement of their dispute.
If necessary this can be done through conciliation, either before the Conciliation Board, or by non-judicial mediation or by bringing the dispute before a non-judicial resolution board.[25]
It is interesting to learn that the procedure before the Conciliation Board is normally held in public.

It is worth mentioning the possibility, provided for in several jurisdictions, to approach a competent court in order to try a voluntarily conciliation.[26]
It is perhaps due to its non-committal character that its success seems rather limited, if there is any success at all to be reported.[27]

The general idea, reflected by other procedures in the pre-action phase, whether in court as a kind of preliminary procedure, or out-of court as guided

---

25 NORWAY (Laura Ervo, Universities of Helsinki and Turku) commenting: "The last but not the least obligation at pre-action stage is that the parties shall attempt to reach an amicable settlement of the dispute prior to bringing legal action, if necessary through conciliation before 1) the Conciliation Board, by 2) non-judicial mediation or by 3) bringing the dispute before a non-judicial dispute resolution board."

26 BELGIUM (Paul van Orshoven and Benoît Allemeersch, Catholic University of Leuven) commenting: "Article 731 of the Judicial Code, allowing any claimant or future defendant to (voluntary) present the dispute – prior to commencement of the contentious proceedings – to the court which will be competent to adjudicate the matter, with a view of exploring the possibilities of a settlement under the supervision of that court; this procedure ("oproeping in verzoening of minnelijke schikking", "conciliation") is separate and prior to the actual conduct of the litigation itself and, in case of success, results in a formal, instantly enforceable title for the parties".
GREECE (Constantin Polyzogopoulos, University of Athens) commenting on article 214 A of the Greek code of civil procedure: "En pratique les cas d' un accord des parties selon cette règle sont extrèmement rares jusqu' à présent. Les avocats ne sont ni habitués ni instruits à concilier les parties dont la mentalité n' est pas du tout favorable à la conciliation en général. Il paraît aussi que les avocats n' ont pas encore compris que leur rémunération en cas de succès de la tentative de conciliation (5% de l' objet de la conciliation) peut quelque fois être supérieure à leurs honoraires pour l' instance même! "

27 In his contribution to the Studia in honorem, Pelayia Yessiou-Faltsi, Marcel Storme comments on article 731: "This mechanism which extended the scope for arriving at an out-ot-court settlement resulting in an enforceable instrument, has failed to meet with any success."

by pre-action protocols, seems to be clarifying and streamlining and by doing so trying to come to a solution.[28]

The better informed, the better prepared. It therefore comes as no surprise that access to information in the pre-action-phase is a topic, if not the central one, discussed in several national reports. These show a wide variety of instruments on the one hand, while on the other hand underlining that a right to become informed by your prospective opponent on every business detail one might wish to know, does not exist.

Information, however, should not only be used as a weapon in the procedural battle, if a civil procedure should be described in battle terms at all.

As Lord Woolf put it:[29]

"What is needed is a system which enables the parties to embark on meaningful negotiation as soon as the possibility of litigation is identified, and ensures that as early as possible they have the relevant information to define their claims and make realistic offers to settle."

The influence of the Woolf Reports has been widely felt.

In the trilateral relations between the court and each of the parties to a civil procedure, the sharing of information seems essential to reach meaningful results. Even if the information in the pre-action-phase is destined to inform the court, the sheer existence of a duty to inform, provided for by the law, may lead, as experience shows, to a voluntarily exchange of information.[30]

---

28 SPAIN (José Luis Vasques Sotelo, University of Barcelona) commenting: "The only "preparatory procedure" or of "pre-action" that can be recognized in the Spanish civil procedure is the procedure of "Preliminary Proceedings". It already existed under the previous *Ley de Enjuiciamiento Civil* (of 1881) and it has been preserved in the applicable LEC, (Law 1/2000), that has tried to enforce and confere more utility on those proceedings. It is regulated now in the articles 256 to 263 of the LEC, with a certain similarity with the antique "*actio ad exhibendum*" from the Roman-canon civil procedure. The Preliminary Proceedings procedure is judicial and its function is clarifying doubts that can difficult the correct interposition of the request."

29 Final Report 1996, Chapter 10.

30 ARGENTINA (Roberto Omar Berizonce, Universidad Nacional de La Plata) commenting: "The rules that govern the pre-judicial procedures *do not require, in general, that the potential litigants interchange information*. The information that is required through preparatory measures (art. 323 CPCCN) is not for the counterparty, but for the judge. Nevertheless, the common practice is that the parties voluntarily (based on good faith) or at

In several jurisdictions pre-action behaviour is not non-committal.
English pre-action protocols rest on a principle of co-operation between disputants and their lawyers.[31] For the Netherlands it has been suggested[32]

---

the request of the counterparty, exchange information, exhibit documents and registries or reciprocally allow the access to archives or accounting records. That attitude can be considered as common in the commercial contractual relationships, corporate conflicts and in general in perpetual contracts, under certain circumstances. "

31 See the general report by Neil Andrews, (iv) Indirect Compulsion to Pursue Pre-Action Mediation etc.

32 W.D.H. Asser, H.A. Groen, J.B.M. Vranken, and I.N. Tzankova, A new balance, A summary of the Interim report Fundamental review of the Dutch law of civil procedure, ZZPInt 8 (2003), p. 354, "We have talked above (7.2) of the joint responsibility of parties and court, and the parties' duty of cooperation arising from this. We have chosen this duty as a basis for organizing proceedings and developing rules for proceedings behaviour. It will be clear that this responsibility will already leave its mark on the preliminary phase as the possibility of eventual proceedings must be taken into account here. More particularly we are thinking of those behaviours and measures that serve to prepare for the proceedings (collection of evidence, taking compulsory measures). But where this is not directly at stake, no thinking can take place regarding the part of parties or potential parties in the preliminary phase without a normative framework for their behaviour. We therefore attempt in our report to sketch a more general framework.
From the time when people get into dispute with one another, there is a need for rules of behaviour relating to the dispute. If we limit ourselves to legal disputes then the rules that apply are those relating to the content of the dispute and those relating to its settlement or termination. The question whether and if so, what, rules would have to apply in the preliminary phase must not only be looked at from the point of view of the court involved with the parties but also from the point of view of the parties who have to take eventual proceedings into account. If for example we feel that parties must do their utmost to terminate their dispute out of court and should only gain access to the court if they have done this and can provide evidence of it, then they will immediately take this into account from the start when dealing with their dispute. The same applies for the preparation for the proceedings: if before dealing with the case the judge lays down the requirement that parties have worked out and exchanged points of view and facts prior to the proceedings, then parties will take this into account much sooner than if they had to wait to do so until the proceedings.
In practice the introduction of such rules would mean that the possibility of proceedings will determine the behaviour in the preliminary phase much more than is perhaps the case now. It may be assumed that precisely *that* may mean that many proceedings can be avoided. The previous collection and exchange of facts and evidence for example without any doubt has a clarifying effect and contributes to a more efficient, but also better quality handling of the dispute. The same applies for the information about the point of view of the other party and countering tactics to surprise the other party.
Consideration must also be given to the fact that disputes between parties often arise from an existing legal relationship. Rules that apply to that relationship, not only make themselves felt in the proceedings but also in the preliminary phase. If the legal relationship between parties is of such a nature that they must have their behaviour determined by what reasonableness and fairness demand under certain circumstances, this will also where

possible and taking into account the specific circumstances that prevail in a civil procedure, apply in the procedure and a fortiori in the preliminary phase of the procedure. If such a legal relationship does not exist or if the question of whether a legal relationship exists between parties actually forms the starting point for the dispute, then there in any case exists between them a legal relationship of its own type due to the occurrence of the dispute.
What may one then, on this assumption, reasonably expect from the parties in the preliminary phase? In any case that they will take one another's interests into account with a view to bringing their dispute to an end. They must not let their dispute escalate – let alone, unnecessarily - but on the contrary try to bring it to an amicable conclusion. They should not cause one another more damage in relation to that dispute than is strictly necessary to enforce their own interest that is involved in the dispute. There is then on this point also something like an obligation with respect to the other party as far as possible to prevent and where possible to limit further damage. We are allowing ourselves to be inspired here by the developments in England that we describe in the report, including in particular the pre-action protocols.
Even though we do not subscribe to the view that the civil procedure is a last resort,[32] we do think that proceedings before the judge must be avoided if at all possible and disputes must be solved amicably. Things are no longer allowed to come to proceedings as a matter of course and for this reason, we feel, parties may be expected, if asked, to inform the judge why the proceedings could not be avoided. An aspect that relates to this is that parties are obliged to clarify the foundation of facts of their dispute as quickly as possible. They have in this respect a duty of information to one another to clarify to one another their own point of view and the facts on which this rests. The deal here is that parties are helped more by factual information and clarification about the dispute than by taking up legal positions that as it were dictate the selection of facts. The duty here is not to dig in but to communicate. One must prevent people become fixed in legal and factual positions without the facts actually being sufficiently charted. Prematurely taken positions encourage a selection of facts aimed at these positions and so prevent a thorough investigation of the facts. The activities must be aimed at preventing escalation and at obtaining a better understanding of the dispute.
Obtaining a greater understanding of the dispute must in our view be combined with being prepared to reconsider one's own point of view. In particular institutional parties in the proceedings, such as insurers and mail order companies, who regularly carry on proceedings may simply be expected to regulate their behaviour in the preliminary phase in the way described above and make room for investigation of the facts and review. One can think of the special provisions for this in their general conditions, that is something like general proceedings conditions or pre-action protocols. Even if there is a gateway in the form of proceedings before an industry disputes committee – a very common form of dispute conciliation in the Netherlands - the thing is that on the point of complaints handling and the collection of the necessary facts and data as well as communication with the other party there is a code of behaviour. This code must aim to bring the dispute to an end in a way that also does justice to the justified interests of the other party and, if it does not seem possible to bring it to an end, ensures adequate preparation for the proceedings in the disputes committee or proper preparation for proceedings before the court.
To sum up we would say: the behaviour of parties and the rights and obligations that they have with respect to one another have been determined in the preliminary phase on the one hand by the general social principle that they must take one another's interests into account

that the dispute between the parties creates a relation with standards of behaviour.[33]
It may be too early to formulate a general theory, bringing the various mechanisms, rules and obligations governing pre-trial and pre-action under a kind of umbrella. In the national reports no mention is made of such a theory.

New trends in pre-trial and pre-action put emphasis on a twofold purpose: better preparation for proceedings in court, offering possibilities for an early settlement out of court.
The trend is unmistakeably to promote early solutions of disputes. Exchanging information seems to be a key issue in this respect,[34] although even with limited obligations to provide information in an early stage of the proceedings, let alone before, it seems possible, as the Scandinavian example clearly shows,[35] to come to impressive results.

---

in bringing the dispute to and end and that they must aim to settle it out-of-court and on the other hand by the obligation to prepare properly for the proceedings."

33 In his response to the proposals, the minister of justice of The Netherlands endorsed the idea that the parties to a civil procedure have certain obligations towards each other and towards the court. A co-operative attitude fits into the idea that each of the parties has a responsibility to contribute to a solution of the dispute. The minister added that he preferred " own responsibility " to " joint responsibility ". He announced that he would propose to Parliament the incorporation of the principle that each of the parties is responsible for contributing to the solution of the dispute in the general principles, laid down in the code of civil procedure.

34 BRAZIL (Paulo Henrique dos Santos Lucon, University of São Paulo Law School) commenting: "Brazilian civil litigation procedure does not include pre-action conciliation procedures, such as those that exist in England, for example.
In regions where they do exist, they aim to reduce or eliminate litigation delays and costs by bringing the parties closer together. The objective is to encourage the parties to negotiate openly and frankly before formally commencing proceedings. For this, the parties must give timely and sufficient information on their cases to the other parties. Parties cannot refuse to settle unless there is good reason not to."

35 FINLAND and SWEDEN (Laura Ervo, Universities of Helsinki and Turku) commenting: "The parties in Swedish (and Finnish) civil litigation and their representatives may not lie during the proceedings. However, they are under no obligation to disclose facts that he considers unfavorable to him voluntarily. It is for each party to detect identity and the facts which he wishes to rely on. If he suspects, that relevant facts are being withheld he may try to induce or force the other side to disclose those facts using the following methods. Firstly he can put questions to the opposite party. Then he can ask the discovery of documents and even the pre-trial examination of witnesses is in extraordinary circumstances possible.
The parties are free to put questions at each other during the pre-trial proceedings. However, there is no general sanction available to force an answer. Swedish law does not know the concept of the contempt of court. Thus if party to whom a question is directed does not wish to answer he may refuse to do so. It is for the court to draw its own conclusions from the fact

The trend is at least to structure proceedings in an early phase of - what used to be called – the battle of the parties.

It should, however, be kept in mind that a civil procedure is not an evil that is to be avoided at all costs. Reaching acceptable solutions, or at least decisions, through a quick, simple and not too costly procedure, before an independent tribunal, is – as far as Europe is concerned - just exercising one of the human rights, protected by the European Convention. Across the Atlantic access to court is also highly valued.[36]

In preparing for an early settlement, frontloading of costs should be avoided. Stimulating rules may lead to an open mind for settling disputes, just as best practices may lead to well formulated guidelines. But it should be kept as simple as possible.

---

that no answer is given. A party is, however, under the duty to state what evidence he himself relies upon. In respect of written evidence, he is also required, at the request of his opponent, to state what further evidence he possesses. This rule is rarely used and it is not properly sanctioned. Moreover, its scope of application is unclear. There is no known precedent on its application."

36 UNITED STATES OF AMERICA (Richard Marcus, Hastings College of the Law, San Francisco) commenting: "Putting formal legal impediments in the way of plaintiffs wanting to file suit is therefore frowned upon; access to the court is a high value."

ACROSS THE RIVER AND INTO THE POISONOUS TREES: FROM EXCLUSION TO USE OF ILLEGALLY GATHERED EVIDENCE IN CRIMINAL PROCEEDINGS IN BELGIUM

S. DE DECKER and F. VERBRUGGEN

He shrugged his shoulders slightly, then added with the same leisurely assurance: "To break up the superstition and worship of legality should be our aim."

[J. CONRAD, *The secret agent*, IV, 1907]

1. INTRODUCTION

1. Evidence law separates modern, rational criminal procedure under the rule of law from the hysteria of the witch hunt and the travesty of the show trial. It runs like a connecting thread throughout the whole criminal procedure.

Evidence requirements function as an initial threshold: they mark consecutive stages of the pre-trial proceedings. Some proof (e.g. elements providing a particular level of certainty as to incriminating facts) is required to move from one stage of the criminal process to the next, and the burden is on the prosecution.

Evidence law also lays down rules on which evidence can be used at the trial stage. Whether rules governing the rights of suspects, the conduct of police interviews or the use of other investigative powers are respected in practice, depends to a large extent on the existence of systematic and effective enforcement mechanisms. The exclusion of evidence gathered in consequence of a breach, is often seen as the best deterrent.[1] In this respect, the regulation of illegally obtained evidence is the tailpiece of the entire criminal process.

---

1 E. CAPE, J. HODGSON, T. PRAKKEN and T. SPRONKEN, "Procedural rights at the investigative stage: towards a real commitment to minimal standards" in E. CAPE, J. HODGSON, T. PRAKKEN and T. SPRONKEN (eds.), *Suspects in Europe. Procedural rights at the investigative stage of criminal process in the European Union*, Antwerp, Intersentia, 2007, (1) 14.

2. In Belgium, parliamentary indifference left the issue by and large to the Belgian Supreme Court *(Hof van Cassatie – Cour de Cassation).* Calling it a Supreme Court is somewhat misleading, because technically it cannot create binding precedent and it should respect the role of the Constitutional Court. Still, as the guardian of uniform judicial interpretation of the law, it is a very important policy maker in practice. Trial judges were told to exclude illegally obtained evidence from criminal proceedings until 2003, when the Supreme Court crossed the Rubicon. It made the exclusion of illegally obtained evidence the exception rather than the rule. This chapter describes the genesis of this spectacular U-turn in case law and casts a critical glance at this evolution and its implications.

2. BASICS OF BELGIAN CRIMINAL PROCEDURAL LAW[2]

3. The Belgian criminal law and criminal justice systems are derived from the post-revolutionary French systems.[3] Over 175 years of independence have since brought many changes and a Belgian touch becomes apparent in the continuous reshaping of the system. Still, in its essence, the investigative stage of the criminal proceedings under Belgian law remains thoroughly inquisitorial.[4] The trial stage is public and oral. Although the judge who conducts the trial will still search for the truth in an inquisitorial way, many of the principles of adversarial argument apply to the trial phase.

4. The original, 19th century system presupposed a so-called judicial inquiry *(gerechtelijk onderzoek – instruction)* by an investigating judge *(onderzoeksrechter – juge d'instruction)*, under the supervision of the Indictment chamber of the Court of Appeals *(Kamer van Inbeschuldigingstelling – Chambre des Mises en Accusations).* Most criminal investigations (over 90 %) are called preliminary investigation *(opsporingsonderzoek – information)* and are conducted by the public prosecution service *(openbaar ministerie – ministère public).* Only in 1998 did this factual situation receive legal

---

2 See also J. FERMON, F. VERBRUGGEN and S. DE DECKER, "The investigative stage of the criminal process in Belgium" in E. CAPE, J. HODGSON, T. PRAKKEN and T. SPRONKEN (eds.), *Suspects in Europe. Procedural rights at the investigative stage of criminal process in the European Union*, Antwerp, Intersentia, 2007, 29-30.

3 J. MONBALLYU, *Zes eeuwen strafrecht, de geschiedenis van het Belgische strafrecht (1400-2000)* (Six Centuries of Criminal Law, the History of Belgian Criminal Law (1400-2000)), Leuven, Acco, 2006, 47-55.

4 R. VERSTRAETEN, *Handboek strafvordering* (Companion to criminal procedure), Antwerp, Maklu, 2007, no. 5, p. 38; H.-D. BOSLY and D. VANDERMEERSCH, *Droit de la Procédure Pénale* (Criminal procedure law), Bruges, La Charte, 2005, p. 13.

acknowledgement in articles 28*bis* and following Code of Criminal Procedure (CCP).[5]

5. Belgium has rather few explicit rules on evidence. No rules direct the judges in their assessment of the evidence. The judges of the facts[6] can freely assess the weight of the admissible evidence put before them and are only bound by their "deep-down conviction" *(innerlijke overtuiging – l'intime conviction).*[7] It is perfectly possible for a judge to attach more importance to a witness statement than to a confession.[8] However, this free assessment does not allow the judge to distort the content of the written statements in the case file *(processen-verbaal – procès-verbaux).* Judges can dismiss a witness statement as unreliable, yet they cannot "alter" the content of this statement. Specific exceptions to the free assessment of evidence are rare and often of recent making, like the prohibition to base a conviction exclusively or to a decisive extent on statements of anonymous witnesses,[9] undeniably inspired by the case law of the European Court of Human Rights.

3. SANCTIONING ILLEGALLY GATHERED EVIDENCE

6. If during pre-trial investigations the rules have been bent or breached, the crucial issue is whether and how this will be punished. From a theoretical viewpoint, a wide range of sanctions is conceivable.[10] The police itself could impose disciplinary measures on the officers involved in the illegal actions.

---

5 The (Belgian clone of the French) Code of Criminal Procedure of 17 November 1808.

6 In 99,9 % of the cases a professional judge, for the most serious cases (less than 0,1 %) a jury instructed by a judge.

7 C. VAN DEN WYNGAERT, "Belgium" in C. VAN DEN WYNGAERT (ed.), *Criminal procedure systems in the European Community*, London, Butterworths, 1993, p. 22. Remarkable is that the origin of this system lies in the French revolutionary law on criminal justice and the jury of 16-29 September 1791. The replacement of professional judges by lay jurors was used to replace the extensive, complex, and even arcane rules on evidence, by a new open system relying on "common sense". See J. MONBALLYU, *Zes eeuwen strafrecht, de geschiedenis van het Belgische strafrecht (1400-2000)* (Six Centuries of Criminal Law, the History of Belgian Criminal Law (1400-2000)), Leuven, Acco, 2006, 67-68 and P. TRAEST, *Het bewijs in strafzaken* (Evidence in criminal cases), Ghent, Mys & Breesch, 1992, 254. This is all the more remarkable, as the fact that lay people act as judges of the facts was traditionally deemed to be the reason behind the complex rules on evidence in common law countries. See M. DAMAŠKA, *Evidence law adrift*, New Haven, Yale University Press, 1997, 2.

8 R. VERSTRAETEN, *Handboek strafvordering* (Companion to criminal procedure), Antwerp, Maklu, 2007, no. 1835, p. 892.

9 Article 189*bis* CCP.

10 *Infra* no. 46.

Trial judges who are confronted with illegally obtained evidence, could reduce the sentence of the defendants whose conviction they base (if only partly) on the tainted evidence. Judges could also declare the disputed evidence illegal and exclude it altogether. This would oblige judges – and juries – to ignore the illegal evidence. In extreme cases, one could consider the ultimate procedural sanction: the inadmissibility of the criminal proceedings as a whole.

7. For decades, the Belgian criminal justice system rigorously opted for exclusion of illegally gathered evidence, applying even a "fruits of the poisonous tree" doctrine.[11] Nevertheless, this principled position came under increasing pressure. Case law refined the rigorous exclusion in several areas. In a first phase (1990-2003), automatic exclusion as a sanction was not called into question. During this period, the Supreme Court merely altered the definition of illegal evidence. In 2003 the Supreme Court drastically restricted the scope of the exclusionary rule itself. It overturned its established case law by a remarkable decision of 14 October 2003.[12] The key question is no longer whether evidence has been gathered illegally, but whether a judge has to apply the sanction of exclusion. Subsequent Supreme Court decisions have confirmed this new line and refined it.

3.1. BEFORE…

8. It might strike outsiders as surprising that Belgian statutory legislation contains hardly any positive-legal regulation of an issue as important as the exclusion of illegally obtained evidence.[13] On further consideration however, the absence of such rules is less amazing. Originally, the French (and later on also the Belgian) parliaments assumed that merely including procedural formalities in the legislation was sufficient to guarantee that they would be respected. In 19th century legalistic school of thought, it was self-evident that what happened outside of the bounds of the law, would be inadmissible in subsequent criminal proceedings.[14] This is why the CCP seldom explicitly provides nullity as a sanction for failing to meet a procedural formality.[15]

---

11 *Infra* no. 36.

12 Supreme Court decision of 14 October 2003, *T.Strafr.* 2004, p. 129, with comment by P. TRAEST.

13 See however *infra* no. 50.

14 B. DE SMET, "Stromingen in het stelsel van nietigheden. Nieuwe criteria voor de uitsluiting van onrechtmatig verkregen bewijs" (Trends in the system of nullities. New standards for the exclusion of illegally obtained evidence), *T.Strafr.* 2005, (248) 249, who refers to F. HÉLIE,

9. In 1923, the Supreme Court embedded this strict exclusionary rule explicitly in its case law.[16] In doing so, the Court only voiced the prevailing view of the legislative intent. During the better part of the 20th century, judges obediently and consistently stood by the strict exclusion of illegally gathered evidence. Recent legal doctrine therefore somewhat distorts history by laying the foundations of the exclusionary rule in those decisions of 1923: they had a declaratory function, merely confirming what had been the rule for over a century. This tends to be overlooked by authors who argue that the exclusionary rule was a mere judicial creation of the Supreme Court, and that it was therefore up to the Court to reverse its case law.[17]

3.2. ... AND AFTER

10. The Supreme Court decision of 14 October 2003 and the decisions in its wake are informally known as the "Antigon case law". Antigon *(Antigoon)*[18] was the code name for a large-scale police action in Antwerp which gave rise to the landmark decision of 14 October 2003. During the police operation against inner city crime an individual was stopped and frisked. The police found a set of car keys. They decided to search the car and came across a loaded gun with the serial number filed off. Legislation on police powers only allows vehicle searches if the police have reasonable grounds to believe that the vehicle is used to store, or to transport, dangerous objects (like weapons), or evidence of a crime.[19] The trial judge decided that the police had insufficient grounds to believe there was a gun in the car.[20] As a consequence,

---

Traité de l'instruction criminelle (Treatise on the criminal investigation), Brussels, Bruylant, 1863, III, 766.

15 The few provisions that do so, date from after 1993. See M. STERKENS, "De gewijzigde cassatierechtspraak met betrekking tot de onrechtmatige bewijsverkrijging en de weerslag ervan op het vooronderzoek" (The new case law on illegally obtained evidence and its effects on the investigative stage), *T.Strafr.* 2005, 508-517.

16 Established case law since Supreme Court decision of 12 March 1923, *Pas.* 1923, I, 233; Supreme Court decision of 10 December 1923, *Pas.* 1924, 1, 66 with opinion AG LECLERCQ.

17 See L. Kennes, *La preuve en matière pénale* (Evidence in criminal cases), Brussels, Kluwer, 2005, no. 110, p. 72.

18 According to Antwerp legend, the Roman soldier Brabo chopped off the hand of the giant Antigon, and threw it in the river Scheldt. In Belgium, large-scale police operations are frequently code named after mythical giants, presumably because of the display of power involved. Curiously, the police seem to have overlooked the fact that the giant Antigon tasted defeat by a smaller, yet shrewder opponent.

19 Article 29 Police Powers Act of 5 Augustus 1992, *Official Bulletin* 22 December 1992.

20 Antwerp Court of Appeals decision of 11 April 2003, *RABG* 2004, 335, with comment by F. SCHUERMANS.

the search was illegal. At that time, the evidence resulting from the search normally would have to be excluded from the proceedings. The Supreme Court did however reverse and restricted the scope of the exclusionary rule considerably. It stated that judges were allowed to accept illegally gathered evidence, except for three situations: if the statute explicitly provides nullity for failure to meet a formality; if the reliability of the evidence has been tainted; and if the use of the evidence violates the right to a fair trial. In the case before it, the Supreme Court decided that none of the three exceptions applied. As a result, it allowed the judge of the facts to take into consideration the evidence resulting from the manifestly illegal search of the vehicle.

4. DEFINITION OF ILLEGAL EVIDENCE

11. Before taking a closer look at the three circumstances that may lead to exclusion of illegally gathered evidence, we will point out what can make evidence "illegal". After describing the traditional definition, we will address the differentiations – some subtle, some more radical – that the Belgian Supreme Court introduced.

4.1. TRADITIONAL DEFINITION

12. Originally the concept of illegally gathered evidence had to be taken literally as "gathered contrary to the law". The illegality could stem from the fact that the evidence in question had been obtained through an *offence* or in *violation of criminal procedure legislation.*[21] Both cases are frequently interchangeable, as most offences committed in the course of an investigation will infringe upon procedural legislation, and the more serious violations of criminal procedural legislation are penalized.[22] A 1986 Supreme Court decision really expanded the meaning of illegal evidence. In the underlying case, tax officers had talked a suspect into confessing, by promising, among other things, that no criminal proceedings would be instituted.[23] This misleading behaviour was neither criminal, nor explicitly forbidden by any statutory provision. The Supreme Court decided nonetheless that evidence

---

21 See for instance the old case law: Supreme Court decision of 12 March 1923, *Pas.* 1923, I, 233; Supreme Court decision of 10 December 1923, *Pas.* 1924, 1, 66 with opinion AG LECLERCQ.

22 E.g. unlawful arrest (Article 147 Criminal Code), unlawful search (Article 148 Criminal Code) or unlawful interception of telecommunications (Article 259*bis* Criminal Code).

23 Supreme Court decision of 13 May 1986, *Arr.Cass.* 1985-1986, no. 558, with opinion AG DU JARDIN.

obtained in *violation of general principles of justice* (i.e. the rights of the defence, and more specifically in this case the use of deception). In a move which was not obvious for a continental court, it conceived "law" as something broader than "statute". This was in line with the tendency of increasing judicial review of the compatibility of statute law with supranational, international and constitutional norms.

13. The Supreme Court summarized and at the same time refined its own case law on the definition of illegal evidence in a surprisingly didactic 2004 decision.[24] It starts with the standard maxim of the European Court of Human Rights: Article 6 E.C.H.R (and, for that matter, Article 14 I.C.C.P.R.) does not contain any provisions on evidence in criminal cases, and it is up to the national legal systems to work out a framework for illegally obtained evidence.[25] A new element however is that the Belgian Supreme Court makes an explicit reservation with regard to evidence obtained through torture or other cruel, inhuman or degrading treatment.[26] This distinct mention is chiefly of demonstrative value, because evidence obtained through torture naturally infringes on the right to a fair trial and the right to human dignity. Moreover, torture or other cruel, inhuman or degrading treatment is a criminal offence in itself since 2002,[27] so evidence of this kind is also considered illegal for being gathered through an offence.

14. The Supreme Court decision distinguishes five types of illegally gathered evidence. Evidence is considered illegal if it has been gathered through an offence; in violation of criminal procedural legislation; in violation of the right to privacy (Article 8 E.C.H.R.); in violation of the rights of the defence (Article 6 E.C.H.R.) and, finally, in violation of the right to human dignity. Compared to the earlier decision of 13 March 1986, the first two circumstances remain unchanged. Some of the more common *offences* that can render evidence gathering illegal are theft, extortion, fraud and the

---

24 Supreme Court decision of 23 March 2004, AR P.04.0012.N., *RABG* 2004, 1061, with comment by F. SCHUERMANS, *Rev.dr.pén.* 2005 (excerpt), 661, with comment by C. DE VALKENEER. See *in extenso* R. VERSTRAETEN, *Handboek strafvordering* (Companion to criminal procedure), Antwerp, Maklu, 2007, no. 1788-1811, p. 866-881.

25 E.C.H.R. 12 May 2000 (Khan / U.K.); E.C.H.R. 25 September 2001 (P.G. and J.H. / U.K.); E.C.H.R. 5 November 2002 (Allen / U.K.).

26 Article 3 E.C.H.R. and arts. 2 and 16 of the UN Convention of 10 December 1984 against torture and other cruel, inhuman or degrading treatment or punishment.

27 Article 417*bis*-417*quinquies* Criminal Code.

breach of the duty of professional confidentiality.[28] The category of *violations of criminal procedure legislation* (e.g. investigative actions conducted by persons without the necessary legal authority) is virtually limitless: since most investigative actions require numerous procedural formalities, there are as many potential violations as there are formalities. The Court now breaks up its third traditional category, violation of general principles of justice, into three separate categories.[29] The right to *privacy* is frequently invoked with respect to investigative techniques that are not (yet) completely defined in criminal legislation (e.g. the use of a polygraph or of surveillance cameras). An infringement on the *rights of the defence* can include the use of deception (as in the 1986 case) or the violation of the right to remain silent[30]. It also singles out violations of the right to *human dignity* as a separate category, although obviously such actions will often be covered by one of the previous categories.

4.2. ILLEGALITIES COMMITTED BY PRIVATE PERSONS

15. Under the traditional definition of illegal evidence, it did not matter who had committed the illegality.[31] The Supreme Court limited the definition in the 1990s, only a few years after it had broadened the scope to violations of general principles of justice. The question had arisen whether the illegality could also be derived from the actions of private persons (or other public authorities not acting as criminal prosecution authorities). The Supreme Court decided in 1990[32] that if data or goods have been *gathered* illegally by someone who is not part of the criminal prosecution authorities, their subsequent *use* in evidence by the prosecution is only wrong under a double condition. The person who committed the illegality must be the one who reported the offence to the law enforcement authorities. On top of that, he or she must have engaged in the illegal action with the purpose of using the data or the goods as evidence in a criminal case.

---

28 R. VERSTRAETEN, *Handboek strafvordering* (Companion to criminal procedure), Antwerp, Maklu, 2007, no. 1797-1800, p. 871-873.

29 R. VERSTRAETEN, *Handboek strafvordering* (Companion to criminal procedure), Antwerp, Maklu, 2007, no. 1788, p. 866.

30 Or a combination of both: see E.C.H.R. 5 November 2002 (Allen / U.K.).

31 Supreme Court decision of 29 October 1962, *Pas.* 1963, 1, 272.

32 Supreme Court decision of 17 January 1990, *Arr.Cass.* 1989-90, no. 310, *RW* 1990-91, 463, with comment by L. HUYBRECHTS. Similar case law: Supreme Court decision of 17 April 1991, *Rev.dr.pén.* 1992, 94, with comment by C. DE VALKENEER; Supreme Court decision of 4 January 1994, *Arr.Cass.* 1994, 1, *R. Cass.* 1994, 72-75, with comment by P. TRAEST, *RW* 1994-95, 185, with opinion AG DU JARDIN, with comment by F. D'HONT.

16. If either of the conditions is not met, courts should not consider the evidence to have been obtained illegally by the authorities. For example, when someone did commit an illegality in order to use the evidence afterwards in a criminal case, but handed it over to another private person who in his turn reported the offence, the evidence is not tainted.[33] Conversely, if the person who reported the offence to the authorities is indeed the one who committed the illegality, but he or she came across the data or goods by accident, the prosecution can use the evidence as well. The Court therefore fashioned the system not as a way to bolster respect for the law in general, but rather as a sanctioning system for improper behaviour of criminal investigators. If the authorities *obtained* in good faith what had been *gathered* illegally, they can *use* it in evidence. Obviously, this leaves Belgian procedure vulnerable to "evidence laundering".[34]

4.3. EVIDENCE OF AN OFFENCE VS. REPORTING OF AN OFFENCE

17. Along this line of stressing the "evidence" rather than the "illegal" prong in the combination "illegal evidence", the Supreme Court in 1995 made a distinction between the *evidence* of an offence and the *reporting* of an offence.[35] In that case, a Belgian prosecutor launched a preliminary investigation on the basis of data that had been obtained illegally by the French police. At the time, France had no legal framework for wiretapping in conformity with Article 8 E.C.H.R. The Belgian Supreme Court held that the fact that the offence was illegally discovered by the French police, did not affect the evidence that was subsequently – and legally – gathered by the Belgian authorities themselves. This distinction between the (French) report and the (Belgian) evidence has a lot to say for it and is used in many countries, but in practice it sometimes is so subtle that it gives cause to

---

33 Supreme Court decision of 9 December 1997, *Arr.Cass.* 1997, no. 542, *RW* 1997-98, 1441; Supreme Court decision of 14 February 2001, *JT* 2001, 593, *Rev.dr.pén.* 2001, 875.

34 P. TRAEST, "De rol van de particulier in het bewijsrecht in strafzaken: naar een relativering van de uitsluiting van onrechtmatig verkregen bewijs?" (The role of private persons in evidence gathering in criminal matters: towards a diminishing of the exclusion of illegally obtained evidence) in Y. POULLET and H. VUYE (ed.), *Liber Amicorum Jean du Jardin*, Deurne, Kluwer, 2001, (61) 71. Dutch case law has developed the "*dirty hands rule*" against this: the authorities can not avail themselves of evidence illegally obtained by third persons. See G. CORSTENS, *Het Nederlands strafprocesrecht* (Dutch criminal procedural law), Deventer, Kluwer, 2005, 676.

35 Supreme Court decision of 30 May 1995, *Arr.Cass.* 1995, no. 267, *JLMB* 1998, 488, with comment by F. KUTY, *R. Cass.* 1996, 142, with comment by P. TRAEST, *Rev.dr.pén.* 1996, 118.

difficult demarcation problems.[36] Often it will be hard for judges to justify that the illegality which tainted the report of the offence, did not have any bearing on the subsequent furnishing of proof.

4.4. DEFINITION OF ILLEGAL EVIDENCE AFTER THE "ANTIGON CASE LAW"

18. In view of its tendency to apply the exclusionary rule in an increasingly restrictive way, it came as no surprise that in its "Antigon case law" the Supreme Court did not recede from the differentiations mentioned above. It still excludes *privately gathered* evidence and distinguishes *information about a crime or a suspect* from *evidence of an offence*.[37] Regrettably, the gaps and loopholes connected with these differentiations subsist as well.

5. EXCLUSION OF ILLEGALLY GATHERED EVIDENCE

5.1. EXCULPATORY EVIDENCE: NEVER

19. In one situation illegally gathered evidence is always accepted: if the evidence is exculpatory, suspects can always rely on it.[38] It does not matter whether suspects or defendants are personally involved in the illegal actions or not.[39] For instance, when a witness statement containing some exculpatory information is illegal (e.g. violation of the public nature of the court sessions), the suspect can use the information in his defence all the same.[40] As it happens, evidence which is exculpatory for one of the suspects can indeed be quite damaging for another suspect. Judges will have to consider it in favour

---

36 P. TRAEST, "De rol van de particulier in het bewijsrecht in strafzaken: naar een relativering van de uitsluiting van onrechtmatig verkregen bewijs?" (The role of private persons in evidence gathering in criminal matters: towards a diminishing of the exclusion of illegally obtained evidence) in Y. POULLET and H. VUYE (ed.), *Liber Amicorum Jean du Jardin*, Deurne, Kluwer, 2001, (61) 73; F. DERUYCK, "Wat krom is wordt recht. Over de bruikbaarheid van onrechtmatig verkregen bewijs" (Making the crooked straight. On the admissibility of illegally obtained evidence) in X. (ed.), *Strafrecht en strafprocesrecht. XXIIste postuniversitaire cyclus Willy Delva*, Mechelen, Kluwer, 2006, (201) 206.

37 E.g. Supreme Court decision of 23 March 2004, quoted *supra* footnote 24; Supreme Court decision of 19 October 2005, AR P.05.1287.F., *NC* 2006, 188, with opinion AG VANDERMEERSCH, *Pas.* 2005, 1982.

38 Supreme Court decision of 12 November 1997, *Rev.dr.pén.* 1998, 586.

39 R. VERSTRAETEN, *Handboek strafvordering* (Companion to criminal procedure), Antwerp, Maklu, 2007, no. 1739, 870.

40 Supreme Court decision of 3 November 1999, *T.Strafr.* 2000, 255, with comment by J. MEESE.

of the former, but ignore it when dealing with the latter. That is easier said than done.

5.2. GROUNDS FOR EXCLUSION OF ILLEGALLY OBTAINED EVIDENCE

20. The landmark decision of 14 October 2003 replaced a system in which illegally obtained evidence was almost automatically excluded by a very limited exclusionary rule.
Trial judges now have to exclude illegally obtained evidence in three cases:

- if statutory legislation explicitly provides nullity for the failure to meet a formality;
- if the reliability of the evidence has been tainted;
- if the use of the evidence violates the right to a fair trial.

In 2004, the Supreme Court pointed out that *only* in these three situations exclusion is possible and indeed obligatory. The court confirmed this in 2005. In this last case, some evidence (soft drugs) had been discovered after an illegal hot pursuit by the French police on Belgian territory. The judge of the facts, the Mons Court of Appeals, had excluded the evidence, without however subsuming the illegality under one of the Supreme Court's three categories. The Supreme Court simply quashed the decision, hence making its three grounds for exclusion of evidence "exclusive".[41]

21. No infringement of a fundamental right is necessary to taint evidence. If the statutory legislation explicitly provides nullity, this illegal evidence will still be excluded, even though no fundamental rights were infringed. Also if the reliability is jeopardised – not necessarily by the infringement of a fundamental right–, the evidence cannot be admitted in evidence.

22. It should be mentioned that since the "Antigon decision" of 14 October 2003, the Supreme Court conscientiously keeps reminding everyone that, as a rule, illegally gathered evidence is not admissible. One can be forgiven for overlooking this, as the court has reduced the scope of the grounds for exclusion to such an extent that the tail (exceptional use of illegal evidence) is indeed wagging the dog (exclusion as a principle).[42] Some other European

---

41 Supreme Court decision of 12 October 2005, AR P.05.0119.F., *JT* 2006, 109, *JLMB* 2006, 585, *Pas.* 2005, 1904, *Rev.dr.pén.* 2006, 211, *T.Strafr.* 2006, 25, with comment by F. VERBRUGGEN.

42 F. VERBRUGGEN, "Vindt het spook van Antigoon rust? Franstalig "schoonmoedersarrest" als slotluik van de nieuwe cassatierechtspraak over de uitsluiting van onrechtmatig bewijs"

jurisdictions also start from the position that illegally obtained evidence is not admissible in evidence (e.g. Italy and Germany), whilst others start from the opposite premise (e.g. England and Wales).[43] The result in practice is that jurisdictions starting from exclusion in principle, eventually admit as much or perhaps even more illegal evidence than those who use exclusion as an option rather than as an obligation for the judges.
In the following paragraphs, we will look into the only three circumstances that may lead to exclusion of illegally obtained evidence in Belgium.

5.3. LEGISLATION EXPLICITLY PROVIDES NULLITY AS A SANCTION

23. This category is perhaps the most limited one. When evidence is gathered without meeting a formality, judges have to exclude this evidence only if the statute explicitly provides nullity. At present, only four articles in the CCP do so.[44] In the absence of any explicit sanction, the evidence is no less illegal[45] – it is still gathered in violation of criminal procedural legislation –, but the Supreme Court discarded compulsory exclusion. The judge will only be able to exclude the evidence on the basis of one of the other grounds.

24. At first sight, judges do not seem to have any margin of appreciation in the matter. Either the formality is met or it is not. For example: the CCP demands that the written records state the name and rank of police officers involved in wiretapping (Article 90*quater*, 5° CCP). When this has been omitted, judges have no choice but to exclude all the evidence based on the illegal wiretapping.[46] In a similar case, the Supreme Court nevertheless makes

---

(French-language "mother-in-law decision" as the concluding piece on the exclusion of illegally obtained evidence. Comment on the Supreme Court decision of 12 October 2005), *T.Strafr.* 2006, (26) 26-27.

43 See E. CAPE, J. HODGSON, T. PRAKKEN and T. SPRONKEN, "Procedural rights at the investigative stage: towards a real commitment to minimal standards" in E. CAPE, J. HODGSON, T. PRAKKEN and T. SPRONKEN (eds.), *Suspects in Europe. Procedural rights at the investigative stage of criminal process in the European Union*, Antwerp, Intersentia, 2007, (1) 14.

44 For a detailed overview of these provisions see M. STERKENS, "De gewijzigde cassatierechtspraak met betrekking tot de onrechtmatige bewijsverkrijging en de weerslag ervan op het vooronderzoek" (The new case law on illegally obtained evidence and its effects on the investigative stage), *T.Strafr.* 2005, (508) 509-515.

45 E.g. a violation of the rules on DNA-tests: Supreme Court decision of 25 May 2005, AR P.05.0672.F., *JLMB* 2005, 1408, *JT* 2005, 481, with comment, *NC* 2006, 402, *Rev.dr.pén.* 2005, 1297.

46 Criminal chamber of the Hasselt Court of First Instance 12 May 2005, *RABG* 2005, 1524, with comment by P. WAETERINCKX.

the superfine distinction between the validity of the warrant, and its subsequent execution. As long as the warrant indicates any name, the Court seems satisfied. That another police officer actually executes the warrant "does not impact on the validity of the warrant".[47] In this way, the Court diverts the attention from the black-and-white appraisal of nullity, and centres on the two remaining grounds for exclusion. This contrived argument limits the scope of this ground for exclusion even more. There is however one bright spot: some legislation (wiretapping, use of anonymous witnesses) requires an explicit statement of the reasons for the investigative act. If the statement of reasons given fails to mention one or more obligatory aspects, nullity ensues, and the evidence is not to be admitted.[48] Still, even if the *statement of the reasons* as such is complete, judges – following legal doctrine[49] – tend to scrutinize their *substance*. If investigating judges pass off their duty to give reasons with word processor formulas, judges of the facts are more inclined to dismiss these reasons as nonexistent, and apply the exclusionary rule.[50] Through such substantive examination, some trial judges seem to have procured themselves a margin of appreciation in an apparent black-and-white matter.

25. On top of the rare formalities which statutory legislation itself protects with nullity as a sanction, case law over the years has developed a category of so-called "substantial formalities". They concern principles of criminal procedural law which the judges deem so essential that a violation of the rule also leads to nullity, although this is not explicitly provided in the statute.[51] Some authors suggested that a failure to respect these substantial formalities would also result in exclusion of the evidence.[52] The Supreme Court shattered their illusions in a decision of 16 November 2004. It said that it is up to the

---

47 Supreme Court decision of 19 June 2007, AR P.07.0311.N., *RABG* 2008, with comment by F. VAN VOLSEM, *T.Strafr.* 2008, 41, with comment.

48 E.g. a case where the reasons for wiretapping did not touch on the subsidiarity of the measure, although this is obligatory: Supreme Court decision of 5 October 2005 AR P.05.1056.F., *Rev.dr.pén.* 2006, 208, *T.Strafr.* 2006, 20, with comment by P. VANWALLEGHEM.

49 H.-D. BOSLY and D. VANDERMEERSCH, *Droit de la Procédure Pénale* (Criminal procedure law), Bruges, La Charte, 2005, p. 730.

50 Brussels Court of Appeals decision of 24 December 2003, *Rev. dr. pén* 2004, 742.

51 B. DE SMET, "De handhaving en relativering van strafvorderlijke voorschriften" (The enforcement of and the decline in formalities in criminal procedure) in A. DE NAUW and P. TRAEST (ed.), *Wie is er bang van het strafrecht?* (Who's afraid of criminal law?), Ghent, Mys & Breesch, 1998, (91) 105-106.

52 H.-D. BOSLY and D. VANDERMEERSCH, *Droit de la Procédure Pénale* (Criminal procedure law), Bruges, La Charte, 2005, p. 1292.

judge of the facts to decide what the result is of a violation of a formality, be it a traditional statutory one or a "substantial" one. According to the Court, only if a treaty provision[53] or a statutory clause stipulates how a violation affects the gathering of evidence, judges have to comply.[54] This decision renders the distinction which traditional case law made between substantial formalities and formalities of lesser importance, practically pointless. It would be advisable for parliament to adapt the statutes to the radically changed framework, and to provide nullity explicitly for each formality it deems essential.[55] Meanwhile, most of the time illegal actions by investigators will not lead to exclusion of the evidence obtained as a consequence of this action, unless it affects the reliability of the evidence or the use of the evidence violates the right to a fair trial.

5.4. RELIABILITY HAS BEEN TAINTED

26. If the illegality[56] has tainted the reliability of the evidence, it cannot be used either. The reliability is the relation between the evidence itself and the facts to be proved: evidence that is considered unreliable can no longer be persuasive.[57] As to the cause of the unreliability, one can make a distinction. On the one hand, there is evidence that is dependent from a person's own free will (witness statements, confessions,...). The reliability of this type of evidence could suffer from illicit pressure or influence from the police.

---

[53] E.g. Article 15 UN-Convention 10 December 1984 against torture and other cruel, inhuman or degrading treatment or punishment reads: "Each party state shall ensure that any statement which is established to have been made as a result of torture shall not be invoked as evidence in any proceedings, except against a person accused of torture as evidence that the statement was made".

[54] Supreme Court decision of 16 November 2004, AR P.04.0644.N., *RABG* 2005, 504, *RW* 2005-06, 387, with comment by P. POPELIER, *T.Strafr.* 2005, 285, with comment by R. VERSTRAETEN and S. DE DECKER, *Vigiles (N)* 2004 (excerpt), 171, with comment by F. SCHUERMANS; confirmed in Supreme Court decision of 15 November 2005, AR P.05.1275.N.

[55] P. TRAEST, "Onrechtmatig verkregen doch bruikbaar bewijs: het Hof van Cassatie zet de bakens uit", (Illegally obtained yet admissible evidence: the Supreme Court sets out a new course. Comment on the Supreme Court decision of 14 oktober 2003), *T.Strafr.* 2004, (133) 136-137; R. VERSTRAETEN, *Handboek strafvordering* (Companion to criminal procedure), Antwerp, Maklu, 2007, no. 1819, p. 884.

[56] Belgium does not have a general rule prohibiting the use of hearsay evidence and never really had a debate on the issue: hearsay is not considered inherently unreliable. (P. TRAEST, *Het bewijs in strafzaken* (Evidence in criminal cases), Ghent, Mys & Breesch, 1992, 369-370.)

[57] P. TRAEST, *Het bewijs in strafzaken* (Evidence in criminal cases), Ghent, Mys & Breesch, 1992, p. 276.

Statements made under those circumstances may conflict with the truth and should not be admitted in evidence. On the other hand, the evidence that is independent of a person's free will (blood or DNA test, wiretapping,...), can be unreliable when it is impossible to examine the technicalities involved with this type of evidence. DNA tests for instance are regulated in detail.[58] A violation of these regulations does not entail nullity, but the fact that the evidence was not collected in conformity with the technical standards, may very well impact on its reliability.[59]

27. Legal commentators gave the lack of reliability as a ground for exclusion of evidence a fairly cool reception.[60] This category has some added value, though. In the past, judges could only take reliability into account when they assessed the probative value of the (legally) obtained evidence. At present, judges can evaluate the reliability as a part of the preceding exercise of excluding illegally obtained evidence. This is relevant when the violation of a formality is neither threatened with an explicit nullity, nor does the use of the evidence violate the right to a fair trial, because of the Strasbourg evaluation of the fairness of the procedure "as a whole".[61] It is fitting that evidence that is *in se* unreliable is not admitted in evidence, even if the violation might not jeopardize the fairness of the trial as a whole.[62] A classic example is taking of a blood or DNA sample. If a technical formality is not met, this could not be detrimental to the fairness of the trial, but could raise some doubts about the reliability of the evidence.

5.5. USE VIOLATES THE RIGHT TO A FAIR TRIAL

28. The third and last ground for exclusion is that the use of the evidence would violate the right to a fair trial. In its decision of 23 March 2004,[63] the

---

58 Royal Decree 4 February 2002, *Official Bulletin* 30 March 2002.

59 Supreme Court decision of 25 May 2005, AR P.05.0672.F.

60 See H.-D. BOSLY and D. VANDERMEERSCH, *Droit de la Procédure Pénale* (Criminal procedure law), Bruges, La Charte, 2005, p. 1293; D. DE WOLF, "Nieuwe wending in de rechtspraak betreffende de sanctie bij onrechtmatig verkregen bewijs: het cassatiearrest van 14 oktober 2003" (A new turn in the case law on the exclusion of illegally obtained evidence), *RW* 2003-04, (1235) 1237.

61 R. VERSTRAETEN, *Handboek strafvordering* (Companion to criminal procedure), Antwerp, Maklu, 2007, no. 1820, 884-885.

62 R. VERSTRAETEN and S. DE DECKER, "Antigoon sluit de achterpoort, maar opent een raam" (Antigon closes a loophole, but opens a window. Comment on the Supreme Court decision of 16 November 2004), *T.Strafr.* 2005, (289) 290.

63 Quoted above in footnote 24.

Supreme Court interpreted this abstract and rather noncommittal reference to case law of the European Court of Human Rights. It laid down some guidelines for determining whether the right to a fair trial is violated or not. According to the Supreme Court, trial judges can, among other things, take into consideration one or more of the following elements: the deliberate nature of the illegal action of the authorities; the seriousness of the offence when compared to that of the illegal investigative action; and the fact that the illegally gathered evidence only relates to the material element of the offence. The words "can" and "among other things" indicate that the list of circumstances is not exhaustive. Later on, in 2005, the Supreme Court added new guidelines.

5.5.1. The illegality was committed deliberately

29. A first element which judges have to use to assess whether the illegal evidence gathering affects the fairness of the trial is whether the illegality was committed deliberately. The criterion stems from the decision of the Antwerp Court of Appeals which led to the Supreme Court's "Antigon case".[64] The Court of Appeals held that the alleged illegal vehicle search *"did not seriously violate any essential principles regulating proceedings"*, nor *"encroached on his right to a fair trial by deliberately or grossly neglecting the suspect's interests"*. The Court drew its inspiration from Dutch case law, using almost exactly the same words as the Dutch Supreme Court.[65] In Dutch criminal law this formula is used on another level of sanctioning, namely to assess whether the *criminal proceedings as a whole are admissible* or not. Its Belgian clone is merely one of the touchstones for the lesser sanction of *exclusion of evidence*.

30. Furthermore, the Supreme Court narrowed the Dutch-Antwerp formula down to a *deliberate* violation only. Consequently, even a serious violation of the essential principles of the course of proceedings, caused by gross negligence of the investigators towards the suspect's interests, would not suffice. This forces judges scrupulously to distinguish (culpable and gross) negligence from deliberate violation.[66] The Supreme Court leaves the lower

---

64 Antwerp Court of Appeals decision of 11 April 2003, *RABG* 2004, 335, *T.Strafr.* 2004, 147.

65 Dutch Supreme Court decision of 19 December 1995, *NJ* 1996, 249, with comment; Dutch Supreme Court decision of 30 March 2004, *NJ* 2004, 376, with comment by Y. BURUMA.

66 C. DE VALKENEER, "Que reste-t-il du principe de legalité de la preuve? Variations autour de quelques arrêts récents de la Cour de Cassation" (What is left of the legality principle in evidence law? Thoughts on some recent Supreme Court decisions), *Rev.dr.pén.* 2005, (685) 692; R. VERSTRAETEN and S. DE DECKER, "Antigoon sluit de achterpoort, maar opent een

judges a lot of freedom. It upheld a conviction by the Court of Appeals in a case where a civilian had participated in an undercover operation, which was forbidden at the time. The defence had argued in vain that the involvement of the civilian amounted to a deliberate violation of the rules, and the resulting evidence had to be excluded. The Supreme Court however was satisfied with the reasons given by the Court of Appeals, and held – in startlingly general terms – that *"a deliberate violation of the rules by the authorities does not necessarily entail the exclusion of the evidence"*.[67]

5.5.2. Offence is far more serious than the illegality

31. Another criterion to evaluate whether the use of illegal evidence violates the right to a fair trial consists of a proportionality test. If the offence is far more serious than the illegality that was committed, the fairness of the trial does not suffer. "Far more" serious indicates that only blatant disproportions are to be considered. At closer inspection, the proportionality test is not as self-evident as it might seem. Does it mean that the trial can be less fair if the offence is more serious?[68] Do Magistrate's Courts have to apply a stricter version of the notion "fair trial" than the Crown Courts?[69] Are not the stakes for defendants higher when they stand accused of more serious offences? Moreover, every proportionality test runs the risk of inspiring utilitarian attitudes, with the end justifying the means.[70]

32. The proportionality test has easily found its way into the case law of the lower courts. In one of the cases, traffic police had been accompanied by a television crew which had filmed the detection of offences and the subsequent procedures. The material was intended for use in a semi-documentary programme on a commercial television channel. The trial judge referred to the case law of the Supreme Court. He concluded that the traffic

---

raam" (Antigon closes a loophole, but opens a window. Comment on the Supreme Court decision of 16 November 2004), *T.Strafr.* 2005, (289) 290.

67 Supreme Court decision of 31 October 2006, AR P.06.1016.N., *NC* 2007, 62, *T.Strafr.* 2007, 53 with comments by F. SCHUERMANS and J. VAN GAEVER.

68 R. VERSTRAETEN and S. DE DECKER, "Antigoon sluit de achterpoort, maar opent een raam" (Antigon closes a loophole, but opens a window. Comment on the Supreme Court decision of 16 November 2004), *T.Strafr.* 2005, (289) 295.

69 B. DE SMET, "Stromingen in het stelsel van nietigheden. Nieuwe criteria voor de uitsluiting van onrechtmatig verkregen bewijs" (Trends in the system of nullities. New standards for the exclusion of illegally obtained evidence), *T.Strafr.* 2005, (248) 258.

70 H.-D. BOSLY and D. VANDERMEERSCH, *Droit de la Procédure Pénale* (Criminal procedure law), Bruges, La Charte, 2005, p. 1293.

offences were not as serious as to outweigh the illegality committed, i.e. the intrusion on the privacy of suspects by the illegal presence of a television crew and the filming of the first stages of the investigations.[71] As using the evidence would violate the right to a fair trial, the judge excluded the evidence. In a very similar case the lower judge decided that, relying on the fact that none of the footage was actually broadcast, the evidence could be taken into account. The Supreme Court upheld the decision, because it was up to the lower judge to make this assessment.[72]

5.5.3. Illegal evidence which only relates to the material element of the offence

33. According to the Supreme Court, judges can take into account that the illegally gathered evidence "merely concerned the material element of the offence". This rather enigmatic phrase hints at the distinction between evidence merely revealing the existence of the offence and evidence linking a suspect with the offence. In this line of reasoning, it would be appropriate to exclude the evidence if the illegality is connected with a "direct" proof pointing at the suspected offender.[73] The distinction somewhat echoes the distinction between *reporting* of the offence and *evidence* of the offence, but it goes yet one step further down a slippery slope. It will be very difficult to apply in practice. Often an element of evidence (e.g. the weapon found in an illegal search) reveals something about the facts and, in combination with other elements, also about the suspect.[74] Fortunately, this particular guideline found little response in the case law of the lower courts so far.

---

71 Supreme Court decision of 8 November 2005, AR P.05.1106.N., *Pas.* 2005, 2181, *RABG* 2006, 930, with comment by S. BERNEMAN, *Rev.dr.pén.* 2006, 672, *T.Strafr.* 2006, 85.

72 Supreme Court decision of Decision of 21 November 2006, AR P.06.0806.N.

73 R. VERSTRAETEN, *Handboek strafvordering* (Companion to criminal procedure), Antwerp, Maklu, 2007, no. 1822, 886-887.

74 F. DERUYCK, "Wat krom is wordt recht. Over de bruikbaarheid van onrechtmatig verkregen bewijs" (Making the crooked straight. On the admissibility of illegally obtained evidence) in X. (ed.), *Strafrecht en strafprocesrecht. XXIIste postuniversitaire cyclus Willy Delva*, Mechelen, Kluwer, 2006, (201) 220.

5.5.4. Illegality does not impact on the basic right that is protected

34. The Supreme Court only added the guideline of the (lacking) impact of the illegality on the basic right on 2 March 2005,[75] but trial judges seem happy to use it ever since.[76] A shop manager had installed a concealed security camera to catch an employee he suspected of stealing. The footage had been obtained illegally. The legally binding collective labour agreement[77] obliged employers to inform their workers of the use of cameras and the shop keeper had not done so. The Supreme Court coined yet a new criterion to allow illegally gathered evidence: the illegality did not impact on the basic right, i.e. privacy, involved. The camera had been placed in the public area of the shop. Moreover, it had only been pointed at the cash register. These two elements led the court to the conclusion that the basic right of privacy, which the collective labour agreement wanted to protect, did not suffer from the illegality. Consequently, the use of the footage as evidence for the prosecution did not violate the right to a fair trial. This has clearly been inspired by what the Germans call the *Schutznorm*-concept. Unfortunately, it can easily be abused to allow investigators to trample on the rights of innocent citizens without ever being sanctioned by exclusion of the evidence they gathered through that illegal behaviour. An illegal search of the house of a suspect's mother would violate only the mother's privacy and property rights and not necessarily that of her criminal son.

5.5.5. Illegality of a purely formal nature

35. The latest suggestion the Supreme Court offers to help trial judges reach the conclusion that the illegal gathering of evidence need not render the trial unfair, is to consider that the illegal action was "of a purely formal nature". This formula surfaced for the first time in the advisory opinion of the

---

[75] Supreme Court decision of 2 March 2005, with opinion AG VANDERMEERSCH, *JLMB* 2005, 1086, with comment by M.-A. BEERNAERT, *JT* 2005, 211, *RABG* 2005, 1161, with comment by S. BERNEMAN, *Rev.dr.pén.* 2005, 668, with comment by C. DE VALKENEER.

[76] Supreme Court decision of 12 October 2005, AR P.05.0119.F., *JT* 2006, 109, *JLMB* 2006, 585, *Pas.* 2005, 1904, *Rev.dr.pén.* 2006, 211, *T.Strafr.* 2006, 25, with comment by F. VERBRUGGEN.

[77] Article 9 of the Collective Labour Agreement no. 68, 16 June 1998 on the protection of the privacy of employees in relation to cameras in the workplace, *Official Bulletin* 20 October 1998.

Advocate-General in the Antigon case.[78] In the case leading to the Supreme Court decision of 16 November 2004,[79] the occupants had only given their oral consent to a search of their private residence, but not a written one, although criminal procedure legislation required both. The judges of the Court of Appeals held that the illegality, i.e. the fact that they only consented orally, was of a purely formal nature.[80] The Supreme Court picked up this formula in 2005.[81] The added value of this "mere formality"-guideline is unclear. It largely coincides with the proportionality test:[82] if an illegality is of a purely formal nature, it will almost certainly be exceeded by the seriousness of the offence. In both cases the fairness of the trial as a whole does not suffer, so the evidence is not to be excluded.

6. CONSEQUENCES OF EXCLUSION OF ILLEGALLY GATHERED EVIDENCE

6.1. FRUITS OF THE POISONOUS TREE

36. As explained above, the system for illegally gathered evidence is wholly based on the case law of the Supreme Court. The Court has always stood by the "fruit of the poisonous tree doctrine": if the conditions for exclusion are met, that means exclusion of the illegal evidence itself and of all its fruits. If the original illegal action is covered by any of the three grounds for compulsory exclusion, judges cannot take into consideration *"neither directly nor indirectly"* any evidence found as a consequence of the original error.

6.2. EXCLUSION: HOW?

37. Evidence can be declared illegal both at the investigating stage and at the trial stage. It is not possible to declare evidence illegal at the moment of its gathering or immediately afterwards, to try to avoid it would be included in

---

78 Opinion AG DE SWAEF on the Supreme Court decision of 14 October 2003, item 6.1: "The requirement of formal legality is no doubt of lower value than respect for human dignity and the general obligation for investigators to act in a lawful way when gathering evidence."

79 *Supra* footnote 54.

80 Ghent Court of Appeals decision of 16 March 2004, *T.Strafr.* 2005, 304.

81 Supreme Court decision of 12 October 2005, AR P.05.0119.F.

82 F. DERUYCK, "Wat krom is wordt recht. Over de bruikbaarheid van onrechtmatig verkregen bewijs" (Making the crooked straight. On the admissibility of illegally obtained evidence) in X. (ed.), *Strafrecht en strafprocesrecht. XXIIste postuniversitaire cyclus Willy Delva*, Mechelen, Kluwer, 2006, (201) 223.

the proceedings. As the pre-trial stage of the criminal proceedings in Belgium is a written one, every investigative measure, legal or not, must be reflected in the case file. As far as the definition of illegally gathered evidence is concerned, no distinction is made between infringements committed in the investigation phase and infringements committed during the trial. Differences do occur with regard to the bodies that exclude the evidence and the way in which the exclusion takes place.

6.2.1. Pre-trial investigation

38. In case of a "preliminary investigation" by the public prosecution service,[83] illegally obtained evidence can only be excluded during the subsequent trial. It is not possible to prevent evidence from being included in the trial. At the end of the preliminary investigation, the public prosecution service may very well decide not to prosecute and initiate a trial if it fears the illegal behaviour might hurt its case. Belgian criminal procedural law does not contain a legality principle which would make prosecution compulsory.

39. The situation is quite different in a "judicial inquiry" by an investigating judge. The Indictment chamber of the Court of Appeals, which specialises in the supervision of pre-trial investigations and inquiries, can "cleanse" a case file by eliminating procedural acts or documents that are null and void, e.g. illegally gathered evidence.[84] Excluded evidence disappears physically from the case file and is kept in a sealed envelope, thus avoiding unconscious influence on the trial judge's decision.[85] Complications arose when the illegally gathered evidence, which had been excluded at the request of one suspect, might be exculpatory for another suspect who had not yet been involved in the procedure at the moment the evidence was excluded. Courts allowed the illegal evidence to be produced at the trial: suspects can always rely on illegal evidence if it is exculpatory for them.[86]

40. Judges can exclude evidence of their own motion or at the request of one of the parties. The public prosecution service can also request the exclusion of the evidence, but will comprehensibly be less inclined to do so.

---

83 *Supra* no. 3.

84 Article 235*bis* § 5 CCP.

85 Article 235*bis* § 6 CCP.

86 Supreme Court decision of 12 November 1997, *Rev.dr.pén.* 1998, 586.

6.2.2. Trial stage

41. At the trial stage, it is the judge of the facts (Criminal chamber of the Court of First Instance, or the Court of Appeals) who excludes the evidence. The trial consists mainly of a debate on the basis of the case file – to which all parties have access – and a discussion of sentencing issues. When a judge decides that the illegally gathered evidence cannot be used, it is "excluded from the proceedings". This means that the judge is supposed to ignore it, but as the evidence remains in the case file, it might in practice still influence the decision. This proves even more problematic in the most serious criminal cases, which are dealt with by the Assizes Court. The presiding judge who decides that the evidence cannot be used, is a professional, but the lay jury is the judge of the facts. The debate on the use or exclusion of illegal evidence is held in full presence of the jury. As the decision to exclude the illegally gathered evidence was by definition not made by them, laymen may struggle even more than professional judges with the difficult mental leap of erasing what they saw or heard from their minds.

42. As during the investigation stage, judges can exclude evidence of their own motion or at the request of one of the parties. If a party denounces illegally obtained evidence, the court is obliged to explain in its decision whether it does consider the gathering of the evidence illegal and, if so, whether it decides to exclude the evidence. If it does not, the court is free to found its decision on the evidence.[87]

43. As a rule, courts do not allow the inclusion of additional evidence to demonstrate that the evidence has been gathered in an illegal way. Because of the criteria set out by the Supreme Court (particularly the question whether the use of the illegal evidence affects the fairness of the trial) some evidence as to investigative practice might enter the debate. Courts can request, but not compel, the public prosecution service to provide additional information on investigative practice which the courts might find necessary. They can only sanction a refusal by acquitting the suspect or declaring the prosecution inadmissible.

44. The decision of a judge that evidence was (not) illegally gathered and the decision on whether it has to be excluded, can be appealed. It should however be pointed out that normally there is no separate procedure or separate appeal

---

87 Supreme Court decision of 16 June 1987, *Arr.Cass.* 1986-87, no. 627.

for evidence incidents. They will be decided together with the appeal as to the facts and merits.

6.2.3. When does the exclusion have to take place?

45. If evidence is excluded during the investigative stage, it disappears completely from the case file. If it is excluded during the trial stage, it remains in the case file, but cannot be taken into consideration by the judge.[88] At which point exactly do judges have to exclude illegally obtained evidence? It seems obvious that evidence gathered through a violation of a formality explicitly protected by nullity is excluded as soon as possible.[89] The same goes for evidence whose reliability has been tainted. The moment of exclusion is less obvious when the right to a fair trial is concerned. According to case law of the E.C.H.R., the fairness of the trial depends on the proceedings seen "as a whole".[90] The investigating stage may not be the best time to make an assessment of the overall fairness. Nonetheless, the Supreme Court has quashed a decision of an Indictment chamber of the Court of Appeals, because it had not excluded the results of an illegal house search at the committal stage.[91] In other words, judges who supervise the investigative stage are forced to assess the impact of the illegality on the right to a fair trial at the earliest possible stage of the proceedings.

6.2.4. Other consequences

46. In extreme cases of investigative misbehaviour, one could consider the ultimate procedural sanction: the *inadmissibility* of the criminal proceedings as a whole. In Belgium this is mainly applied in cases of police provocation (entrapment). Offences are provoked if the intention to commit the offence was generated or reinforced – or endorsed when the suspect no longer

---

88 *Supra* no. 39.

89 F. SCHUERMANS, De nieuwe cassatierechtspraak inzake de sanctionering van het onrechtmatig verkregen bewijs: doorbraak of bres?", (The new case law on the exclusion of illegally obtained evidence: breakthrough or breach? Comment on the Supreme Court decision of 14 October 2003), *RABG* 2004, (337) 348; R. VERSTRAETEN, *Handboek strafvordering* (Companion to criminal procedure), Antwerp, Maklu, 2007, no. 1382, 667-668.

90 E.C.H.R. 12 July 1988 (Schenk / Switzerland), para. 46.

91 Supreme Court decision of 11 January 2006, AR P.05.1371.F., *JLMB* 2006, 588, with comment by A. JACOBS, *JT* 2006, 106, with comment.

wanted to commit the offence – by a police officer or a third person acting at the request of the police.[92]

47. Furthermore, the person who gathered the evidence may be *criminally liable*. This depends on the nature of the illegal action. If the conduct is punishable by law (e.g. conducting a search or a wiretap without a warrant is a criminal offence), this person can be prosecuted. Sometimes the identity of persons is protected by law (informers and infiltrators (undercover agents): Article 47*octies* and Article 47*decies* CCP). Although the public prosecution service can reveal their identity if crimes were committed, it cannot be forced to do so by judges, if it decides the identity should be protected.

48. Persons who have been unfairly dealt with, can *hold the state liable* for any loss the illegal evidence has caused them. They will have to demonstrate the causal relation between the illegal evidence and their material or moral loss before a civil court (Article 1382 Civil Code).

7. FUTURE

7.1. PARLIAMENTARY MEEKNESS

49. As the framework for illegally obtained evidence is set by a number of landmark decisions of the Supreme Court, few remedies are available to those who disagree. Since they are a jurisprudential creation, the rules on exclusion of illegally obtained evidence cannot be submitted to the Constitutional Court. In the case where the constitutionality of the Special (Covert) Investigative Powers Act[93] was challenged, some parties had made references to the Antigon case law. The Constitutional Court however held that case law of the Supreme Court is outside its jurisdiction. It is not competent to check whether the way the courts implement legislation is (un)constitutional.[94]

50. Parliament has codified the rules set by the Supreme Court as they stood at the time, but only regarding evidence gathered abroad and used in a subsequent Belgian procedure.[95] However this does not indicate that the

---

92 Article 30 Preliminary Title of the CCP.

93 Statute of 27 December 2005 amending the CCP in order to ameliorate investigative powers in the fight against terrorism and organized crime, *Official Bulletin* 30 December 2005.

94 Constitutional Court 19 July 2007, no. 105/2007 para. B.16.12.

95 Article 13 of the Statute of 9 December 2004 concerning mutual assistance in criminal matters, *Official Bulletin* 24 December 2004.

legislator wholeheartedly approved of the Antigon case law. The main reason for the codification was rather prosaic. Belgian parliament had to transpose the EU-Convention on mutual assistance in criminal matters[96] into national law and the government thought it wise to use the wordings used by the Supreme Court. There was hardly any debate on the issue. The contrast with a subsequent bitter discussion over the evidence rules in the Bill for a new Code of Criminal Procedure revealed that when they voted on Article13 of the Statute concerning mutual assistance in criminal matters the MPs were not aware of stakes.

The Supreme Court has since slightly changed its Antigon rules since 2004,[97] but it is likely the provisions will be interpreted in the same way as the case law.

7.2. BILL FOR A NEW CODE OF CRIMINAL PROCEDURE

51. A Bill for a new Code of Criminal Procedure would have laid down the rules concerning illegal evidence.[98] The original draft predated the Antigon case law and codified the traditional absolute exclusionary rule.[99] As such it was approved by the Senate, but the evidence issue sparked a sharp debate in the Chamber of Deputies.[100] Hearings were organised and especially prosecutors and some judges suggested that the Antigon rules should be codified, albeit with some slight amendments. Others suggested that Parliament should simply state which rules it considered really crucial and explicitly sanction their infringement with nullity. Then the use of all other evidence would be allowed.

This discussion soon grinded the parliamentary debate on the new Code of Criminal Procedure to a complete halt. The fundamental disagreement on how to sanction illegal evidence provided if not the real reasons, in any event a convenient excuse for shelving the entire draft for an indeterminate period of time. General elections were looming anyway, so there was not enough time for technical discussions on codes or procedures. Consensus was lacking on fundamental issues, the logistical hardware to run the new procedure was

---

96 Convention of 29 May 2000 on Mutual Assistance in Criminal Matters between the Member States of the European Union, *PB C.* 12 July 2000, no. 197, 1.

97 *Supra* nos. 28 et seq.

98 Draft Bill on the Code of Criminal Procedure, *Parl.Doc.* Kamer 2004-05, no. 51-2138/1, www.dekamer.be.

99 *Supra* nos. 7 and 8.

100 See F. VERBRUGGEN, "De omissie van de commissie, het Wetboek van Strafprocesrecht in de parlementaire coma" (The Draft Code of Criminal procedure in a parliamentary coma), in X. (ed.), *Liber Amicorum Frans Vanistendael*, Herentals, Knops Publishing, 2007, 495-502.

not in place and therefore the new Code would affect the already strained federal budget. All insiders therefore conclude that Belgium does undeniably need a new Code of Criminal Procedure, but that it would be most foolish to hold one's breath awaiting its adoption or entry into force.

7.3. CRITICAL REMARKS

52. Jurisprudential developments in Belgium have made exclusion of illegally gathered evidence increasingly less likely. Courts privilege their role in truth-finding over the protection of the rights of the individual.[101] Both the sanction itself and the way the Supreme Court implemented it, are not entirely free from criticism.

53. The underlying rationale of the exclusion of illegally obtained evidence is that this sanction will have a dissuasive effect on overzealous police officers, prosecutors and perhaps even investigating judges. Still, chances are that this type of sanction will not reduce the unwanted behaviour, but merely stimulate creativity in searching ways to avoid the sanction, e.g. "evidence laundering" by third parties.[102] Moreover, the distance – both in terms of time and psychologically – between the illegal action and the potential exclusion of the evidence is considerable. Under Belgian criminal procedural law, the people behaving improperly during the investigation are rarely called at the trial to answer in person for their procedural misbehaviour. The biggest problem however is that a consistent application of the exclusionary rule produces results which both practitioners and public opinion find hard to swallow. The exclusionary rule is mostly – or only – to the advantage of "guilty" suspects. When a case does not entail criminal proceedings, innocent persons whose rights were violated, will not benefit from this sanction.
In conclusion, the exclusion of reliable, but illegally gathered evidence does not always sanction or reward the right persons.[103]

---

[101] E. CAPE, J. HODGSON, T. PRAKKEN and T. SPRONKEN, "Procedural rights at the investigative stage: towards a real commitment to minimal standards" in E. CAPE, J. HODGSON, T. PRAKKEN and T. SPRONKEN (eds.), *Suspects in Europe. Procedural rights at the investigative stage of criminal process in the European Union*, Antwerp, Intersentia, 2007, (1) 14.

[102] *Supra* no. 16.

[103] See F. VERBRUGGEN, "Vindt het spook van Antigoon rust? Franstalig "schoonmoedersarrest" als slotluik van de nieuwe cassatierechtspraak over de uitsluiting van onrechtmatig bewijs" (French-language "mother-in-law decision" as the concluding piece on the exclusion of illegally obtained evidence. Comment on the Supreme Court decision of 12 October 2005), *T.Strafr.* 2006, (26) 27-28.

54. In its current form, the Antigon case lacks coherence. On the one hand the Supreme Court expresses a legalistic view. One of the three grounds for obligatory exclusion is the violation of a formality explicitly threatened by nullity. This is rather peculiar, as the Supreme Court knows only too well these provisions are very rare. One could say the Court passes the buck to Parliament. Statutes can easily provide nullity for every formality which Parliament deems essential. If that is what the Supreme Court suggested, the suggestion has fallen on deaf ears so far…

55. On the other hand the Supreme Court seems to consider the right to a fair trial as a kind of panacea, as it makes assessing whether evidence is illegal or not almost completely subordinate to this benchmark. In this way the Supreme Court reduces the Belgian standards – which used to be relatively high – to the minimum level of Strasbourg case law. According to the E.C.H.R., for instance a violation of the right to privacy does not necessarily entail an infringement on the right to a fair trial.[104] Will the only standard – consequently the maximum standard – in Belgian criminal law be the lower limit of Strasbourg case law?[105]

56. Parliament's "absent-minded" adoption, without any reflection or significant debate, of a rule on the use of evidence gathered abroad is perplexing. Only in the subsequent controversy regarding the Bill for a Code of Criminal Procedure the evidence discussion really popped up on the political radar screen. Developments in the EU, like the proposed European Evidence Warrant, make it likely that the issue will return to the Belgian parliamentary agenda sooner rather than later. We would suggest Parliament to make exclusion the rule again, but to allow judges to use the evidence in a number of exceptional situations. Investigators cannot be sure from the outset that their illegal actions will not affect the evidence and judges have to explain why they do use evidence in spite of the fact that it was illegally gathered. The Supreme Court seems very concerned that ever more detailed procedural rules in combination with more adversarial style defence tactics

---

104 E.C.H.R. 12 May 2000 (Khan / U.K.); E.C.H.R. 25 September 2001 (P.G. and J.H. / U.K.); E.C.H.R. 5 November 2002 (Allen / U.K.); E.C.H.R. 9 December 2004 (Van Rossem / Belgium).

105 F. VERBRUGGEN, "Vindt het spook van Antigoon rust? Franstalig "schoonmoedersarrest" als slotluik van de nieuwe cassatierechtspraak over de uitsluiting van onrechtmatig bewijs" (French-language "mother-in-law decision" as the concluding piece on the exclusion of illegally obtained evidence. Comment on the Supreme Court decision of 12 October 2005), *T.Strafr.* 2006, (26) 29-30.

will lead to trials in which procedural discussions overshadow the merits and the substantive issues of criminal law. Is this a nostalgic longing for trials with debates centred more on the defendants and less on the investigators?

57. Much as we appreciate this concern, we would like to warn for phobic traits in the judicial dislike of defence arguments related to procedural errors. Any pharmacologist knows that small doses of poison can sometimes be beneficial for an organism. We believe that the Supreme Court had good reasons to mitigate the absolute exclusionary rule. A deficient statutory framework and the failure of Parliament to intervene, made it hard for the Court to stand by, although one cannot deny it has dedicated quite some time and energy to the matter over the last five years. Still, the appetite for poisoned fruit which the Supreme Court expressed in Antigon case law can be dangerous, if not lethal, in the long run. It is unduly lenient for sloppy performance and even for mischievous practices by investigators. That someone who does not play by the rules, deserves a sanction which really hurts, constitutes the basis of the house of cards we call the criminal justice system. Question that, you question the whole system.

ILLEGALLY OBTAINED EVIDENCE: AN ANALYSIS OF NEW TRENDS IN THE CRIMINAL JUSTICE SYSTEM OF THE NETHERLANDS

M. GROENHUIJSEN

PRELIMINARY OBSERVATIONS

This contribution is about new trends and developments regarding illegally obtained evidence. The format of this paper is determined by the questionnaire that was circulated by the organiser of the workshop on this topic, prof. Teresa Armenta-Deu from the Universidad de Girona, Spain. In order to facilitate the general rapporteur adequate room for comparing the various jurisdictions – and to allow her to evaluate the presently obtaining discrepancies between these systems – I have followed the list of questions closely.[1] However, in my 'closing remarks' I have taken the opportunity to reflect more broadly on the deeper meaning of the developments that are dealt with in the present contribution.

1. LEGAL SYSTEM

1. *Is there a positive-legal regulation of illegally obtained evidence in the legislation?*
Yes, there is a positive-legal regulation of illegally obtained evidence in Dutch legislation. As of November 2nd, 1996, article 359a was introduced into the Code of Criminal Procedure (WvSv). The basic contents of the provision are as follows.

If and when during the course of the preliminary investigation certain procedural rules have been violated, the court – during subsequent trial – has several options available.[2] The first one is to correct the mistake that was made. An example of this is when the prosecutor has mistakenly refused to enter some exculpatory documents into the case-file. By adding these

---

1 This has resulted in the report *Illegally obtained evidence. New trends in illegal evidence in criminal procedure*, General Paper for the 13th World Congress of the Internationale Association of Procedural Law, Salvador, Bahia (Brazil), September 2007.

2 J.M. REIJNTJES, *Minkenhof's Nederlandse Strafvordering*, 10th edition, Deventer: Kluwer 2006, p. 34.

materials to the file, the defence no longer suffers any harm as a result of the omission. Secondly, the court can simply declare that some irregularity has taken place and refuse to attach any negative consequences to this ruling. This usually happens in instances of minor oversights or transgressions. The mechanism of simply declaring an infraction of a procedural provision was introduced in order to avoid an overly formalistic approach of criminal procedural law. In more serious situations, however, the court can – thirdly - determine that the sentence shall be reduced, if it deems such reduction appropriate compensation for harm or damage done by the violation. Alternatively, it can also – fourthly - exclude the results of the breach of procedural rules from the evidence to proof the charges (the exclusionary rule). Finally, in extreme circumstances, when the violation is deemed so serious that it essentially compromises a fair trial for the defendant, the charges of the prosecutor can be deemed inadmissible and the case will be dismissed.

It is further stipulated in article 359a WvSv that in choosing between these options, the court shall take into account the interests served by the procedural rule which was involved, the seriousness of the violation and the harm caused by the violation.[3]

2. *If the response is negative, can a legal system for illegally obtained evidence be deduced from the case-law?*

The adoption of article 359a WvSv in 1996 was to a large extent considered as a codification of the pre-existing case-law. This will be illustrated in response to the next question.

3. *If the response to the first question is affirmative, has the jurisprudence integrated, developed or modified the legal regulations in any way?*

Since 1962, a substantial body of case-law on this topic has been developed by – primarily – the Dutch Supreme Court. In 1990, a high-powered governmental advisory committee reported that the status of illegally obtained evidence is of such crucial importance for criminal procedure as a whole, that the rule of law in its proper sense requires that the obtaining case-law be codified. The legislative acted accordingly and adopted article 359a WvSv as referred to sub 1. A striking feature of the provision is that it leaves much room for the discretion of the court. The court can select any of the available options as it deems fit, "according to the circumstances of the

---

3 M.C.D. Embregts, *Uitsluitsel over bewijsuitsluiting. Een onderzoek naar de toelaatbaarheid van onrechtmatig verkregen bewijs in het strafrecht, het civiele recht en het bestuursrecht*, diss. Tilburg, Deventer: Kluwer 2003, p. 101.

case". In doctrinal writings, many scholars have criticized the lack of strict guidance by the Code of Criminal Procedure.[4]

According to the case-law, three kinds or types of illegally obtained evidence can be distinguished.

The first is where officials have acted contrary to a statutory provision governing criminal procedure. An example would be to interrogate a suspect without giving him prior notice that he is not under an obligation to answer the questions asked (article 29 WvSv).

A second kind of misbehaviour occurs when the official acts *in the absence* of any legal power to do so. This was for instance the case before random blood testing for motor vehicle drivers was introduced in our legislation during the 1970ies. The Supreme Court held that in the absence of a statutory basis such power could only be exerted with the consent of the suspect.[5]

And finally, evidence can also be tainted when it is collected by not violating statutory provisions, but when unwritten general principles of procedural law have been ignored. [6] Prominent examples are represented by the principles of proportionality and subsidiarity. For instance, when law enforcement authorities have a warrant to search a place, they will usually have to give the occupants an opportunity to let them in on a voluntary/cooperative basis before they can resort to the use of force to gain entry.[7]

Apart from the kind of infraction or omission involved, there is always the requirement that the standard which was violated by law enforcement officials must have been intended to protect the interests of the accused.[8] If this condition is not met, the defendant in the case has no standing in this respect, i.e. he can not invoke any one of the remedies referred to in article 359a WvSv. A case in point is an illegal phone-tap of the line of subscriber A, which yields the police serious incriminating data against partner-in-crime B.[9] According to the Supreme Court, this phone-tap should not be considered illegal *in connection with the charges brought against B.* In this situation, B is not protected by the rules and sanctions against improper gathering of evidence. Similarly, when the attic of homeowners X is searched in an

---

4 For references, see EMBREGTS, *op.cit.* p. 97.

5 HR (Dutch Supreme Court) 26 june 1962, *NJ* 1962, 470 with comments by W. Pompe.

6 EMBREGTS, *op.cit.* p. 50.

7 HR 12 December 1978, *NJ* 1979, 142 with comments by G.E. Mulder.

8 This is called the 'doctrine of protective scope'. Under German law this is usually labelled as the 'Schutznorm-Prinzip'.

9 As was the case in HR 18 October 1988, *NJ* 1989, 306.

irregular way, criminal procedural law offers no protection to person Y who uses this attic as a place to store heroin.[10]

In academic discourse, a slightly amended criterion has been suggested to replace the one just mentioned. Ybo Buruma advocates a closer link with the case-law of the ECHR in Straatsbourg. In the *Khan-case*, the European Court held that the use of evidence acquired in violation of art. 8 of the European Convention (right to 'private life') does not by definition affect the fairness of the trial. Extending this line of reasoning, Buruma argues that the criterion to be applied is whether the infraction fatally impairs the fairness of the trial as a whole.[11]

As in any developing legal system, case-law of a later date has affected the statutory provisions in place. The relevant changes since 1996 will be discussed at the relevant stages in this country report (e.g. sub 10, 16 & 18).

2. DEFINITION OF ILLEGALLY OBTAINED EVIDENCE

4. *What elements are used to define illegal evidence?*

The constituent elements to define illegally obtained evidence have been listed sub 3. They amount to:

- evidence acquired by violating a statutory provision during the preliminary investigation; or
- evidence gathered without any legal power to do so while violating constitutional rights of the suspect; or
- evidence collected within the framework of statutory powers, but in violation of unwritten general principles of criminal procedural law.

It is important to underline that in Dutch law the decision whether or not some actions (or omissions) with subsequent results do or do not qualify as 'illegally obtained evidence' is to a very large extent distinct and separated from the decision by the court whether this evidence can be used as a basis for conviction and/or any other type of sanction to be applied. Article 359a WvSv provides for three different sanctions which *can* be attached to the determination that evidence was illegally obtained. It follows that a fourth possibility is that the court will determine the nature of the infraction so minimal that no procedural consequences are deemed appropriate.[12] On top of that, the doctrine of protective scope can also lead to the conclusion that

10 EMBREGTS, *op.cit.* p. 124.

11 Y. BURUMA, 'Onrechtmatige opsporing', *Delikt en Delinkwent* 2002, p. 201.

12 And as we have shown sub 1 above, some mistakes can simply be corrected during the trial stage.

the official conduct was illegal vis-à-vis a third party, but not illegal in connection with the individual rights of the defendant in the case.

5. *Does the definition necessarily entail an infringement of a fundamental right?*

According to the wording of the Code of Criminal Procedure, the definition of illegally obtained evidence does not necessarily entail an infringement of a fundamental right. Technically, violation of any kind of procedural rule or provision renders the results of that action as illegally obtained.

In academic doctrinal writings, this has given rise to interesting debates on the nature of illegally obtained evidence. Some writers have observed that the language used in describing and analysing this phenomenon obscures its true nature. Instead of referring to illegal conduct by law enforcement officials the Code of Criminal Procedure tends to use concepts like 'neglecting to observe procedural rules' as if these were mere formal – or even 'formalistic'- requirements. Statutory vocabulary tends to understate the importance of failures to observe the standards by classifying them as 'oversights' which can or should or must be corrected or sanctioned at a later stage of the procedure.

By contrast, some researchers have emphasized that coercive powers during the preliminary stages are by definition established to legitimize infractions of constitutional rights of people suspected of having committed crime.[13] In cases where the legal limits of these powers have not been respected, this should not be euphemized as a failure to observe a procedural formality, but it should be plainly recognized as a violation of basic constitutional rights. For these academics, all illegally obtained evidence ought to be regarded in the light of fundamental (human) rights. Seen in this light, it not only indicates the seriousness of transgressions of coercive powers; it also provides a legal foundation to accept the exclusionary rule as the most natural response to instances of illegally obtained evidence.[14] Others have looked to the European Convention on Human Rights for justifying this rather robust position. The concept of 'fair hearing' in article 6 ECHR presupposes that the government does not exceed its statutory powers in investigating crime. If the limits to these powers are neglected, it is argued, this disturbes the 'equality of arms' between the parties involved. In order to

---

13 J.B.H.M. SIMMELINK, *De rechtsstaatgedachte achter art. 1 Sv*, Arnhem: Gouda Quint 1987.

14 EMBREGTS, *op.cit.* p. 323.

preserve a fair trial as guaranteed by the Convention, the equality must be re-established in court by excluding the illegally obtained evidence.[15]

Finally, there are those – including the present author - who have consistently argued that the case for excluding illegally obtained evidence should primarily be founded on the basic structure of the Code of Criminal Procedure[16] and its connection with the constitution. Article 1 WvSv stipulates that criminal procedure shall only take place according to the provisions of the Code. As one famous American constitutionalist has claimed in the footsteps of Sophocles, nobody has a more sacred obligation to obey the law than those who make and enforce it.[17] Tribe then goes on to say:

> *"The so-called exclusionary rule has often been criticized for valuing the rights of criminals above those of law-abiding citizens. But those who wrote the Constitution's limitations on how suspects may be pursued obviously knew that taking those limits seriously – that is, obeying them rather than flouting them – would necessarily prevent some guilty people from being apprehended and convicted. The exclusionary rule simply makes that result more dramatic and visible than might some other rules – rules that successfully prevent illegal searches from occurring in the first place. But whatever its price, the exclusionary rule plainly protects the liberties of all of us."*

In conclusion, the definition of illegally obtained evidence as such does not entail a restriction to violations of fundamental rights. Accordingly, it is understandable that art. 359a WvSv has created a flexible regime of responding to a finding that certain parts of the evidence have been acquired in violation of procedural rules. In legal doctrine, however, it has been argued that the discretionary power of the courts in this respect is too broad. Several foundations have been summarized for maintaining the exclusionary rule as the principal and most appropriate way to deal with illegal behaviour by law enforcement officials.

---

15 A. KRIKKE, 'De rechtsgrond van de bewijsuitsluiting in strafzaken', in: E. ANDRÉ DE LA PORTE a.o. (eds.), *Bij deze stand van zaken*, Arnhem: Gouda Quint 1983, p. 291.

16 D.H. DE JONG, 'Bewijsuitsluiting kent meer dan één rechtsgrond', in: J.P. BALKEMA a.o. (eds.), *Liber amicorum Th.W. van Veen*, Arnhem: Gouda Quint 1985, p. 97-111; M.S. GROENHUIJSEN, 'Het niet realiseren van gegronde materieelrechtelijke aanspraken in het strafprocesrecht', in: E.S.G.N.A.I. VAN DE GRIEND & B.W.N. DE WAARD (eds.), *Rechtsvinding. Gedachtenwisseling over het nieuwe Algemeen Deel van de Asser-serie (asser-Vranken)*, Zwolle: W.E.J. Tjeenk Willink 1996, p. 9-20.

17 LAURENCE H. TRIBE, *God save this honorable Court. How the choice of Supreme Court justices shapes our history,* New York and Scarborough, Ontario: Mentor 1985, p. 7.

More recent case-law, though, has confirmed that applying the exclusionary rule more and more actually appears to become the exception rather than the rule. In a landmark decision, the Supreme Court held that excluding the evidence can only be considered when an *important* procedural provision or unwritten principle has been *significantly* violated by the conduct of law enforcement officials.[18]

6. *Is it possible to infer that evidence is illegal from an infringement of rights not considered to be fundamental rights?*
It is possible to infer that evidence is illegal from an infringement of rights not considered to be of a fundamental nature, i.e. constitutional and human rights of the individual citizen. For instance, evidence will also be considered as illegally obtained when the acting law enforcement official temporarily or permanently lacked competence to do so. This occurs, *inter alia*, when a certain rank is required to exercise a coercive measure and this rank is only conferred upon the official during a given shift of duty. Another example would be where an officer is only competent to report limited categories of crime and he moves on beyond this limit. Finally, instructions like the obligation to advise the suspect that he is under no obligation to answer the questions asked of him are to be considered as fundamental rights of the accused, while they probably do not count as protecting constitutional or human rights in the technical sense of the word.

As stated before, the difference between violating fundamental rights and less fundamental rights is not primarily important in connection with the definition of illegally obtained evidence, but the distinction can make a decisive difference in determining the legal consequences of the misconduct.

7. *Is it possible to infer that evidence is illegal from a breach of procedural rules regulating the gathering of said evidence?*
It is possible to infer that evidence is illegally obtained from a breach of procedural rules regulating the gathering of said evidence. In actual fact, this is without any doubt the most common reason why evidence is considered to be tainted. It is precisely the omission to observe procedural rules on breaking and entering premises and of provisions of search and seizure which clouds the results attained in this way. The same holds for tapping confidential telecommunications and for interrogating a suspect without following the relevant rules (putting too much pressure on him; failing to allow an

---

18 HR 30 March, 2004, *NJ* 2004, 376 with comments by Y. BURUMA.

interpreter be present when the suspect does not understand the language, etcetera).

8. *Does a definition of illegally obtained evidence entail the infringement of a fundamental right – or, where appropriate, of a lesser right – by the criminal prosecution authorities, or can the illegality also be derived from the activity of private subjects or of other public authorities not acting as criminal prosecution authorities?*
The illegality of evidence gathering can – sometimes - also be derived from the activity of private subjects and of other public authorities not acting in a law enforcement capacity.

For governmental action the basic rule is that illegal conduct by any agency or official will usually contaminate the information gathered in this way. The prosecutors' office cannot invoke a lack of involvement or a lack of prior knowledge as a ground for justification. The responsibility for the illegal nature of evidence gathering is even more obvious when the prosecutor actually did have a say in the illegal activity. A notorious example in the Dutch system is the police officer who pretended to be a criminal and had himself incarcerated with a suspect in pre-trial custody. The officer was able to obtain highly incriminating information by conducting quasi-confidential talks with the suspect. The Supreme Court had to pass judgement on the legality of this approach.[19] It ruled that the acceptability is co-dependent on the seriousness of the crime involved and on the availability of other means of effectively investigating the case. The court held that considering the principles of proportionality and subsidiarity, and given the fact that in these circumstances the prohibition against improper compulsion during questioning is being violated, the exclusionary rule applies. The underlying rationale for this ruling is the deliberate belying of the trust placed by the suspect in the integrity of his 'fellow detainee'.

In cases where fact finding takes place by private individuals with no involvement whatsoever by criminal justice authorities, the following applies. Individual citizens are not restricted by the provisions of the Code of Criminal Procedure. Instead, they are free to act as they seem fit. The standard to apply here is to be derived from tort law. When fact finding activity by private individuals constitutes tort, the Supreme Court has held that the resulting information can sometimes – depending on the circumstances of the case – be considered as illegally obtained and can be

---

19 HR 9 March, 2004, *NJ* 2004, 263 with comments by T.M. SCHALKEN..

subject to exclusion from the evidence in a subsequent criminal trial.[20] There are three standards to determine whether private conduct constitutes tort. One is when the action violated a statutory provision. This is for instance the case when the individual stole documents from the suspect or from a witness. The second is where the conduct violates someone else's property right or right to protection of a private life. The right to private life is closely linked with some other constitutional rights, such as the right to physical integrity and the right to be respected in your privacy. When a private citizen records confidential (telephone) conversations, hires private detectives, systematically follows the tracks of a suspect or intercepts letters or other sensitive documents, this may invade the privacy of the suspect to an extent which is not allowed by law. The third reason why private investigation can qualify as tort is when the actions taken are contrary to the due care criteria which apply in civil society. These are unwritten rules of conduct of a general nature, which govern inter-human relations at all times, even when there is no contractual relationship between the parties involved. An example appears from the verdict rendered by the Court of Appeal of Den Bosch.[21] In this case, a teacher had reported ill but was suspected by his employer of performing similar duties elsewhere. The school board hired a detective agency to check on the man's behaviour. Even though it could not be established that this constituted a clear violation of the teacher's right to privacy, the Court nevertheless held the school liable because it had not acted consistent with the due care standards to be observed by a 'good employer'. Consequently, hiring the detective agency constituted tort and the information it yielded was excluded from being used in a subsequent criminal trial against the fraudulent teacher.[22]

---

20 HR 1 June 1999, *AA* 2000, p. 117-121 with comments by Y. BURUMA. The Court added that this kind of tort by private citizens could never constitute sufficient grounds for dismissing the case altogether.

21 Court of Appeal Den Bosch 2 December 1992, *NJ* 1993, 327.

22 It is beyond the scope of this paper to give a detailed account of the special rules and regulations on the private security branch. More on this in the well referenced contribution by C. FIJNAUT, 'Bedrijfsmatig georganiseerde particuliere opsporing en (het Wetboek van) Strafvordering', in: M.S. GROENHUIJSEN & G. KNIGGE (eds.), *Dwangmiddelen en rechtsmiddelen. Derde interimrapport onderzoeksproject Strafvordering 2001*, Deventer: Kluwer 2002, p. 689-749.

9. *Is a distinction made between illegally obtained evidence deriving from infringements committed when obtaining evidence and illegally obtained evidence derived from infringements committed during the trial?*
There is a natural as well as a formal distinction between illegally obtained evidence in the pre-trial stage and during the trial in open court.

The main provision of article 359a WvSv only concerns transgressions during the pre-trial stages. The general structure of this provision has been outlined above (in particular sub 1, 3 and 4). Two additional observations are pertinent.

The first one is that complaints about irregularities in arrest and pre-trial detention can only be dealt with according to specific provisions in the Code of Criminal Procedure. The Code offers detailed guidance as to the complaints procedure to be followed and to the opportunities for appealing some of the decisions on these matters *during the pre-trial stage* of the proceedings. The Supreme Court has consistently ruled that the Code is exhaustive in providing remedies. When it does not explicitly allow for an appeal, or when an existing opportunity for judicial review has not been used, the complaint about arrest and detention can not be successfully repeated during trial in open court.

Then there is the rather mysterious provision of article 256, section 2 WvSv, which holds that failures to observe procedural rules during the pre-trial stage can no longer serve as a basis to invoke nullities once the trial in open court has commenced. In The Netherlands, no-one really understands the full meaning of this odd guideline.[23] When taken literally, it precludes the defence of illegally obtained evidence as such, which – as we have seen – is the *raison d'être* and the subject matter of article 359a WvSv. Furthermore, it has long been acknowledged that there are quite a few mistakes which yield evidential nullities in their own right, regardless of when or by whom the nullity is invoked. Examples are an affidavit which does not conform to legal requirements, or testimony provided in violation of procedural rules during the pre-trial stage.[24] Hence, for practical purposes I would recommend not to pay too much attention to article 256 section 2 WvSv when examining the Dutch legal system with respect to the topic at hand.[25]

---

23 Maybe this assertion is slightly overstated. The most coherent analyses of this provision is provided by T. Kooijmans in A.L. Melai & M.S. Groenhuijsen e.a., *Het wetboek van strafvordering*, Deventer: Kluwer (losbladig), commentary on art. 256 WvSv.

24 A.M. van Woensel, 'Sanctionering van onrechtmatig verkregen bewijsmateriaal', *Delikt en Delinkwent* 2004, p. 125.

25 Kooijmans, *op.cit.*, note 8, concludes that article 256 does have some theoretical significance for the distinction between the pre-trial and the trial stage of the procedure, but has little practical meaning.

Illegally obtained evidence derived from infringements committed *during the trial* are slightly more complicated to analyze. This issue can hardly be understood without some general information on the way criminal procedures are being conducted in The Netherlands. In our country, in the vast majority of cases the main part of the entire procedure consists of the pre-trial stage. It is the police investigation where evidence is collected: forensic samples are secured and statements by witnesses and by the suspect, all of which is recorded in formal protocols, signed by the police officer on the oath of his office. Similarly, in the more serious types of cases, an examining magistrate can play a role in procuring information to be used in subsequent proceedings. He can order entering private homes for the purpose of searching and seizing. Depending on circumstances, he has the power to interview witnesses under oath and he can direct an expert to prepare a report on contested issues in the case. All of this leads to a mass of documentary evidence, which is inserted in the case-file. After the trial in open court has started, the case-file plays a predominant role. The trial itself usually is of a very short duration. Serious crimes, carrying a penalty of several years of imprisonment, are commonly dealt with in an hour and a half by a bench consisting of three judges. Less serious crime, where a sentence of less than a year is expected, are usually handled by a single judge, who can dispose of over 20 cases a day. This special feature of Dutch criminal procedure can be explained by the fact that the trial stage is mainly meant to check if the evidence collected during the pre-trial stages is sufficient and convincing, and whether there are any special defences to decide on. In most cases, no witnesses are interviewed during the trial, since their previously recorded statements are considered to be sufficient. [26]

Against this background, it is easy to understand why an ordinary trial in open court only rarely yields any significantly new evidence. Usually, the defendant – if present[27] – is heard, but his statements quite often echo the ones he made to the police in earlier stages of the proceedings. Since it is so rare that the trial stage itself yields substantial new evidence, it is more or less obvious that there are no separate provisions – nor is there case-law - on the isolated topic of illegally obtained evidence during the trial stage. This entire issue is absorbed by the general rules governing the trial. If the relevant procedural rules are violated, the defence can bring it to the attention of the

---

26 This feature of Dutch criminal procedure, allowing for the statements of witnesses to be presented through police records, was only made possible after the Supreme Court ruled that – within certain restrictions – hearsay evidence can be acceptable (HR 20 December 1926, *NJ* 1927, 85).

27 In The Netherlands, trials *in absentia* are rampant.

court and the court has discretion to decide on the complaint. The opinion of the court will be given either in an interim-judgement or it will be included in the reasoning of the final verdict. In either case, the decision can only be challenged by filing an appeal with a higher court.

10. *Does the "fruit of the poisonous tree doctrine" apply in the legislation? If the response is affirmative, does some type of legal or jurisprudential limitation exist?*

The fruit of the poisonous tree-doctrine has not been explicitly included in the Code of Criminal Procedure. The doctrine did find its way, though, into case-law. The rationale behind the doctrine is obvious. It is intended not to circumvent or bypass procedural rights of the accused. The right to remain silent, for instance, would be substantially compromised in the following situation. When a person admits guilt as a result of the government exercising excessive pressure during an interrogation, it is obvious that this confession must be excluded from the evidence. Should this guilty plea be the sole reason that the authorities subsequently find material evidence (an illegal weapon, narcotics), then it only makes sense to consider the latter material to be equally tainted. This line of reasoning has for a long time been accepted in Dutch case-law. The textbook case is the one tried in Amsterdam in 1979.[28] The defendant was arrested and put in pre-trial custody. Defying all the rules in the book, police officers took the keys from his pocket, went to his home without any kind of warrant, searched the place and found an illegal fire-arm. Returning triumphantly to the police station with their discovery, it was easy to make him confess to possessing an illegal weapon. In the end, the court decided the confession was a direct result of the illegal search and seizure and should be dismissed as it is fruit of a clearly poisonous tree.

On the other hand, courts have introduced several limitations to the doctrine and appear to be more and more reluctant to apply it. The key to the question is the concept of causation. The doctrine only applies if the contaminated material is the direct result of the initial illegal government activity. That is to say: the illegally obtained evidence must be the sole source and cause of the ensuing evidentiary material. According to doctrine and recently developed case-law, there are four types of situations in which the causal link is considered to be insufficiently strong.

The first one is where it can credibly be argued that a causal relationship is absent. An example is when an arrest was made in violation of the relevant statutory provisions, and the suspect subsequently makes a confession while

---

28 Amsterdam Court of Appeal 4 May 1979, *NJ* 1980, 48 with comments by A.L. MELAI.

in police custody. The confession could also have taken place had the arrest been perfectly legal. The second restriction occurs when the causal chain is weakened or interrupted. This is for instance the case when a suspect confesses the crime in a police interrogation which was not preceded by the required ('Miranda-like') notice that he is not obliged to answer any questions, and he moves on to repeat the same admission of guilt in later stages of the proceedings after having been duely alerted to this right to silence and in the presence of legal counsel.[29] The required causal link can also be weakened or broken by consent of the accused. When a suspect who has been illegally arrested agrees to his home being searched, the results of that police action – e.g. the seizure of narcotics[30] - can be used as evidence against him in court. The third situation which has been removed from the realm of the poisonous tree-doctrine is labelled as 'alternative causation'. This is present when the evidence is *not only* the result of the tainted material, but is *also* the product of another independent source. Typically, this is the case if identical information was procured in a legal as well as in an illegal way. The court may accept it as evidence since it has *also* been collected in a procedurally proper way. Fourthly and finally, causation is insufficient in cases which are in the USA referred to as 'inevitable discovery'. This means that the relevant evidence was actually obtained by illegal means, but *could also have been* acquired in a legal way. If consulting a number of data bases (DNA-profiles, fingerprints) is standard routine when a person is suspected of having committed a specific type of crime, the resulting information would qualify as 'inevitable discovery'.

Another recent case in which the Dutch Supreme Court limited the scope of the 'fruit of the poisonous tree-doctrine' dealt with a situation in which the defendant had admitted guilt after having being confronted with the results of an illegal telephone-tap and an equally illegal search of his home. This confession was not regarded as an exclusive result of the improper use of coercive powers, because the statements were repeated in court where the accused was duly advised of his right to silence and was assisted by defence counsel.[31]

---

29 HR 26 January, 1988, *NJ* 1988, 818. Similarly – but probably yet another step further – the Supreme Court held in a recent ruling (HR 13 November 2007, *NJ* 2008, 116) with comments by M.J. BORGERS) that a confession which was made in the police station in the absence of legal counsel to which the accused was entitled, was nevertheless admissable as evidence.

30 As was the case in HR 8 February 2000, *NJ* 2000, 316.

31 HR 14 June 2005, LJN AS8854.

3. PROCEDURAL TREATMENT OF ILLEGALLY OBTAINED EVIDENCE

11. *At what point in the trial and in what way can evidence be declared illegal?*
Evidence can in general[32] only be declared illegally obtained after the trial when the court pronounces its verdict.[33] The provisions in article 359a WvSv (see sub 1 supra) pertain to violations of legal standards during the pre-trial stages of the procedure. If the court would detect an irregularity having taken place during the trial-stage, the only remedy would be to correct the mistake.[34]

The Code of Criminal Procedure does not provide for a separate procedure prior to the trial in which complaints about the way evidence has been collected can be filed and decided on. In doctrinal writings, this is a contested issue. Some writers have argued that illegally obtained evidence should be removed from the case-file at the earliest possible moment.[35] The main reason supporting this position is to ensure that the trial judges will not have any knowledge of this contaminated information and that they cannot even subconsciously be affected by it. However, this point of view has never prevailed. A prestigious governmental advisory committee, charged with reassessing the basic structure of the criminal procedure, considered the matter and offered various arguments not to change the existing state of affairs. It held that (a) a separate pre-trial procedure could never offer guarantees that the trial judges would really not face the excluded evidence; (b) the existence of such a special procedure could never deny the defendant the right to complain during the trial about illegal police conduct; (c) a pre-trial procedure does not offer a solution for cases in which the trial judge finds *ex officio* that certain evidence is illegally obtained; and (d) it would delay the procedure.[36]

All in all, the prevailing view is that assessing the legality of the way evidence was collected is best placed in the hands of the trial judge. This kind

---

32 Exceptions to this principle will be explained sub 12-15 infra.

33 VAN WOENSEL, *op.cit.* p. 167.

34 See sub 9 supra. If the court would fail to notice the problem, its verdict can be appealed.

35 A.L. MELAI, 'Fouillering en onrechtmatig verkregen bewijs', in: *Praesidium libertatis. Opstellen over het thema vrijheid en recht uitgegeven ter gelegenheid van het 400-jarig bestaan der Rijksuniversiteit Leiden*, Deventer: Kluwer 1975, p. 161.

36 Moons-committee, *Recht in vorm* (9th report), in: G.J.M. CORSTENS (ed.), *Rapporten herijking strafvordering 1993)*, Arnhem: Gouda Quint 1993, p. 24; VAN WOENSEL, *op.cit.* p. 168.

of monitoring and evaluating of investigative actions is assumed to contribute to the legitimacy of the verdicts of the courts.

12. *Who can declare that evidence is illegal? Can the court do it of its own motion? Can the public prosecutor's office do it? Can it be done at the request of one of the parties involved?*
As was mentioned sub 11 supra, the court is the principal authority to declare that evidence was obtained in an illegal way. According to the wording of article 359a WvSv – taken literally – the court can do so only of its own motion. However, this interpretation of the said provision would be misleading. Both the prosecutor and the accused (or his defence lawyer) can call the attention of the court to evidence they regard as tainted. If they do so in an explicit and well reasoned way, the court can only use the contested material if it properly argues in the verdict why it considers the evidence as legally obtained (article 359, section 2 WvSv).[37]

In some cases it is not clear during the trial what exactly happened during the investigation stage. If there remains significant doubt as to the legality of the coercive powers used during the preliminary stages, the court can order an additional inquiry into the matter. This inquiry will be conducted by an examining magistrate (article 347 WvSv, article 316 WvSv).

13 and 14. *Can the illegality of the evidence be declared when taking investigation measures? Is it possible to prevent said evidence from being included in the proceedings?*
Can the illegality of the evidence be declared during the investigation stage? Is it possible to prevent said evidence from being included in the trial?
The illegality of evidence can be declared in specific circumstances during the pre-trial stages. The first opportunity is when the accused is detained in pre-trial custody. According to the *habeas corpus principle* pre-trial detainees can invoke judicial review of decisions on incarceration. When exercising this right, they can also claim irregularities in the conduct of the authorities affecting the legitimacy of the deprivation of their liberty.[38]

The second example of decisions on the illegality of evidence is when an accused is formally informed that he will be indicted (articles 244/245 WvSv)

---

37 Of course, the court can also decide for one of the other options allowed by article 359a WvSv, as elaborated sub 1 supra.
The exact requirements for the court to explicitly respond to a defence concerning the legality of the available evidence have been specified in the previously mentioned ruling in HR 30 March 2004, *NJ* 2004, 376 with comments by Y. BURUMA. More on this sub 16 *infra*.

38 It must be noted, though, that when the judge accepts this claim of the defence, the appropriate remedy usually is release rather than exclusion of any evidence.

and during the so-called 'committal proceedings'.[39] In both these situations a court is called upon to judge whether the prosecutor has sufficient evidence to warrant prosecution. The defendant can complain about serious violations of his rights with the aim of having the resulting evidence discarded.[40]

Finally, it has to be observed that in Dutch criminal procedure the preliminary investigation is supervised by the public prosecutor. He has the authority to direct the police and is responsible for their activities. It follows that in cases of blatant police misconduct the prosecutor has the power to exclude the resulting incriminating evidence from the case-file. In order to promote transparency and accountability in situations like this, the prosecutor will have to make a formal report of what went wrong and what kind of information was considered illegally obtained. This account will be inserted in the case-file to enable the court to have a complete picture of the pre-trial stages of the proceedings.

15. *Can the illegality of the evidence be declared during the trial? Before the evidence is presented? After it is presented?*

As stated sub 11 supra, the general rule is that the court declares the illegality of evidence when it pronounces its final verdict. During the trial, the parties can argue whether or not parts of the available evidence have been obtained in an illegal way. Sometimes, there is a dispute on this issue between the defence and the prosecutor. Usually, the court will not give a ruling on this until the trial is over. In exceptional circumstances, though, it may be possible for the defence to ask for an early interim-ruling on this issue. In the Code of Criminal Procedure, this is referred to as a preliminary defence. It must be added that this can only occur when the conduct of the officials is claimed to have been so extremely unlawful that the trial has to be aborted instantly and the charges will have to be dismissed. The court can then adjourn the trial. After the matter has been decided, the trial will either be resumed in the normal way or the proceedings shall be halted. I have to add, though, that this possibility is hardly ever used. So for practical purposes, it is mostly a theoretical option.

---

39 That is to say, in criminal procedure in the United Kingdom this is called the committal proceedings. In The Netherlands, it concerns the situation when the accused is served a summons to appear in court; he has the right to challenge this summons on the ground that the prosecution is obviously and blatantly ill-founded. These remedies are governed by articles 250 and 262 WvSv respectively.

40 W.E.C.A. Valkenburg, *Het bezwaarschrift tegen de dagvaarding*, diss. Tilburg, Arnhem: Gouda Quint 1992; G.J.M. Corstens, *Het Nederlandse strafprocesrecht*, (fifth edition) Deventer: Kluwer 2005, p. 514 ff.

16. *If illegally obtained evidence is denounced in the trial, does the court have the obligation to explain in its decision if it considers the evidence to be illegal and to take it into consideration or not?*

If evidence is challenged during the trial, the court does not always have to explain why it considers the relevant information acceptable. The obligations of the court depend on the circumstances of the case.

In a decision of the Supreme Court in 1978, it was held that every defence concerning the legality of the way evidence has been gathered has to be either accepted or explicitly responded to by the court.[41] This no longer applies. In a landmark decision in 2004, the Supreme Court offered significantly stricter guidance on this issue.[42] The Supreme Court first stipulates (as mentioned before, sub 5 supra) that illegally obtained evidence shall only be excluded when the illegal conduct of the law enforcement official violated *an important procedural rule or general principle of law* and when the violation was of a *substantial nature*. The next step in the ruling is that the cases where the lower court has to explain in its decision that it considers the evidence acceptable are limited to the ones where the defence *clearly, articulately and in a well reasoned way* argues that the italicized criterion has been met. This is a very powerful requirement. In academic writings, many authors have complained that this ruling by the Supreme Court has made it extremely difficult for the defence to successfully invoke illegal police conduct as a ground for the exclusion of the resulting evidence. If a defence of this kind does not meet the standard referred to, the lower court does not even have to verify the accuracy of the facts that – according to the accused – constituted illegal behaviour.[43]

17. *Generally, does the legislation regulate special cases to declare the illegality of evidence? Is additional evidence allowed to be included to demonstrate the illegality of evidence?*

Dutch legislation includes several specific provisions pertaining to the legality of the gathering of evidence. In areas such as road traffic regulation, environmental crime and economic crime there are detailed statutes

---

41 HR 18 April 1978, *NJ* 1978, 365.

42 HR 30 March 2004, *NJ* 2004, 376 with comments by Y. BURUMA.

43 As of January 1, 2005, the Code of Criminal Procedure was amended on the topic of how judicial decisions have to be argued and reasoned. A general provision was inserted in article 359, section 2 WvSv, which instructs the court to always explain when and why its decision deviates from *expressly substantiated positions* taken by one of the parties in the trial. Subsequent case-law on the interpretation of the wording of 'expressly substantiated positions' have made it clear that the standard set by *NJ* 2004, 376 has not been seriously changed.

concerning the way samples may be taken that can be used as evidence in court. One example is the breathalyser, which is used in order to determine the alcohol level in a car drivers' body. There are extensive sets of rules rules on how this equipment is to be operated, what quality standards apply, how to calibrate it, how monitoring is to be secured, etc. If one of these rules is violated, it automatically follows that the evidence is excluded.[44] A similar example concerns the tachograph, a device which is being used, *inter alia*, to check the working hours of truck drivers. The rules on installing the device, its technical specifications, requirements on periodical testing and many more items are so complex that they comprise a total of 252 pages in print. Again, if these provisions are not complied with, the evidence is inadmissible. In environmental law and in the area of economic crime, the same applies when the authorities have to take samples in order to prove an illegal composition of liquids or other commodities. Detailed administrative rules govern the equipment which can be used to collect and analyse the samples, and any failure to comply with these standards makes the exclusionary rule applicable.

Is additional evidence allowed to be included to demonstrate the illegality of evidence? Yes, in the sense that every source of knowledge is admissible to substantiate the defence that evidence was gathered in an illegal way. It has to be noted, though, that the accused does not have to establish improper governmental conduct according to the same standard ('beyond reasonable doubt') as applies for the prosecutor when he has to proof the defendants guilt. The criterion to apply here comes closer to the 'balance of probabilities'.

4. CONSEQUENCES OF ILLEGALLY OBTAINED EVIDENCE

18. *What consequences are there to a judicial decision stating that evidence is illegal? Do they vary according to the moment in the trial in which it is declared illegal?*

The range of consequences of a judicial decision to the effect that evidence is obtained in an illegal way has in general been described sub 1 supra.[45] In summary, the court has the discretionary power to

a. correct the mistake;
b. include a declaration of irregularity in the verdict without attaching any further consequences;
c. reduce the sentence imposed;

---

44 'Automatically follows', meaning that the judge does not have any discretionary power in this respect.

45 This follows from article 359a WvSv.

d. exclude the resulting evidence;
e. declare the charges by the prosecution inadmissible.

The Supreme Court has issued some guidelines on the circumstances in which these options should be considered appropriate.[46]

Option b should be chosen when the doctrine of protective scope applies, i.e. when the procedural rule which was violated does not purport to protect the interests of the accused in the criminal trial.[47]

Reduction of the sentence, option c, is the preferable one when the accused suffered harm because of the violation and the effects can suitably be restored by a diminished sentence. An additional condition is that the reduction of sentence must also be justified in view of the weight of the violated procedural rule and the seriousness of the violation.

As explained above, exclusion of evidence (option d) is only allowed when an important procedural rule or unwritten principle has been violated in a significant and substantial way.[48]

Option e is an instrument of last resort. It can only be contemplated in exceptional circumstances, when the authorities have seriously breached principles of a decent procedure and have consciously undermined the possibility of a fair trial for the defendant.

Do the consequences vary according to the moment in the trial in which it is declared illegal? As explained before, the usual routine is to only formally declare evidence as tainted in the final verdict of the court. If, however, in the rare case where for instance the prosecutor finds that police activity has been improper, he may decide to apply the exclusionary rule even when the infraction was less serious as has been described in connection with option c.

---

46 The most pertinent case is HR 30 March 2004, *NJ* 2004, 376 with comments by Y. BURUMA, already discussed sub 16 supra.

47 Thus the Dutch Supreme Court in the ruling presently under discussion. Sub 4 supra it has been explained that the same result can be arrived at through a different line of reasoning, allowing for the infraction to be deemed illegal vis-à-vis a third party, but not in the case of the accused.

48 A coherent exposition of *ius constituendum* on the range of sanctions to be applied and on the way the legislative should provide guidance in this respect is provided by Y.G.M. BAAIJENS-VAN GELOVEN, 'De rechtsgevolgen (sanctionering) van onrechtmatigheden in het opsporingsonderzoek', in: M.S. GROENHUIJSEN & G. KNIGGE, *Afronding en verantwoording. Eindrapport onderzoeksproject Strafvordering 2001*, Deventer: Kluwer 2004, p. 341-420.

19, 20 & 21. *Can the decision of a judge declaring that evidence is or is not illegal be appealed?*
Can a decision be appealed alleging that it was based on illegal evidence?
Can a decision be appealed alleging it did not take into account supposedly illegal evidence whose legality is asserted by the appellant?
The most frequently used moment to declare a decision on the illegality of evidence is in the final verdict of the court. It is highly exceptional – bordering on the theoretical – to have this decision at an earlier stage in the procedure. Since this decision is an intrinsic part of the reasoning of the final verdict, it is only logical that it can be appealed in exactly the same way as all the other component parts of the verdict. The decision of the court of first instance can – with very few exceptions, like in petty cases with very minor sentences – be challenged at the Court of Appeal. Subsequently, a decision of the Court of Appeal can be subjected to review at the Supreme Court, which can only rule on legal questions and in principle not decide on factual issues.

When the outcome is a conviction, these rules of appealing the decision and its underlying justification apply to both the defence and the prosecutor. In case of an acquittal, there is no remedy available for the defendant ('point d'interêt, point d'action'), but the prosecutor can contest the ruling on the illegality of the evidence in the same ways as in cases of conviction. If the prosecutor appeals against an acquittal, he can do so alleging that the lower court mistakenly did not take into account incriminating evidence the legality of which was asserted by the prosecutor.

22. *Is the person who obtained the illegal evidence criminally liable?*
Depending on the circumstances, an official who obtains evidence in an illegal way can be criminally liable. The obvious example of course is the officer who deliberately forges an official document, like an affidavit. That would constitute fraud, pure and simple.

Interestingly, there is an entire chapter in the Dutch Criminal Code (hereafter: WvSr) dedicated to crimes which can only be committed by persons in their capacity as public servants (abuse of office). Quite a few of these crimes are typically applicable on misconduct by office holders charged with law enforcement. The most significant are the following:

Article 365 WvSr criminalizes the public servant who by abuse of authority vested in him compels another person to act, to refrain from acting or to submit to anything. This could be applicable if a police officer manifestly and deliberately exceeds his powers in, for instance, search and seizure. The maximum penalty provided for is a prison sentence of two years.

Article 370 WvSr is about illegally entering and/or searching the home or premises of a suspect. A public servant who, exceeding the limits of his authority or not observing the requirements specified by law, enters into a dwelling, an enclosed room or premises in use by another, against the person's will, or who, remaining there unlawfully, does not remove himself forthwith upon the demand or on behalf of the person entitled, is liable to a term of imprisonment of one year maximum.[49]

Similarly, article 371 WvSr stipulates that a public servant who, exceeding the limits of his authority, causes to be submitted to him or seizes a letter, post card, postal packet or parcel entrusted to any public entity for its conveyance, or a telegraph message held by a public servant of the telegraph services or by other persons charged with the operation of a telegraph facility intended for the use of the general public, is liable to a sentence of one year maximum imprisonment.[50] It is obvious that various ways of illegally obtaining evidence come under the ambit of these provisions.

It has to be observed, though, that in actual practice prosecutions in these matters are extremely rare. The same holds for the formal application of disciplinary measures. It is very exceptional for a law enforcement officer who has collected evidence in an illegal way to be subjected to formal disciplinary sanctions.

23. *Is any type of civil redress provided for those who have been unfairly judged due to illegal evidence?*

Is any type of civil redress provided for those who have been unfairly judged due to illegal evidence? This question can be interpreted in various ways.

If a person is convicted and it can later be established beyond doubt that the conviction was based on illegally obtained evidence, there is the possibility of initiating a civil lawsuit against the government, based on tort law. However, this option looks rather theoretical. The burden of proof is high and civil proceedings are both costly and lengthy.[51]

The question can also be interpreted in another way. Does the criminal procedure offer opportunities for financial remedies for illegally obtained evidence? The answer is basically negative. The consequences of violating procedural rules are listed in article 359a WvSv and were cited sub 1 and sub 18 above. Financial compensation is not included in the list. This has been a

---

49 The punishment is also applicable to a public servant who on the occasion of a search, exceeding the limits of his authority or not observing the requirements specified by law, examines or seizes documents, books or other papers.

50 Again, the same applies to a public servant who, exceeding the limits of his authority, allows himself to be informed, by a public servant of the telephone services or by other persons charged with the operation of a telephone facility intended for the use of the general public, of any communication which has been transmitted through that facility.

51 EMBREGTS 2003, *op.cit.* p. 121-122.

deliberate choice, based on the recommendations of a government advisory committee.[52] However, there still is a general provision on compensation in cases which do not have a conviction as an outcome (article 591a WvSv). In such instances the former defendant can receive restitution for travel expenses, costs for lodging, for legal counsel and for time wasted during presence at trial. However, the practical relevance of this provision for the question under consideration appears to be close to zero. As explained in previous parts (sub 16), tainted evidence is only excluded if special conditions are met, and even then usually there is enough unrelated evidence left to warrant a conviction. In the rare cases where the illegal nature of the evidence does lead to an acquittal, the court has a margin of appreciation in applying article 591a WvSv. In actual practice it is likely that when the defendant has been acquitted because the evidence was obtained in an illegal way, there will be circumstances in the case which will allow the court – despite the formal acquittal – to use its discretionary power to either mitigate or altogether deny an award of compensation.[53]

CLOSING REMARKS

It has often been observed that the main trends in criminal procedure in many ways resemble the swing of the pendulum. On the one hand there is the obvious interest of effectively fighting crime. On the other end of the spectrum, it is equally self-evident that we want to protect the integrity of the criminal justice system while engaging in this primary objective. In a way, these interests are constantly competing. The tension between the interests has been repeatedly identified as the engine which provides the impetus for ongoing reform of the way criminal procedure is being shaped and criminal justice is being administered.[54] The system is never completed; it is in constant motion; guiding this motion requires a balancing act.

---

52 The previously mentioned Moons-committee (see its 9th report, *Recht in vorm*), *op.cit.* p. 55. In case-law preceding the introduction of article 359a WvSv a right to financial compensation has been recognised very rarely. A more frequent use of this remedy has sometimes been advocated in academic writings, e.g. by TH.W. VAN VEEN, 'Over misslagen, vormverzuimen en nietigheden van het strafproces', *RM Themis* 1991, p. 219.

53 The technicalities of this arrangement are discussed by N.J.M. KWAKMAN, *Schadecompensatie in het strafprocesrecht*, diss. Groningen, Groningen 2003. A draft-bill providing for a completely new system of granting compensation has now been circulated by the government for consultation by the various interest-groups (het (voor)ontwerp van de 'Wet schadecompensatie strafvorderlijk overheidsoptreden' d.d. 17 Oktober 2007).

54 HERBERT L. PACKER, *The limits of the criminal sanction*, 1968.

The issue of how to deal with illegally obtained evidence is a textbook-example of how the criminal justice system in The Netherlands performs in this respect. Generally speaking, there have been periods of time in which the interest of crime control was more prominently visible in legislative trends than the attention for the individual civil liberty rights of defendants. In other era's the opposite was the case, when the concept of due process of law was conspicuously valued. To be more specific, the pre-war decade of last century is considered by most as a time when the former perspective clearly dominated the debate (and the outcome of the debates). During the 1960ies and 1970ies, the human rights angle became very powerful in reform efforts of the criminal justice system. And finally, since the middle 1980ies the pendulum has swung back into the direction of a more repressive climate. In the opening years of the 21st century, this has been reinforced rather than diminished, by the global fight against terrorism.

These general observations are clearly mirrored in the developments concerning the legal problem of how to assess illegally obtained evidence. This can be demonstrated by three key examples.

One. When the current Code of Criminal Procedure went into force (1926), it included no provisions concerning the issue under consideration. Only in 1962, the Supreme Court ruled that a bloodsample taken from a car driver could only be used as evidence in court, if either the driver cooperated on a voluntary basis or there was a statutory power to oblige the driver to cooperate (see sub 3 supra). In the absence of both, the Court held the available evidence to be inadmissable, thus establishing the Dutch equivalent of the exclusionary rule. With hindsight the timing of this decision is not quite accidental, since – as I have just pointed out - the sixties and seventies were the period in which human rights for defendants ranked particularly high on the agenda. In 1996, in the middle of times when attention had shifted in the direction of more effective crime control strategies, the principle that illegally obtained evidence cannot be used in court was fundamentally abandoned with the introduction of article 359a WvSv. Since then, exclusion of evidence is only one of several available options when the law has been violating when collecting evidence. In 2004, in the same spirit, the Supreme Court held that this remedy should only be applied when an *important* procedural rule or unwritten principle has been violated in a *significant and substantial* way.

The second example concerns the obligation of a Court to respond to a defence claiming that evidence has been illegally obtained. During the late 1970ies, when the priority awarded to individual civil liberties was virtually at its peak, the Supreme Court decided that each and every defence of this nature should either be accepted, or – if the lower court wants to include the contested evidence in its verdict – be rejected with explanation of the reasons for doing so. Some three decades on, when the general mood had shifted dramatically, the case law became much more restrictive. As was explained in the above (sub 16), two powerful restrictions were introduced. According to the 2004 ruling of the Supreme Court the obligation to respond is now only present in cases where the defendant *a.* clearly, articularly and in a well reasoned way argues, that *b.* the *important* rules/principles have been violated in a *serious* way.

The final example is about the 'fruit of the poisonous tree doctrine' (sub 10 supra). Again, during the high days of attention for procedural rights for defendants in a due process of law, case law tended to be supportive of this doctrine (I mentioned a pinpoint case of 1978). Later on, when the pendulum had swung, the Supreme Court insisted on more restrictions in this respect (we referred to the new standard set in 2005).

It follows that a clear pattern has emerged. The fate of illegally obtained evidence apparently rides on the waves of the tide. This observation in its own right suffices to explain why it is impossible to fully evaluate the merits and demerits of this part of the current criminal justice system in a few brief paragraphs. The way any system deals with the phenomenon of illegally obtained evidence is indicative of many more parts of criminal procedure. Since the overall picture will be constantly changing – adapting to circumstances – the only safe conclusion is that the same applies to the topic of this contribution.

LA PROCÉDURE ÉLECTRONIQUE EN MATIÈRES CIVILE ET PÉNALE EN BELGIQUE

J.-F. HENROTTE[1]

ELECTRONIC PROCEDURE IN CIVIL AND CRIMINAL MATTERS IN BELGIUM

This paper is intended to take stock of the electronic judicial procedure in Belgium and, incidentally, to consider the electronic procedure before the Council of State in the specific context of cassation proceedings.

Two laws of 10 August 2005, currently in force, establish an information system in Belgium, known as Phenix, which serves six purposes: the internal and external communication needed for the workings of justice, management and storage of judicial dossiers, the introduction of a national roll, the establishment of two jurisprudence databases, the preparation of internal and external statistics and assistance with the management and administration of courts and tribunals.

The law institutes three bodies flanking this information system:

- a management committee, composed of members of the judiciary and third parties in equal numbers;
- a supervisory committee, composed of members of the Commission on the protection of privacy and members external to this Commission, who serve as magistrates in the judiciary, in equal numbers;
- a committee of users.

Two other laws of 10 July and 5 August 2006, which complement the laws instituting the Phenix information system, are intended to adapt the Judicial Code and criminal procedure to the electronic judicial procedure, without altering the substance of the procedure.

[1] jf.henrotte@elegis.be, www.elegis.be

Chapter I of the law of 10 July 2006 sets out the general principles and the definitions, including:

- the equivalence of paper and electronic documents;
- a definition of the qualified electronic signature;
- the point in time when an electronic legal process takes effect;
- the definition of the missions and responsibilities of the communication service provider entrusted with the task of forwarding documents served, notifications, deposits or other forms of judicial electronic communication.

Chapter II of the law of 10 July 2006 and of the law of 5 August 2006 adapt the Judicial Code to electronic legal processes.

The articles on serving documents, notification, petitions, registers and directories, the contents of judicial dossiers, the communication of documents, the depositing of pleadings and the hearing sheet have been adapted to ensure that they remain unaffected by the form of medium – electronic or paper.

A single roll is created, which allocates a number to each case for the entire Kingdom.

Chapter III of the law of 10 July 2006 introduces autonomous regulations in criminal matters, which leave intact the existing regulations but give the public prosecutor's office and the examining magistrate the authority to decide on the medium to be used – electronic or paper - for dossiers that concern them.

It also governs the conversion of a dossier from one medium to another, the archiving, consultation and copying of dossiers, forwarding reports, signing documents, convening notices and serving documents electronically.

1. INTRODUCTION

1. Depuis plusieurs années, un ambitieux projet d'uniformisation et de développement des technologies de l'information et de la communication au sein de la Justice est en cours en Belgique. La résorption de l'arriéré judiciaire, objectif poursuivi par le gouvernement, requiert en effet une informatisation accrue de la procédure judiciaire ainsi que la constitution d'outils statistiques permettant d'évaluer la charge de travail des juridictions et assurant une aide à la gestion et l'administration des cours et tribunaux.

Un système d'information, appelé par la loi « Phenix », assurera à la Justice des gains appréciables en termes de rapidité, de simplicité, d'efficacité et de réduction des coûts. L'ensemble des communications judiciaires, tant pénales que civiles, pourront à terme être transmises par voie électronique. Tous les actes et pièces de procédure d'un dossier seront établies, utilisées et conservées sur support électronique.

Ce projet vise non seulement à rationnaliser le fonctionnement interne du pouvoir judiciaire, mais également à faire bénéficier le justiciable des nombreux avantages offerts par cette modernisation de la Justice. L'informatisation de la justice qui avait jusque là eu lieu était, en effet, uniquement conçue à l'usage interne des juridictions.

2. Cette entrée des technologies de l'information et de la communication dans le monde judiciaire nécessite, outre l'indispensable développement d'un système informatique sûr et efficient, l'adoption de lois définissant ce système d'information, ainsi que l'adaptation de la législation régissant la procédure.

Les deux lois du 10 août 2005 instituant le système d'information Phenix[2] et modifiant l'article 610 du Code judiciaire,[3] entrées en vigueur le 11 septembre 2005,[4] définissent le système d'information Phenix et ses finalités et instituent des organes de gestion et de contrôle.[5]
Le Code judiciaire et le Code d'instruction criminelle seront modifiés par la loi du 10 juillet 2006 relative à la procédure par voie électronique[6] (ci-après LPVE) et la loi du 5 août 2006 modifiant certaines dispositions du Code judiciaire en vue de la procédure par voie électronique[7] (ci-après LMCJ).[8]

---

2 *M.B.*, 1er septembre 2005, p. 38305, http://www.moniteur.be.

3 *M.B.*, 1er septembre 2005, p. 38312, http://www.moniteur.be.

4 A l'exception des articles 6 (rôle national) et 30 (standards ouverts) de la loi instituant le système d'information Phénix, pour lesquels la date d'entrée en vigueur sera déterminée par arrêté royal (Article 31 de la loi du 10 août 2005 instituant le système d'information Phenix).

5 Voir également sur ce sujet: V. TOLLENAERE, « Informatiesysteem Phenix », *T. V. W.*, 2005, liv. 10, 409-411; H. VAN BOSSUYT, « Het informatiesysteem Phenix: een nieuw hulpmiddel voor justitie », *R.A.B.G.,* n° 15/2005, p. 1435.

6 *M.B.*, 7 février 2006, p. 45527, http://www.moniteur.be.

7 *M.B.*, 7 février 2006, p. 45532, http://www.moniteur.be.

8 Voy. *Phenix et la procédure électronique* (sous la coord. de J-F. HENROTTE), CUP, Larcier, 2006, vol. 85; H. VAN BOSSUYT ET J-F. HENROTTE., « Le projet Phenix ? Une révolution en marche », *J.T.*, 38/2006, 25 novembre 2006, p. 728; Phenix – Les tribunaux à l'ère électronique, Cahiers du CRID, Bruylant, 2007; D. MOUGENOT, « La procédure par voie

3. Hélas, le prestataire informatique chargé de la réalisation du système d'information semble s'être montré incapable de réaliser sa tâche et en tout cas l'Etat belge a résolu pour faute grave le marché public et l'a assigné en dommages et intérêts. Cela a considérablement ralenti le projet puisque seule la banque de donnée de jurisprudence externe a été à ce jour réalisée (par un autre prestataire) et la notification hybride a été préparée par un troisième prestataire. Le système d'information, moins holistique et rebaptisé officieusement « Cheops justice », est désormais reporté sur de nouveaux fonds baptismaux mais n'est pas encore clairement défini et la rédaction des arrêtés royaux d'application est encore suspendue. Le projet ne devrait toutefois pas être fondamentalement changé par rapport au défunt Phenix qui devrait donc renaître, comme l'oiseau mythique, de ses cendres simplement renommé par une inspiration égyptienne.

4. La procédure électronique n'existe donc à ce jour en Belgique que dans le contentieux objectif du Conseil d'Etat[9] et encore dans la procédure particulière qu'est la procédure en cassation devant le Conseil d'Etat.[10]

Les lois qui ont été adoptées permettent néanmoins de dresser les contours de cette procédure électronique, ce à quoi s'attache la présente contribution.

2. LE SYSTÈME D'INFORMATION PHENIX ET SES ORGANES

2.1. LE SYSTÈME D'INFORMATION PHENIX ET LE RESPECT DE LA VIE PRIVÉE

5. Le projet de loi instituant le système d'information Phenix a été soumis pour avis à la Commission de la protection de la vie privée[11] qui, après avoir

---

électronique - Les modifications de la procédure civile – (Lois des 10 juillet et 5 août 2006) », *J.T.*, 2007, p. 161.

9 Il y a pourtant urgence si on a égard au récent arrêt de la Cour de cassation qui a décidé qu' « *un message électronique ne répond à aucune des conditions requises pour constituer une demande en justice, et spécialement une demande en récusation, en sorte qu'il ne produit aucun effet et qu'aucune suite judiciaire ne doit lui être réservée* », Cass., 25 janvier 2008, *J.T.*, 2008, p. 192, http://www.cass.be.

10 Arrêté royal du 30 novembre 2006 déterminant la procédure en cassation devant le conseil d'Etat, *M.B.*, 1er décembre 2006, http://www.moniteur.be.
RENDERS, D. & PIJCKE, G., « La procédure en cassation administrative », *A.P.T.*, 4/2006, p. 229.

rappelé que les traitements de données judiciaires sont soumis à la loi du 8 décembre 1992 relative à la protection de la vie privée à l'égard des traitements de données à caractère personnel,[12] a attiré l'attention sur le fait que l'introduction des technologies dans l'ordre judiciaire, si elle facilite le travail du juge et lui permet de rassembler facilement l'ensemble des informations relatives à un dossier, accroît le pouvoir des parquets et tribunaux vis-à-vis du justiciable.

Elle a ajouté que « *la volonté de maintenir un certain équilibre des intérêts entre le justiciable et l'appareil judiciaire plaide pour certaines limites dans le traitement des données et leur accès, en même temps que pour une transparence des circuits d'information existants. La Commission souhaite dès lors la prise en considération d'une certaine balance entre l'intérêt général servi par le pouvoir judiciaire et les libertés du justiciable.* »[13]

6. La Commission a, notamment, estimé à cet égard qu'il était nécessaire de mieux définir les finalités de la banque de données. En effet, l'arrêt Rotaru[14] de la Cour européenne des droits de l'Homme a rappelé la nécessité pour chacune de ces finalités de déterminer les données consignées, les catégories de personnes dont les données sont consignées, les circonstances de consignation et la durée de conservation de ces données. De telles précisions sont nécessaires pour que la «loi» réponde à la condition de «prévisibilité» exigée par la jurisprudence de Strasbourg sur base de l'article 8 de la Convention européenne des droits de l'homme.[15] La Commission de la protection de la vie privée a également suggéré de déterminer les catégories de destinataires de l'information traitée.
La Commission de la protection de la vie privée rappelle que conformément à la législation protectrice de la vie privée, il appartient à la loi de déterminer les finalités des traitements de données et au Roi, sur base d'une délégation précise, de fixer les modalités d'application de ces finalités.[16]

---

11 Avis de la Commission de la protection de la vie privée 11/ 2004, point 7, *in* Doc. Parl., Ch. repr., session 2004-2005, 7 mars 2005, projet de loi, doc. 51-1645/001, p. 80; http://www.privacycommission.be.

12 *M.B.*, 18 mars 1993, p. 5801, http://www.moniteur.be.

13 Op. cit.

14 Arrêt Rotaru c/ Roumanie de la Cour européenne des droits de l'homme, 4 mai 2000, n° 28341/95, § 57, disponible sur http://www.echr.coe.int.

15 Avis de la Commission de la protection de la vie privée 11/2004, point 8, *op. cit.*, p. 81, http://www.privacycommission.be.

16 Avis de la Commission de la protection de la vie privée 11/2004, point 14, *op. cit.*, p. 84, http://www.privacycommission.be.

La loi suit la proposition de la Commission et détaille ci-après les différentes finalités tout en donnant, pour chacune d'entre elles, délégation au Roi de régler certaines modalités, l'avis du Comité de surveillance[17] étant systématiquement requis préalablement à l'adoption de ces arrêtés royaux.

La loi instituant le système d'information Phenix constitue donc une première. Il est vrai que le Code judiciaire respectait souvent en lui-même la législation protectrice de la vie privée,[18] mais la loi du 10 août 2005 est la première législation procédurale à affirmer tenir compte de la loi du 8 décembre 1992.

2.2. LES FINALITÉS DE PHENIX

7. L'avant-projet de loi parlait des « objectifs » du système d'information Phenix.[19] Le Conseil d'Etat a suggéré à cet égard de remplacer les termes «qui a pour objectifs » par les termes «qui a pour finalités»,[20] afin de mieux s'inscrire dans le cadre des directives communautaires et plus particulièrement de la directive du 24 octobre 1995 relative à la protection des personnes physiques à l'égard du traitement des données à caractère personnel et à la libre circulation de ces données,[21] ainsi que de la loi du 8 décembre 1992.[22]
Le système d'information Phenix a donc pour finalités:[23]

- la communication interne et externe requise par le fonctionnement de la justice ;
- la gestion et la conservation des dossiers judiciaires ;

---

17 Voy. sur ce comité, *infra* n° 31.

18 F. DANIELI, « L'application de la loi vie privée au pouvoir judiciaire et au secteur policier: disaster ... or much ado about nothing? », *R.D.T.I.*, 2006/25, p. 169.

19 Doc. Parl., Ch. repr., session 2004-2005, 7 mars 2005, projet de loi, doc. 51-1645/001, exposé des motifs, p. 28.

20 On regrettera dès lors l'usage par le Président VAN BOSSUYT du mot « doelstellingen » dans le sous-titre de sa contribution, au lieu de « doeleiden »; H. VAN BOSSUYT, « Het informatiesysteem Phenix: een nieuw hulpmiddel voor justitie », *R.A.B.G.*, n° 15/2005, p. 1435.

21 Directive 95/46/CE du Parlement européen et du Conseil du 24 octobre 1995 relative à la protection des personnes physiques à l'égard du traitement des données à caractère personnel et à la libre circulation de ces données, modifiée par le règlement (CE) n° 1882/2003 du Parlement européen et du Conseil du 29 septembre 2003, respectivement JO L 281 du 23 novembre 1995, p. 31–50 et JO L 287 du 5 novembre 2003, p. 1–10.

22 Avis du Conseil d'Etat, n° 37.943/2, *in* Doc. Parl., Ch. repr., session 2004-2005, 7 mars 2005, projet de loi, doc. 51-1645/001, p. 40.

23 Article 2, al. 1 de la loi du 10 août 2005 instituant le système d'information Phenix.

- l'instauration d'un rôle national ;
- la constitution d'une banque de données de jurisprudence, interne et externe ;
- l'élaboration de statistiques, internes et externes ;
- l'aide à la gestion et l'administration des institutions judiciaires.

2.2.1. La communication interne et externe

8. « *La communication interne vise les communications requises pour le fonctionnement et la gestion des cours et tribunaux et de leurs parquets, ainsi que par la constitution et la gestion des dossiers de procédure* ».[24] L'exposé des motifs précise que cela vise tout échange de données entre les membres de l'ordre judiciaire, nécessaire au fonctionnement des procédures judiciaires.[25]

« *La communication* externe *vise la notification, la signification et la communication des actes requis par les procédures judiciaires, ainsi que la communication avec les autorités publiques destinée à la collecte des données nécessaires pour l'élaboration et la gestion des dossiers judiciaires* ».[26]

9. Ces échanges se font conformément au Code judiciaire et au Code d'instruction criminelle, ainsi qu'aux différentes lois particulières,[27] notamment la loi relative à la procédure par voie électronique. Nous y reviendrons ci-après.

10. « *Il est créé au sein de Phenix un répertoire central des adresses judiciaires électroniques, accessible aux membres de l'ordre judiciaire et aux auxiliaires de justice ainsi qu'à d'autres catégories de personnes désignées par le Roi sur proposition du comité de gestion et après avis du comité de surveillance.* »[28] Le Roi déterminera les règles d'accès et d'authentification d'accès au répertoire central des adresses électroniques.

---

24 Article 3, al. 1 de la loi du 10 août 2005 instituant le système d'information Phenix.

25 Doc. Parl., Ch. repr., session 2004-2005, 7 mars 2005, projet de loi, doc. 51 1645/001, exposé des motifs, p. 7.

26 Article 3, al. 2 de la loi du 10 août 2005 instituant le système d'information Phenix.

27 Comme le rappelle le Conseil d'État dans son avis 37.943/2 (*op. cit.*, p. 44), il faut également mentionner la loi du 8 août 1997 relative au casier judiciaire central qui régit la communication des décisions rendues en matière pénale et de défense sociale. Dès lors, les délégations au Roi accordées par le projet de loi Phenix se bornent à déterminer les modalités d'application de ces articles.

28 Article 4 de la loi du 10 août 2005 instituant le système d'information Phenix.

Cette disposition doit être lue en parallèle avec l'Article 5[29] de la LMCJ qui dispose qu'il faut entendre par adresse judiciaire électronique « *l'adresse de courrier électronique, attribuée par un greffe et à laquelle une personne a accepté ou est réputée avoir accepté, selon les modalités fixées par le Roi, que lui soient adressées les significations, notifications et communications* ».

Pour mettre en œuvre cette disposition, il est nécessaire que les membres de l'ordre judiciaire disposent d'un annuaire des adresses judiciaires électroniques qui soit à jour. Cet annuaire n'existe pas à l'heure actuelle. Il sera donc créé au sein de Phenix et accessible aux membres de l'ordre judiciaire, aux avocats, aux huissiers, aux notaires voire même à d'autres catégories de personnes déterminées par le Roi.

L'article 430 du même Code, remplacé par la loi du 22 novembre 2001, est complété comme suit : « 4. *L'Ordre des barreaux francophones et germanophone et l'Orde van Vlaamse balies établissent chacun une liste électronique des avocats inscrits sur les tableaux et listes des ordres des avocats qui les forment. Ils veillent à la mise à jour permanente de cette liste* [...]».[30] Des dispositions similaires imposent la création de listes des membres de l'ordre judiciaire,[31] des notaires[32] et des huissiers.[33]

L'élaboration de ces listes est primordiale puisqu'elle déterminera le droit pour chaque acteur, donc pour un avocat, de rentrer dans le système Phenix et d'être, par ce système de données centralisées, le destinataire ou l'expéditeur d'un acte de procédure.

2.2.2. La gestion et la conservation des dossiers judiciaires

11. L'une des principales fonctions de Phenix est de permettre la gestion électronique des dossiers judiciaires.

D'un point de vue juridique, les règles relatives à cette gestion ne diffèrent pas fondamentalement de celles relatives aux dossiers «papiers»: c'est le Code judiciaire, le Code d'instruction criminelle et les lois particulières de

---

29 Modifiant l'Article 36 du Code judiciaire.
30 Article 13 de la LMCJ.
31 Article 12 de la LMCJ.
32 Article 38 de la LPVE.
33 Article 14 de la LMCJ.

procédure qui déterminent les données qui sont traitées, les circonstances de l'ouverture du dossier et sa durée de conservation.

Par contre, l'outil informatique nécessite de préciser les modalités d'accès électronique au système Phenix et surtout les mesures de protection et d'authentification de cet accès.[34] La loi charge donc le Roi d'en fixer les modalités.

12. L'arrêté royal portant exécution de l'article 5 de la loi du 10 août 2005 instituant le système d'information Phenix permettra un accès au dossier judiciaire électronique aisé et respectueux des lois existantes.

L'accès sera aisé, dans la mesure où, il suffira qu'un magistrat appartienne à un compartiment (équivalent à une juridiction civile, pénale, de la jeunesse ou du travail) pour qu'il puisse se connecter à un dossier judiciaire électronique relevant de cette juridiction.

De même, chaque avocat pourra accéder, après vérification électronique de sa qualité, à n'importe quel dossier judiciaire électronique, comme il peut le faire actuellement en se prévalant de son mandat *ad litem*, consacré par l'article 440, alinéa 2, du Code judiciaire. Cette commodité permettra, en cas de saisine tardive du client, d'accéder au dossier la veille au soir d'une audience ou le dernier jour d'un délai quand bien même le greffe serait fermé. Elle permettra également à un *dominus litis* de déléguer sa signature à son collaborateur ou à tout confrère obligeant sans devoir le renseigner au greffe comme tel.

Cette facilité d'accès n'est évidemment pas sans limites. On pense au Code judiciaire et au Code d'instruction criminelle mais aussi à la loi du 8 décembre 1992. Il ne peut, par exemple, être question d'accéder au dossier pénal si on n'y est pas autorisé par la personne compétente, comme nous le rappelle Monsieur VANDERMEERSCH.[35]

L'avant-projet d'arrêté royal organisant l'accès au dossier judiciaire électronique rappellera vraisemblablement aux avocats qu'ils n'accèdent au dossier judiciaire électronique que dans le cadre du mandat qui leur est confié

---

[34] Doc. Parl., Ch. repr., session 2004-2005, 7 mars 2005, projet de loi, doc. 51 1645/001, exposé des motifs, p. 9.

[35] D. VANDERMEERSCH, « Phenix à l'épreuve de la procédure pénale » in *Phenix - Les tribunaux à l'ère électronique*, Cahiers du CRID, Bruylant, 2007, p. 105-142.

et dans le respect de la loi du 8 décembre 1992 relative à la protection de la vie privée à l'égard des traitements de données à caractère personnel. Il donnera, par ailleurs, au Comité de gestion la possibilité de restreindre l'accès par internet des avocats au dossier judiciaire électronique, s'il est manifestement demandé à des fins étrangères à leur mandat.

De même, il sera normalement réaffirmé dans l'avant-projet d'arrêté royal que les membres de l'Ordre judiciaire visés, accèdent exclusivement aux dossiers électroniques judiciaires dans le cadre de l'exécution de leurs fonctions et dans le respect des dispositions prévues à cet effet par le code judiciaire et le code d'instruction criminelle ainsi que de la loi du 8 décembre 1992.

Pour assurer une effectivité à ces principes, la liberté d'accès est contrebalancée par une contrainte technique : l'inventaire des accès à un dossier judiciaire électronique et des opérations y effectuées sera enregistré par Phenix. Certes, l'accès sera plus aisé, mais il sera aussi plus contrôlé que maintenant. Il ne sera plus possible d'accéder à un dossier sans laisser de traces de cet accès.

13. Y aura-t-il unicité du dossier de procédure en matière civile, comme le plaide Monsieur le président VEROUGSTRAETE[36] en se fondant sur l'esprit de la réforme, ou non, comme le déclare Monsieur MOUGENOT[37] en se fondant sur la lecture de la loi ?
Comme le relève ce dernier auteur, l'article 173, alinéa 2, 4°, du Code judiciaire autorise le greffier à constater que l'acte numérisé était porteur d'une signature manuscrite en original et que cette déclaration aurait valeur authentique. Le greffe dispose donc déjà de l'outil législatif nécessaire à la numérisation des actes et pièces de procédures qui seraient déposés sur support papier et donc à la constitution d'un dossier de procédure électronique unique.

---

36 I. VEROUGSTRAETE, « Présentation générale sur système Phenix, entre projet et réalité » in *Phenix - Les tribunaux à l'ère électronique*, Cahiers du CRID, Bruylant, 2007, p. 39, n° 28; I. VEROUGSTRAETE, V. LAMBERTS, « Le dossier électronique: concept, création, gestion » in *Phenix et la procédure électronique* (sous la coord. de J-F. HENROTTE), CUP, Larcier, 2006, vol. 85, p. 59.

37 D. MOUGENOT, « le code judiciaire à l'épreuve du cyberespace: une réforme réussie » in *Phenix - Les tribunaux à l'ère électronique*, Cahiers du CRID, Bruylant, 2007, p. 53-104.

On notera également que l'avant-projet d'arrêté royal réglant l'accès au dossier judiciaire accrédite la thèse de l'unicité du dossier de procédure et en tout cas la conversion de tous les actes et pièces de procédures[38] déposés sur support papier au greffe. En effet, il disposera probablement que lors de chaque consultation d'un dossier judiciaire par voie électronique la mention des actes ou pièces de procédure et des pièces du dossier qui n'ont pas été ou n'ont pas encore été convertis sous forme électronique, ainsi que la mention de la date de leur dépôt, sera affichée.

En fait, le véritable obstacle à l'unicité du dossier judiciaire sera la réticence habituelle au changement illustrée par Monsieur MOUGENOT[39] au moyen de l'avis des huissiers devant la Commission de la justice ou par Monsieur VANDERMEERSCH[40] par le biais de l'examen des raisons qui présideraient à systématiquement prévoir une copie sur support papier lorsqu'il est fait le choix d'établir le dossier pénal original sur support électronique.

Les raisons avancées ne nous semblent pas résister à l'examen.

Il ne faut pas perdre de vue que l'un des objectifs de la réforme est que « *la montagne de papier produite chaque année par les services judiciaires pourra être réduite* ».[41]

Certes, certains préfèreront imprimer tout ou partie des documents contenus dans le dossier judiciaire électronique mais cela se fera à leurs frais et les impressions qui pourraient être multiples des dossiers ne seront pas conservées.

Cette volonté de ne pas conserver les copies imprimées est démontrée par l'avant-projet d'arrêté royal relatif à l'accès au dossier judiciaire électronique qui permet la consultation du dossier par le bais d'une copie imprimée qui sera emportée par le justiciable et qui en tout cas ne sera pas archivée après la clôture du dossier.

---

38 Et non les pièces déposées par les parties dans leur dossier qui pourront, mais ne devront pas, être numérisées.

39 D. MOUGENOT, « le code judiciaire à l'épreuve du cyberespace: une réforme réussie » in *Phenix - Les tribunaux à l'ère électronique*, Cahiers du CRID, Bruylant, 2007, p. 53-104.

40 D. VANDERMEERSCH, « Phenix à l'épreuve de la procédure pénale » in *Phenix - Les tribunaux à l'ère électronique*, Cahiers du CRID, Bruylant, 2007, p. 105-142.

41 *Doc. parl.*, Chambre, S.O. 2004-2005, 1701/004, p. 5.

Par ailleurs, il ne faut pas prévoir *a priori* la copie sur support papier afin de respecter le droit de tout justiciable de consulter le dossier sur support papier.[42] Sinon, pourquoi l'article 32, § 1er, de la loi du 10 juillet 2006 relative à la procédure par voie électronique disposerait-il que la consultation du dossier électronique « *peut également se faire par le bais d'une copie imprimée de tout ou partie du dossier* » ?

Le dossier de procédure électronique en matière civile est et doit être, à notre estime, unique. Ce n'est qu'ainsi que le dossier de procédure pourra être consulté par internet et que l'on pourra abattre les montagnes de papier. La numérisation systématique des actes et pièces de procédure établis sur support papier est toutefois une tâche qui nécessite du matériel performant et du temps. Il conviendra donc que l'on donne aux greffes les moyens nécessaires pour accomplir cette nouvelle fonction.

2.2.3. Le rôle national

14. Le rôle national se distingue du rôle prévu à l'article 711 du Code judiciaire et n'a donc pas de fonction proprement juridique, il constitue juste un instrument de gestion de l'outil informatique Phenix.

Chaque affaire sera ainsi revêtue d'un numéro de rôle valant pour l'ensemble du royaume qui la suivra tout au long de la procédure. Ce numéro sera un numéro séquentiel, qui de lui-même ne donnera aucune information sur le dossier aux personnes ne disposant pas d'un accès au dossier.[43]

L'article 6 de la loi du 10 août 2005 instituant le système d'information Phenix, qui institue le rôle national, n'est pas encore d'application. En effet, il entrera en vigueur concomitamment aux articles de la LPVE relatifs au rôle national. Des mesures d'exécution étant nécessaires afin d'établir les règles d'établissement du numéro de rôle unique,[44] c'est le Roi qui fixera la date d'entrée en vigueur de ces dispositions.

---

42 *Doc. parl.*, Chambre, S.O. 2004-2005, 1701/004, p. 27.

43 Doc. Parl., Ch. repr., session 2004-2005, 7 mars 2005, projet de loi, doc. 51 1645/001, exposé des motifs, p. 10; http://www.privacycommission.be.

44 *Op. cit*,, p. 26.

2.2.4. La constitution d'une banque de données de jurisprudence[45]

15. La Commission de la protection de la vie privée a demandé au législateur de préciser dans la loi la finalité de la banque de données de jurisprudence, s'il s'agissait d'une banque de données anonymes ou si on concevait – et à l'adresse de qui – l'accès par certains ou par tous aux décisions personnalisées.[46] Elle a également souligné le fait qu'un arrêté royal devrait préciser si les justiciables disposent d'un droit d'opposition, si les justiciables et les membres de l'ordre judiciaire disposent d'un droit d'anonymat et si l'accès aux données peut se faire sur le type d'affaires, le nom des avocats, etc.

16. Il a été tenu compte de ces différentes remarques dans la loi du 10 août 2005. Celle-ci crée deux banques de données, chacune avec un régime distinct, l'une interne, destinée à permettre aux membres d'une même juridiction de traiter les dossiers et d'harmoniser leur jurisprudence, l'autre externe, destinée à diffuser dans le public les décisions ayant une importance pour la connaissance du droit.

Ces deux banques de données poursuivent une finalité distincte du casier judiciaire central, régi par la loi du 8 août 1997, qui assure l'enregistrement, la conservation et la modification des données concernant les décisions rendues en matière pénale et la communication de ces renseignements aux autorités judiciaires.[47] C'est le motif pour lequel, suite à la remarque émise par le Conseil d'état,[48] l'article 7 ajoute que la création de ces banques de données se fait sans préjudice de la loi sur le casier judiciaire central.

17. La banque de données *interne* comprend toutes les décisions de chaque juridiction dans leur intégralité Les membres de la juridiction concernée ont droit à accéder à l'ensemble des décisions, mais uniquement à des fins professionnelles.

Dans son avis 11/2004 la Commission de la protection de la vie privée demandait que le Roi détermine les modalités d'accès à la banque de données,

---

45 Voy. Également C. De Terwangne, « Banque de données de jurisprudence et protection des données personnelles », p 143, *in Phenix et la procédure électronique*, sous la coordination de J.-F. Henrotte, Bruxelles, Larcier, 2006

46 Avis de la Commission de la protection de la vie privée n°11/2004, point 14, *op. cit.*, p. 84.

47 Doc. Parl., Ch. repr., session 2004-2005, 7 mars 2005, projet de loi, doc. 51 1645/001, exposé des motifs, p. 10; http://www.privacycommission.be.

48 Avis du Conseil d'Etat, n° 37.943/2, *op. cit.*, p. 45.

les mesures de sécurité particulières ainsi que les catégories de personnes y ayant accès. La loi se range à l'avis de la Commission sur ce point.[49]

Des inquiétudes ont également été émises par les parlementaires qui s'inquiétaient de ce que l'accès à la banque de données interne risquait d'être ouvert à davantage de personnes que dans la situation antérieure au système Phenix (on peut par exemple penser au dossier dont est saisi un juge d'instruction et auquel les autres magistrats du Tribunal n'ont pas accès). On peut également s'interroger sur la portée réelle de l'exercice des tâches professionnelles.

L'ancienne ministre de la justice les a rassurés[50] en précisant que « *l'accès sera déterminé, en fonction de la personne et du moment, par des clés d'accès, des signatures électroniques dont disposera chacun des acteurs du monde judiciaire. L'accès sera donc 'à géométrie variable', comme c'est la cas actuellement* ». Elle a ajouté que « *le comité de surveillance doit donner des avis sur les arrêtés d'exécution proposés en ce qui concerne l'accès aux banques de données et la fixation des modalités de sécurité, de surveillance et de contrôle à prendre en considération. On déterminera quelle information est accessible pour qui* ».[51]

Il appartiendra donc au Roi d'être particulièrement attentif aux risques d'abus dans la mise en œuvre de ces dispositions.

18. La Ministre de la Justice de l'époque a rappelé qu' « *en principe, le juge doit trancher le litige en se basant sur les dossiers des parties mais pas sur des éléments externes dont il n'a pas connaissance* ».[52]
La Ministre poursuit : « *Par contre, il est évident que si le juge cite des décisions qui ne sont pas publiées dans la banque de données externe, la personne qui souhaite contester la décision doit en disposer pour que l'égalité des armes soit respectée* ».[53] Mais cette égalité est-elle vraiment respectée si les décisions sur lesquelles le juge se base ne sont disponible qu'*a posteriori*

---

[49] Doc. Parl., Ch. repr., session 2004-2005, 7 mars 2005, projet de loi, doc. 51 1645/001, exposé des motifs, p. 11; http://www.privacycommission.be.

[50] Doc. Parl., Sénat, session 2004-2005, 17 mai 2005, Rapport fait au nom de la Commission justice, n°3-1163/3, p. 4.

[51] Doc. Parl., Ch. repr., session 2004-2005, 21 avril 2005, Projet de loi, doc. 51 1645/004, p. 31.

[52] Doc. Parl., Sénat, session 2004-2005, 17 mai 2005, Rapport fait au nom de la Commission justice, n°3-1163/3, p. 14.

[53] Op. cit.

pour le justiciable ? Il est permis d'en douter, *a fortiori* si la décision rendue l'est en dernier ressort.

19. La banque de données *externe* comprend les décisions sélectionnées par chaque juridiction en fonction de leur intérêt pour l'évolution du droit, conformément aux critères établis par le comité de gestion[54] et, comme suggéré par le Conseil d'État, après consultation du comité des utilisateurs.

Il s'agit d'une part des critères négatifs suivants :

- la motivation est rédigée selon une formule standard ou une clause de pure forme, (formulation qui peut être décelée à l'aide de modules tels que ceux d'un traitement de textes. A titre d'exemples, on retiendra : les jugements prononcés par défaut, les désignations d'experts etc.);
- les décisions donnant aux moyens une réponse conforme à la jurisprudence existante ou statuant sur des éléments de preuve conformément à une jurisprudence établie;
- les décisions constatant l'incompétence manifeste du tribunal, l'irrecevabilité manifeste de la demande et le caractère évident du non fondement de la demande;

et d'autre part des critères positifs suivants :

- décisions dont le contenu a un retentissement dans la société;
- décisions dans lesquelles sont expliqués une notion ou un terme juridique, c'est-à-dire qu'une règle de droit y est formulée ou modifiée;
- décisions dans lesquelles la méthode d'interprétation utilisée aboutit à une application inusitée d'une règle de droit à un ensemble de faits;
- décisions dans lesquelles est avancée une argumentation inédite;
- décisions qui traitent d'une question concernant la compétence du tribunal;
- décisions dans lesquelles est exposé le caractère constant d'une solution ou exprimant au contraire le caractère controversé de la solution adoptée par le juge ou encore reflétant une solution

[54] Ces règles de sélection de la jurisprudence dans la banque de données de jurisprudence externe du Comité de gestion ont été publiées au M.B. le 5 octobre 2007, http://www.moniteur.be.

s'écartant de celle proposée par le ministère public ou une juridiction supérieure;
- décisions dans lesquelles sont mis en cause un principe de droit et/ou un ensemble de faits d'intérêt général.

À cet égard, il faut rappeler la Recommandation R (95) 11 du Conseil de l'Europe relative à la Sélection, au traitement et à la présentation et à l'archivage des décisions judiciaires dans les systèmes de documentation juridique automatisés, qui insiste pour que la publication de la jurisprudence prenne en compte la protection de la vie privée.[55]

Dans son avis 42/97 du 23 décembre 1997, la Commission de la protection de la vie privée s'est prononcée sur l'équilibre entre le droit du public de savoir et le droit des personnes à la protection des données, cet équilibre variant en fonction de différents critères objectifs liés à la nature du litige, à la juridiction en cause et aux catégories de personnes concernées. Par exemple pour ce qui concerne les décisions en matière de divorces, de pensions alimentaires, de mineurs, etc., elle considère que les noms des parties ne devraient être mentionnés que par leurs initiales.[56]

C'est le motif pour lequel la loi prévoit que les décisions seront en principe anonymisées, selon des modalités fixées par le Roi, mais qu'Il peut néanmoins déterminer des exceptions à ce principe, afin de garantir la compréhension des décisions. Dans ce dernier cas, néanmoins, la personne concernée conserve un droit individuel d'opposition,[57] ainsi que le demandait la Commission de la protection de la vie privée,[58] qu'il appartient également au Roi de modaliser. La Commission de la protection de la vie privée,[59] appuyée par le Conseil d'état,[60] recommande à cet égard de permettre aux parties de faire part de manière simple, gratuite et efficace de leur refus de voir publier des données à caractère personnel les concernant.

Les arrêtés royaux pris dans le cadre des articles 9 et 10 de la loi du 10 août 2005, en raison des risques évidents d'atteinte à la vie privée existant dans ce

---

55 http://www.coe.int.

56 http://www.privacycommission.be.

57 Article 9, al. 3 de la loi du 10 août 2005 instituant le système d'information Phenix.

58 Avis de la Commission de la protection de la vie privée n°11/2004, point 14, *in fine*, *op. cit.*, p. 85.

59 Avis de la Commission de la protection de la vie privée n°42/1997, point 19, § 3, *in* Doc. Parl., Ch. repr., session 2004-2005, 7 mars 2005, projet de loi, doc. 51-1645/001, p. 75.

60 Avis du Conseil d'Etat, n° 37.943/2, *op. cit.*, p. 45.

domaine, seront à chaque fois pris sur proposition du comité de gestion et après avis du comité de surveillance.
On notera toutefois que cette banque de données de jurisprudence « externe »[61] a été lancée par les autorités belges avant même l'adoption de ces arrêtés royaux ... On peut regretter qu'à ce stade le numéro de rôle figure dans les décisions anonymisées car, lorsque le rôle sera publié sur internet en vertu de l'article 713 du Code judiciaire, il sera extrêmement facile de croiser les données.

20. Comme on le verra plus loin,[62] conformément à l'article 2 de la loi du 10 août 2005 modifiant l'article 610 du Code judiciaire, c'est à la Cour de cassation qu'il appartiendra de connaître des oppositions des personnes concernées à la publication de leurs données à caractère personnel lors de la publication d'une décision de justice. Cette compétence ne porte bien évidemment pas atteinte à celle du président du tribunal de 1ère instance statuant en référé sur base de l'article 584 du Code judiciaire.

2.2.5. L'élaboration de statistiques internes et externes

21. Au point 17 de son avis 11/2004, la Commission de la protection de la vie privée demande de préciser les finalités du traitement de données à des fins statistiques. Le projet de loi répond à cette question en distinguant les statistiques destinées à un usage interne, et celles destinées à un usage externe et en précisant les règles applicables à chacune d'entre elles.[63]

22. Les statistiques internes ont pour but de permettre la gestion du service, de la chambre et de la juridiction. Elles ne sont pas destinées à être communiquées à des tiers.[64] Elles permettront également d'obtenir un indicateur précis de la charge de travail de l'ordre judiciaire, du fonctionnement des institutions judiciaires et des affaires portées devant les autorités. On vise en cela à utiliser les statistiques tant comme un instrument de gestion des ressources humaines, financières et matérielles attribuées aux cours et tribunaux que comme un instrument de politique criminelle.

---

61 http://jure.juridat.just.fgov.be.
62 Cfr. n° 29.
63 Doc. Parl., Ch. repr., session 2004-2005, 7 mars 2005, projet de loi, doc. 51-1645/001, exposé des motifs, p. 13.
64 Op. cit.

23. Les statistiques *externes* seront celles des statistiques internes qui auront été sélectionnées pour être destinées aux tiers à la juridiction. La loi précise en son article 10 que les données traitées aux fins de statistiques externes sont des données anonymes, ou à caractère personnel codées.

Ces statistiques sont destinées à être communiquées à des instances tierces. Certaines de ces instances tierces doivent toutefois être considérées comme privilégiées, selon l'exposé des motifs,[65] notamment en raison des missions qui leur sont conférées, de l'appartenance de leurs membres à l'ordre judiciaire ou de leur obligation de secret professionnel (ministre de la Justice, un ou de plusieurs chefs de corps, le Conseil supérieur de la Justice ou le comité de gestion de Phenix). Partant, la codification des données sera plus ou moins complexe en fonction du tiers auxquelles les données statistiques sont destinées.

24. La codification et l'anonymisation des données destinées à l'élaboration des statistiques devra être effectuée selon des modalités déterminées par le Roi, sur proposition du comité de gestion, et après avis du comité de surveillance, dans le respect des dispositions relatives aux règles statistiques et à la protection de la vie privée, et en particulier à l'arrêté royal du 13 février 2001[66] exécutant la loi du 8 décembre 1992 relative à la protection de la vie privée à l'égard des traitements de données à caractère personnel.

2.2.6. L'aide à la gestion et l'administration des institutions judiciaires

25. La Commission de la protection de la vie privée demandait également que la finalité «aide à la gestion et à l'administration » soit davantage précisée.[67] La loi va aussi loin que possible en ce sens, selon ses auteurs,[68] en précisant qu'il s'agit de la gestion des ressources humaines, de la documentation, des fournitures et de la comptabilité.

Les modalités d'application seront également arrêtées par le Roi, à nouveau sur proposition du comité de gestion et après avis du comité des utilisateurs.

---

65 Op. cit.

66 *M.B.*, 13 mars 2001, p. 7839, http://www.moniteur.be.

67 Avis de la Commission de la protection de la vie privée n°11/2004, point 10, *op. cit.*, p. 82.

68 Doc. Parl., Ch. repr., session 2004-2005, 7 mars 2005, projet de loi, doc. 51 1645/001, exposé des motifs, p. 14.

2.3. LES ORGANES DE PHENIX

26. La première loi du 10 août 2005 institue trois organes de gestion et de contrôle de Phenix: le comité de gestion, le comité de surveillance et le comité d'utilisateurs.

La structure de Phenix est en cela comparable à celle des autres grandes banques de données et réseaux d'informations de l'État : le Registre national, la banque-carrefour de la sécurité sociale et la banque-carrefour des entreprises. Néanmoins, la structure de Phenix s'en distingue, dans la mesure où Phenix porte sur le traitement informatisé des dossiers judiciaires et qu'il importe dès lors que la structure de ces comités respecte le principe de la séparation des pouvoirs.[69] C'est le motif pour lequel, si le comité de gestion est composé paritairement de membres de l'ordre judiciaire et de personnes qui n'en font pas partie, le comité de surveillance est majoritairement composé de magistrats.

2.3.1. Le Comité de gestion

27. Compétences - Le comité de gestion a une compétence d'action et une compétence d'avis.

En ce qui concerne la compétence *d'action*, le comité de gestion gère les missions quotidiennes de Phenix. Il prend toute initiative qui peut contribuer à améliorer son efficacité. Il prend également toutes les décisions requises par la loi du 10 août 2005 instituant le système d'information Phenix.

L'activité du comité de gestion est cependant encadrée par le Roi en ce qui concerne les principales modalités d'exécution des différentes finalités de Phenix, le Roi agissant sur proposition du comité de gestion et après avoir entendu l'avis du comité de surveillance. Il s'agit:

- des règles d'accès et d'authentification d'accès relatives à la gestion et la conservation des dossiers judiciaires;
- des règles d'accès et d'authentification d'accès au rôle national;
- des modalités d'accès, des catégories des personnes ayant accès et les mesures de sécurité particulières ayant trait à la banque de données de jurisprudence interne;

[69] Op. cit.

- des modalités d'anonymisation des décisions et des exceptions au principe d'anonymisation concernant la banque de données de jurisprudence externe;
- des règles d'anonymisation ou de codification des données nécessaires à l'élaboration de statistiques externes;
- des modalités d'exécution relatives à l'élaboration de statistiques internes et externes.

On notera, en outre, que différentes dispositions de la loi relative à la procédure électronique instituent une procédure similaire, à savoir une délégation au Roi sur proposition du comité de gestion.

Il est vrai que le rôle laissé à l'exécutif est important. Il n'y a pas lieu de s'en inquiéter selon les auteurs de la loi, dès lors que la loi ne délègue au Roi que la compétence de prendre des mesures sur le fonctionnement et la structure du système d'information Phenix, et ne lui donne aucun pouvoir sur la fonction juridictionnelle même ni sur le contenu des dossiers.[70]
Pour d'autres missions, qui ne sont pas attentatoires à la vie privée ou qui sont purement techniques, le comité de gestion agit d'initiative. Il s'agit de:

- l'adoption des codes;[71]
- la certification de la conformité des documents électroniques issus de la conversion des documents papiers ou des documents électroniques qui doivent migrer vers un autre format afin que leur lisibilité, leur authenticité et leur intégrité soient garanties dans le cadre de l'évolution constante de la technologie informatique;[72]
- l'adaptation du système aux modifications législatives, réglementaires ou technologiques, notamment en matière de simplification du langage judiciaire;[73]
- la conclusion des accords techniques avec le SPJ Justice relatifs à la gestion du système.[74]

---

70 Y. Poullet et D. Moreau, « La justice au risque de la vie privée », p. 107, in *Phenix et la procédure électronique*, sous la coordination de J.-F. Henrotte, Bruxelles, Larcier, 2006; La Commission justice du Sénat s'inquiétait d'ailleurs de la compatibilité des nombreuses délégations au Roi avec la Convention n° 108 du Conseil de l'Europe pour la protection des personnes à l'égard du traitement automatisé des données à caractère personnel, Doc. Parl., Sén., Sess. 2004-2005, doc. 3-1163, p.11 et s.

71 Article 17, al. 5 de la loi du 10 août 2005 instituant le système d'information Phenix.

72 Article 17, al. 10 de la loi du 10 août 2005 instituant le système d'information Phenix.

73 Article 17, al. 7 de la loi du 10 août 2005 instituant le système d'information Phenix.

74 Article 17, al. 8 de la loi du 10 août 2005 instituant le système d'information Phenix.

28. À côté de sa compétence d'action, le comité de gestion a une compétence *d'avis* à l'égard du ministre de la Justice et de la Cour de cassation. Il leur remet un rapport annuel sur l'activité de Phenix, contenant notamment les prévisions budgétaires. En outre, il leur remet des avis ponctuels, d'initiative ou suite à la constatation d'anomalies ou de manquements aux règles de Phenix.

Le comité de gestion se doit également de répondre de façon motivée aux suggestions du comité d'utilisateurs.

29. Recours - La loi du 10 août 2005 modifiant l'article 610 du Code judiciaire a ajouté au dit article un alinéa libellé comme suit : *« La Cour de cassation connaît des demandes en annulation des actes du comité de gestion qui excéderaient ses pouvoirs, seraient contraires aux lois ou pris de manière irrégulière ».*

Les travaux parlementaires soulignent qu' « *eu égard à la spécificité de la base de données Phenix, et au principe de la séparation des pouvoirs, il apparaît opportun d'attribuer à la plus haute juridiction de l'ordre judiciaire la compétence de connaître de ce type de demandes* ».[75]

Cette compétence de la Cour de cassation est sans préjudice de la compétence du Président du tribunal de 1ère instance statuant en référé en vertu de l'article 584 du Code judiciaire.

Suite à l'avis du Conseil d'État, qui observait que le texte ci-dessus, qui constituait l'article 29 de l'avant-projet de loi, relevait de l'article 77 de la Constitution en ce qu'il attribuait une compétence à une juridiction de jugement et était ainsi de nature à influencer l'«organisation judiciaire» au sens de l'article 77, alinéa 1er, 9°, de la Constitution,[76] l'avant-projet de loi initial a été scindé. Cet article a donc été intégré sans modification dans un projet de loi distinct, soumis à la procédure bicamérale parfaite.

30. Composition - Le comité de gestion est composé d'un président, d'un vice-président, de huit membres et de huit suppléants, nommés pour un mandat de

---

75 Doc. Parl., Ch. repr., session 2004-2005, 7 mars 2005, projet de loi, doc. 51-1645/001, exposé des motifs, p. 27.

76 Avis du Conseil d'Etat, n° 37.943/2, *op. cit.*, p. 43.

6 ans renouvelable. Y siègent également avec voix consultative le président et le vice-président du comité d'utilisateurs.[77]

Il doit être tenu compte lors de leur nomination par le Roi :

- de la parité linguistique des président et vice président, d'une part, et des membres, d'autre part ;
- de la parité entre membres et non-membres de l'Ordre judiciaire (la moitié des membres étant désignés par le pouvoir judiciaire, l'autre moitié par le ministre de la justice) ;

En outre, la représentation du parquet, de l'auditorat, du siège, du greffe, du secrétariat du parquet, des juridictions de 1ère instance et d'appel doit être assurée au sein des membres faisant partie de l'Ordre judiciaire.

Les personnes nommées par le Roi doivent par ailleurs offrir toute garantie d'indépendance et posséder des *compétences notoires* dans le domaine du droit et de la gestion de l'information. La loi ne précise malheureusement pas ce qu'elle entend par « *compétences notoires* ».

Le mode de désignation des membres de ce comité vise à garantir un certain équilibre et maximaliser la collaboration entre l'ordre judiciaire, dont Phenix gère les dossiers, et l'administration, chargée de l'organisation et de la gestion de Phenix.[78] C'est pourquoi le président et vice–président sont désignés par le Roi, l'un des deux sur proposition du Conseil des ministres, l'autre sur proposition conforme du président et du procureur général de la Cour de cassation. Ils exercent chacun leur fonction durant trois ans, puis l'échangent.

2.3.2. Le Comité de surveillance

31. A côté du comité de gestion, chargé de la gestion quotidienne de Phenix, est institué un comité de surveillance, chargé du contrôle du respect des règles de la loi du 8 décembre 1992 appliquées à Phenix.[79]

---

[77] A.R. du 30 janvier 2006 portant nomination des Président, Vice-Président et membres du comité de gestion du système d'information Phenix, *M.B.*, 2 février 2006, en vigueur le 2 février 2006, http://www.moniteur.be; A.R. du 4 mai 2006 fixant le montant du jeton de présence et des frais de déplacement attribués aux membres du comité de gestion de Phenix, *M.B.*, 24 mai 2006, en vigueur le 2 février 2006, http://www.moniteur.be.

[78] Doc. Parl., Ch. repr., session 2004-2005, 7 mars 2005, projet de loi, doc. 51-1645/001, exposé des motifs, p. 15.

[79] Article 24, § 1er, al. 2 de la loi du 10 août 2005 instituant le système d'information Phenix.

Il s'agit en fait d'un comité sectoriel institué au sein de la Commission de la protection de la vie privée.

32. Compétences - Le comité de surveillance a tout d'abord une *compétence d'avis* sur toute question relative à l'application de la loi du 8 décembre 1992 à Phenix, que sa consultation préalable soit prévue ou non par la loi du 10 août 2005 ou par la LPVE.

Il a également une compétence d'avis particulière, chaque fois que la loi instituant Phenix ou celle relative à la procédure électronique le mentionne expressément.
Toutefois, sauf si la loi instituant Phenix y déroge de manière expresse (comme c'est le cas par exemple pour le traitement des plaintes),[80] l'article 24, § 1er, al. 2 ne porte pas atteinte aux compétences de la Commission pour la protection de la vie privée, telles que déterminées par la loi du 8 décembre 1992.

Entre autres, il donne un avis préalable à l'élaboration d'arrêtés royaux relatifs :

- à la gestion et la conservation des dossiers judiciaires, aux règles d'accès et d'authentification d'accès;
- au rôle national, aux règles d'accès et d'authentification d'accès;
- à la banque de données de jurisprudence interne, aux modalités d'accès, aux catégories des personnes ayant accès et aux mesures de sécurité particulières;
- à la banque de données de jurisprudence externe, aux modalités d'anonymisation des décisions et aux exceptions au principe d'anonymisation;
- à l'élaboration de statistiques externes, aux règles d'anonymisation ou de codification des données nécessaires à leur élaboration;
- à l'élaboration de statistiques internes et externes, et à leurs modalités d'exécution.

33. À côté de cette compétence d'avis, le comité de surveillance connaît également des *plaintes* relatives aux infractions à la loi instituant le système d'information Phenix et à la LPVE, sans préjudice de toute action devant les tribunaux. Il adresse annuellement un rapport à la Commission de la protection de la vie privée relatif au traitement de ces plaintes.

---

80 Article 24, § 1er, al. 3 de la loi du 10 août 2005 instituant le système d'information Phenix.

Cette compétence est limitée dans son champ d'application par celle de la Commission de la protection de la vie privée elle-même, qui connaît des plaintes touchant les autres domaines de la protection de la vie privée. Cette compétence est également limitée dans sa portée : le traitement des plaintes ne peut déboucher que sur un avis ou un procès-verbal de conciliation.

34. Le comité de surveillance *dénonce* également au parquet les infractions à la loi du 10 août 2005 dont il a connaissance.[81]

35. Le Comité de surveillance de Phenix a des pouvoirs restreints par rapport aux autres comités sectoriels de la Commission de la protection de la vie privée.

Il n'a pas le pouvoir d'accorder ou non l'accès aux données de Phenix, contrairement au comité sectoriel du Registre national[82] et au comité de surveillance de la banque-carrefour des entreprises.[83] Comme mentionné *supra*, le droit d'accès au dossier judiciaire est en effet régi par les dispositions du Code judiciaire ou du Code d'instruction criminelle.
Pour les traitements de données qui ne sont pas régis par les Codes judiciaire ou d'instruction criminelle, comme le répertoire des adresses judiciaires électroniques, la loi délègue au Roi le pouvoir de décider, sur proposition du comité de gestion et après avis du comité de surveillance, des modalités d'accès. Cette manière de procéder est conforme à l'Article 8 de la loi du 8 décembre 1992 qui donne au Roi délégation de réglementer les traitements de données judiciaires.

Le comité de surveillance de Phenix n'a pas non plus le pouvoir d'autoriser ou d'interdire les communications au sein de Phenix, comme le font le comité sectoriel de la banque-carrefour de la sécurité sociale et le comité sectoriel

---

81 Article 24, § 3 de la loi du 10 août 2005 instituant le système d'information Phenix.

82 Article 5 de la loi du 8 août 1983 organisant un registre national des personnes physiques (*M.B.*, 21 avril 1984, p. 5247, http://www.moniteur.be), modifié par l'Article 5 de la loi du 25 mars 2003 modifiant la loi du 8 août 1983 organisant un Registre national des personnes physiques et la loi du 19 juillet 1991 relative aux registres de la population et aux cartes d'identité et modifiant la loi du 8 août 1983 organisant un Registre national des personnes physiques (*M.B.*, 28 mars 2003, p. 15921, http://www.moniteur.be).

83 Article 18, § 2 de la loi du 16 janvier 2003 portant création d'une Banque-Carrefour des Entreprises, modernisation du registre de commerce, création de guichets-entreprises agréés et portant diverses dispositions, *M.B.*, 5 février 2003, p. 4778, http://www.moniteur.be.

pour l'autorité fédérale,[84] qui doit donner une autorisation de principe pour «*toute communication électronique de données personnelles par un service publique fédéral*», après vérification de la conformité de la communication aux dispositions légales et réglementaires.

Ce sont également les Codes judiciaire et d'instruction criminelle qui régissent la communication entre les acteurs du monde judiciaire et ensuite le Roi, sur base de l'Article 8 de la loi du 8 décembre 1992. Subordonner cette communication à l'autorisation d'une instance tierce serait contrevenir à l'indépendance du pouvoir judiciaire.

Il fallait en effet trouver un équilibre entre deux organes légalement ou constitutionnellement indépendants, la Commission vie privée et le pouvoir judiciaire, et garantir que chacun puisse poursuivre les objectifs que la loi ou la Constitution lui attribue dans le respect de son indépendance.

36. A la demande de 2 membres du comité, l'examen d'un dossier peut être suspendu afin de le soumettre préalablement à la Commission de protection de la vie privée qui s'en saisira pleinement.

À l'origine, le projet de loi n'avait pas prévu de possibilité pour la Commission vie privée de connaître des avis du comité de surveillance de Phenix. Mais le Conseil d'État a demandé à ce que l'on veille à une meilleure articulation entre les deux organes, « *à défaut de quoi, l'intégration du comité de surveillance spécialisé dans le cadre général de la loi du 8 décembre 1992 paraîtra artificielle* ».[85] Compte tenu des spécificités de la banque de données Phenix, le présent projet de loi prévoit dès lors une procédure qui s'apparente au mécanisme d'une question préjudicielle.[86]

---

84 Créé par l'Article 36*bis* de la loi du 8 décembre 1992 relative à la protection de la vie privée à l'égard des traitements de données à caractère personnel (*M.B.*, 18 mars 1993, p. 5801, http://www.moniteur.be), tel que modifié par l'article 10 de la loi du 26 février 2003 modifiant la loi du 8 décembre 1992 relative à la protection de la vie privée à l'égard des traitements de données à caractère personnel et la loi du 15 janvier 1990 relative à l'institution et à l'organisation d'une Banque-Carrefour de la sécurité sociale en vue d'aménager le statut et d'étendre les compétences de la Commission de la protection de la vie privée, *M.B.*, 26 juin 2003, p. 34416, http://www.moniteur.be.

85 Avis du Conseil d'Etat n° 37.943/2, *op. cit.*, p. 43.

86 Doc. Parl., Ch. repr., session 2004-2005, 7 mars 2005, projet de loi, doc. 51-1645/001, exposé des motifs, p. 24.

Toutefois, l'avis rendu par la Commission de la protection de la vie privée n'a pas préséance sur celui du comité de surveillance de Phenix,[87] ceci afin de respecter le principe de l'indépendance du pouvoir judiciaire. « *Le point de vue de la Commission est explicitement mentionné dans l'avis du comité de surveillance. Le cas échéant, le comité motive explicitement les raisons pour lesquelles le point de vue de la Commission n'a pas du tout ou seulement partiellement été suivi.* »[88]

37. Composition - La Commission de la protection de la vie privée a demandé[89] que, tout comme pour les autres banques de données de l'État,[90] le comité de surveillance soit composé conformément à l'Article 31 *bis* de la loi du 8 décembre 1992, à savoir un comité sectoriel institué au sein de la CPVP. Un tel comité est composé paritairement de trois membres désignés par la Commission vie privée en son sein, dont le président, et de trois membres externes. La Commission a néanmoins reconnu que la spécificité du système d'information Phenix autorisait que ce comité soit uniquement composé de magistrats.

Le législateur a suivi l'avis de la Commission sur certains points:

- le comité de surveillance a été institué au sein de la Commission de la protection de la vie privée et est devenu un comité sectoriel ;
- il est composé en majorité de magistrats;
- il est composé paritairement de trois membres désignés par la Commission de la protection de la vie privée en son sein et de trois membres externes.

Par contre le projet ne s'est pas rangé à l'avis de la Commission en ce que le président du comité de surveillance n'est pas un membre de la Commission mais un des trois membres externes, désignés par la Chambre, sur proposition du Conseil des ministres, après avis conforme et conjoint du premier

---

87 Il en est de même pour les avis du comité sectoriel de la sécurité sociale et de ceux de la Commission de la vie privée (Article 44 de la loi du 15 janvier 1990 relative à l'institution et à l'organisation d'une banque carrefour de la sécurité sociale, *M.B.*, 22 février 1990, p. 3288, http://www.moniteur.be).

88 Article 24, § 2, 3e et 4e al. de la loi du 10 août 2005 instituant le système d'information Phenix.

89 Avis de la Commission de la protection de la vie privée n°11/2004, points 21 et 22, *op. cit.*, p. 89.

90 Registre national des personnes physiques, banque-carrefour de la sécurité sociale, banque-carrefour des entreprises.

président et du procureur général près la Cour de cassation.[91] Or, c'est généralement le président de la Commission de la protection de la vie privée qui assume la tâche de président du comité sectoriel.

38. Le comité de surveillance est donc composé de 6 membres, nommés pour un mandat de 6 ans renouvelable, majoritairement des magistrats (au moins 4), avec parité membres de la Commission de protection de la vie privée, non membres de la Commission.[92]

La Chambre des représentants nomme 3 membres effectifs, dont le président, et 3 suppléants, ayant qualité de magistrats. La Commission de la protection de la vie privée nomme également 3 membres effectifs et 3 membres suppléants, choisis en son sein, dont au moins 1 magistrat.

La parité linguistique doit évidemment être respectée.

2.3.3. Le Comité des utilisateurs

39. Compétences - Le comité des utilisateurs a pour fonction de permettre à tous les acteurs du monde judiciaire de faire entendre leur voix dans le fonctionnement de Phenix. C'est un organe de réflexion, qui a pour mission principale de proposer toute initiative de nature à promouvoir l'utilisation de Phenix.[93]

Il adresse ses suggestions au comité de gestion. Afin d'éviter que ces avis et recommandations ne restent lettre-morte, la loi oblige le comité de gestion à répondre de façon motivée aux suggestions du comité d'utilisateurs.[94] Le président et le vice-président siègent en outre avec voix consultative dans le comité de gestion,[95] ce qui leur permet d'y faire entendre leur voix.

---

91 Doc. Parl., Ch. repr., session 2004-2005, 7 mars 2005, projet de loi, doc. 51-1645/001, exposé des motifs, p. 19. Les auteurs de la loi y justifient cette différence de manière très complète et détaillée.

92 A.R. du 4 mai 2006 fixant le montant des jetons de présence et des frais de déplacement attribués au président et aux membres du comité de surveillance de Phenix, *M.B.*, 24 mai 2006, http://www.moniteur.be.

93 Article 27, al. 1 de la loi du 10 août 2005 instituant le système d'information Phenix.

94 Article 17, al. 6 de la loi du 10 août 2005 instituant le système d'information Phenix.

95 Article 15, § 7 de la loi du 10 août 2005 instituant le système d'information Phenix.

En revanche, comme le déplore la Commission de la protection de la vie privée,[96] le comité d'utilisateurs ne peut saisir le comité de surveillance.

40. Composition - Le comité d'utilisateurs est composé de 24 membres,[97] parmi lesquels 16 sont membres de l'Ordre judiciaire et 8 auxiliaires de justice. Il compte ainsi dans ses rangs 12 magistrats, 4 avocats (2 faisant partie de l'OBFG, et 2 appartenant à l'OVB), 2 huissiers, 2 notaires, 2 représentants du personnel des secrétariats des parquets et auditorats et enfin 2 greffiers.[98] Parmi les représentants de l'Ordre judiciaire, 2 sont désignés par la Cour de cassation (l'un appartenant au siège, l'autre appartenant au parquet de la Cour), 2 par les premiers présidents des cours d'appel et du travail, 2 par le collège des procureurs généraux, 2 par le Conseil des procureurs du Roi, 2 par le Conseil des auditeurs du travail et 2 par le Conseil supérieur de la Justice.

Il a été soigneusement veillé à ce que cet organe représente le plus fidèlement possible l'ensemble des catégories professionnelles utilisant le système Phenix. Ainsi, Il est composé paritairement :

- de francophones et de néerlandophones, tant au sein de chaque représentation qu'au niveau global, ainsi qu'entre le président et le vice-président,
- de magistrats et de non-magistrats,
- parmi les magistrats, de membres du siège et du parquet,
- parmi les magistrats, de membres de cour d'appel et de tribunaux de première instance.

Une répartition la plus équilibrée possible d'un point de vue géographique et du genre est également prévue.

---

96 Avis de la Commission de la protection de la vie privée n°11/2004, point 18, *op. cit.*, p. 88; Dans le même sens: Y. POULLET et D. MOREAU, « La justice au risque de la vie privée », *op. cit.*, p. 103.

97 A.R. portant composition du comité des utilisateurs du système d'information Phenix, *M.B.*, 15 juin 2006, http://www.moniteur.be; A.R. du 15 février 2006 déterminant les modalités de fonctionnement du comité des utilisateurs institué par l'article 27 de la loi du 10 août 2005 instituant le système d'information Phenix, *M.B.*, 28 février 2006, http://www.moniteur.be.

98 A. M. du 15 mai 2006 portant désignation de certains membres du comité des utilisateurs de Phenix institué par l'article 27 de la loi du 10 août 2005 instituant le système d'information Phenix, *M.B.*, 15 juin 2006, en vigueur le 15 juin 2006, http://www.moniteur.be; Modification de l'avis du 15 juin 2006 relatif à la composition du comité des utilisateurs du système d'information Phenix - Remplacement d'un membre, *M.B.*, 28 juin 2007, http://www.moniteur.be.

Enfin, et afin de rencontrer le souhait émis par les barreaux et le notariat, il est précisé que le président ou le vice-président doit être un avocat, un huissier de justice ou un notaire, c'est à dire un auxiliaire de justice externe aux juridictions.[99]

2.4. L'UTILISATION DE STANDARDS OUVERTS

41. La loi du 10 août 2005 instituant le système d'information Phenix, dispose en son article 30 que les protocoles et formats de communication et de sauvegarde du système d'information Phenix sont basés exclusivement sur des standards ouverts.

Il faut entendre par standard « *une spécification technique, suffisante pour en développer une implémentation complète, approuvée par un organisme de certification indépendante* » et par standard ouvert « *un standard qui soit gratuitement disponible sur l'internet et sans restriction juridique quant à sa diffusion et son utilisation* ».

Lorsque l'on parle de « standard ouvert », c'est par opposition au « standard propriétaire ». Un standard propriétaire est caractérisé par le fait qu'il est la propriété de quelqu'un qui y met (ou peut y mettre) des restrictions d'usage et d'accès.

42. Les auteurs de la loi exposent que « *l'utilisation de standards permet de garantir que dans trente ans, il y aura toujours des logiciels capables d'ouvrir les fichiers sauvegardés aujourd'hui, ce qui n'est pas le cas de tous les logiciels actuellement sur le marché. Le recours à des standards garantit donc la pérennité du système Phenix* ».[100]

En effet, il n'est pas rare qu'un éditeur de logiciel mette la clef sous la porte et que, le logiciel n'étant plus maintenu, il devienne très difficile de récupérer les données dans un autre logiciel. Un standard ouvert peut par contre être utilisé dans n'importe quel logiciel, ce qui permet de récupérer des données dans un nouveau logiciel.

---

99 Article 27, al. 6 de la loi du 10 août 2005 instituant le système d'information Phenix; Doc. Parl., Ch. repr., session 2004-2005, 7 mars 2005, projet de loi, doc. 51-1645/001, exposé des motifs, p. 25.

100 Doc. Parl., Ch. repr., session 2004-2005, 7 mars 2005, projet de loi, doc. 51-1645/001, exposé des motifs, p. 26.

43. L'utilisation de standards ouverts permettra par ailleurs, avantage non négligeable, d'économiser le prix d'achat ou de conception de ces formats et protocoles.[101]

44. Mais surtout, comme le soulignent les travaux préparatoires, « *le recours à des standards ouverts permet d'éviter le monopole d'une entreprise sur les protocoles et formats de communication et d'archivage du système* ».[102] Les standards ouverts offrent donc l'avantage de ne pas lier l'utilisateur à un prestataire de service unique. Plusieurs acteurs informatiques pourront donc offrir des services autour de Phenix, ce qui non seulement stimule la concurrence en établissant des conditions techniques égales pour tous les acteurs du marché et se traduit par des réductions de coût au profit des entreprises et, en définitive, des consommateurs,[103] mais garantit également une liberté non négligeable dans le chef de l'administration. « *Ce secteur informatique est l'un des domaines où l'action des pouvoirs publics peut en effet être extrêmement compromise à raison de relations mal gérées avec un fournisseur ou un prestataire de services dans le cadre d'un marché public : la dépendance du pouvoir adjudicateur provoquée par des conditions contractuelles inadéquates peut produire de conséquences néfastes, notamment en cas de défaillance du cocontractant du pouvoir adjudicateur. A cet égard, le souci, affiché en l'espèce, d'assurer la pérennité des données publiques révèle plus largement l'importance d'une prévention des risques inhérents à ces cas de défaillance.* »[104]

45. Dans de nombreux pays,[105] les autorités compétentes commencent à réaliser les avantages offerts par les formats ouverts.

---

101 *Op. cit.*

102 *Op. cit*, p. 25.

103 E. LIIKANEN, commissaire européen chargé des entreprises et de la société de l'information, Journée mondiale de la normalisation, 14 octobre 2003, http://europa.eu.int/rapid/pressReleasesAction.do?reference= IP/03/1374&format=HTML&aged=1&language=FR&guiLanguage=fr

104 D. DE ROY, « L'utilisation des logiciels libres par les pouvoirs publics - Réflexions sur quelques propositions récentes », *Droit & nouvelles technologies*, disponible à l'adresse http://www.droit-technologie.org/dossiers/Utilisation_logiciels_libres_pouvoirs_publics.pdf, p. 3.

105 Pour une analyse des différentes initiatives étatiques: P. GENOUD, G. PAULETTO, « Standards ouverts et logiciel libre - Clarification des notions », Observatoire Technologique, Centre des technologies de l'information, République et Canton de Genève, 30 septembre 2005, disponible à l'adresse ftp://ftp.geneve.ch/obstech/soll-clarification-V1_0.pdf.

Ainsi, en Belgique, en juin 2004 déjà, le Conseil des Ministres approuvait les directives et recommandations aux services publics fédéraux pour l'usage de standards, de logiciels d'application et de logiciels libres, faits sur mesure,[106] qui prévoient notamment que « *pour les nouveaux systèmes informatiques, les services publics fédéraux utiliseront désormais exclusivement des standards ouverts et/ou spécifications ouvertes pour les formats de données et les protocoles de communication lors de l'archivage, de l'échange et de la communication de données électroniques. Pour les applications existantes qui, lors de l'archivage, de l'échange ou de la communication de données électroniques à des parties externes, n'utilisent pas encore de standards ouverts et/ou de spécifications ouvertes, pour les formats de données et les protocoles de communication, les services publics fédéraux lanceront et achèveront une migration conformément à un planning convenu lors de la fixation de chaque standard ouvert et/ou spécification ouverte* ».

La note stratégique 2005[107] présentée par Monsieur Peter Vanvelthoven, Secrétaire d'État à l'Informatisation de l'État, confirmait ce mouvement en stipulant clairement que toute nouvelle application informatique utilisera des standards ouverts et que les applications existantes devront être migrées progressivement vers ceux-ci. La liste des standards ouverts utilisés par l'État sera rassemblée au sein du Cadre Fédéral Belge d'Interopérabilité en concertation avec les Communautés et Régions.

Lors du Conseil des Ministres du 23 juin 2006, a été approuvée la note sur l'utilisation de standards ouverts pour l'échange de documents bureautiques, proposée par Monsieur Peter Vanvelthoven, Ministre de l'Emploi et de l'Informatisation. Cette note dispose qu' « *afin de réduire la dépendance de ces formats "propriétaires", il est nécessaire d'utiliser un standard ouvert comme format d'échange. XML est un tel standard pour l'échange d'informations entre différents systèmes informatiques. Un document basé sur XML est donc une garantie d'assurer l'accessibilité des informations à long terme. L'Open Document Format (ODF) est un format de document basé sur XML qui a été accepté par l'ISO (Organisation internationale de normalisation). C'est pourquoi nous proposons de retenir l'ODF comme*

[106] Standards et Logiciels, Chancellerie du Premier Ministre — Conseil des Ministres, Belgique, 2004, http://www.belgium.be/eportal/application?pageid=contentPage&docId=35409.

[107] Note stratégique 2005, Secrétaire d'État à l'Informatisation de l'État, PETER VANVELTHOVEN, Belgique, 2005, http://www.belgium.be/eportal/application?pageid=contentPage&docId=36796.

standard pour l'échange de documents bureautiques comme les documents texte, les feuilles de calcul et les présentations, dès son approbation définitive par l'ISO ». Cette mesure se concrétisera par le fait que « *chaque administration publique fédérale doit prévoir une fonctionnalité de lecture pour les documents ODF d'ici septembre 2007. Cela n'exclut pas l'utilisation d'autres formats. L'administration en question détermine la manière dont la fonctionnalité de lecture est garantie. En fonction des résultats d'une analyse d'impact effectuée par Fedict, l'ODF sera utilisé comme format standard pour l'échange de documents bureautiques à partir de septembre 2008* ».

46. L'article 30 de la loi instituant le système d'information Phenix n'est pas encore entré en vigueur,[108] contrairement aux autres dispositions de la loi. Le Roi fixera la date d'entrée en vigueur de cette disposition. Il a en effet été jugé souhaitable de prévoir une période transitoire, qui sera déterminée par le Roi, afin de laisser aux acteurs du monde judiciaire qui n'utilisent pas de standard ouvert le temps de s'y adapter.[109]

En effet, même si l'on ne peut que se réjouir d'un point de vue intellectuel du choix qui a été fait d'utiliser des formats standards ouverts, cela ne fera pas sans heurt dans la pratique. Rare en effet sont les acteurs du monde judiciaire qui emploient ces formats à l'heure actuelle.

47. Les autorités belges ne sont hélas pas très constantes puisque pour la procédure en cassation devant le conseil d'Etat[110] le Gouvernement a fait choix du format « Portable Document Format » (.pdf)[111] incorporant les polices et donnant à l'utilisateur le droit de copier et d'extraire des informations et d'imprimer le document.

---

108 Ainsi que l'article 6 de la loi du 10 août 2005 instituant le système d'information Phenix, instituant un rôle national, comme vu *supra*, n° 14.

109 Doc. Parl., Ch. repr., session 2004-2005, 7 mars 2005, projet de loi, doc. 51-1645/001, exposé des motifs, p. 27.

110 Article 39 de l'arrêté royal du 30 novembre 2006 déterminant la procédure en cassation devant le conseil d'Etat, *M.B.*, 1er décembre 2006, http://www.moniteur.be.

111 Le format PDF est un standard ouvert mais qui n'a pas été approuvé par un organisme de certification indépendant.

3. LES LOIS RELATIVES À LA PROCÉDURE PAR VOIE ÉLECTRONIQUE

3.1. INTRODUCTION: OBJET DE LA LÉGISLATION

48. Les lois du 10 juillet 2006 relative à la procédure par voie électronique[112] (ci-après LPVE) et du 5 août 2006 modifiant certaines dispositions du Code judiciaire en vue de la procédure par voie électronique[113] (ci-après LMCJ) règlent la manière dont les pièces de procédure prescrites par les lois ou règlements sont créées, déposées, signifiées, notifiées, communiquées, conservées et consultées électroniquement dans le cadre d'une procédure judiciaire.[114]

« *Les termes 'procédure judiciaire' doivent être entendus au sens large et visent les procédures tant civiles que pénales* ».[115]

Pour atteindre cet objectif, la LPVE énonce en son premier chapitre des définitions et principes généraux, modifie en son deuxième chapitre, avec la LMCJ, le Code judiciaire et règle, en son troisième chapitre, la période transitoire pour le dossier électronique en matière pénale.

3.2. PRINCIPES GÉNÉRAUX

3.2.1. La liberté et la contrainte au passage aux technologies de l'information et de la communication

49. L'article 4 de la LPVE établit un principe et une exception :

3.2.1.1. Principe

Le principe est que *« sauf dispositions légales contraires, personne ne peut être contraint de poser des actes de procédure ou de recevoir des documents relatifs à des actes de procédure par voie électronique ».*[116]

---

112 *M.B.*, 7 février 2006, p. 45527, http://www.moniteur.be.

113 *M.B.*, 7 février 2006, p. 45532, http://www.moniteur.be.

114 Article 3 de la LPVE.

115 Doc. Parl., Ch. Repr., lég. 51, sess. Ord. 2004-2005, n° 1701/001, http://www.lachambre.be, ci-après « Exposé des motifs », p. 13.

116 L'article 4, § 1er de la loi du 9 juillet 2001 fixant certaines règles relatives au cadre juridique pour les signatures électroniques et les services de certification disposait déjà, mais sans la

Cette règle est justifiée, dans l'exposé des motifs, par le fait qu'*« il ne faut en effet pas perdre de vue que tout le monde ne possède pas les connaissances nécessaires, voire l'infrastructure requise pour communiquer électroniquement. L'on ne peut créer indirectement une inégalité entre les citoyens par ce manque de connaissance ou d'infrastructure ».*[117]

Cela nous paraît d'autant plus justifié que la Cour d'arbitrage (désormais Cour constitutionnelle) a prononcé le 16 juin 2004 un arrêt n°106/2004[118] au sujet des dispositions limitant à trois exemplaires la version en papier du *Moniteur belge*, introduites par les articles 474, 475, 476 et 478 de la loi-programme (I) du 24 décembre 2002.[119]

Selon la Cour, *« les dispositions attaquées ne créent par elles-mêmes aucune différence de traitement puisque toutes les personnes auxquelles s'appliquent les actes législatifs et administratifs peuvent en prendre connaissance de la même manière. Mais ce qui est reproché à ces dispositions est, précisément, de n'avoir pas tenu compte de ce que chacun n'a pas un accès égal aux techniques informatiques. Or, le principe d'égalité et de non-discrimination peut être violé lorsque le législateur traite de la même manière des personnes qui se trouvent dans des situations essentiellement différentes ».*

La mesure en cause « *introduit* », selon la Cour, *« ainsi une différence de traitement entre celui qui, ayant accès à un matériel informatique, peut consulter aisément tous les numéros du Moniteur belge édités depuis la mise en vigueur des dispositions attaquées et y trouver le texte qui l'intéresse, et celui qui, n'ayant pas accès à l'informatique, ne peut identifier le numéro dans lequel ce texte est publié ».*

En n'organisant pas des mesures d'accompagnement pour ces personnes qui n'ont pas d'accès à l'informatique, le législateur avait ainsi empiété, de manière disproportionnée, sur un droit fondamental : *« Compte tenu de ce que la publication est une condition essentielle de la force obligatoire des*

---

nuance dérogatoire de la LPVE, qu' « *à défaut de dispositions légales contraires, nul ne peut être contraint de poser un acte juridique par voie électronique* », *Droit des technologies de l'information*, CODES LARCIER *thématiques*, p. 35.

117 Exposé des motifs, p. 13-14.

118 C. arb., n°106/2004, 16 juin 2004, *R.D.T.I.*, décembre 2004, n° 20, obs. F. ABU DALU et J.F. HENROTTE, « Disparition de la version en papier du Moniteur belge, obligations positives et large marge d'appréciation: le prix du Docteur Faust ».

119 *M.B.*, 31 déc. 2002, http://www.moniteur.be; *Droit des technologies de l'information*, CODES LARCIER *thématiques*, p. 349.

textes officiels, la faculté pour chaque personne d'en prendre connaissance en tout temps est un droit inhérent à l'Etat de droit puisque c'est cette connaissance qui permettra à chacun de s'y conformer »

Or, il n'est pas douteux que le droit d'accès à un juge, qui est notamment garanti par l'article 6 de la Convention de sauvegarde des droits de l'homme et des libertés fondamentales est tout aussi inhérent à l'Etat de droit que le droit de prendre connaissance des textes rendus obligatoires par la formalité de la publication.

Le législateur ne s'y trompe pas et rassure déjà : « *A l'avenir, il semble souhaitable d'accorder à l'e-justice une portée aussi large que possible, ainsi que d'encourager et de généraliser la communication par voie électronique entre les citoyens et les institutions judiciaires. On peut pour cela envisager la mise à disposition, par les autorités, aux citoyens de l'infrastructure et de l'assistance nécessaires, de sorte que chacun puisse de facto être censé avoir la possibilité de procéder par voie électronique* ».[120]

3.2.1.2. Exception

50. L'alinéa 2, 1° de l'article 4 de la LPVE établit une exception à ce principe de non-imposition de la procédure électronique : le Roi peut, après avis du comité de gestion, par arrêté délibéré en Conseil des ministres disposer, notamment, que des catégories de personnes morales[121] ou « *des catégories de personnes physiques qui, à titre professionnel, à la requête de tiers ou d'une autorité judiciaire, posent des actes de procédure sont, dans le cadre de leur profession, tenues de poser et de recevoir des actes de procédure par voie électronique* ».

Selon l'exposé des motifs, « *afin d'encourager néanmoins la procédure par voie électronique et de l'intégrer aussi vite que possible, le Roi peut contraindre certains acteurs professionnels (greffiers, secrétaires de parquet, avocats, huissiers, experts,...) ou certaines personnes morales à poser et à recevoir certains actes de procédure par voie électronique. Cette possibilité est prévue à l'article 4, alinéa 2, 1° et 2°. Ces dispositions sont rédigées de manière suffisamment souple afin de permettre d'opérer certaines distinctions entre les actes de procédure. En effet, il faut pouvoir prévoir un régime*

---

[120] Exposé des motifs, p. 14.

[121] Article 4, al. 2, 2° de la LPVE.

suffisamment flexible, pour, par exemple, permettre le dépôt à l'audience d'une note manuscrite si une partie souhaite déposer sur le champ un écrit de procédure sur un point précis. Ces mesures d'exécution auront bien entendu lieu après concertation avec les représentants des corps professionnels concernés, et des modalités particulières de transition seront prévues ».[122]

En ce qu'elle permet au Roi d'établir une exception de cette nature, la disposition en cause ne paraît pas en soi contraire aux articles 10 et 11 de la Constitution. On rappellera, à cet égard, que *« les règles constitutionnelles de l'égalité et de la non-discrimination n'excluent pas qu'une différence de traitement soit établie entre des catégories de personnes, pour autant qu'elle repose sur un critère objectif et qu'elle soit raisonnablement justifiée (...) L'existence d'une telle justification doit s'apprécier en tenant compte du but et des effets de la mesure critiquée ainsi que de la nature des principes en cause ; le principe d'égalité est violé lorsqu'il est établi qu'il n'existe pas de rapport raisonnable de proportionnalité entre les moyens employés et le but visé ».*[123]
En l'occurrence, il peut paraître justifié d'imposer à certaines catégories déterminées de personnes qui sont, par rapport à l'appareil judiciaire, dans une relation de type professionnel et qui tirent de cette relation un profit ou un revenu de devoir faire l'investissement du matériel nécessaire à la procédure électronique. Permettre au Roi d'imposer à ces catégories de personnes de recourir à ladite procédure paraît ainsi dans un rapport raisonnable de proportionnalité avec le but visé, qui est d'encourager le recours à l'électronique, et ne semble guère empiéter sur le droit fondamental d'accès à un juge, d'autant que cette mesure ne vise que les actes posés dans le cadre de la profession et que l'objectif est aussi la meilleure organisation administrative des juridictions.

Le Roi devra toutefois se garder d'établir, en ce qui concerne ces catégories de personnes, ou ces catégories d'actes, des distinctions prohibées : par exemple, ne paraîtrait pas *a priori* compatible avec le principe d'égalité et de non-discrimination d'imposer la voie électronique aux seuls avocats stagiaires, car la mesure établirait alors une distinction entre avocats ayant un pouvoir égal de représentation des tiers en justice sans rapport raisonnable avec le but

---

[122] Exposé des motifs, p. 14.

[123] Voy., entre autres, C. arb., n° 169/2003, 17 déc. 2003; pour une synthèse récente et complète de la jurisprudence de la Cour d'arbitrage en matière de contrôle du respect du principe d'égalité et de non-discrimination, voy. N. BANNEUX, « L'égalité: clef du contentieux constitutionnel ? », in *L'égalité: nouvelle(s) clé(s) du droit ?*, CUP 10/2004, vol. 73, p. 7-74.

poursuivi. Il appartiendra au Roi d'être prudent s'il décide de distinguer certaines procédures (où la procédure électronique serait imposée aux « professionnels de la justice ») d'autres procédures (où il maintiendrait le principe de libre choix),[124] ce que le caractère volontairement souple de l'habilitation lui permet semble-t-il de faire. Nous rappellerons, à cet égard, que la différence de traitement entre certaines catégories de personnes qui résulte de l'application de règles de procédure différentes dans des circonstances différentes n'est pas discriminatoire en soi. Il pourrait néanmoins y avoir une discrimination si la différence de traitement résultant de l'application de ces procédures allait de pair avec une limitation disproportionnée des droits des parties concernées.[125] Plus encore, l'on ne comprendrait pas que le Roi impose aux avocats le « tout électronique » mais qu'Il en exempte d'autres intervenants ayant accès à la barre, tels les délégués syndicaux,[126] ou que l'Etat ne s'impose pas à lui-même ce qu'il impose à d'autres et n'oblige donc pas, dans un même temps, ses fonctionnaires « plaideurs »[127] à ce passage ...

L'arrêté royal pourra faire l'objet, le cas échéant, d'un recours en annulation devant le Conseil d'Etat fondé notamment sur les articles 10 et 11 de la Constitution.

Cela étant, l'exposé des motifs vise à rassurer, ainsi qu'on a pu le lire dans l'extrait cité ci-dessus : une période transitoire permettant, entre autres, aux avocats de s'adapter à ces technologies de l'information et de la communication sera établie en concertation avec les ordres. Au demeurant, cet arrêté royal sera pris après avis du comité de gestion, dont il faut souligner, qu'à l'instigation de l'Ordre des barreaux francophones et

---

124 Voy. par exemple le recours obligatoire à l'électronique en matière de procédure sommaire d'injonction de payer en Autriche pour les affaires dont les enjeux ne dépasse pas 30.000 €, http://www.ccbe.org/doc/it_conference/documents/fr/heufler_fr.pdf et I. VEROUGSTRAETE et V. LAMBERTS, « Le dossier électronique: concept, création, gestion », p. 73, in *Phenix et la procédure électronique*, CUP 02/2006, vol. 85, Bruxelles, Larcier. Observons que les auteurs y font état d'une proposition de loi belge suggérant l'imposition de la procédure électronique pour toute demande inférieure à 1.860 €, soit ressortissant de la compétence du juge de paix.

125 C. arb., n° 123/2003, 8 oct. 2003 et n° 163/2003, 10 déc. 2003; sur cette question, voy. particulièrement H. BOULARBAH, « La Cour d'arbitrage et le droit judiciaire privé », *Rev. dr. ULB*, 2002, p. 257 et s.; F. ABU DALU, « Cour d'arbitrage et droit judiciaire privé » in *La Cour d'arbitrage: un juge comme les autres ?*, Liège, Editions du Jeune Barreau ASBL, 2004, p. 282 et s., sp. p. 289.

126 Article 728 du Code judiciaire.

127 Par exemple, le membre ou le délégué du CPAS (Article 728 du Code judiciaire) ou le fonctionnaire de l'administration fiscale (Article 379 CIR 92).

germanophone, il comprend, certes seulement avec voix consultative, le président et le vice-président du comité d'utilisateurs,[128] l'un des deux étant nécessairement un auxiliaire de justice.[129] On notera également que cette imposition est contingente en matière pénale, tant que le Roi n'aura pas fixé la date de l'introduction complète du dossier électronique en matière pénale.[130]

3.2.1.3. Habilitation large au Roi

51. Selon l'article 4, alinéa 2, 3° de la LPVE, le Roi peut, par arrêté délibéré en Conseil des ministres, *« abroger, compléter, modifier ou remplacer des dispositions légales en vigueur afin de permettre la communication par voie électronique entre les sujets de droit d'une part, et les autorités judiciaires d'autre part»*.

Compte tenu de la largesse de cette habilitation, les arrêtés visés au 3°, d'une part, sont pris non seulement avec l'avis du comité de gestion mais également de celui de surveillance[131] et d'autre part, devront être confirmés dans les 18 mois à peine de ne plus produire leurs effets.[132]

Le procédé consistant à attribuer au Roi le pouvoir de modifier la législation est désormais connu et largement admis. Il ressortit tantôt au concept de loi d'habilitation « ordinaire », tantôt au concept de loi-cadre,[133] tantôt au concept de loi de pouvoirs spéciaux, selon l'étendue du secteur où la délégation est opérée.[134] La distinction n'est cependant guère utile puisque tous ces procédés se fondent sur l'article 105 de la Constitution, selon lequel *« le Roi n'a d'autres pouvoir que ceux que lui attribuent formellement la*

---

[128] Article 15, § 7 de la loi du 10 août 2005 instituant le système d'information Phenix, *M.B.*, 1er septembre 2005, http://www.moniteur.be.

[129] Article 27, al. 6 de la loi du 10 août 2005 instituant le système d'information Phenix, *M.B.*, 1er septembre 2005, http://www.moniteur.be.

[130] Article 37 de la LPVE – voy *infra*, section 3.

[131] Article 4, al. 3 de la LPVE.

[132] Article 4, al. 4 de la LPVE.

[133] C'est-à-dire d'une *« loi d'habilitation ordinaire, qui recouvre un domaine déterminé de l'action des pouvoirs publics en général et qui, après avoir fixé les lignes de force des divers éléments de la réglementation, confère au Roi un pouvoir relativement étendu »* (C.E., section de législation, avis des 31 mai et 4 juin 1996, Doc. Parl., Ch. Repr., sess. ord. 1995-1996, n° 607/1, p. 55).

[134] Sur cette question, voy. P. LEWALLE, *Contentieux administratif*, Bruxelles, Larcier, 2e édition, 2002, n°441, 442 et 443, et les nombreuses références citées par cet auteur.

Constitution et les lois particulières portées en vertu de la Constitution même ».[135]

La loi prévoit qu'une confirmation législative devra intervenir dans un délai de dix-huit mois, à peine de caducité de la réglementation arrêtée par le Roi.

Avant ladite confirmation, il ne fait aucun doute que les arrêtés royaux auront une valeur réglementaire et seront donc justiciables du Conseil d'Etat, et des cours et tribunaux sur le pied de l'article 159 de la Constitution.

Une fois la loi de confirmation intervenue, la question devient toutefois plus complexe. Selon la jurisprudence de la Cour constitutionnelle, l'arrêté confirmé se voit conférer force de loi et est comme « transformé » en loi à partir de la date d'entrée en vigueur de la loi de confirmation. L'arrêté confirmé ressortit donc, dans cette mesure, à la Cour constitutionnelle ,[136] soit sur recours direct formé contre la loi de confirmation, soit sur question préjudicielle.

La jurisprudence du Conseil d'Etat est quant à elle divisée : un arrêt du 10 novembre 1989[137] décide à cet égard que l'arrêté royal confirmé ne change pas de nature, mais que la loi de confirmation paralyse simplement le contrôle du Conseil d'Etat, de sorte que si la loi ne pouvait pas sortir ses effets, par exemple parce qu'elle serait jugée contraire à une disposition de droit international directement applicable et qu'elle devrait en conséquence de cette contravention être écartée, le Conseil d'Etat pourrait néanmoins connaître de l'arrêté. Cependant, la jurisprudence récente du Conseil d'Etat semble s'être ralliée à la position de la Cour constitutionnelle.[138]

3.2.1.4. Modalité de communication

52. Ce même article 4, en son alinéa 2, prévoit au 4° qu'avec l'avis du comité de gestion (et du comité de surveillance[139]), le Roi fixe les modalités selon lesquelles les citoyens peuvent communiquer avec les autorités judiciaires et leur transmettre des documents et des actes par voie électronique.

---

135 Voy., en ce qui concerne les lois de pouvoirs spéciaux: Cass., 3 mai 1974, *JT*, 1974, p. 577.

136 Voy., p. ex., C. arb., n° 21/95 du 2 mars 1995; C. arb., n° 61/99 du 9 juin 1999, http://www.courconstitutionnelle.be.

137 C.E., n° 33.399 du 10 nov. 1989, *JT*, 1990, p. 607; http://www.raadvst-consetat.be.

138 Voy., p.ex., C.E., n° 91.592 du 13 décembre 2000, http://www.raadvst-consetat.be.

139 Article 4, al. 3 de la LPVE.

On vise ici, par exemple, le format des actes de procédure qui seront déposés dans Phenix (il semble que trois formats, au moins, devraient être retenus : le format .odt (OpenOffice.org Writer de Sun), le format .pdf (Acrobat d'Adobe) et le format .doc (Word de Microsoft)).

3.2.2. Equivalence du document papier et électronique

53. Aux termes de l'article 5 de la LPVE, « *sauf lorsqu'un acte de procédure doit obligatoirement être posé par voie électronique, une pièce de procédure créée, déposée, communiquée et conservée électroniquement est assimilée à une pièce établie sur support papier* ».

Cette disposition contient une clause transversale qui assimile une pièce du procès créée, déposée, communiquée et conservée électroniquement à une pièce établie sur support papier.

Bien entendu, « *cette équivalence n'intervient évidemment pas lorsqu'un arrêté royal impose l'utilisation de la voie électronique* ».[140]

3.2.3. Impossibilité de fonctionnement pour cause de force majeure

54. Lorsqu'il est impossible, pour cause de force majeure, de créer, déposer, signifier, communiquer, conserver ou consulter une pièce de la procédure par voie électronique, cette pièce peut être établie sur papier, être déposée, signifiée, communiquée, notifiée par porteur, par courrier ou par télécopie, consultée et conservée comme telle.[141]

Cette disposition est importante, car elle prémunit d'une panne qui reste toujours possible avec les technologies de l'information et de la communication.

A la demande de l'Ordre des barreaux francophones et germanophone, il a été précisé que rentrait dans la notion de force majeure « *notamment le dysfonctionnement du système Phenix* ».

L'idée est de se protéger, au moins pour ce cas, du pouvoir d'appréciation du juge, connaissant l'interprétation restrictive de la force majeure par la Cour de

---

140 Exposé des motifs, p. 14.

141 Article 6 de la LPVE.

cassation.[142] Cette précision devrait, à notre estime, permettre d'invoquer également, *mutatis mutandis*, la panne d'un système privé.

L'on notera, à cet égard, que l'Ordre des barreaux francophones et germanophone a également obtenu que soit prévu à l'article 20 de la loi du 10 août 2005 instituant le système d'information Phenix (1)[143] que le comité de gestion informe non seulement le ministre de la justice, mais également « *le chef de corps concerné* » de toute anomalie de Phenix.

L'article 26 de la LPVE, par le biais d'un nouvel article 882bis du Code judiciaire,[144] prévoit par ailleurs une procédure simplifiée qui permet aux parties et au juge d'obtenir des précisions de la part du comité de gestion quant à la nature et à la durée du dysfonctionnement, lorsque celui-ci a eu pour conséquence qu'un acte n'a pas pu être accompli dans les délais.

3.2.3.1. Les conclusions rédigées à l'audience

55. L'article 6 de la LPVE est la seule disposition à autoriser le recours au papier lorsque l'avocat aura été contraint de passer au « tout électronique ».
Se pose alors la question des conclusions rédigées sur les bancs, parfois même à la demande du siège, qui ne rentrent manifestement pas, ou en tout cas pas dans la plupart des cas, dans la notion de force majeure.

Les auteurs de la LPVE ont reconnu la pertinence de cette observation et ont annoncé dans l'exposé des motifs de l'article 4 de la LPVE[145] qu'un arrêté royal autoriserait que des conclusions soient encore déposées à l'audience.

On suppose que, dans cette hypothèse, comme pour les conclusions sur support papier déposées par un particulier sans l'assistance d'un avocat ou suite à un cas de force majeure, les conclusions seront « scannées » et signées comme conformes par le greffier à l'aide de sa signature qualifiée.

---

[142] Voy. par exemple le refus de considérer comme étant un cas de force majeure, la grève de la poste ayant conduit à un appel tardif du fait de la réception par le greffe, hors du délai d'appel, de la requête, en raison de ladite grève (Cass., 9 oct. 1980, *Pas.*, 1981, I, p. 155-157, http://www.cass.be).

[143] *M.B.*, 1er sept. 2005, http://www.moniteur.be.

[144] Voy. note 253.

[145] Exposé des motifs, p. 14.

3.2.4. La signature électronique qualifiée

56. Aux termes de l'article 4, § 4 de la loi du 9 juillet 2001 fixant certaines règles relatives au cadre juridique pour les signatures électroniques et les services de certification,[146] la signature électronique dite « qualifiée » est assimilée à la signature manuscrite.

Ce type de signature électronique permet de garantir l'identité de l'auteur de l'acte de procédure et l'intégrité de l'acte et s'est donc très naturellement imposée au législateur[147] qui la définit, par référence à cette loi, comme étant : « *la signature électronique avancée définie à l'article 2, 2°, de la loi du 9 juillet 2001 fixant certaines règles relatives au cadre juridique pour les signatures électroniques et les services de certification, certifiée par un certificat qualifié visé à l'article 2, 4°, de cette loi et créée avec un dispositif sécurisé au sens de l'article 2, 7°, de cette loi* ».[148]

Faisant usage de la faculté prévue au paragraphe 3 de l'article 4 de la loi du 9 juillet 2001 autorisant le Roi à soumettre l'usage des signatures électroniques dans le secteur public à des exigences supplémentaires éventuelles, les auteurs de la loi ont exclu l'usage de toutes autres signatures électroniques (recevables aux termes du paragraphe 5 de l'article 4 de la loi du 9 juillet 2001), la signature qualifiée étant la seule forme de signature électronique admise dans le cadre de la LPVE.[149]

3.2.4.1. Exclusion discutable de toute autre signature qualifiée que celle de la carte d'identité électronique

57. A ce stade, les concepteurs du système d'infirmation Phenix excluent également, dans les faits, l'usage par les avocats (ou les justiciables) de toute autre signature qualifiée que celle contenue dans la carte d'identité électronique.

L'exposé des motifs[150] semble, lui aussi, fermer la voie à l'usage du certificat professionnel de signature: le Conseil d'Etat relève au point I.1. de son avis

---

146 *M.B.,* 29 sept. 2001, http://www.moniteur.be; *Droit des technologies de l'information,* CODES LARCIER *thématiques*, p. 35.
147 Article 7 de la LPVE.
148 Article 2, 3° de la LPVE.
149 Exposé des motifs, p. 15.
150 Exposé des motifs, p. 11.

que, dès lors que l'annexe 1, d) de la loi du 9 juillet 2001 précitée prévoit que tout certificat qualifié doit comporter la possibilité d'inclure, 'le cas échéant', une qualité spécifique du signataire, l'avant-projet de loi doit faire de cette faculté une obligation. Cependant le gouvernement estime « *cette exigence excessive et superflue. En effet, ce sont les listes d'avocats, d'huissiers, de notaires et des membres de l'ordre judiciaire, qui seront mises à jour en permanence, qui permettront d'assurer le contrôle de la fonction affirmée par l'auteur de l'acte* ».

On peut, bien sûr partager cet avis : jusqu'à présent, les avocats étaient crus sur parole lorsqu'ils affirmaient leur qualité sur leur papier à en-tête et qu'ils signaient, sans certification de leurs ordres, leurs correspondances. Les destinataires méfiants pouvaient se référer au Tableau, désormais consultable sur les sites web des différents ordres, afin de vérifier la qualité des signataires. Pourquoi dès lors ne pas se référer à un répertoire central[151] ou à une liste électronique[152] alimentés et mis à jour par l'Ordre ? Mais de là à estimer que « *plus encore, un greffier ne pourrait en tout état de cause pas se fier à l'information relative à la qualité professionnelle d'un avocat contenue dans un certificat. Il devra vérifier la réalité de celle-ci directement dans les listes officielles* » [153] alors que la certification pourrait émaner de l'Ordre, il y a un pas qu'on ne peut pas franchir.
Cela semble d'autant plus choquant que, « *par rapport au prestataire de services de communication, le greffier ou le magistrat du ministère public pourra s'identifier grâce à la signature qualifiée qui lui sera attribuée dans le cadre de Phenix* ».[154] Il est vrai qu' « *en cas de doute, il appartiendra au prestataire de services de communication de consulter la liste des membres de l'ordre judiciaire qui sera prévue au nouvel article 315bis du Code judiciaire en projet* » mais l'on voit que la signature qualifiée est attribuée « *dans le cadre de Phenix* » et non contenue dans la carte d'identité électronique. Pourquoi dès lors fermer cette seconde voie aux avocats ou aux notaires qui ont développé des systèmes reconnus de certification électronique professionnelle ? On notera que l'exposé des motifs semble même se contredire un peu plus loin, en indiquant que la signature contenue dans la

---

151 Article 4 de la loi du 10 août 2005 instituant le système d'information Phenix, *M.B.*, 1er sept. 2005, http://www.moniteur.be.

152 Article 13 de la loi du 5 août 2006 modifiant certaines dispositions du code judiciaire en vue de la procédure par voie électronique, *M.B.*, 7 sept. 2006, http://www.moniteur.be.

153 *Doc. Parl.* Chambre 1701/1, s. o. 2004/2005, p. 11.

154 *Doc. Parl.* Chambre 1701/1, s. o. 2004/2005, p. 11.

carte d'identité électronique « *constituera* [...] [qu'] ***un*** *des mécanismes d'identification au sein de Phenix* » ?[155]

58. Le rejet de toute autre signature électronique que celle résultant de l'usage de la carte d'identité nous semble également critiquable à plusieurs autres titres.
En effet, le paragraphe 3 de l'article 4 de la loi du 9 juillet 2001 justifiant les exigences supplémentaires dans le secteur public (telle l'exigence d'une signature qualifiée) n'est pas sans limite et, au contraire, précise que : « *Ces exigences doivent être objectives, transparentes, proportionnées et non discriminatoires et ne s'appliquer qu'aux caractéristiques spécifiques de l'application concernée. Ces exigences ne peuvent pas constituer un obstacle aux services transfrontaliers pour les citoyens* ».

Cette préférence exclusive pour le certificat contenu dans la carte d'identité électronique belge ne nous semble pas proportionnée par rapport aux objectifs poursuivis : les cybercommerçants s'adaptent aux différentes signatures électroniques circulant sur le marché, somme toute standardisées grâce à la norme x.509 et au moule formé par les exigences posées par les annexes de loi du 9 juillet 2001 auxquelles elles doivent répondre ; on n'aperçoit pas pourquoi le S.P.F. Justice ne pourrait le faire ou en supporter le coût si l'on a égard aux sommes considérables investies dans ce projet, ou pourquoi on ne pourrait faire confiance aux certificats contenus dans une autre carte d'identité européenne.

Par ailleurs s'agissant d'une carte nationale liée à la résidence, il est clair qu'il y a discrimination et obstacle aux services transfrontaliers pour les citoyens.

En effet, si la carte d'identité électronique doit être intégralement déployée en Belgique pour 2009[156] et s'il est possible dans chacune des communes belges d'obtenir anticipativement une carte d'identité électronique, ce n'est pas le cas pour les Belges résidant à l'étranger, ni les étrangers résidant en Belgique.[157]

---

155 *Doc. Parl.* Chambre 1701/1, s. o. 2004/2005, p. 12.

156 Au 7 janvier 2008, 6,2 millions de cartes d'identité électroniques avaient déjà été distribuées (source: http://eid.belgium.be/fr_BE/common/imported_content_eid/pdf/eID_Newsletter_nr_7_-_FR.pdf).

157 Le 20 décembre 2006, le ministre de l'intérieur a toutefois annoncé la délivrance généralisée des cartes électroniques pour les étrangers dans le courant de l'année 2007, voy. http://www.registrenational.fgov.be/cie_fr/cieetrangers/cdocu.htm.

D'évidence, il y aura discrimination entre les avocats belges résidant en Belgique et les avocats résidant dans l'Union européenne. Par ailleurs, les avocats étrangers établis dans l'Union européenne ne bénéficieront jamais d'une carte d'identité belge qu'elle soit électronique ou sur quelque support que ce soit. L'on court également le risque de voir les avocats étrangers admis auprès des barreaux belges grandement gênés, voire empêchés, dans l'exercice de leur profession.[158]

59. Cette restriction à libre prestation des services et à la liberté d'établissement tombe par ailleurs sous le coup d'une autre législation.

En effet, la libre prestation de services, en tant qu'elle concerne les avocats, est régie par la directive du Conseil du 22 mars 1977, tendant à faciliter l'exercice effectif de la libre prestation de services par les avocats.[159]

La liberté d'établissement est, elle, garantie, en tant qu'elle concerne les avocats, par la directive 98/5/CE du Parlement européen et du Conseil du 16 février 1998 visant à faciliter l'exercice permanent de la profession d'avocat dans un État membre autre que celui où la qualification a été acquise.[160]

Ces deux directives ont été transposées en Belgique par la loi du 22 novembre 2001 visant à faciliter l'exercice de la profession d'avocat ainsi que l'établissement en Belgique d'avocats ressortissants d'un autre Etat membre de l'Union européenne.[161]
Or, en Belgique sur les 14.529 avocats inscrits, ce ne sont pas moins de 406 avocats communautaires qui sont inscrits sous leur titre d'origine[162] et 5 avocats qui ont demandé l'admission à la profession d'avocat.[163]
L'article 4. 1 de la directive « services » prévoit que *« les activités relatives à la représentation et à la défense d'un client en justice (...) sont exercées dans chaque Etat membre d'accueil dans les conditions prévues pour les avocats*

---

[158] Avis n° 13/2006 du 24 mai 2006 de la Commission de la protection de la vie privée relatif à l'identification et signature électronique au sein du système d'information Phenix, n°42, http://www.privacycommission.be.

[159] *J.O.C.E*, 26 mars 1977, L 78, p. 17-18; *EUR-Lex*, http://eur-lex.europa.eu/fr/index.htm.

[160] *J.O.C.E*, 14 mars 1998, L 77, p. 36-43; *EUR-Lex*, http://eur-lex.europa.eu/fr/index.htm.

[161] *M.B.*, 20 déc. 2001, http://www.moniteur.be.

[162] Article 2 de la directive.

[163] Article 10 de la directive. http://www.ccbe.org/fileadmin/user_upload/NTCdocument/table_number_lawyers1_1179905628.pdf.

établis dans cet Etat, à l'exclusion de toute condition de résidence ou d'inscription à une organisation professionnelle dans ledit Etat » ;

L'article 5, 2e tiret de la directive « services » énonce cependant que, « *pour l'exercice des activités relatives à la représentation et à la défense d'un client en justice, chaque Etat membre peut imposer aux avocats visés à l'article 1er (...) d'agir de concert soit avec un avocat exerçant auprès de la juridiction saisie et qui serait responsable, s'il y a lieu, à l'égard de cette juridiction* ».

L'article 5.3. de la directive « établissement » est comparable à l'article 5, 2e tiret de la directive « services » : « *Pour l'exercice des activités relatives à la représentation et à la défense d'un client en justice et dans la mesure où le droit de l'État membre d'accueil réserve ces activités aux avocats exerçant sous le titre professionnel de cet État, ce dernier peut imposer aux avocats exerçant sous leur titre professionnel d'origine d'agir de concert soit avec un avocat exerçant auprès de la juridiction saisie et qui serait responsable, s'il y a lieu, à l'égard de cette juridiction, soit avec un 'avoué' exerçant auprès d'elle* ».

D'après la Cour de justice, l'article 5, 2e tiret de la directive « services » vise à mettre l'avocat prestataire de services *« en état d'accomplir les tâches que lui a confiées son client dans le respect du bon fonctionnement de la justice"* et, plus précisément, à lui *« fournir l'appui nécessaire en vue d'agir dans un système juridictionnel différent de celui auquel il est habitué, et de donner au tribunal saisi l'assurance que l'avocat prestataire de services dispose effectivement de cet appui et est ainsi en mesure de respecter les règles procédurales et déontologiques applicables ».*[164]

Or, l'imposition de l'usage de la carte d'identité électronique belge ne répond manifestement pas à un souci d'appui des avocats étrangers dans leur action au sein du système juridictionnel belge.
A défaut de répondre à cette condition, la discrimination fondée sur la nationalité, ne serait légitime que si elle se justifiait par des raisons d'ordre public, de santé ou de sécurité publique (articles 49 et 55 du traité CE), ce qui ne nous semble nullement être le cas, en l'espèce.

60. L'ensemble des ordres nationaux, en ce compris belges, au sein de l'Union européenne développe des projets de certification professionnelle afin de

---

[164] C.J.C.E., 25 févr. 1988, Commission/Allemagne, 427/85; Rec. p. 1123, et 10 juillet 1991, Commission/France, C-294/89, Rec. p. 3591; *EUR-Lex*, http://eur-lex.europa.eu/fr/index.htm.

garantir la nécessaire indépendance des avocats.[165] Le Conseil des barreaux européens lui-même a élaboré le 15 octobre 2007 un cadre visant à établir un système européen pour les cartes d'identité électroniques et des normes techniques pour une interopérabilité des cartes d'identité électroniques.[166] Comment justifier leur rejet en Belgique, alors qu'elles sont de plus en plus nombreuses à se voir reconnues par les autorités nationales dont elles dépendent et que ces signatures électroniques qualifiées répondent aux exigences de la directive 1999/93/CE du 13 décembre 1999 du Parlement européen et du Conseil sur un cadre communautaire pour les signatures électroniques ?[167]

61. En outre, chaque titulaire d'une carte d'identité électronique est libre de ne pas activer les certificats sur sa carte, conformément à l'article 6, § 2, dernier alinéa de la loi du 19 juillet 1991 relative aux registres de la population et aux cartes d'identité et modifiant la loi du 8 août 1983 organisant un Registre national des personnes physiques.[168] Cette liberté sera pourtant aliénée si seule la carte d'identité électronique permet de s'authentifier dans le système et de signer les actes de procédure au moment où l'on rendra obligatoire pour les avocats la procédure électronique.

Comment déroger à la loi du 19 juillet 1991 par un arrêté royal ou par une simple décision du Comité de gestion ?

62. Nous avions suggéré, lors de nos exposés de février 2006 de la Commission Université-Palais,[169] une solution paradoxalement fondée sur celle qui est la cause de toutes ces difficultés : la carte d'identité électronique.

La création d'une carte d'identité est un processus contrôlé par le Registre national. Dès qu'un nom ne figure pas dans le Registre national ou qu'il n'y a

---

165 Voy. « Etat actuel des développements en matière de communications électroniques - Données recueillies auprès des Délégations membres du CCBE », http://www.ccbe.org/doc/it_conference/documents/fr/e_communication_questionnaire_fr.pdf.

166 http://www.ccbe.org/index.php?id=94&id_comite=36&L=1.

167 *J.O.C.E*, 19 janv. 2000, L 13, p. 12-20; *EUR-Lex*, http http://eur-lex.europa.eu/fr/index.htm; Droit des technologies de l'information, CODES LARCIER *thématiques*, p. 19 et s.

168 Avis n° 13/2006 du 24 mai 2006 de la Commission de la protection de la vie privée relatif à l'identification et signature électronique au sein du système d'information Phenix, n° 42, http://www.privacycommission.be.

169 HENROTTE, J.F., FESLER, D., « Phenix: du mythe à la pratique. Questions sur la procédure électronique en matières civile et pénale », in *Phenix et la procédure électronique* (sous la coord. de HENROTTE, J.F.), CUP 02/2006, vol. 85, p. 203 et s., n° 16.

pas de résidence en Belgique, le processus de production des cartes ne permet pas la production d'une carte d'identité. Les personnes qui ne résident pas en Belgique – qu'elles soient belges ou étrangères - sont concernées, puisqu'elles n'ont éventuellement pas de dossier au Registre national et certainement pas d'adresse en Belgique.

Une problématique similaire à celle-ci a été rencontrée pour la délivrance même des cartes d'identité électroniques.[170]

En effet, le principe général défini est que le fonctionnaire du service "population" doit utiliser sa propre carte d'identité électronique, ce qui est évidement problématique pour les fonctionnaires communaux résidant en dehors des frontières et ne disposant pas de carte d'identité électronique.

La solution pour ses fonctionnaires résidant à l'étranger a été trouvée dans la « carte d'habilitation ».
Un dossier technique *ad hoc* est créé avec une adresse fictive, à savoir celle de la maison communale où le fonctionnaire est employé. Ce dossier technique n'est évidemment en aucun cas transmis dans les autres bases de données qui utilisent le Registre national et n'a donc aucun autre impact que celui de permettre la création de la carte d'habilitation.

Pourquoi ne pas utiliser le même système de carte d'habilitation (répondant nécessairement aux exigences techniques du système Phenix) en utilisant comme adresses fictives celles des cabinets des avocats belges résidant à l'étranger ou des avocats communautaires ? On pourrait également assigner aux avocats étrangers voulant exercer la représentation et la défense d'un client en justice en Belgique, l'adresse fictive du siège de l'O.B.F.G. ou de l'OVB.

Pourquoi même ne pas créer une carte d'habilitation pour l'ensemble des avocats belges avec comme adresses fictives, celles de leurs cabinet sur base des tableaux des Ordres qui en restent les maîtres?

Cela résoudrait la difficulté liée à la présence du numéro de Registre national dans les certificats d'authentification et de signature.

---

170 Compte-rendu intégral de la Commission de l'intérieur, des affaires générales et de la fonction publique du 15 juin 2005, CRIV 51 COM 648, p. 23 et s, http://www.lachambre.be/doc/CCRI/pdf/51/ic648.pdf.

En effet, ainsi que l'a évoqué Maître LAMBERTS, les recoupements entre bases de données publiques, attentatoires à la vie privée des avocats, sont rendus possibles grâce au numéro de Registre national.
C'est pour cette raison que l'on substitue au numéro de registre national, le numéro d'ordre des avocats avant qu'ils n'accèdent réellement au système d'information.[171] Il ne faut évidemment pas réintroduire celui-ci dans le système par le bais des certificats de signature.

Le numéro de registre national ne figurerait nécessairement plus sur la carte d'habilitation ou en tout cas ne correspondrait pas au « véritable » numéro de registre national du professionnel concerné.

La Commission de protection de la vie privée a relevé que « *41. A ce sujet, il conviendrait également que le législateur s'interroge sur les risques de créer une extension de l'utilisation de la carte d'identité à toutes les sphères d'activités de la vie d'un individu alors que la carte d'identité n'a jusqu'à ce jour été confinée qu'à la sphère intime de l'individu et non à sa sphère de vie professionnelle.*
...
56. La Commission relève que le certificat de signature électronique de la carte d'identité électronique est implémenté de telle façon que sont systématiquement communiqués au destinataire d'un document signé électroniquement à l'aide de la carte d'identité électronique: le nom, les deux premiers prénoms ainsi que le numéro de registre national du titulaire de la carte (le numéro de registre national étant utilisé comme numéro de série des certificats de la carte d'identité électronique).

57. La Commission s'interroge sur ce point et désirerait connaître la raison d'être de cette communication systématique du n° de Registre national en plus des nom et deux premiers prénoms ».[172]

La commission a d'ailleurs suggéré « ... *que l'utilisation de certificat des signatures électroniques professionnelles pourrait être envisagée dans la mesure où cette solution présente l'avantage, d'une part, d'atteindre la finalité*

---

171 Voy. I. VEROUGSTRAETE, I., « Présentation générale du système Phénix, entre projet et réalité», in *Phenix - Les tribunaux à l'ère électronique*, Cahiers du CRID, Bruylant, 2007, p. 47, n° 40 *op. cit*, n° 33.

172 Avis n° 13/2006 du 24 mai 2006 de la Commission de la protection de la vie privée relatif à l'identification et signature électronique au sein du système d'information Phenix, http://www.privacycommission.be.

voulue qui est de signer électroniquement tout en attestant de sa qualité spécifique sans que le numéro de registre national ne soit utilisé et, d'autre part, d'éviter une extension de l'utilisation de la carte d'identité à la sphère professionnelle. De tels certificats pourraient, en effet, attester de la qualité professionnelle spécifique d'un signataire.
Ces certificats pourraient être gérés par un tiers de confiance en collaboration avec les organisations professionnelles concernées. Ce tiers de confiance peut le cas échéant, être le prestataire de service de communication dont les activités sont réglementées par le projet de loi Phenix 2 dans la mesure où il résulte de l'article 10, §1er, 2°, qu'il lui appartiendra de « vérifier, par des moyens appropriés et légaux, l'identité des parties à la signification, à la notification ou à la communication ». [173]

Une carte d'habilitation, portant des certificats d'authentification et de signature professionnels, émise grâce à un partenariat entre le SPF intérieur, les communes et les ordres professionnels, répondrait à cette suggestion de la Commission.

63. Cette solution semblait avoir été acceptée par la précédente ministre de la justice qui l'avait avancée face à une question d'un membre de la Commission de la justice durant la discussion générale sur les projets de loi.[174]

64. Hélas, tout au plus, peut-on observer dans les avant-projets d'arrêtés royaux une ouverture technique du processus d'authentification préalable à l'accès au système d'information Phenix.

En effet, l'accès à Phenix est donné après authentification de l'identité et de la qualité du demandeur d'accès.

L'authentification de l'identité des personnes est assurée, sauf exceptions, par authentification forte. L'authentification forte est réalisée au moyen d'un certificat d'authentification de l'identité, porté par un dispositif matériel sécurisé d'authentification, reconnu par le comité de gestion, après avis du Service public fédéral Technologie de l'information et de la communication. La liste des certificats d'authentification reconnus est publiée par le comité de gestion au Moniteur belge.

---

[173] Avis n° 13/2006 du 24 mai 2006 de la Commission de la protection de la vie privée relatif à l'identification et signature électronique au sein du système d'information Phenix, n° 61 et 62, http://www.privacycommission.be.

[174] Exposé des motifs, p. 22.

La neutralité de ces textes est totale puisqu'on ne fait plus références à la carte d'identité électronique. Toutefois, dans les faits (mais, peut-être seulement dans un premier temps), seul le certificat porté par la carte d'identité électronique semble être retenu car tout le système de sécurisation de Phenix a été construit autour de la carte d'identité électronique.

65. Les avant-projets d'arrêtés royaux contiendront vraisemblablement une seconde ouverture technique notable pour les avocats qui ne sont pas domiciliés sur le territoire belge ou qui sont ressortissants d'un Etat membre de l'Union européenne ou de l'Espace économique européen s'ils sont repris dans les listes électroniques visées à l'article 430 du Code judiciaire ou s'ils justifient de leur inscription auprès d'un barreau d'un Etat membre de l'Union européenne ou de l'Espace économique européen.

En effet, le comité de gestion peut autoriser ces avocats à accéder à Phenix par internet après authentification contrôlée de leur identité afin de leur assurer des droits équivalents à ceux dont bénéficient les avocats titulaires d'une carte d'identité électronique.

L'authentification contrôlée est réalisée par la vérification de l'identifiant et du mot de passe confidentiels, délivrés par le Comité de gestion ou le service qu'il désigne sous sa responsabilité.

Dans ce cas, le comité de gestion publie un avis au Moniteur belge indiquant de quelle façon les avocats concernés peuvent obtenir ledit moyen d'accès.

66. Cette « solution » de l'authentification contrôlée appelle deux observations de notre part.

La première a trait à l'une des justifications du développement de la sécurité du système d'information fondé sur la carte d'identité électronique. Il nous semble que l'on ne peut, à la fois, soutenir que seule la carte d'identité électronique serait sûre et, par ailleurs, ouvrir plusieurs centaines de points d'entrée au système d'information Phenix par le biais de cette authentification moins sûre ?

La seconde, plus fondamentale, est que cet accès contrôlé n'est qu'un leurre. En effet, tels des enfants punis regardant un gâteau qu'ils ne pourront goûter, ces avocats pourront accéder au dossier judiciaire électronique, le consulter mais en aucune matière y déposer un actes ou une pièce de procédure. En effet, si une solution de substitution au certificat d'authentification est organisée, rien n'est prévu pour substituer au certificat de signature de la carte d'identité électronique un autre moyen de signature. Cela n'est déjà pas si mal pour un avocat bulgare nous direz-vous ? Non, il est communément admis que des actes de procédure peuvent être actuellement déposés par courrier simple.[175] Notre avocat bulgare régressera donc avec l'avènement de procédure par voie électronique obligatoire ! Que dire de l'avocat belge domicilié à Maastricht qui déposait ces actes de procédure quotidiennement au terme de ses plaidoiries aux greffes des différentes juridictions liégeoises ?

67. En l'état d'avancement du projet, nous ne pouvons que regretter que seuls les textes des avant-projets d'arrêté royaux offrent une ouverture permettant l'usage d'autres certificats que ceux portés par la carte d'identité et que la recherche d'une solution en partenariat avec le SPF intérieur n'ait pas encore été initiée.

Il nous semble donc que la suggestion faites aux huissiers de justice de se recycler en des prestataires de service de certification, par Maître LAMBERTS et relayée par Monsieur le président VEROUGSTRAETE,[176] est encore prématurée et devrait, à ce stade, n'être étudiée par la chambre nationale des huissiers de justice qu'avec la plus grande circonspection. Rappelons que tant les notaires que les avocats belges ou européens ont développé des projets coûteux de signatures électroniques qualifiées professionnelles qui sont immédiatement disponibles et qui ne sont pourtant pas pris en compte,[177] ces professions ne pouvant, à ce stade, qu'espérer un partenariat entre leurs ordres et les SPF justice et intérieur autour d'une carte d'habilitation professionnelle fondée sur d'autres bases techniques que celles dans lesquelles ils ont investis.

3.2.5. Le paiement des droits

68. Le Roi fixe, par arrêté délibéré en Conseil des ministres et après avis du comité de gestion, les modalités et la forme de paiement des droits dus en application de dispositions légales ou réglementaires lors du dépôt, de la

---

175 Voy. MOUGENOT, D « Le Code judiciaire à l'épreuve du cyberespace: une réforme réussie ? », n° 12, in *Phenix - Les tribunaux à l'ère électronique*, Cahiers du CRID, Bruylant, 2007 et, à présent, le nouvel article 32bis du Code judiciaire.

176 Voy. I. VEROUGSTRAETE, I., « Présentation générale sur système Phenix, entre projet et réalité » in *Phenix - Les tribunaux à l'ère électronique*, Cahiers du CRID, Bruylant, 2007, p. 47.

177 En tout cas, on le répète, dans un premier temps.

remise ou de la prise de copie de pièces de procédure, lorsque ceux-ci s'effectuent par voie électronique.[178]

Le nouveau système de paiement des droits pourrait entrainer la disparition du bon de greffe au profit du compte courant centralisé et l'apparition, outre bien sûr la possibilité du versement électronique, à terme, de moyens de paiement en ligne grâce aux cartes de crédit et de débit.

3.2.6. Moment auquel un document transmis par voie électronique produit ses effets

3.2.6.1. Application de la théorie de l'envoi

69. L'article 9 de la LPVE consacre, en ce qui concerne la procédure électronique, la théorie de l'envoi : « *Sauf disposition légale contraire, un document de procédure électronique produit ses effets au moment où* :

- *il est introduit dans le système Phenix, lorsqu'un acte doit être accompli au greffe ;*
- *le prestataire de service de communication reçoit la demande de l'expéditeur d'envoi au destinataire, lorsqu'un tel prestataire intervient ;*
- *l'expéditeur donne l'ordre irrévocable d'envoyer le document, en dehors des deux hypothèses ci-dessus* ».

Théoriquement, plusieurs systèmes sont envisageables en ce qui concerne la prise en compte de la date d'un acte, lorsqu'il est confié à un intermédiaire :

a. la date à laquelle il est reçu par le destinataire (théorie de la réception),
b. la date à laquelle il est expédié vers celui-ci (théorie de l'envoi),
c. ou encore une formule mixte en vertu de laquelle, en ce qui concerne l'expéditeur, qui doit agir dans un certain délai, doit être pris en compte le jour de l'expédition, tandis qu'en ce qui concerne le destinataire qui doit réagir à l'envoi dans un certain délai, doit être pris en compte le jour de la réception (dite théorie de la double date).[179]

---

[178] Article 8 de la LPVE.

[179] Sur le système de la double date voy. G. de LEVAL, *Eléments de procédure civile*, Bruxelles, Larcier, 1ère éd., 2003, n° 60, p. 86-87 et les nombreuses références citées par cet auteur. Nous négligeons volontairement la date où le destinataire prend effectivement connaissance de

Pour rappel,[180] interrogée sur la compatibilité avec les articles 10 et 11 de la Constitution des articles 32, 2°, 46 et 792, alinéa 2, du Code judiciaire, la Cour d'arbitrage (désormais Cour constitutionnelle) a décidé dans un retentissant arrêt n°170/2003 du 17 décembre 2003[181] que, s'il est raisonnablement justifié de faire courir les délais de procédure à partir d'une date qui ne soit pas tributaire du comportement des parties, le choix de la date d'expédition du pli judiciaire comme point de départ du délai de recours apporte une restriction disproportionnée au droit de la défense des destinataires, les délais de recours commençant à courir à partir d'un moment où ces derniers ne peuvent avoir connaissance du contenu du pli.[182] Cet arrêt contredit la jurisprudence de la Cour de cassation sur ce point, qui a consacré, quant à elle, encore qu'après quelques hésitations,[183] la théorie de l'envoi.[184]

La jurisprudence de la Cour constitutionnelle est fondée sur l'idée que le délai séparant l'expédition et la réception d'une notification, par hypothèse tributaire des services de la Poste, peut entraîner en certains cas de graves inconvénients pour une partie qui voit son délai de recours partiellement amputé. Ainsi, une notification expédiée un vendredi précédant un week-end suivi d'un lundi férié ne pourrait arriver, par hypothèse, que le mardi à son destinataire, lui faisant perdre un temps précieux, puisque le délai pourrait théoriquement avoir commencé à courir dès le samedi.

---

l'acte (théorie de l'information), qui est unanimement rejetée en raison de son caractère peu vérifiable et, partant, peu objectif.

180 Voy. sur cette question la synthèse d'H. Boularbah et J. Englebert, « Questions d'actualité en procédure civile » in *Actualités en droit judiciaire,* CUP 12/2005, Vol. 83, p. 55-57.

181 C. arb., n° 170/2003, 17 déc. 2003, *Arr. C.A.*, 2003, liv. 5, p. 2021; http://www.courconstitutionnelle.be; *A.P.M.* 2004 (sommaire), liv. 1, p. 3; *M.B.*, 1er mars 2004, 11535; http://www.moniteur.be; *J.L.M.B.*, 2004, p. 140, avec une note D. Pire; http://jlmbi.larcier.be; *J.T.*, 2004, p. 45, avec une note J. Van Drooghenbroeck; http://jt.larcier.be.

182 Le respect des droits de la défense justifie, pour la même raison, qu'en règle, un délai de recours ne peut pas courir à partir du prononcé d'une décision, c'est-à-dire à partir d'un moment où l'intéressé ne peut avoir connaissance du dispositif et des motifs de celle-ci que de manière excessivement théorique (C. arb., 5 mars 1997, *JLMB,* 1997, p. 496; http://jlmbi.larcier.be; C. arb., 17 juin 1998, *JT,* 1998, p. 637; http://www.courconstitutionnelle.be).

La Cour a décidé dans un même sens pour la notification de décisions administratives (C. arb., 16 nov. 2005, *J.T.*, 2006, p. 2; http://www.courconstitutionnelle.be).

183 Cass., 2 mars 1987, *Pas.*, I, 787; http://www.cass.be.

184 Voy. entre autres, Cass., 12 février 2001, *Pas.*, 258; Cass., 15 sept. 2003; Cass., 26 nov. 2004, http://www.cass.be.

Ces controverses trouvent donc leur justification empirique dans le fait que le service postal ne permet la réception d'un envoi, dans le meilleur des cas,[185] qu'un jour après que le pli lui a été confié. En d'autres termes, tout envoi par l'intermédiaire de la Poste fait nécessairement naître une différence de date entre l'envoi et la réception, ce qui peut avoir des conséquences dommageables pour ce qui concerne le respect des délais.

Toutefois, comme le notait avec prescience le Doyen de LEVAL, *« cette délicate question pourrait perdre de son acuité sous l'effet des nouveaux modes de transmission à effet immédiat se substituant aux modes classiques à effet différé ».*[186]

En effet, après avoir initialement opté pour le principe dit de la double date mais « *sans préciser lequel de ces deux évènements permettait à l'acte de produire ses effets* »,[187] la LPVE opte pour la théorie de l'envoi estimant que « *dans un environnement informatique, caractérisé par l'instantanéité des communications, le concept de double date perd une partie de sa pertinence* ». « *Il n'est pas possible de choisir le moment de la réception de l'acte* ».[188] « *Il est au contraire possible de choisir le moment de l'envoi, en partant du présupposé que les communications électroniques sont fiables et dans la plupart des cas, instantanées, ce sur quoi repose l'ensemble du projet Phenix*».[189]

Il est cependant vraisemblable que la Cour constitutionnelle n'y voie pas malice dans la mesure où les inconvénients de la théorie de l'envoi par rapport à la théorie de la réception sont considérablement réduits par le principe d'instantanéité des communications électroniques. Une notification expédiée un vendredi sera ainsi, en règle, reçue ce jour-là. De plus, le paragraphe 2 de l'article 9 de la LPVE sauvegarde les droits de la partie contre qui court le cas échéant le délai,[190] ce qui renforce considérablement la loi.

La jurisprudence de la Cour constitutionnelle ne trouvera donc à s'appliquer que pour les notifications « *sur support papier* » :[191]

---

185 On fait, en effet, le postulat que le service *prior* serait effectivement assuré par la Poste ...

186 G. de LEVAL, *op.cit.*, n° 60, p. 88.

187 Exposé de motifs, p. 17.

188 Exposé de motifs, p. 19.

189 Exposé de motifs, p. 20.

190 Voy. *infra*, n° 71.

191 Sous réserve de ce que l'on dira *infra,* n° 132 sur la convocation pénale.

« *Il est inséré dans la première partie, chapitre VIII, du Code judiciaire, un article 53bis, rédigé comme suit :*
'Article 53bis. A l'égard du destinataire, et sauf si la loi en dispose autrement, les délais qui commencent à courir à partir d'une notification sur support papier sont calculés depuis :
1° lorsque la notification est effectuée par pli judiciaire ou par courrier recommandé avec accusé de réception, le premier jour qui suit celui où le pli a été présenté au domicile du destinataire, ou, le cas échéant, à sa résidence ou à son domicile élu;
2° lorsque la notification est effectuée par pli recommandé ou par pli simple, depuis le troisième jour ouvrable qui suit celui où le pli a été remis aux services de la poste, sauf preuve contraire du destinataire'. »[192]

3.2.6.2. Distinctions suivant le type et le destinataire de la communication

70. Le paragraphe 1er prévoit donc trois hypothèses, en distinguant le type et le destinataire de la communication :

- Si l'acte est accompli au greffe, c'est le moment où il est introduit dans le système qui compte. Puisque la communication a lieu «en direct», l'expéditeur est en effet immédiatement informé de la réussite ou de l'échec de la communication.

- Si le document est envoyé par l'intermédiaire d'un prestataire de service de communication, c'est le moment auquel celui-ci reçoit la demande d'envoi de la part de l'expéditeur, moment qu'il peut et doit attester, en vertu de l'article 10 § 1er, 1° de la LPVE.

- Enfin, si un tel prestataire n'intervient pas, « *c'est le moment où l'expéditeur donne l'ordre irrévocable d'envoi.*
Ce moment peut être défini comme celui où l'instruction d'envoi du message donnée au système informatique ne peut plus être rapportée. Ce moment coïncidera la plupart du temps au départ du message du système informatique de l'expéditeur.
La date et l'heure seront indiquées dans l'entête du message, tel qu'il sera sauvegardé dans le système de messagerie de l'expéditeur. Cette preuve ne sera cependant pas suffisante à elle seule, tout comme à l'heure actuelle, le

---

192 Loi du 13 déc. 2005 portant des dispositions diverses relatives aux délais, à la requête contradictoire et à la procédure en règlement collectif de dette (1), *M.B.*, 21 décembre 2005, htpp://www.moniteur.be.

rapport d'une transmission par fax n'est pas considéré comme une preuve suffisante si le destinataire le conteste ».[193] On verra toutefois que la déontologie pourra aider les avocats à établir cette preuve.[194]

3.2.6.3. Mesure de sauvegarde des droits

71. Toutefois, « *l'absence de délivrance d'un document, sa délivrance tardive ou son caractère illisible, dus à un dysfonctionnement informatique, sans faute ou négligence imputable à la partie qui s'en prévaut, sont assimilés à des cas de force majeure lorsqu'ils l'empêchent d'exercer ses droits* ».[195]

L'article 9, § 2, du projet prévoyait une procédure de prolongation des délais en cas de dysfonctionnement informatique. Un amendement du Gouvernement, en assimilant ces différents dysfonctionnements à un cas de force majeure, permet d'éviter la création de concept et de procédure nouvelle et de se référer au droit commun.[196]

Rentrent dans cette notion de « dysfonctionnement informatique », « *virus, coupure de courant générale, bug, etc.* » .[197]
On peut s'interroger sur la nécessité de préciser que ce n'est que sans faute ou négligence que l'on peut se prévaloir puisque la force majeure se définit comme étant un fait résultant d'une circonstance indépendante de la volonté du demandeur et que celui-ci n'a pu ni prévoir, ni conjurer.[198]

« *Prenons l'exemple d'un calendrier de procédure fixé conformément à l'article 747 du Code judiciaire. Si l'expéditeur envoie ses conclusions le dernier jour du délai à 23h55', il n'est pas impossible que le destinataire les reçoive le lendemain à 00h05'.[...]*
Bien que le destinataire ait reçu les conclusions le lendemain du dernier jour du délai, à 00h05', on ne peut cependant considérer qu'il subit un préjudice. En effet, il prendra très vraisemblablement connaissance du contenu des conclusions le lendemain matin. De telles situations se produisent déjà à

193 Exposé de motifs, p. 20.
194 Voy. *infra*, n° 72.
195 Article 9, § 2 de la LPVE.
196 Justification du deuxième amendement du Gouvernement, p. 2.
197 Justification du deuxième amendement du Gouvernement, p. 2.
198 Voy. par exemple: Cass., 13 janvier 2004; Cass. 17 janvier 1990, *Pas.*, 1990, I, 584, http://www.cass.be.

l'heure actuelle si des conclusions sont envoyées par fax en soirée et que le destinataire n'en prend connaissance que le lendemain matin.
Par contre, si en raison d'un problème technique (virus, document illisible, macro malveillante), la délivrance du document ou sa prise de connaissance par le destinataire a lieu trop tard pour que le destinataire puisse sauvegarder ses droits, et en particulier ses droits de la défense, le juge pourra réaménager le ou les délais dont disposent les parties pour la suite de la procédure ».[199]
Cela étant, il nous semble que pour apprécier l'atteinte aux droits d'une partie, dans l'hypothèse d'un délai même long de délivrance, cette partie devra établir ne pas avoir également reçu l'accusé de réception desdites conclusions qui lui sera notifié par Phenix[200] ou expliquer pourquoi, malgré cette notification, elle n'a pas demandé à l'autre partie de lui renvoyer sans délai ces conclusions afin de sauvegarder ses droits.

3.2.6.4. Aménagement du règlement de l'OBFG relatif à l'usage des technologies de l'information et de la communication

72. Afin d'éviter la violation des droits de la défense du destinataire et une discussion sur l'existence d'un cas de force majeure, à défaut d'accord entre confrères, le règlement dispose désormais en son article 2.9 que : « *L'avocat configure son serveur de courrier électronique pour qu'il accuse automatiquement réception, lorsqu'un tel accusé est requis par l'expéditeur, de toute correspondance électronique qui parvient dans sa boite de courrier électronique et établisse la date et l'heure de sa réception. A défaut de pareil accusé de réception automatique, il adresse sans retard un accusé de réception à l'expéditeur* ». L'expéditeur ne recevant pas d'accusé de réception pourra réagir pour renvoyer sans délai l'acte ou la pièce de procédure, au besoin par une autre voie.

Or, l'accusé de réception automatique de certains serveurs de messagerie comporte, outre les mentions requises par cette disposition, le message lui-même, permettant ainsi de rapporter un peu plus la preuve nécessaire dans l'hypothèse prévue au troisième tiret du paragraphe 1er de l'article 9.

---

[199] Exposé de motifs, p. 21-22.
[200] Voy. *infra*, n° 106.

3.2.6.5. Définition de la délivrance

73. La délivrance d'un document électronique est définie comme étant « l*e moment où le destinataire peut prendre connaissance du contenu de celui-ci* »,[201] c'est-à-dire le moment où un courriel arrive dans la boîte e-mail d'un serveur et non celui où le courriel est téléchargé dudit serveur ou lu grâce au logiciel de messagerie ou à un navigateur.

L'on notera toutefois, et c'est une présomption réfragable, que « l*a délivrance est réputée accomplie au moment où le prestataire de services de communication*[202] *atteste avoir délivré l'acte* ».[203]

3.2.6.6. Document illisible ou affecté d'un virus adressé à une partie

74. Le paragraphe 4 prévoit des dispositions analogues à celles de l'article 2.8 du règlement de l'Ordre des barreaux francophones et germanophone relatif à l'usage des technologies de l'information et de la communication[204] qui l'a inspiré, en énonçant trois présomptions liées à la qualité du document, pour les communications entre parties : « *Un document électronique adressé à une partie est réputé lisible et non affecté d'un virus ou de toute autre instruction nuisible, sauf réclamation motivée sans délai de celle-ci.*
En cas de réclamation motivée, l'expéditeur lui adresse sans délai une nouvelle version du document électronique lisible et non affectée des vices susmentionnés ».

3.2.6.7. Document illisible ou affecté d'un virus adressé au greffe

75. Pour le dépôt au greffe, un document électronique illisible est considéré comme un acte valablement accompli, pour autant que l'expéditeur démontre qu'il a pris des mesures adéquates dans le but d'assurer la sécurité et la lisibilité du document et qu'il adresse au greffe, même hors délai, dès qu'il

---

201 Article 9, § 3, al. 1 de la LPVE.

202 Sur ce prestataire, voy. *infra*, n° 76.

203 Article 9, § 3, al. 2 de la LPVE.

204 « *Dans l'hypothèse où, pour des raisons techniques, un avocat ne peut lire une correspondance électronique en tout ou partie, il demande, sans retard, un exemplaire imprimé à l'avocat qui la lui a envoyée. Dès lors que, sans retard, l'exemplaire imprimé est communiqué au destinataire, le premier envoi est pris en considération pour les effets juridiques y attachés, sauf si l'application de cette règle conduit le destinataire de bonne foi à être en défaut à la date de réception de l'exemplaire imprimé* ».

peut se rendre compte de l'échec de sa tentative, un document lisible et non affecté des vices susmentionnés.[205]

Cette solution est possible dans la mesure où « *Phenix génèrera un listing de chaque événement (envoi, réception, rejet de document,...)* ».[206]

Ainsi, si l'on tente d'introduire dans Phenix un document atteint d'un virus ou toute autre instruction nuisible, le système le rejettera, mais l'acte sera considéré comme étant accompli à ce moment, pour autant que deux conditions soient respectées : (1) l'auteur de l'acte démontre avoir pris les mesures de sécurité adéquates, (2) il adresse un nouveau document «sain», sans délai, dès qu'il peut se rendre compte de l'échec de la tentative.

3.2.7. Le prestataire de services de communication et son statut

76. Le prestataire de services de communication est « *toute personne physique ou morale (...) intervenant comme organe intermédiaire lors d'une signification, d'une notification, d'un dépôt ou d'une communication dans le cadre d'une procédure judiciaire* ».[207]

77. L'article 10 de la LPVE détermine les exigences auxquelles le prestataire de services de communication doit répondre.

Cette disposition, à laquelle il est renvoyé pour l'essentiel, s'imposait dans la mesure où il n'existe pas une législation unique régissant le statut juridique des différents tiers de confiance, seul le statut des prestataires de service de certification, intervenant dans le cadre de l'utilisation d'une signature électronique, faisant l'objet d'une réglementation à ce jour, par application de la loi du 9 juillet 2001.[208]

On épinglera simplement l'exigence qui est faite au prestataire des services de communication, au 5° du paragraphe 1er de la disposition, d'enregistrer toutes les informations pertinentes relatives aux communications effectuées pendant le délai utile de 30 ans, en particulier pour pouvoir fournir une preuve de la certification en justice.

---

205 Article 9, § 5 de la LPVE.
206 Exposé des motifs, p. 23.
207 Article 2, 4°, de la LPVE.
208 Exposé des motifs, p. 24.

Ce délai prolongé s'impose compte tenu des longs délais de recevabilité d'une tierce opposition.[209] On se référera toutefois aux deux questions que pose une durée d'archivage aussi longue, s'agissant d'un archivage électronique et donc menacé par l'obsolescence, décrites par le Doyen de LEVAL.[210] On ne trouve pas de réponse concrète à ces questions dans l'exposé des motifs, celles-ci étant réservées à un arrêté royal restant à prendre. On peut cependant s'en remettre aux pistes dégagées par I. VEROUGSTRAETE et V. LAMBERTS.[211]

3.3. MODIFICATIONS DU CODE JUDICIAIRE

3.3.1. Les signification, notification, dépôt et communication électroniques

3.3.1.1. Définitions des signification, notification, dépôt et communication électroniques

78. Tant la signification et la notification que le dépôt et la communication pourront dorénavant se faire par voie électronique:[212]

Aux termes du nouvel article 32 du Code judiciaire,

- la signification est « *la remise d'un original ou d'une copie de l'acte; elle a lieu par exploit d'huissier de justice ou, dans les cas prévus par la loi, selon les formes que celle-ci prescrit* ».[213]
« *Dans le texte actuel, la signification ne concerne que la remise de la copie d'un acte. Toutefois, lorsque cette signification a lieu par voie intégralement électronique, il n'est pas exclu que le document qui est transmis au destinataire et qui porte la signature électronique de l'huissier soit considéré comme un original* ».[214]

- la notification est *« l'envoi d'un acte de procédure en original ou en copie ; elle a lieu par les services postaux ou par courrier électronique à l'adresse*

[209] Exposé des motifs, p. 25.
[210] G. de LEVAL, « Le Code judiciaire à l'épreuve du cyberespace » in *Multimédia Le cyberavocat*, CUP 2/1999, Vol. 29, p. 424-425.
[211] I. VEROUGSTRAETE, V. LAMBERTS, « Le dossier électronique: concept, création, gestion » in *Phenix et la procédure électronique* (sous la coord. de J-F. HENROTTE), CUP, Larcier, 2006, vol. 85, p. 60.
[212] Article 2 de la LMCJ.
[213] Article 3 de la LMCJ.
[214] Exposé des motifs, p. 27.

judiciaire électronique, ou, dans les cas prévus par la loi, par télécopie ou selon les formes que la loi prescrit ».[215]

La loi modifiant certaines dispositions du Code judiciaire en vue de la procédure par voie électronique (ci après LMCJ) remplace l'expression «*la poste*» par «*les services postaux*», de façon à prendre en considération la possibilité de faire procéder à des notifications par des entreprises autres que la Poste. En vertu de l'article 144*octies* de la loi du 21 mars 1991 portant réforme de certaines entreprises publiques économiques,[216] seuls les envois recommandés sous forme physique réalisés dans le cadre d'une procédure judiciaire font toujours l'objet d'un monopole de La Poste. La LMCJ permet ainsi de faire appel à une entreprise privée pour les autres formes d'envoi.[217]

« *Les dépôts visent les dépôts d'actes de procédure auprès des greffes et parquets par les justiciables ou leurs mandataires.*
Les communications visent toutes formes de communications judiciaires généralement quelconques, qui ne font pas l'objet d'une réglementation spécifique ».[218]

3.3.1.2. Définition de l'adresse judiciaire électronique

79. Le nouveau concept d' « *adresse judiciaire électronique* » est défini comme étant « *l'adresse de courrier électronique, attribuée par un greffe et à laquelle une personne a accepté ou est réputée avoir accepté, selon les modalités fixées par le Roi, que lui soient adressées les significations, notifications et communications* ».[219]

En réalité, l'adresse judiciaire électronique concerne plusieurs catégories de destinataires, soumis à des régimes juridiques différents :[220]

- Elle désigne tout d'abord l'adresse des professionnels intervenant habituellement dans le cadre de la procédure judiciaire: huissiers, notaires, avocats, experts, agents de police… Ils seront réputés consentants par le Roi. Mais le recours à l'adresse judiciaire électronique pour les professionnels liés

---

215 Article 3 de la LMCJ.
216 *Droit des technologies de l'information*, CODES LARCIER *thématiques*, p. 33.
217 Exposé des motifs, p. 28.
218 Exposé des motifs, p. 27.
219 Article 36, § 1er, 3° C.J. introduit par l'Article 5 de la LMCJ.
220 Exposé des motifs, p. 14.

au monde judiciaire sera évidemment autorisé même indépendamment de toute obligation de recourir à la forme électronique.

- Rien n'empêche les justiciables eux-mêmes d'utiliser une adresse judiciaire électronique. Ils devront toutefois émettre un accord exprès qui devrait porter sur le principe même de la communication par voie électronique en matière judiciaire. C'est le système de l' « *opt-in* ». Il est probable que certaines personnes morales, habituellement en contact avec le monde judiciaire (banques, assurances...) souhaiteront recourir à cette modalité. Elle est également ouverte aux personnes physiques, si elles le souhaitent.

- Enfin, il est possible que l'accord soit présumé – en vertu d'un arrêté royal – pour certaines catégories de justiciables disposant de la technologie adéquate, notamment les personnes publiques.

80. Il est tout-à-fait regrettable que les autorités belges n'aient pas harmonisées ces adresses judiciaires électroniques, qui sont déjà distinctes des adresses de courriel usuelles des avocats et des justiciables, avec les « compte[s] de messagerie électronique pour toute juridiction, pour toute autorité administrative et pour tout avocat d'une partie qui [en] formule la demande » ouverts par le conseil d'Etat dans le cadre de la procédure de cassation devant lui.[221]

81. On notera que le dépôt au greffe ne se fera pas par une telle adresse judiciaire électronique mais par l'upload du fichier électronique sur le site de Phenix.

Le gouvernement a fait un choix différent pour la procédure en cassation devant le conseil d'Etat puisque, selon la langue du recours, les copies des écrits de procédure et dossiers sont envoyées en annexe à un courrier électronique à l'adresse « greffe.cassation@raadvst-consetat.be », « kanzlei.kassation@raadvst-consetat.be » ou « griffie.cassatie@raadvst-consetat.be ».[222]

82. L'adresse judiciaire électronique ne constitue pas une forme d'élection de domicile : les communications qui sont faites à cette adresse sont faites

---

[221] Article 39 de l'A.R. 30 novembre 2006.
[222] Article 39 de l'A.R. 30 novembre 2006.

directement au destinataire et non à un tiers choisi par lui, même si la boîte de réception du courrier électronique est hébergée par un tiers de confiance.

83. « *Le Roi détermine, après avis du comité de gestion et du comité de surveillance [...], les modalités de création et d'attribution, d'enregistrement, de conservation, et de consultation des adresses judiciaires électroniques.* »[223]

« *Toute personne qui a accepté la signification, la notification ou la communication à une adresse judiciaire électronique est présumée y consentir tant qu'elle n'a pas manifesté expressément son intention de renoncer à l'utilisation de cette adresse judiciaire électronique ou de la modifier.* » [224] Il s'agit de la transposition du principe de permanence du domicile judiciaire[225] à l'électronique.

« *Le Roi détermine, après avis du comité de gestion et du comité de surveillance [...], les formes selon lesquelles l'acceptation, la renonciation ou la modification visée au § 2, alinéa 2, doivent être faites et sont opposables* » .[226]

3.3.1.3. Obligations des avocats quant à leur adresse électronique

84. Pour les avocats, le règlement de l'Ordre des barreaux francophones et germanophone relatif à l'usage des technologies de l'information et de la communication prescrit que l'avocat informe, sans retard, son Ordre de « *son ou ses adresses électroniques ainsi que des modifications qui y sont apportées* »,[227] de même qu'il doit aviser ses correspondants lorsqu'il n'utilise plus une adresse électronique donnée.

Cette règle revêtira dorénavant une importance accrue puisque c'est sur la base des renseignements dont l'Ordre des barreaux francophones et germanophone disposera que seront attribuées et surtout mises à jour les adresses de courriel auxquelles seront adressées les notifications des messages adressés à l'adresse judiciaire électronique.

Le même règlement régit également le choix de l'adresse électronique en tant qu'il n'autorise l'utilisation, par un avocat, d'une adresse électronique « *qui*

---

[223] Article 36, §1er, 3° C.J. introduit par l'Article 5 de la LMCJ.
[224] Article 36, § 2, al. 2 C.J. introduit par l'Article 5 de la LMCJ.
[225] Article 36, §2, al. 1 C.J.
[226] Article 36, § 1er, 3° C.J. introduit par l'Article 5 de la LMCJ.
[227] Article 1.3 du règlement.

reproduit de manière non distinctive un terme générique évocateur de la profession d'avocat» que moyennant l'inclusion « *[du] nom de l'avocat ou celui de l'association dont il fait partie ou toute autre dénomination»*.[228]

Cela étant d'autres exigences doivent être formulées à l'égard des adresses de courrier électronique. En effet, il pourrait être aisément considéré que l'utilisation d'adresses électroniques par trop commerciales, gratuites ou, le cas échéant, permettant aux prestataires de services concernés de modifier le contenu d'un courrier électronique,[229] ne paraît pas conforme au principe de dignité qui gouverne l'exercice de la profession d'avocat. Par ailleurs, cette altération du contenu met à néant la signature électronique qui aurait été apposée par l'expéditeur. Enfin, la gratuité s'oppose, dans une certaine mesure, à des exigences fortes en matière de sécurité pour des boîtes qui doivent contenir des correspondances couvertes par le secret professionnel et des données à caractère personnel.

De même, l'utilisation d'adresses de courrier électronique collectives qui risque de séduire les rétifs aux technologies de l'information et de la communication ne nous paraît pas conforme aux règles légales[230] et déontologiques[231] qui gouvernent le secret professionnel de l'avocat, le secret partagé ne valant pas simplement entre confrères mais seulement entre confrères traitant le même dossier.[232] La loi du 8 décembre 1992 relative à la protection de la vie privée à l'égard du traitement des données à caractère personnel ne paraît pas plus respectée dans la mesure où, elle aussi, impose de limiter l'accès aux données personnelles aux seuls membres du cabinet concernés par la gestion du dossier concernant la personne à qui appartiennent ces données.[233]

---

228 Article 1.2 du règlement.

229 Ainsi que c'est le cas avec des services de courriers gratuits tels que Hotmail ou Yahoo qui complètent les courriers véhiculés par leurs serveurs de messages à caractère publicitaire.

230 Article 458 du Code pénal.

231 Art 94 de la Tradition de Liège, http://www.barreaudeliege.be/deontologie.asp, par exemple.

232 P. De Pooter, « Secret professionnel et secret de la confession », *JT*, 2002, p. 201-206, spéc. 1.1.2; Bruxelles (8e ch.), 23 oct. 1990, *J.T.*, 1991, p. 496, note Cruyplants, J.: « La cessibilité des créances des prestataires de soins sur les organismes assureurs »; http://jt.larcier.be; *RPDB*, T. XII, v° Secret professionnel, p. 38, n° 87.

233 Article 16 de la loi du 8 déc. 1992, *Droit des technologies de l'information*, CODES LARCIER *thématiques*, p. 220-221; voy. C. De Terwangne, « Les cabinets d'avocats et la loi sur la protection des données à caractère personnel », in *Cabinets d'avocats et technologies de l'information,* J.F. Henrotte – Y. Poullet (éd.), Cahiers du CRID, n° 26, Bruxelles, Bruylant, 2005, p. 172-173.

Si l'on peut comprendre qu'il soit difficile de mettre à la disposition de chacun des membres d'une association, parfois très nombreuse, une boîte postale personnelle sur la façade, on conviendra que cela est beaucoup plus aisé pour les boîtes de courrier électronique. Par ailleurs, le courrier postal est dans une enveloppe, qui garantit, dans une certaine mesure, la confidentialité de la correspondance.

Ces quelques réflexions reviennent à dire que les avocats seraient sans doute avisés de recourir à des adresses sécurisées de courrier électronique qui leur soient entièrement personnelles, ce notamment en procédant à l'enregistrement d'un nom de domaine renvoyant à leur propre identité ou à la raison sociale de leur cabinet. Les solutions commerciales permettant cette pratique sont désormais largement diffusées sur le marché des services électroniques et ne sont pas d'un coût prohibitif. Les boîtes de courriel @avocat.be mises à disposition de ses membres par l'Ordre des barreaux francophones et germanophone constituent évidemment une autre solution permettant de répondre adéquatement à ces préoccupations.

Le règlement de l'Ordre des barreaux francophones et germanophone relatif à l'usage des technologies de l'information et de la communication prend en compte ces considérations en ses articles 1.2, 2.3 à 2.5.

3.3.1.4. Dépôt ou communication électroniques

85. Le nouvel article 32*bis* du Code judiciaire dispose que tout dépôt ou communication peut avoir lieu valablement par simple pli ou, dans les cas prévus par la loi, par pli recommandé.

Les dépôts ou communications par pli simple ou recommandé adressés au greffe et parquet peuvent avoir lieu valablement par voie électronique par introduction dans le système Phenix.

Toute autre communication par pli simple peut avoir lieu valablement par courrier électronique à l'adresse judiciaire électronique.

Toute autre communication par lettre recommandée peut avoir lieu valablement par courrier électronique à l'adresse judiciaire électronique, pour autant qu'une preuve d'envoi soit remise à l'expéditeur. Cette preuve d'envoi ne peut être créée automatiquement par le système d'expédition de l'expéditeur.[234] « *Le dernier alinéa exclut que la preuve d'envoi puisse être constituée par une copie imprimée d'un courrier électronique, portant les mentions de date créées par l'ordinateur. Ces éléments ne sont pas assez probants pour être admis à titre de preuve d'un envoi équivalent au recommandé en matière judiciaire* ».[235]

3.3.1.5. Signification par voie électronique – Prise d'effets

86. Aux termes du nouvel article 42*bis*,[236] « *Sans préjudice de l'application des conventions internationales en la matière,*[237] *la signification peut avoir lieu par voie électronique.*
Elle a lieu à l'adresse judiciaire électronique par l'intermédiaire d'un prestataire de services de communication [...].

Dans les vingt-quatre heures de l'envoi par l'huissier de justice, le prestataire de services de communication [...] fait parvenir à l'huissier de justice expéditeur de l'acte un avis de délivrance de celui-ci.

Si dans le délai visé à l'alinéa 3, l'huissier de justice expéditeur de l'acte n'a pas reçu cet avis de délivrance, la signification a lieu sans délai conformément aux articles 33 et suivants. L'exploit mentionne l'absence d'avis de délivrance, ainsi que la date et l'heure de l'envoi électronique et de l'accusé de réception du prestataire de services de communication. La date de la signification est celle du moment où le prestataire de services a reçu la demande d'envoi au destinataire, conformément à l'article 9, § 1er, de la [LPVE] ».

En effet, la personne qui a requis la signification ne peut subir les effets défavorables de cette signification électronique avortée. Ce sont donc les dates et heures de la tentative de signification électronique qui, à son égard, devront être prises en considération, dès lors que, conformément à l'article 9, § 1er de la LPVE, une pièce de procédure électronique produit ses effets au moment de son envoi (même si elle n'est pas reçue par le destinataire pour des raisons techniques). Il est donc important que ces renseignements figurent sur

---

234 Article 4 de la LMCJ.
235 Exposé des motifs, p. 31.
236 Article 6 de la LMCJ.
237 « *La modification apportée à l'alinéa 1er de l'article 42bis, vise à rappeler la prééminence des conventions internationales et notamment du règlement 1348/2000 du Conseil du 29 mai 2000 relatif à la signification et à la notification dans les Etats membres des actes judiciaires et extrajudiciaires en matière civile et commerciale* » (Justification du septième amendement du Gouvernement, p. 8).

l'acte de signification pour que le signifié soit averti de ce que la signification qualifiée par l'exposé des motifs de « *traditionnelle* » a été précédée d'une tentative de signification électronique qui, à l'égard du requérant, a eu pour effet d'interrompre valablement les délais.[238] La prescription, par exemple, est donc interrompue par la première tentative de signification électronique, et non par la signification effective.

Cela étant, nous nous interrogeons sur la question de savoir si le texte préconise bien une deuxième tentative de signification par la voie traditionnelle comme écrit dans l'exposé des motifs et dans la justification du septième amendement du Gouvernement ? La référence du texte « *aux articles 33 et suivants* » du Code judiciaire ne nous semble pas interdire une nouvelle signification électronique, même si cela peut paraître contraire au bon sens et à l'exposé des motifs.

Le destinataire de la signification ne peut, lui non plus, subir les effets défavorables de cette signification électronique avortée, de sorte que la signification lui sera faite sans délai à l'échéance des vingt-quatre heures de la première tentative de l'huissier instrumentant.

87. L'article 7 de la LMCJ modifie l'article 43, premier alinéa, du Code judiciaire afin de compléter les mentions obligatoires de l'acte de signification, en ajoutant l'adresse judiciaire électronique du destinataire de l'exploit, de l'huissier de justice et, le cas échéant, du requérant, lorsque la voie électronique a été adoptée. Les modalités de la signification électronique et, le cas échéant, les mentions prévues à l'article 42*bis*, alinéa 4 devront également y figurer.

3.3.1.6. Pli judiciaire

88. L'article 8 de la LMCJ modifie l'article 46 du Code judiciaire qui définit de manière assez précise les modalités d'envoi du pli judiciaire en matière civile et en matière pénale.
L'objet de cette disposition est d'introduire le pli judiciaire électronique ainsi qu'une forme hybride. La disposition de l'article 46 a été revue afin de séparer distinctement la réglementation de chacune des formes de pli judiciaire envisagées.

---

[238] Exposé des motifs, p. 36.

Le paragraphe premier vise le pli judiciaire traditionnel, notifié à la demande du ministère public. Cette disposition n'est pas modifiée, sauf pour y remplacer les références à La Poste par une référence plus générale aux «*services postaux*» et ajouter dans les refus à relater par le préposé des services postaux au bas de l'accusé de réception, celui de dater.

89. Le deuxième paragraphe de l'article 46 du Code judiciaire envisage le pli judiciaire traditionnel, notifié à la demande du greffier. Les mêmes modifications qu'au paragraphe 1er sont apportées mais le mécanisme reste inchangé pour le surplus. Rien n'empêche en effet le greffier ou le ministère public de recourir encore au pli judiciaire classique, même si des formes plus évoluées sur le plan technologique existent.

90. Il nous semble que la nécessaire médiation du prestataire de services de communication et partant, la convergence entre la signification électronique et la notification électronique amènent à réfléchir sur la plus-value de l'intervention de l'huissier de justice qui subsiste encore et sur son monopole et son rôle.[239]

3.3.1.7. Pli judiciaire hybride

91. Le nouveau paragraphe 3 de l'article 46 du Code judiciaire dispose que « *le pli judiciaire peut être adressé par courrier électronique par le greffier ou le ministère public à un prestataire de services de communication [...] chargé de l'imprimer et de le faire parvenir à son destinataire. L'envoi du pli imprimé est régi par les §§ 1er et 2.*

Le prestataire de services de communication peut attester que le pli adressé au destinataire est conforme à celui envoyé par le greffier ou le ministère public. Il peut également attester la date à laquelle il a remis le pli aux services postaux ou l'a fait parvenir au destinataire ».

L'exposé des motifs explique que « *l'envoi d'un pli judiciaire intégralement sous forme électronique suppose en effet que le destinataire dispose de l'équipement technique adéquat et accepte cette forme de notification. Or il serait dommage de ne pas permettre au personnel des greffes et des parquets*

239 I. VEROUGSTRAETE, « Présentation générale sur système Phenix, entre projet et réalité » in *Phenix - Les tribunaux à l'ère électronique*, Cahiers du CRID, Bruylant, 2007, p. 47, n° 40; V. LAMBERTS, « La signification par voie électronique » in *Phenix - Les tribunaux à l'ère électronique*, Cahiers du CRID, Bruylant, 2007, p. 220, n° 39.

de profiter des facilités et du gain de temps résultant de l'automatisation de l'envoi des plis judiciaires, même lorsque le recours au pli judiciaire électronique n'est pas permis. La solution à cette difficulté est trouvée dans le recours au pli judiciaire hybride. Ce mécanisme présente en outre l'avantage de centraliser les envois postaux de tous les tribunaux et parquets de Belgique auprès d'une entreprise unique, avec les économies qui peuvent en résulter ».[240]

On soulignera[241] que « *le prestataire de service de communication est investi d'un pouvoir de certification important. En effet, rien n'empêche techniquement de modifier le contenu du pli lors de son impression. Par ailleurs, la signature électronique du greffier ou du secrétaire du parquet perd son caractère original lors de l'impression du pli. Il était donc capital d'autoriser le prestataire de service de communication à certifier non seulement la réalité de l'envoi mais aussi la conformité du pli imprimé remis au destinataire par rapport à l'envoi électronique initial réalisé par le greffe ou le ministère public. Ce même pouvoir de certification concerne la date de l'envoi imprimé. Celle-ci ne coïncide pas nécessairement avec la date d'envoi du pli électronique par le greffe ou le parquet. Si cet envoi électronique est réalisé trop tard dans la journée, le prestataire de service de communication ne disposera pas du temps suffisant pour imprimer le pli et l'adresser par voie postale classique le jour même. Cette certification ne vaut pas jusqu'à inscription de faux, car cette force probante particulière est réservée aux actes authentiques. Si elle est susceptible de preuve contraire par toutes voies de droit, il n'en reste pas moins que les garanties qui entourent l'activité du prestataire de service de certification confèrent aux actes qu'il accomplit une valeur probante élevée* ».[242]

Les règles relatives au pli judiciaire traditionnel régissent la seconde partie du mécanisme, à savoir l'envoi du pli au destinataire par le prestataire de service

---

240 Exposé des motifs, p. 37.

241 Nous nous sommes déjà prononcés contre cette technique du recommandé hybride pour les raisons que les rédacteurs de la LPVE ont l'honnêteté de décrire dans l'exposé des motifs (l'impression fait naître le doute sur l'intégrité du message et compromet l'intégrité de la signature électronique. La mise sous pli du message pourrait également être l'occasion d'une atteinte au secret des communications électroniques) (Voy. en ce sens: D. FESLER, « La correspondance et le recommandé électronique », in *Cabinets d'avocats et technologies de l'information,* J.F. HENROTTE – Y. POULLET (éd.), Cahiers du CRID, n° 26, Bruxelles, Bruylant, 2005, p. 237 et J.F. HENROTTE, « L'encadrement des transactions électroniques », in *Cabinets d'avocats et technologies de l'information, op. cit.*, p. 89-90).

242 Exposé des motifs, p. 38.

de communication. En effet, dès son impression par le tiers intermédiaire, le pli judiciaire redevient un pli classique.

3.3.1.8. Pli judiciaire électronique

92. Aux termes du paragraphe 4, « *sans préjudice de l'application des conventions internationales en la matière, le pli judiciaire peut être adressé par voie électronique.*

Il est délivré à l'adresse judiciaire électronique, par l'intermédiaire d'un prestataire de services de communication […].

Si dans les 24 heures de l'envoi par le greffe ou le ministre public, le prestataire de services de communication ne fait pas parvenir au greffier ou au ministère public un avis de délivrance de celui-ci, la notification a lieu sans délai, selon les cas conformément aux §§ 1, 2 ou 3.

Dans ce cas, la date du pli judiciaire est celle du moment où le prestataire de service de communication reçoit la demande de l'huissier d'envoi au destinataire conformément à l'article 9, §1er de la [LPVE]. […]

Dans ce cas également, le pli mentionne l'absence d'avis de délivrance ainsi que la date et l'heure de l'envoi électronique et celles de l'accusé de réception du prestataire de services de communication […] ».

Il s'agit de la même solution que celle qui a été retenue au nouvel article 42*bis* pour la signification électronique qui échoue. La disposition est toutefois mieux rédigée et exclut sans ambiguïté la possibilité de procéder à une nouvelle notification électronique en ne prévoyant que la notification conforme au § 1, 2 ou 3 et pas 4.

3.3.1.9. Formes et mentions du pli judiciaire – Remplacement des notifications par des significations

93. Les deux paragraphes suivants sont libellés ainsi :

« *§ 5. Le ministre de la Justice peut déterminer les formes à respecter et les mentions de services devant être stipulées lors de l'envoi de pli judiciaire. Si le lieu de destination est situé à l'étranger, le pli judiciaire est remplacé par un pli recommandé aux services postaux, sans préjudice des modes de* *transmission prévus par les conventions internationales et de l'application des §§ 3 et 4.*

§ 6. Néanmoins, lorsque l'une des parties demanderesses ou requérantes en exprime la volonté soit dans l'exploit introductif d'instance ou dans la requête, soit par écrit, au plus tard au moment de la première comparution devant le juge, les notifications par pli judiciaire sont remplacées par des significations, faites à la requête de la partie à laquelle il appartient d'y faire procéder ».

Les travaux préparatoires annoncent que les paragraphes 5 et 6 reprennent des dispositions non modifiées de l'article 46 (les paragraphes 3 et 4) .[243]

Ce n'est que partiellement exact pour le paragraphe 5 dans la mesure où la compétence qui y est énoncée est transférée du ministre qui a la Poste dans ses attributions au ministre de la Justice et la référence à « *la Poste* » est changée par les désormais habituels « *services postaux* ».

3.3.1.10. Recommandé avec accusé de réception

94. Le paragraphe 7 rend applicables les règles de cet article 46, soit les modalités d'envoi du pli judiciaire, au recommandé avec accusé de réception. En effet, ces deux mécanismes sont pratiquement similaires, de telle sorte qu'il était souhaitable qu'ils soient soumis à des modalités identiques, notamment la forme hybride et la forme électronique. Cet alinéa évite de devoir répéter les dispositions de l'article 46 aux articles qui visent la communication par pli recommandé avec accusé de réception. C'est le cas notamment des articles 1275, 1303, 1339, 1457, 1627 et 1675/9 du Code judiciaire.

3.3.2. La computation des délais et le dysfonctionnement

3.3.2.1. Dépôt par voie électronique

95. L'article 52 du Code judiciaire est remplacé par la disposition suivante:
« *Le délai se compte de minuit à minuit. Il est calculé depuis le lendemain du jour de l'acte ou de l'événement qui y donne cours et comprend tous les jours, même le samedi, le dimanche et les jours fériés légaux.*

---

243 Exposé des motifs, p. 39.

A moins qu'il ne soit effectué par voie électronique, un acte ne peut être valablement accompli au greffe qu'aux jours et heures pendant lesquels ce greffe doit être accessible au public.

Si un acte n'a pu être accompli au greffe dans les délais, même prescrits à peine de nullité ou de déchéance, en raison d'un dysfonctionnement du système Phenix, celui-ci est néanmoins valable s'il est accompli sous forme papier ou électronique le lendemain du dernier jour du délai. En cas de contestation de la réalité et de la durée du dysfonctionnement, il est procédé comme indiqué à l'article 882bis.

La prolongation de délai visée à l'alinéa 3 s'applique en tout état de cause si le dysfonctionnement intervient le dernier jour du délai ».[244]

La possibilité, introduite par l'article 5 de la loi du 20 octobre 2000 introduisant l'utilisation de moyens de télécommunication et de la signature électronique dans la procédure judiciaire et extrajudiciaire,[245] qui n'est jamais entré en vigueur et qui est abrogé par la LPVE,[246] de déposer par voie électronique jusqu'à minuit au lieu des traditionnelles seize heures est, bien sûr, maintenue.

L'on notera toutefois que l'accomplissement par télécopie de l'acte, envisagé dans la loi du 20 octobre 2000, n'est plus autorisé et que la date de l'acte n'est plus déterminée par le moment où il arrive mais par son introduction dans le système.[247]

3.3.2.2. Disfonctionnement – Procédure ad hoc

96. Plus important, le législateur a entendu l'interpellation de l'Ordre des barreaux francophones et germanophone et a tenu à rassurer le barreau en cas de dysfonctionnement du système Phenix.

---

244 Article 9 de la LMCJ.

245 *M.B.*, 22 déc. 2000, http://www.moniteur.be; *Droit des technologies de l'information*, CODES LARCIER *thématiques*, p. 32.

246 L'article 28 de la LPVE abroge les articles 4 à 7 de la loi du 20 octobre 2000 introduisant l'utilisation de moyens de télécommunication et de la signature électronique dans la procédure judiciaire et extrajudiciaire.

247 Exposé des motifs, p. 40.

En cas de dysfonctionnement, l'acte peut être valablement accompli le lendemain du dernier jour du délai sous forme papier ou électronique.

On se rappellera, à cet égard, qu'en vertu de l'article 20 de loi du 10 août 2005 instituant le système d'information Phenix (1)[248] le comité de gestion informe tous les chefs de corps concernés des dysfonctionnements du système Phenix.

Toutefois, en cas de contestation de la réalité et de la durée du dysfonctionnement, est d'application une nouvelle procédure inscrite à l'article 882*bis*.[249] Le juge peut interroger le comité de gestion et trancher au terme d'une procédure d'une trentaine de jours.

3.3.3. Les registres et répertoires

97. Les articles 10 et 11 de la LMCJ portent sur les registres et les répertoires qui, naturellement, seront également exclusivement électroniques à l'avenir.

Renvoi est fait, sur ce point, à la très complète étude d'I. VEROUGSTRAETE et V. LAMBERTS.[250]

---

[248] *M.B.*, 1er sept. 2005, http://www.moniteur.be.

[249] Article 26 de la LPVE: « *Un article 882bis, rédigé comme suit, est inséré dans la quatrième partie, livre II, titre III, chapitre VIII, section II du même Code:*
'Sans préjudice de l'application des dispositions qui précèdent, le juge saisi d'une contestation concernant la réalité ou la durée d'un dysfonctionnement du système Phenix en vertu de l'article 52, alinéa 3, peut, par décision, demander au comité de gestion [...] tout renseignement utile à la solution de cette contestation. Le comité de gestion communique au juge les éléments de réponse dans les huit jours de la réception de la décision, qui lui est transmise par pli judiciaire par les soins du greffier, conformément à l'article 46, § 4.
Ces éléments de réponse sont notifiés aux parties par le greffier par pli judiciaire et le cas échéant, par simple lettre à leurs avocats. Les parties peuvent, dans les huit jours de l'envoi du pli judiciaire, adresser leurs observations au juge. Dans les huit jours qui suivent l'expiration du délai prévu à l'alinéa 4, ou le cas échéant par la même décision que celle qu'il rend sur le fond de l'affaire, le juge statue sur pièces. Si toutefois il estime nécessaire d'entendre les parties, celles-ci sont convoquées par pli judiciaire dans les huit jours. Dans ce cas, il statue dans les huit jours de l'audience ou, le cas échéant, par la même décision que celle qu'il rend sur le fond de l'affaire. La décision du juge d'interroger le comité de gestion n'est pas susceptible de recours'.»

[250] I. VEROUGSTRAETE, V. LAMBERTS, « Le dossier électronique: concept, création, gestion » in *Phenix et la procédure électronique* (sous la coord. de J-F. HENROTTE), CUP, Larcier, 2006, vol. 85, p. 60.

3.3.4. Les listes électroniques[251]

98. Des listes électroniques publiques sont créées :

- des membres de l'Ordre judiciaire;[252]
- des huissiers de justice titulaires et suppléants;[253]
- des notaires titulaires, associés et suppléants;[254]
- des avocats.[255]

Seule cette habilitation légale autorise les Ordres à collecter les données à caractère personnel de leurs membres nécessaires à ces listes, elle était donc indispensable en vertu de la loi du 8 décembre 1992.

La liste des avocats, par exemple, est établie par les deux ordres fédéraux qui sont tenus de veiller à la mise à jour permanente de cette base de données (par une synchronisation avec leur propre base de données chaque nuit).

En cas de discordance, la mention de cette liste l'emporte, sauf preuve du contraire, sur celle figurant sur les actes de procédure.[256] « *Néanmoins, il a paru opportun de réserver la possibilité de rapporter la preuve du contraire. En effet, la discordance peut porter sur la qualité même d'avocat. Dans cette hypothèse, on peut imaginer qu'un avocat puisse continuer à avoir accès à certains dossiers en faisant à tort état d'une qualification qu'il ne possède plus. A l'inverse, un avocat peut à tort être mentionné sur la liste comme étant radié ou suspendu, alors qu'il ne l'est pas. Ces hypothèses démontrent la nécessité de donner un caractère réfragable à cette présomption.* »[257]

3.3.4.1. Respect de la vie privée

99. La Commission e-barreaux de l'Ordre des barreaux francophones et germanophone a eu à cœur de veiller au strict respect de la vie privée des avocats : les mentions contenues dans cette liste électronique, comme dans le

---

[251] Sur cette notion et la distinction à faire avec le répertoire central de l'article 4 de la loi du 10 août 2005, voy. Y. POULLET et D. MOREAU, « La justice au risque de la vie privée » in *Phenix et la procédure électronique* (sous la coord. de HENROTTE, J.F.), CUP 02/2006, vol. 85, p. 120-122.

[252] Article 12 de la LMCJ.

[253] Article 14 de la LMCJ.

[254] Article 38 de la LPVE.

[255] Article 13 de la LMCJ

[256] Al. 2 du nouveau point 4 de l'article 430 CJ.

[257] Exposé des motifs, p. 43.

répertoire central prévu à l'article 4 de loi du 10 août 2005 instituant le système d'information Phenix,[258] seront les mentions minimales dont il a été démontré qu'elles étaient nécessaires aux finalités de Phenix.

En outre, cette liste ne permettra pas de recoupements grâce à la substitution au numéro de Registre national, du numéro identifiant unique au sein de l'Ordre auquel appartient l'avocat. Ces recoupements, grâce au numéro de Registre national, avec d'autres bases de données publiques sont en effet sources d'atteinte à la vie privée des avocats qui rentrent ici dans le système en leur qualité de professionnel et non de citoyen.

L'avocat entre dans le portail de l'Ordre judiciaire grâce au certificat d'authentification contenu dans sa carte d'identité électronique. Le portail recherche ensuite le numéro de registre national de l'avocat, le notifie à la base de données de l'Ordre des barreaux francophones et germanophone ou de l'Orde van Vlaamse balies, qui substitue au numéro de registre national le numéro d'avocat, de sorte que lorsqu'un avocat accède dans le vrai système Phenix, il n'est pas identifié grâce à son numéro de Registre national mais grâce à son numéro d'identification de l'Ordre des barreaux francophones et germanophone ou de l'Ordre van Vlaamse Balies.[259]

Le système serait donc parfait si les avocats ne devaient pas signer avec le certificat de signature contenu dans la carte d'identité électronique qui comporte ce numéro de Registre national …

L'on rappellera enfin que des avocats européens et mêmes belges domiciliés hors de Belgique ne pourront accéder au système qu'à l'intervention d'un confrère belge puisqu'ils ne disposent pas d'une carte d'identité électronique belge contenant le certificat, cette fois d'authentification.[260]

On aperçoit, en tout cas, la nécessité pour un avocat de toujours disposer de sa carte d'identité électronique. On notera toutefois qu'une procédure de substitution existe en cas de vol ou de perte de la carte d'identité électronique durant la période nécessaire à son remplacement et qu'à condition de payer une surtaxe, il semble qu'il soit possible de recevoir une

---

258 *M.B.*, 1er sept. 2005, http://www.moniteur.be.

259 Voy. les explications et les schémas figurant au n° 36 de la contribution d'I. VEROUGSTRAETE et V. LAMBERTS in *Phenix et la procédure électronique* (sous la coord. de HENROTTE, J.F.), CUP 02/2006, vol. 85.

260 Voy. *supra*, n° 57 et s.

nouvelle carte d'identité par porteur dans les 24 heures. Cela étant, le système admet la co-titularité des dossiers, de sorte qu'un collaborateur pourrait remplacer un associé distrait, par exemple.

3.3.5. La requête conjointe d'introduction

100. L'article 706 du Code judiciaire est remplacé par la disposition suivante: « *Devant le tribunal de première instance, le tribunal du travail, le tribunal de commerce, le juge de paix et le tribunal de police, la demande peut être introduite par une requête conjointe des parties, signée et datée par elles à peine de nullité.*

La requête est déposée ou adressée au greffe par lettre recommandée.

Le dépôt de la requête au greffe ou l'envoi recommandé vaut signification.

La requête est inscrite au rôle après que, le cas échéant, les droits de mise au rôle ont été payés.

Si les parties ou l'une d'elles le demandent dans la requête, ou si le juge l'estime nécessaire, ce dernier fixe une audience dans les quinze jours du dépôt de la requête. Les parties et, le cas échéant, leur conseil sont alors convoquées par le greffier à comparaître à l'audience fixée par le juge par simple lettre ».[261]

On n'introduira donc plus de demande par la comparution volontaire et la signature d'un procès-verbal à l'audience, mais par une requête conjointe signée.

Ce n'est que si les parties ou l'une d'elles le demandent dans la requête ou si le juge l'estime nécessaire qu'il fixe une audience.

Même dans l'hypothèse d'une introduction par requête électronique, une audience peut toutefois rester utile et donc être fixée par exemple pour fixer un calendrier consensuel de mise en état, pour débattre d'une mesure avant dire droit, pour accorder à l'une des parties un jugement provisionnel, ou plus simplement pour plaider l'affaire si celle-ci est déjà en état.

---

261 Article 11 de la LPVE.

Les auteurs de la loi ont estimé que la signature électronique « qualifiée » donnait une quasi certitude quant à l'identité des parties et à l'intégrité de l'argumentation de chacune des parties, de sorte que la comparution personnelle des parties, qui avait ces finalités, ne s'impose plus.

On peut bien sûr les suivre sur ce point mais pas quand ils écrivent et décident que « *dans un souci de simplification et d'uniformisation, il apparaît par ailleurs opportun de supprimer l'exigence de la comparution volontaire pour les procès-verbaux de comparution volontaire déposés sur support papier* ».[262]

Précisément, ce qui justifie la suppression de la comparution des parties (la signature qualifiée) n'est pas présent sur le support papier …

L'article 15 de la LMCJ dispose que « *le Roi est autorisé à remplacer dans les dispositions légales en vigueur, la terminologie relative à la comparution volontaire par la terminologie relative à la requête conjointe d'introduction. Les arrêtés royaux pris en vertu de la présente disposition qui n'ont pas été confirmés par une loi le premier jour du dix-huitième mois qui suit celui de leur publication au Moniteur belge, cessent de produire leurs effets* ».

Un autre amendement pourrait également remplacer opportunément les mots « *le procès-verbal de comparution volontaire* » de l'article 1344*ter* du Code judiciaire par « *la requête conjointe d'introduction*[263] *visé à l'article 706* ».

On note enfin que la date d'introduction n'est plus fixée par la date de l'audience, qui n'est pas systématiquement ordonnée, mais bien par la date d'introduction dans le système Phenix.

3.3.6. Le rôle national, le dossier électronique et le procès-verbal d'audience

3.3.6.1. Rôle national

101. Il n'est plus question de rôle général ou particulier, mais simplement de rôle (électronique).[264] Renvoi est fait, sur ce point, aux contributions d'Y.

262 Exposé des motifs, p. 45.
263 Expression utilisée en p. 45 de l'exposé des motifs.
264 Article 12 à 15 de la LPVE.

POULLET et D. MOREAU et d'I. VEROUGSTRAETE et V. LAMBERTS,[265] en notant leurs appréciations différentes sur l'augmentation des risques en matière de protection de la vie privée entrainée par la numérisation de celui-ci.

L'article 712 du code judiciaire traitant des rôles particuliers sera dès lors logiquement abrogé.[266]

On notera toutefois qu'une correction législative s'impose car ce faisant, le rôle étant public, les affaires introduites unilatéralement (saisie, constats d'adultère, ...) bénéficieront d'une publicité qui risque de mettre à néant leur efficacité.

3.3.6.2. Le dossier de la procédure

L'article 16 de la LPVE apporte un certain nombre d'adaptations techniques à l'actuel article 721 du Code judiciaire en ce qui concerne le dossier de la procédure. Ces adaptations s'imposent dès lors que les actes de procédure sont posés par voie électronique. Renvoi est fait, sur ce point, aux contributions d'I. VEROUGSTRAETE.[267]

Naturellement, l'alinéa 2 de l'article 720 est abrogé,[268] dans la mesure où il dispose que le greffier inscrit sur la chemise du dossier la date de la mise au rôle et le numéro d'ordre de la cause.

---

265 I. VEROUGSTRAETE, V. LAMBERTS, « Le dossier électronique: concept, création, gestion » in *Phenix et la procédure électronique* (sous la coord. de J-F. HENROTTE), CUP, Larcier, 2006, vol. 85 et Y. POULLET et D. MOREAU, « La justice au risque de la vie privée », in *Phenix et la procédure électronique* (sous la coord. de J-F. HENROTTE), CUP, Larcier, 2006, vol. 85; Voy. également sur le rôle, les développements de V. LAMBERTS dans « Le rôle électronique et la diffusion des données jurisprudentielles », in *Cabinets d'avocats et technologies de l'information,* J.F. HENROTTE – Y. POULLET (éd.), Cahiers du CRID, n° 26, Bruxelles, Bruylant, 2005, p. 239 et s.

266 Article 27 de la LPVE.

267 I. VEROUGSTRAETE, « Présentation générale sur système Phenix, entre projet et réalité » in *Phenix - Les tribunaux à l'ère électronique*, Cahiers du CRID, Bruylant, 2007; I. VEROUGSTRAETE, V. LAMBERTS, « Le dossier électronique: concept, création, gestion » in *Phenix et la procédure électronique* (sous la coord. de J-F. HENROTTE), CUP, Larcier, 2006, vol. 85.

268 Article 27 de la LPVE.

3.3.6.3. Communication entre parties

102. L'article 18 de la LPVE modifie dans une mesure restreinte l'article 737 actuel du Code judiciaire, en supprimant le renvoi aux pièces «enliassées ». Lorsque des pièces sont communiquées par voie électronique, il ne peut évidement plus être question de liasse matérielle de ce genre.

Pour le surplus, la communication peut, bien sûr, toujours être faite à l'amiable sans formalité. Rien n'impose donc la communication électronique mais elle est naturellement possible, « *les avocats devant cependant prendre les précautions voulues pour assurer le respect du secret professionnel* ».[269]

3.3.6.4. Protection de la communication électronique ?

103. Faudra-t-il pour autant recommander ou exiger de l'avocat qu'il ait recours à des techniques de chiffrement (improprement appelées « cryptage »)[270] pour protéger ses communications électroniques ?

S'agissant de communication de point à point, la réponse nous paraît devoir être négative.[271] En effet, moyennant un choix pour des moyens de communication sérieux, on peut considérer que la correspondance électronique n'entraînera pas statistiquement de risque accru d'interception par rapport à la correspondance traditionnelle. Chaque courrier électronique est, en effet, noyé dans le flux de millions de courriels circulant sur la Toile au même instant.
On distingue dès lors difficilement pour quelles raisons l'avocat devrait prendre des précautions extraordinaires concernant cette forme de

---

269 D. MOUGENOT, « Le Code judiciaire à l'épreuve du cyberespace » in *Multimédia Le cyberavocat*, CUP 2/1999, Vol. 29, p. 398.

270 Il s'agit d'un anglicisme. Seul le mot décryptage existe mais induit une intention malveillante que le déchiffrement n'implique évidemment pas.

271 Le règlement de l'Ordre des barreaux francophones et germanophone relatif à l'usage des technologies de l'information sur la communication ne le prescrit pas, tandis que l'article II.1 des lignes directrices du C.C.B.E. sur la communication électronique et Internet ne fait que l'évoquer en ces termes: « *Bien que les communications électroniques soient protégées techniquement et légalement contre les interceptions par des tiers, leur confidentialité peut être mise en péril de diverses manières. Les avocats se doivent dès lors d'apprécier les risques encourus par leur correspondance électronique et de prendre les dispositions appropriées, telles que le recours à des techniques de cryptage en fonction des cas, et à informer correctement leurs clients et correspondants des risques encourus par la correspondance électronique* »,
http://www.ccbe.org/doc/Fr/ccbe_guidelines_ecommunication_internet_fr.pdf.

communication. Pourquoi demander plus à l'électronique qu'au papier ? Le chiffrement est aussi concevable pour le papier (voy. Enigma[272] pendant la Seconde Guerre mondiale) et on n'a pourtant jamais eu cette exigence à l'égard de ce support alors qu'il est, somme toute, assez simple de fracturer une boîte aux lettres. Les juristes se contentant pour le support papier de la protection juridique du secret de la correspondance, ils se satisferont de la protection résultant de la loi du 13 juin 2005 relative aux communications électroniques.[273]

D'autre part, on soulignera que, dans l'état actuel de la technique, l'on ne peut procéder au chiffrement de ses communications électroniques que moyennant la collaboration du destinataire dont on doit utiliser la clé publique de chiffrement.
À défaut, on ne pourra avoir recours qu'à des techniques de cryptographie dite symétriques qui sont en réalité peu commodes et requièrent en général que la clé unique de déchiffrement soit communiquée en clair, ce qui amoindrit bien évidemment la sécurité générale du procédé.

Les avocats seront cependant bien inspirés de s'informer des possibilités de chiffrement de leurs communications à l'aide des moyens mis à leur disposition par des logiciels d'utilisation courante. Dans certains cas, et tenant compte des moyens employés, il sera également judicieux d'informer leurs correspondants des risques liés à l'utilisation de la communication électronique et des possibilités de contrer ceux-ci.

En tout état de cause, l'avocat devra tenir compte d'éventuelles demandes de la part de ses correspondants de recourir au chiffrement et veillera à prendre les mesures appropriées pour satisfaire celles-ci.

3.3.6.5. Restitution des pièces sur support papier

104. L'article 19 de la LPVE vise à adapter l'actuel article 739 du Code judiciaire à la communication électronique des pièces. Dans cette hypothèse, il n'est naturellement plus question de «restituer» les pièces communiquées.

---

272 http://fr.wikipedia.org, V° « *Enigma (machine)* ».
273 *M.B.*, 20 juin 2005, http://www.moniteur.be.

3.3.6.6. Procès-verbal d'audience

105. L'on notera que l'on ne parle naturellement plus non plus de feuilles d'audience mais de procès-verbal d'audience.[274]

3.3.7. Les conclusions électroniques

3.3.7.1. Accusé de réception

106. L'article 20 de la LPVE tend à adapter l'article 742 du Code judiciaire à la communication électronique de conclusions. Les conclusions que déposent électroniquement les parties au greffe constituent bien évidemment l'original. Il n'est dès lors plus question de dépôt matériel au greffe.[275]

La partie déposante reçoit nécessairement un accusé de réception du dépôt des conclusions, ce qui n'est plus simplement une faculté comme actuellement. Mieux, l'ensemble des parties litigeantes reçoit aussi cet accusé de réception.

3.3.7.2. Exigence de signature

107. Les auteurs des projets de loi ont soutenu que : « *le nombre d'interventions a sciemment été limité autant que possible et le but n'était pas expressément de modifier fondamentalement la réglementation existante en matière de procédure pénale et civile à l'occasion de l'introduction de la procédure par voie électronique* ».[276]

Pourtant, l'article 18 de la loi du 10 juillet 2006 relative à la procédure par voie électronique a introduit un nouvel article 743 dans le Code judiciaire, qui réunit les articles 743 et 744 actuellement en vigueur (cette dernière disposition étant abrogée) et qui dispose que:

« *Les parties mentionnent dans leurs conclusions leurs nom, prénom et domicile ou adresse judiciaire électronique, ainsi que le numéro de rôle de la cause.*

---

[274] Article 22, 24 et 25 de la LPVE.

[275] Exposé des motifs, p. 48.

[276] *Doc. Parl.* Chambre 1701/1, s. o. 2004/2005, p. 5.

Les personnes morales justifient de leur identité selon les modalités prévues à l'article 703.

Les conclusions sont signées par les parties ou leur conseil.»

L'exposé des motifs est muet sur ce troisième alinéa qui ne va pas pourtant nécessairement de soi. Comme la requête d'appel ou la requête en fixation déposée sur le pied de l'article 751 du Code judiciaire,[277] il n'est en effet pas si évident que les conclusions doivent actuellement être signées.

La cour de cassation[278] a en effet estimé en matière pénale que l'écrit, fût-il intitulé « note », qui, suivant les mentions de la décision ou du procès-verbal de l'audience a été soumis au juge par une partie ou son conseil au cours des débats à l'audience, qui est visé et signé par le greffier et qui invoque un moyen à l'appui d'une demande, une défense ou une exception, constitue un écrit de conclusions, même s'il n'est pas signé par la partie ou son conseil.
Le Code judiciaire ne spécifie pas expressément que les conclusions doivent être signées. Les tenants de la nécessité de la signature des conclusions ne fondent leur position que sur le fait que l'article 742 du Code judiciaire vise « *l'original de leurs conclusions* » et que c'est la signature qui distingue l'original de la copie.[279]

Dans la mesure où cette mention de l'originalité des conclusions a disparu avec le nouveau libellé de l'article 742 du Code judiciaire, les auteurs de la loi se sont peut-être sentis contraints de réinsérer, cette fois formellement, l'exigence de la signature mais, on le répète, en contradiction, en tout cas au plan pénal, avec la jurisprudence de la Cour de cassation.

Cela étant, l'absence de signature n'est toujours pas sanctionnée. Plus encore, le nouvel article 863 du Code judiciaire, introduit par la loi mort-née du 20 octobre 2000,[280] est maintenu par la nouvelle loi en ces termes : « *dans tous les cas où la signature est nécessaire pour qu'un acte de procédure soit valable,*

---

277 Voy. la note d'observations et les décisions citées dans J.F. HENROTTE, « une requête d'appel, même transmise par courriel électronique, ne doit pas nécessairement être signée ... », *R.D.T.I.*, 2003/16, p. 101-105; http://www.strada.be.

278 Cass., 20 déc. 1983, *Pas.*, 1984, I, 448; http://www.cass.be.

279 Voy. les références citées par D. MOUGENOT, « Le Code judiciaire à l'épreuve du cyberespace » in *Multimédia Le cyberavocat*, CUP 2/1999, Vol. 29, p. 402.

280 Loi du 20 octobre 2000 introduisant l'utilisation de moyens de télécommunication et de la signature électronique dans la procédure judiciaire et extrajudiciaire, *M.B.*, 22 déc. 2000, http://www.moniteur.be.

l'absence de signature peut être régularisée à l'audience ou dans un délai fixé par le juge ». On observe à cet égard que la nouvelle formulation ne vise plus la nullité qui résulterait de l'absence de signature. On peut donc estimer que la situation ne change pas par rapport au texte antérieur et que le juge sera toujours obligé de rencontrer des conclusions non signées. On notera toutefois qu'à notre estime, le nouvel article 863 du Code judiciaire ne pourra être invoqué que par le justiciable qui sera toujours autorisé à déposer des conclusions sur support papier, car il est probable que Phenix n'autorisera pas le dépôt sans signature qualifiée et que ce soit la technique, et non la loi, qui sanctionnera l'alinéa 3 du nouvel article 743 du Code judiciaire.

Au moins, le texte actuel a le mérite de la clarté, ce que n'avait pas la notion d' « original » utilisée antérieurement. Par ailleurs, il n'est sans doute pas choquant qu'un des actes les plus importants de la procédure doive être signé.

3.3.7.3. Abrogation du délai présumé de communication des conclusions ?

108. L'article 745, alinéa 2 du Code judiciaire, qui prévoyait que la communication des conclusions était réputée accomplie cinq jours après l'envoi, est abrogé.[281]

Cela pourrait sembler normal, au vu des modifications introduites par l'article 9 de la LPVE.

On notera toutefois que pendant la période de droit transitoire durant laquelle le papier et l'électronique coexisteront pour les avocats et plus généralement à l'égard des justiciables, cette présomption n'existera plus pour la communication par envoi postal. Il nous semble qu'il aurait mieux valu restreindre cette disposition aux seules conclusions sur support papier plutôt que de l'abroger et donc qu'un amendement en ce sens se justifie pleinement.[282]

---

281 Article 27 de la LPVE.

282 Si tant est que cette disposition ait encore un intérêt après l'arrêt de la cour de cassation du 9 décembre 2005, C040135F, http://www.cass.be; *J.L.M.B.*, 2006/1, p. 4-14, note H. Boularbah; http://jlmbi.larcier.be; *J.T.*, 2006/1, p. 4-8, note J. Englebert; http://jt.larcier.be.

3.3.8. Couverture de la nullité

109. Le premier alinéa de l'article 863 (contrairement à son second alinéa), introduit par la loi du 20 octobre 2000 mais jamais entré en vigueur, est maintenu :

« *Dans tous les cas où la signature est nécessaire pour qu'un acte de procédure soit valable, l'absence de signature peut être régularisée à l'audience ou dans un délai fixé par le juge* ».[283]

L'absence de signature d'un acte, lorsque le dépôt par Phenix sera obligatoire, peut toutefois sembler improbable, car il est manifeste que le système d'information n'acceptera pas l'introduction de l'acte sans qu'il soit signé.
Il ne faut toutefois pas perdre de vue, outre la période transitoire de coexistence du support électronique et papier pour les avocats, le fait que le justiciable pourra continuer à déposer des actes de procédure sur support papier et donc que cette couverture de la nullité restera très utile pour des parties profanes.

3.4. LA PROCEDURE PÉNALE ÉLECTRONIQUE

3.4.1. Observations préliminaires

110. Il ne faut pas se méprendre, bien que le chapitre III de la LPVE soit intitulé « *Du dossier électronique en matière pénale* », l'ensemble des modifications affectant la procédure pénale n'y est pas rassemblée. Les modifications relatives à la procédure de droit commun introduites par les deux premiers chapitres de la LPVE et la LMCJ auront également des répercussions sur la procédure devant les juridictions pénales.

En effet, faut-il le rappeler, l'article 2 du Code Judiciaire dispose que « *les règles énoncées dans le présent Code s'appliquent à toutes les procédures, sauf lorsque celles-ci sont régies par des dispositions légales non expressément abrogées ou par des principes de droit dont l'application n'est pas compatible avec celle des dispositions dudit Code* ».

Il faut cependant noter qu'une lecture *a contrario* de l'exposé des motifs pourrait laisser entendre que le chapitre II de la LPVE n'aurait d'impact que

---

283 Article 23 de la LPVE.

sur la procédure civile.[284] Il n'en est évidemment rien et nombreux sont les exemples des incidences que ce deuxième chapitre et la LMCJ ont sur la procédure pénale.

Les praticiens pénalistes devront notamment avoir égard aux nouvelles règles d'organisation du pouvoir judiciaire et plus particulièrement celles qui ont trait à l'organisation du travail des greffes et greffiers ou au déroulement des audiences. La présentation des conclusions et l'exigence qu'elles soient signées par les parties ou leurs conseils sont également soumises aux règles de droit commun.[285]

111. Cette troisième section se bornera donc à l'examen des modifications spécifiquement applicables à la procédure pénale introduites par le chapitre III de la LPVE. Le lecteur se réfèrera, pour la procédure de droit commun, aux sections 1 et 2 de la présente contribution quant aux principes généraux de la procédure électronique ou aux changements apportés de façon générale au Code judiciaire.

112. L'on remarquera également que le chapitre III de la LPVE se singularise par le fait que, sauf exceptions, il n'entend pas modifier systématiquement des dispositions du Code d'instruction criminelle. « *L'option retenue en ce qui concerne le dossier électronique en matière pénale est celle d'un système autonome qui laisse inchangées les dispositions existantes du Code d'Instruction criminelle. Les dispositions proposées existeront donc en tant que telles et il n'est dès lors pas nécessaire d'indiquer quels sont leurs rapports avec les textes de loi existants* ».

Cette différence d'approche était rendue nécessaire par deux facteurs décisifs:[286]

« *D'abord, le droit de la procédure pénale est actuellement en pleine évolution. [...] A la suite des travaux du groupe de travail Franchimont, une proposition de loi portant le Code de procédure pénale a été déposée au Sénat,*[287] *et y est actuellement débattue. L'introduction de la procédure par voie électronique ne peut donc attendre la réforme du droit de la procédure*

---

[284] Exposé des motifs, p. 6.
[285] Article 21 de la LPVE, remplaçant l'Article 743 CJ.
[286] Exposé des motifs, p. 8.
[287] Doc., Sénat, 3-450.

pénale. » Un système qui puisse fonctionner indépendamment des dispositions définitives du Code d'Instruction criminelle s'imposait donc.

« *Il s'est ensuite rapidement avéré que la procédure par voie électronique en matière pénale était beaucoup plus compliquée qu'en matière civile* ».[288] Les auteurs de la loi relèvent ainsi qu'en matière pénale, outre les acteurs directs que sont l'auteur et la victime, des instances judiciaires très différentes comme les services de police, le parquet, le juge d'instruction, les juridictions d'instruction ou le juge du fond se succèdent. A la suite de quoi de nombreuses personnes sont responsables du dossier aux différents stades de traitement d'une affaire pénale. Il est en outre impossible de prévoir quelles parties seront impliquées dans une procédure pénale. Enfin, il appartient exclusivement aux autorités judiciaires de fournir toutes les preuves et de constituer le dossier pénal, contrairement à une procédure civile, dans laquelle les parties versent leurs propres pièces au dossier de la procédure.

3.4.2. Le dossier pénal

3.4.2.1. Dualité transitoire du dossier pénal papier et électronique

113. Selon les termes de l'article 29, § 1er, alinéa 1er de la LPVE « *A l'exception des pièces à convictions, toutes les pièces du dossier sont placées sur support papier ou électronique, sauf l'inventaire, qui doit toujours être établi sous forme électronique* » , le législateur organise une dualité transitoire du dossier pénal, lequel peut être tenu tantôt sur support papier, tantôt sur support électronique.

Il appartient au juge d'instruction, pour les dossiers d'instruction, au procureur fédéral, au procureur général, à l'auditeur du travail ou au procureur du Roi, pour les dossiers d'information et au tribunal de la jeunesse, pour les dossiers relevant de sa juridiction, de décider sur quel support le dossier original sera établi.[289]

Par ailleurs, et comme le souligne opportunément l'exposé des motifs, « *il va de soi qu'une exception doit être faite pour les pièces à conviction qui seront toujours conservées sous leur forme initiale* ».[290] Cela s'impose en effet, car les

---

288 *Op. cit.*

289 Article 30, al. 1er et al. 3 de la LPVE.

290 Exposé des motifs, p. 53.

pièces à conviction ne sont pas physiquement jointes au dossier pénal proprement dit.

Pour des raisons de nature pratique, ne sont pas convertis sur un autre support les dossiers qui, afin d'être examinés à l'audience par le tribunal, doivent être joints pour des motifs de récidive légale ou spéciale, de criminalité d'habitude, de moralité, de connexité ou d'unité d'intention visée par l'article 65 du Code pénal, de même que les dossiers qui font l'objet d'une procédure de révision.[291]

114. La coexistence de dossiers électroniques et de dossiers classiques pendant une période transitoire est justifiée par le fait qu'il n'est pas indiqué de permettre qu'un dossier original soit établi sur différents supports, ce qui conduirait selon les auteurs de la loi à des situations trop compliquées et probablement à de graves erreurs vu la multitude des procédures au cours de l'instruction.[292]

Cette période de transition, que les travaux préparatoires prévoient longue, prendra fin *en fonction de l'infrastructure nécessaire,*[293] à la date qui sera fixée par le Roi.[294]

115. Les auteurs de la loi estiment, en réaction à une observation du Conseil d'Etat, que ce système ne contrevient pas au principe de la liberté de poser et recevoir ou non des actes de procédure par voie électronique, car selon les termes de l'article 32 de la LPVE, une partie à une procédure pénale pourra toujours consulter ou obtenir une copie imprimée de tout ou partie du dossier répressif, quel que soit le support sur lequel celui-ci a été établi.[295]

116. Contrairement à ce que cet article pourrait laisser entendre, un même dossier peut être manipulé sur des supports différents par le parquet, le juge d'instruction et la juridiction de jugement.

Ainsi, le juge d'instruction saisi sur base d'un réquisitoire de mise à l'instruction peut décider de convertir un dossier original non électronique. Dans ce cas, le dossier répressif *original* devient électronique. Les auteurs de

---

291 Article 29, § 1er, al. 2 de la LPVE; exposé des motifs, p. 53.
292 Exposé des motifs, p. 52.
293 Exposé des motifs, p. 52.
294 Article 37, § 1er de la LPVE.
295 Exposé des motifs, p. 53.

la loi insistent néanmoins sur le fait que « *le juge d'instruction devra éventuellement tenir compte des possibilités techniques du greffe si de nombreuses pièces doivent être converties sous forme numérique. En effet, tant que les procès-verbaux des services de police ne peuvent être transmis dans leur intégralité par voie électronique, la conversion sur support numérique peut constituer un immense travail* ».

Dans la situation inverse, où le juge d'instruction saisi d'un dossier électronique d'une information décide de le traiter sur support papier, une copie du dossier électronique continue à être utilisée dans la procédure pénale.

Une fois saisi, le juge du fond peut également, dans l'intérêt d'une bonne administration de la justice, ordonner le changement de support du dossier s'il l'estime nécessaire.[296]

On le voit, cette cohabitation entre écrit et électronique ne signifie pas forcément un gain de temps ou une rationalisation du travail.

117. Comme écrit ci-avant, le dossier contient un inventaire électronique chronologique permettant de retrouver toutes les pièces à la date où elles ont été versées au dossier, quelle que soit leur nature ou leur origine. Une copie certifiée conforme de l'inventaire électronique est jointe à tout dossier dont il a été décidé qu'il serait établi sur support papier.[297] L'inventaire mentionne également les retraits de pièces du dossier.[298]

Les travaux préparatoires précisent : « *L'inventaire électronique sera le seul à avoir valeur d'inventaire authentique dès l'entrée en vigueur de la phase de transition. Pendant la phase de transition, [...] il sera toutefois nécessaire que dans les dossiers (établis sur support papier), une copie certifiée conforme de cet inventaire électronique soit versée au dossier papier, afin d'éviter que le dossier papier soit incomplet par défaut d'inventaire* ».[299]

118. L'on doit cependant toutefois s'interroger sur la raison pour laquelle le législateur entend réserver aux seuls juges ou greffier ou, s'il s'agit

296 Article 30, al. 2 de la LPVE.
297 Article 29, § 1er, al. 2 de la LPVE.
298 Article 29, § 1er, al. 3 de la LPVE.
299 Exposé des motifs, p. 53.

d'information, au Procureur ou au secrétaire de parquet, la faculté de verser des pièces au dossier pénal.

L'exposé des motifs semble indiquer qu'il s'agit là d'une mesure de précaution pour garantir l'unité, en termes de format, du dossier pénal.[300] On peut toutefois s'interroger sur l'opportunité d'une telle approche, ce notamment au regard du principe de l'égalité des armes qui limiterait la possibilité d'alimenter un dossier pénal aux seules parties judiciaires, à l'exclusion notable du prévenu, de la partie civile et de leurs conseils.

Dans la réalité, un dossier pénal contient également des pièces et documents autres que celles du juge, du procureur ou du greffier, ce notamment par le dépôt de requêtes, de conclusions, voire des correspondances diverses dont il ne paraît pas sain de restreindre le versement dans le dossier pénal en le subordonnant à la décision favorable des instances judiciaires précitées.

A notre estime, le législateur serait bien inspiré de prévoir, en lieu et place d'une telle innovation dont il pourrait découler des difficultés sérieuses, le principe suivant lequel les pièces à verser au dossier pénal le seront en la forme retenue pour la tenue dudit dossier ou, à défaut de l'être, seront converties suivant les dispositions *ad hoc* de la LPVE.

3.4.2.2. Conversion des pièces, certification et conservation

119. « *La conversion de dossiers répressifs établis sur support papier, de pièces de procédure et d'autres pièces dans un dossier électronique s'effectue par un enregistrement dans un dossier électronique par lecture électronique et par une certification de la conformité avec le document lu électroniquement par une signature qualifiée de l'autorité judiciaire qui a ordonné la conversion ou, selon le cas, du greffier ou du secrétaire du parquet* ».[301]

L'ensemble des pièces n'ayant pas été établies au départ sous forme électronique font partie d'un dossier dit d'archivage chronologique qui reprend lesdites pièces dans l'ordre suivant lequel elles ont été versées au dossier, ainsi que les copies de déclarations signées manuscritement par les personnes auditionnées.

---

300 Exposé des motifs, p. 8.
301 Article 31, § 1er de la LPVE.

Il est à noter que « *les pièces de procédure sont également classées par ordre chronologique mais sont mises dans un dossier séparé du dossier d'archivage chronologique.* »[302]

Quant à la conversion d'un dossier établi sur support électronique, en tout ou en partie, sur support papier, elle s'effectue par le biais d'une copie certifiée conforme et signée, selon le cas, par le procureur du Roi, le secrétaire de parquet ou le greffier. Si la pièce convertie émane d'un service de police ou d'une autre autorité, ce service ou cette autorité peut également fournir selon les mêmes modalités une copie certifiée conforme.[303]

120. Le paragraphe 2 de l'article 31 de la LPVE dispose que « *les pièces qui, à l'origine, n'ont pas été établies sous forme électronique sont déposées au secrétariat du parquet si le dossier répressif concerne une information* ».[304] Elles sont ensuite transmises au greffe de la juridiction saisie de l'affaire au plus tard au moment de la citation saisissant le tribunal à moins que la consultation des pièces au greffe ne soit imposée antérieurement par la loi.

121. Quant aux pièces relatives à l'instruction,[305] « *celles-ci sont conservées par le greffier qui assiste le juge d'instruction et déposées au greffe dès que l'affaire a été renvoyée par chambre du conseil ou la chambre des mises en accusation.*

Si le juge d'instruction est déchargé sans renvoi devant un juge du fond, les pièces seront communiquées, avec le dossier, au Procureur du Roi et seront ensuite conservées par le secrétaire de parquet ».

3.4.3. La consultation du dossier et la prise de copies

3.4.3.1. Consultation du dossier

122. Les nouvelles possibilités technologiques générées par la création du dossier électronique nécessitent l'établissement d'une réglementation spécifique pour la consultation ou la délivrance d'une copie d'un dossier sous cette forme.

---

302 Article 31, § 3 de la LPVE.
303 Article 31, § 4 de la LPVE.
304 Article 31, §2 de la LPVE.
305 Article 31, § 2 de la LPVE, exposé des motifs, p. 58.

123. La consultation du dossier électronique durant la phase d'instruction, lorsque la loi l'autorise, a lieu au greffe, ou en un lieu désigné à cet effet. « *Elle peut également se faire par la consultation d'une copie imprimée de tout ou partie du dossier*[306] ». [...] Au cours de l'information, si le procureur du Roi en a donné l'autorisation, la consultation du dossier électronique a lieu directement au secrétariat du parquet ou en un lieu désigné à cet effet

La consultation de dossiers s'effectue donc, en règle, par la mise à disposition du matériel nécessaire pour permettre une lecture du dossier sur l'écran. Les auteurs de la loi concèdent cependant que cela nécessite une infrastructure importante compte tenu du nombre de personnes qui, au même moment, doivent pouvoir consulter leur dossier et qui bénéficient d'un droit de consultation. Ils prévoient dès lors que l'infrastructure nécessaire devra être développée progressivement pendant la période de transition, en vue de la conversion définitive vers une procédure entièrement électronique.[307]

124. Ces règles relatives au mode de consultation sont d'application tant durant la phase d'instruction, qu'à compter de la citation ou de la convocation par procès-verbal.

En l'état actuel de la LPVE, les avocats se contenteront éventuellement de l'indication dans l'exposé des motifs[308] de ce que le texte actuel du projet permet en tout état de cause la consultation de dossiers répressifs au greffe du tribunal d'arrondissement dans lequel l'avocat a son cabinet et non pas nécessairement au greffe du tribunal saisi. Le législateur estime qu'une énumération limitative des lieux à partir desquels l'on peut consulter les pièces d'un dossier n'est pas indiquée, dans la mesure où « *l'évolution de la technologie d'une part et de l'e-government d'autre part permettront peut-être dans l'avenir de consulter les dossiers dans d'autres lieux en offrant des garanties suffisantes quant au secret de l'instruction* ».

Les promoteurs du projet Phenix n'ont cependant pas écarté la possibilité d'une consultation en ligne des dossiers pénaux, soit une formule qui satisferait assurément les pénalistes et leur ferait profiter pleinement du passage au dossier électronique.

---

306 Article 32, § 1er, al. 1er de la LPVE.
307 Exposé des motifs, p. 58.
308 Exposé des motifs, p. 59.

En effet, une telle réforme impliquera pour les avocats parfois des investissements en matériel et en logiciels, souvent la nécessité de formation et toujours des nouvelles contraintes (signer numériquement prend plus de temps que manuscritement, par exemple).

Le véritable intérêt de Phenix, pour ceux-ci, réside dans l'accessibilité en ligne des dossiers. Plus particulièrement, tous souhaitent accéder en ligne dans un endroit confortable au dossier répressif. Il en résultera pour le justiciable de substantielles économies et donc une plus grande accessibilité à la justice puisqu'il ne faudra plus payer les frais de déplacement et que l'on sera beaucoup plus parcimonieux dans les copies de pièces si on peut prendre connaissance du dossier à tout instant sans déplacement.

Il y a, bien sûr, l'obstacle juridique de l'interdiction de copie du dossier répressif au stade de l'information ou de l'instruction (on pourrait exclure dans ces seules hypothèses la consultation par internet et la réserver à celle au greffe par le biais de l'intranet), mais il y a surtout un obstacle pécuniaire. On craint que par le biais de la copie écran on contourne les dispositifs anti-copie des fichiers et la perte des droits afférents à la copie.

La précédente Ministre de la Justice s'est prononcée en faveur de la consultation en ligne du dossier répressif.[309]

Le blocage semble, venir du SPF Finance qui, bien loin de déférer à la demande du monde judiciaire de défiscalisation de la délivrance par voie électronique des copies, a inséré dans la loi-programme (I) du 27 décembre 2006[310] un article 309 qui pourrait supprimer l'ambigüité qui pouvait exister dans l'article 372 en prévoyant que le droit de € 0,75 est également dû pour chaque page électronique copiée du document source.

La justification du droit réside pourtant dans le coût de la main d'œuvre nécessaire à la réalisation de cette copie, coût qui disparaît dans l'hypothèse d'une copie effectuée en ligne, puisque réalisée sans intervention humaine, si ce n'est celle de l'internaute lui-même.

En l'absence de justification de ces droits, il nous semble qu'il y lieu de les supprimer, particulièrement s'ils sont l'obstacle à la consultation par internet

---

309 Onkelinkx, L., « Préface », in *Phenix et la procédure électronique* (sous la coord. de Henrotte, J.F.), CUP 02/2006, vol. 85, p. 10.

310 *M.B.*, 28 déc. 2006, http://www.moniteur.be.

du dossier répressif et ainsi de permettre à Phenix de profiter aux avocats, comme à l'ensemble des acteurs judiciaires.

125. S'agissant des dossiers d'information et pour autant que le Procureur du Roi en ait donné l'autorisation, leur consultation peut s'opérer directement au secrétariat du parquet ou en un lieu désigné à cet effet.[311]

La consultation peut se faire par voie électronique à compter du règlement de la procédure ou du moment où la juridiction pénale a été saisie de l'affaire par citation directe ou convocation par procès-verbal. Les travaux préparatoires précisent que « *dans ce cas, consultation et copie devront être assimilées. Le fichier pourra être copié et, par conséquent, les droits devront être acquittés à l'avance comme c'est le cas pour l'obtention d'une copie papier* ».[312]

3.4.3.2. Prise de copies

126. A compter de la clôture de l'instruction ou de la date de la citation ou de la convocation par procès-verbal, « *une copie peut être délivrée, à la demande d'une partie, sur un support électronique, par voie électronique, ou sous forme d'une copie imprimée». Il en va de même si pendant l'information le Procureur du Roi a autorisé la délivrance de la copie ou si la copie est accordée en vertu d'une disposition légale expresse* ».[313]

Il sera intéressant de voir, dans la pratique, laquelle de ces options sera le plus fréquemment utilisée.

La réflexion d'Ivan VEROUGSTRAETE sur la défiscalisation de la délivrance des copies électroniques de décisions judiciaires par une modification de l'article 272 du Code des droits d'enregistrement, d'hypothèque et de greffe[314] est, à cet égard, porteuse d'espoir en ce qu'elle permettrait de résoudre le problème de la consultation en des lieux limitativement désignés à cet effet en lui substituant la délivrance gratuite d'une copie du dossier.

Dans l'hypothèse où un prévenu ou une personne auditionnée est en droit de se voir remettre sans frais une copie de son audition cette remise peut

---

311 Article 32, § 1er, al. 3 de la LPVE.

312 Exposé des motifs, p. 59.

313 Article 32, § 1er, al. 2 et 4 de la LPVE.

314 I. VEROUGSTRAETE, « Présentation générale sur système Phenix, entre projet et réalité », n° 31 in *Phenix - Les tribunaux à l'ère électronique*, Cahiers du CRID, Bruylant, 2007, p. 17.

également s'opérer sous la forme d'une copie imprimée du document électronique.[315] En effet, l'obligation générale prévue par la loi concernant la délivrance d'une copie de l'audition proprement dite de la personne interrogée, pour autant qu'elle le souhaite, implique que l'obtention de la copie papier du texte de l'audition doit rester possible.[316] Il en est de même dans tous les cas où une personne est en droit de recevoir copie d'un procès-verbal.

3.4.4. La tenue des pièces du dossier pénal

3.4.4.1. Procès-verbaux

127. Suivant les directives qui seront arrêtées par le Collège des Procureurs généraux, après avis du comité de gestion Phenix, les autorités de police, les services de police ou les fonctionnaires et agents appartenant aux services relevant d'autorités ou d'établissements d'utilité publique et chargés de rechercher et de constater les infractions ou d'en collecter les preuves pourront établir des procès-verbaux sous forme électronique en vue de leur transmission à l'autorité judiciaire.[317] Ainsi, dans l'avenir, les procès-verbaux des services de police devront en principe pouvoir être transmis intégralement par voie électronique aux autorités judiciaires.

Les auteurs de la loi soulignent le fait qu' « *il existe [...] une grande différence entre la transmission interne entre autorités impliquées dans la procédure pénale, qui doit pouvoir se faire par voie électronique, et la transmission de pièces à des personnes externes, qui est soumise aux règles du secret de l'instruction.*
Par conséquent, durant la longue transition vers le dossier électronique généralisé, la possibilité de transmettre les procès-verbaux sur support papier au parquet ou au juge d'instruction devra être maintenue. Toutefois, le contenu du procès-verbal pourra, dès que possible, être transmis également par voie électronique ».[318]

Dès lors qu'il n'existe pas encore de signature qualifiée attribuée à chaque personne physique, et que les personnes impliquées dans un dossier répressif peuvent être de nationalité étrangère, « *il sera toujours nécessaire que la*

---

315 Article 32, § 2 de la LPVE.
316 Exposé des motifs, p. 59.
317 Article 33 de la LPVE.
318 Exposé des motifs, p. 60.

personne entendue signe sa déclaration sur une copie de la feuille d'audition établie sur support électronique ».[319]

La LPVE[320] prévoit dès lors que la signature par une personne du texte de sa déclaration se fait par « *l'apposition de sa signature sur une copie imprimée du texte de la déclaration. Cette copie est ensuite déposée dans le dossier d'archivage électronique. Il est fait mention de ces opérations dans le procès-verbal d'audition même, lequel est joint au dossier électronique et est certifié par une signature qualifiée du rédacteur.* »

Nous sommes ici face à une des rares dispositions dans laquelle les rédacteurs de la loi ont estimé que la voie purement électronique serait l'exception, et non la règle.

Il en sera de même dans tous les cas où une personne, indépendamment de sa qualité et du stade de la procédure, est appelée à signer une pièce en forme électronique et ne le fait pas à l'aide d'une signature qualifiée.[321]

Le même procédé s'applique également à chaque fois qu'en application d'une disposition légale, il doit être pris acte de l'accord d'une partie ou de la confirmation par une partie au procès-verbal d'audience et que cet accord ou confirmation doit se traduire par l'apposition de la signature de la partie ou de son conseil au bas dudit procès-verbal.

Les fonctionnaires de police doivent dès lors également disposer d'une signature électronique « qualifiée », afin de certifier les signatures apposées au bas de leurs procès-verbaux.

128. La LPVE prévoit toutefois que « *lorsque cela est possible, les déclarations, requêtes, procès-verbaux ou autres actes sont signés sous leur forme électronique par les personnes concernées ou par les personnes habilitées par la loi à les représenter à cet effet, par l'utilisation d'une signature qualifiée […]* ».[322]

---

[319] Exposé des motifs, p. 61.
[320] Article 34, § 1er de la LPVE.
[321] Article 34, § 2 de la LPVE.
[322] Article 34, § 3 de la LPVE.

3.4.4.2. Actes, déclarations ou requêtes du justiciable

129. « *Les actes, déclarations ou requêtes qui, en vertu de la loi, peuvent être envoyés par la partie concernée, la partie lésée ou le requérant au greffe ou au secrétariat de parquet peuvent être envoyés par voie électronique, pour autant qu'ils soient porteurs de la signature qualifiée de la partie, du requérant ou de l'avocat qui procède à l'envoi. Les conclusions et mémoires peuvent être envoyés par voie électronique au greffe du tribunal ou de la cour saisie de l'affaire, pour autant qu'ils soient porteurs de la signature qualifiée de la partie concernée ou de son avocat*».[323]

Dans la mesure où la LPVE mentionne clairement que tous les actes de procédure dont question doivent être signés à l'aide d'une signature qualifiée, la LPVE se révèle plus exigeante que la jurisprudence de la Cour de Cassation, qui reconnaît la validité de conclusions non signées déposées en matière pénale.[324] La Cour suprême admet également que, dès lors qu'une requête d'appel s'opère par déclaration au greffe et est consignée par le greffier en sa qualité d'officier public, l'absence de signature du prévenu ou de son conseil ne vicie pas l'acte.

Au vu du libellé de l'article 34 § 4, et dans l'attente d'un arrêt de la Cour de Cassation sur ce point, il faudra sans doute considérer que l'absence de signature qualifiée viciera l'acte sauf à recourir à la régularisation instaurée par le nouvel article 863 du Code judiciaire.[325]

Le bon fonctionnement du système ainsi instauré dépendra en grande partie de la diffusion prochaine ou non de la signature qualifiée dans la population et de ce que les justiciables accepteront ou non de prêter leur concours à l'établissement d'actes répressifs à leur encontre en usant de leur carte d'identité électronique pour signer ceux-ci.

3.4.4.3. Citations directes et rapports d'expertise

130. Les citations directes émanant de parties autres que le ministère public sont enregistrées dans le dossier électronique et déposées dans le dossier d'archivage électronique si elles se rapportent à une information dont le

---

[323] Article 34, § 4 de la LPVE.

[324] Cass. 20 déc. 1983, *Pas.*, 1984, I, 448; http://www.cass.be - Voy. *supra*, n° 107.

[325] Voy. l'Article 23 de la LPVE et *supra*, n°106, 109 et note 283.

dossier est tenu sous forme électronique.[326] La citation directe est ainsi scannée en vue d'être intégrée dans le dossier électronique selon la méthode de la lecture électronique, et les pièces originales déposées dans le dossier d'archivage chronologique.

Comme le relèvent les auteurs de la loi, on peut dire que la citation directe émanant d'une autre partie que le ministère public concerne pratiquement toujours une information existante. Il est donc logique que les pièces de la citation directe soient converties sous la forme du dossier original.[327]

Il en est fait de même avec les rapports d'expert établis sur support papier. L'article 34 § 6 prévoit toutefois la possibilité pour l'expert disposant d'une signature électronique qualifiée d'envoyer son rapport sous forme électronique à l'autorité judiciaire compétente.[328]

3.4.5. Les convocations et significations

3.4.5.1. Convocations

131. Le législateur a prévu une double possibilité pour remplacer, à terme, l'actuelle convocation par lettre recommandée à la poste. Les convocations peuvent ainsi être exécutées soit directement par le greffier à l'adresse judiciaire électronique du destinataire, soit en ayant recours au prestataire de services de communication qui adressera une forme hybride de convocation.[329] En ce qui concerne cette deuxième forme de convocation, l'on peut supposer que les motifs du législateur sont les mêmes que ceux qui l'ont amené à organiser le système du pli judiciaire hybride.[330]

En précisant que *« sauf dispositions légales contraires, en matière pénale la convocation est réputée reçue par le destinataire le premier jour ouvrable qui suit le moment où le greffier ou le prestataire de services de communication a présenté la lettre de convocation aux services postaux en vue de son envoi recommandé »*, les auteurs du projet ont voulu couper court à la possibilité

326 Article 34, § 5 de la LPVE.
327 Exposé des motifs, p. 62.
328 Article 34, § 6 de la LPVE.
329 Article 35, al. 1 et 2 de la LPVE.
330 Voy. *supra* n° 91.

d'invoquer en matière pénale le bénéfice de la jurisprudence de la Cour constitutionnelle relative aux délais de recours.[331]

La Cour constitutionnelle a en effet jugé que, en ce qu'ils sont interprétés comme faisant courir les délais de recours contre une décision dont la notification se fait par pli judiciaire à partir de la date de l'expédition de ce pli, [...] les articles 32, 2° et 46 §2, combinés avec l'articles 792, al. 2 du Code judiciaire, violaient les articles 10 et 11 de la Constitution, mais qu'ils ne violaient pas la constitution s'ils étaient interprétés comme faisant courir les délais de recours à la date à laquelle le pli judiciaire à été remis par les services de la poste au destinataire ou à son domicile.[332]

Etant donné les délais extrêmement courts fixés par la loi en matière pénale, le législateur n'a pas jugé souhaitable d'attendre les accusés de réception. Il a donc prévu une présomption réfragable qu'il estime compatible avec l'enseignement de la Cour d'arbitrage (désormais Cour constitutionnelle),[333] selon laquelle les convocations sont réputées reçues le premier jour ouvrable suivant la présentation de la lettre de convocation aux services postaux en vue de son envoi recommandé,[334] ce délai d'un jour étant justifié par le fait qu' « *il est incontestable qu'il est pratiquement impossible d'être informé du contenu de la lettre recommandée le jour même de l'envoi* ».[335]

Compte tenu du fait que cette présomption est réfragable[336] et de ce délai complémentaire d'un jour par rapport au régime de droit commun prévu à l'article 9 de la LPVE pour tenir compte de la nature spécifique de la matière pénale, cette approche pourrait couper court aux contestations.

Cela étant, s'agissant du recommandé postal, on se demande si cette disposition ne relève pas de la méthode Coué. Ce n'est pas parce qu'on voudrait qu'il n'y ait qu'un délai d'un jour en raison de la brièveté des délais en matière pénale que les choses se passent concrètement ainsi. Par exemple, la plupart des justiciables sont sur leur lieu de travail durant les heures ouvrables et donc absents lors du passage du facteur. L'article 53*bis* du Code

---

331 Voy. *supra* note 184.
332 Voy. *supra* note 183.
333 Exposé des motifs, p. 64.
334 Article 35, al. 3 de la LPVE.
335 Exposé des motifs, p. 62 et s.
336 Exposé des motifs, p. 64.

judiciaire admet des délais plus réalistes pour la notification sur support papier remise aux services de la Poste.

3.4.5.2. Significations

132. L'article 36 de la LPVE régit les significations effectuées par l'huissier de justice ou par une autre autorité chargée de signifier, par exemple les services de police ou le directeur de prison.

« *Sans préjudice des dispositions de l'article 42bis du Code judiciaire,*[337] *la signification des arrêts, des jugements, des ordonnances, des citations, des convocations par procès-verbal ou des mandats sur support électronique, effectuée en exécution d'une disposition s'inscrivant dans le cadre de la législation relative à la détention préventive ou de la procédure pénale en général, est réglée comme suit.*

La signification est faite par la remise d'une copie de l'acte concerné.

Partant du principe que les huissiers de justice seront équipés techniquement à cet effet, il est prévu qu'ils communiquent électroniquement l'exploit de citation après l'avoir scanné et lu électroniquement. L'exploit même doit en même temps être envoyé à l'autorité judiciaire mandante, en vue de son dépôt dans le dossier d'archivage chronologique.[338]

133. « *Lorsque cela est possible, l'acte de signification électronique est signé par la personne à qui il est signifié par l'utilisation d'une signature qualifiée.* »[339]

3.4.6. Introduction complète du dossier électronique en matière pénale

134. Le Roi fixera, après avis du comité de gestion, la date de l'introduction complète du dossier électronique en matière pénale.[340]

« *Toutes les pièces des dossiers répressifs originaux relatives à une instruction ouverte après la date de l'introduction définitive ou à une information inscrite*

---

337 Introduit par l'Article 6 de la LMCJ.
338 Exposé des motifs, p. 64.
339 Article 36, § 2 de la LPVE.
340 Article 37, § 1er, de la LPVE.

par l'administration du parquet après cette date sont établies sur support électronique conformément aux dispositions du présent chapitre. »[341]

4. CONCLUSIONS

135. Comme on l'aura lu, les lois ici examinées sont sans aucun doute perfectibles sur de nombreux points.

Le législateur en a toujours été conscient et a prévenu les différents acteurs de ce projet en ces termes :

« *Les implications techniques de la mise en œuvre du projet Phenix sont naturellement considérables et elles ne sont pas toujours prévisibles. Il faut déjà prévoir que des adaptations régulières seront nécessaires au cours de la phase des projets-pilotes prévus. Afin de faire correspondre autant que possible la traduction procédurale des adaptations nécessaires avec les interventions techniques, il a été choisi dans un certain nombre de cas de confier la réalisation concrète de certains aspects de la procédure par voie électronique au Roi qui peut intervenir chaque fois que le comité de gestion de Phenix le juge nécessaire ou souhaitable.*

Une réglementation légale trop détaillée aurait pour conséquence de freiner ou même d'empêcher l'évolution naturelle de la procédure par voie électronique dans le cadre de Phenix ».[342]

Laissons donc au Roi et aux comités Phenix le temps de procéder aux ajustements nécessaires. Des corrections légales pourront éventuellement être également opérées si le besoin s'en faisait encore sentir.

---

341 Article 37, § 2, de la LPVE.

342 *Doc. Parl.* Chambre 1701/1, s. o. 2004/2005, p. 5-6.

E-JUSTICE IN THE NETHERLANDS

A.W. JONGBLOED and B. SUJECKI

1.1. INTRODUCTION

Modern IT-technology is becoming an increasingly factor within the judiciary. While e-justice is already in use in German and Austrian civil procedure,[1] is the use of information technology within the Dutch civil procedure at an early stage. The Dutch civil procedure does not have any special proceedings that are proceed electronically and neither has a legal basis existed for the introduction of an electronic procedure in the Dutch civil procedure. However, this does not mean that the possibilities for the use of information technology within the civil procedure are not being discussed in the Dutch literature.[2] Additionally, the use of information technology within civil proceedings is being tested in several pilot schemes.

This following article intends to provide an overview over the recent developments aiming to introduce information technology within the Dutch civil procedure. Before however such an overview can be given, however the function that information technology may have within court proceedings must first be determined. Based on the different functions, the current and possible applications of information technology within civil court proceedings will be described.

---

1 See further on the use of information technology in the civil judiciary in Germany: U.J. SCHERF/H.P. SCHMIESZEK/W. VIEFHUES, Elektronischer Rechtsverkehr, Müller Heidelberg 2006; A. STADLER, Der Zivilprozeß und neue Formen der Informationstechnik, *Zeitschrift für Zivilprozeß (Journal for Civil Procedure)* 111 (2002), p. 413 ff.; and Austria: P. GOTTWALD/W. VIEFHUES, Elektronischer Rechtsverkehr in Österreich - Schlussfolgerungen aus deutscher Sicht, Multimedia und Recht (Multimedia and the Law,) 2004, p. 792 ff.; G.E. KODEK, Der Zivilprozeß und neue Formen der Informationstechnik, *Zeitschrift für Zivilprozeß (Journal for Civil Procedure)* 111 (2002), p. 445 ff.

2 Compare W.D.H. ASSER/H.A. GROEN/J.B.M. VRANKEN/I.N. TZANKOVA, A new balance. A summary of the Interim report Fundamental review of the Dutch law of civil procedure, *Zeitschrift für Zivilprocess International (Journal for Civil Procedure International)* 8 (2003), p. 329, 375 ff.; R.H. VAN DEN HOOGEN, E-Justice, diss. Utrecht University 2007 and Raad voor de rechtspraak, Beginselen van digitalisering van rechtspraak: een aanzet tot bewustwording, Rechtstreeks 2008 – nr 1 (the author of this brochure is Van den Hoogen).

1.2. FUNCTIONS OF INFORMATION TECHNOLOGY WITHIN CIVIL COURT PROCEEDINGS

Information technology can be used in various ways within a judicial procedure.[3] First, it can have a purely supportive function in which case, it is used to facilitate the communication between the parties and the court. It can also be used as a source of information. Such information sources can provide the judiciary (such as judges etc.) as well as the parties with information concerning the legal questions involved in the case. These databanks can contain information on the regulation of jurisdiction and the competence of a court. Additionally, information can be provided on the application, the requirements as well as the process involved in the procedure. These databanks can contain general and also specific information. This information can then be used on the one hand by the parties to get a first impression of the possible costs and the duration of the proceedings as well as the chances of success. With this information, the parties would be able to gain a first impression of the case. In an ideal situation, the parties would at first instance not be required to obtain information from legal professionals but would be able to receive this – initial – information through these databanks. As an example special web-based computer programs can be mentioned which can help the parties – the claimant and the defendant – to determine their chances of a successful result in the procedure.[4] In this case information technology would here have to function so as to facilitate access to the relevant legal information in particular and to the justice in general.[5] On the other hand, the information can have the purpose of providing the professional parties, such as lawyers or judges, with relevant judicial information on specific legal topics. This information would facilitate the access to judicial know-how. As a result, the quality of the judiciary as a

---

3 See further on the different functions of information technology within civil proceedings: H. RÜẞMANN, Herausforderung Informationsgesellschaft: Die Anwendung moderner Technologie im Zivilprozess und anderen Verfahren, in: W.H. RECHBERGER/TH. KLICKA (ed.), *Procedural Law on the Threshold of a New Millennium*, Manz Vienna 2002, p. 205-230; see also regarding to the German civil procedure law: P. GILLES, Zivilgerichtsverfahren, Teletechnik und E-Prozessrecht. Zu den Anfängen einer Elektronifizierung des Zivilprozesses in Deutschland und ihrer Verrechtlichung in der deutschen Zivilprozessordnung, *Zeitschrift für Zivilprozeß (Journal for Civil Procedure)* 118 (2005), p. 399 ff.

4 A similar examination program can be found in the electronic order for payment procedure in Germany. In this so-called *Ohnline*-Mahnverfahren, the data submitted by the claimant is being immediately examined by the software, see B. SUJECKI, *Mahnverfahren*, Müller Heidelberg 2007, nr. 246.

5 Comp. R.H. VAN DEN HOOGEN, *E-Justice*, diss. Utrecht University 2007, p. 64 ff.

whole could be improved.[6] Another function which information technology may have within civil proceedings is the improvement of communication between the parties themselves as well between the parties and the court. The use of information technology here accelerates the process of exchanging of documents. While electronic documents can be transmitted within a few seconds, sending by post on the contrary takes at least one day if not even longer. This reduction in transmitting time may have a direct influence on the proceedings so that their duration will be reduced. The use of information technology as a communication tool within civil proceedings may not only hasten the proceedings but it could also improve access to the court. Using information technology, the participants in court proceedings may be able to file the court documents from any place in the world at any time. Court opening and closing times then become irrelevant. Additionally, transmission costs could be reduced, as there would not be any postal charges. Electronic communication is only possible, however, if the identity of the of the addressor as well as the authenticity of the transmitted document are ensured.[7] This security could be achieved by using electronic signatures[8] or within an admission procedure in which the identity of the applicant is being examined and a personal code is issued.[9]

The function of information technology within civil proceedings may finally extend beyond a purely supportive role. In this case information technology is used not only to support the work of the judiciary, but also to reach decisions.[10] However, such a broad use of information technology within the civil judiciary requires that the proceedings are structured in a systematic

---

6 Comp. R.H. VAN DEN HOOGEN, *E-Justice*, diss. Utrecht University 2007, p. 99 ff.

7 See also: W. VIEFHUES/U.J. SCHERF, Sicherheitsaspekte bei der elektronischen Kommunikation zwischen Anwalt und Gericht, *K&R* 2002, p. 170 ff.; R.H. VAN DEN HOOGEN, *E-Justice*, diss. Utrecht University 2007, p. 67 ff.

8 Comp. W. VIEFHUES/U.J. SCHERF, Sicherheitsaspekte bei der elektronischen Kommunikation zwischen Anwalt und Gericht, *K&R* 2002, p. 170 ff.; S. FISCHER-DIESKAU, Der Referentenentwurf zum Justizkommunikationsgesetz aus Sicht des Signaturrechts, *Multimedia und Recht (Multimedia and the law)* 2003, p. 701 ff.; H. RÜßMANN, Herausforderung Informationsgesellschaft: Die Anwendung moderner Technologie im Zivilprozess und anderen Verfahren, in: W.H. RECHBERGER/TH. KLICKA (ed.), *Procedural Law on the Threshold of a New Millennium*, Manz Vienna 2002, p. 205 ff., 211 ff.

9 Such a procedure can be found in Austrian law, comp. P. GOTTWALD/W. VIEFHUES, Elektronischer Rechtsverkehr in Österreich - Schlussfolgerungen aus deutscher Sicht, *Multimedia und Recht (Multimedia and the Law)* 2004, p. 792, 795 ff. They also compare both systems.

10 An example of this use of information technology is the *Mahnverfahren* in Germany and Austria.

way and are characterized by similar workflows as well as a specifically defined content.[11] Therefore , the limit of such an electronic examination is reached where an evaluation by a judge is required in order to deliver the court decision.[12] However, in comparison to an ordinary judicial examination made by a judge the electronic examination is more precise as it is not dependent on the individual knowledge of the judge or on his emotional and physical condition. Another effect of an electronic judicial examination is that there is a greater possibility that similar cases are also decided in a similar fashion.[13] Since it is not always clear whether the facts of a case are applied in a correct way by the computer software, the parties should have the opportunity to ensure that the examination of the facts of the case is done by a human organ (e.g. a judge or court clerk). Therefore, it is required that the parties have the opportunity to object to the electronic decision which results in an examination by a human organ.[14] Such a far reaching electronic examination requires strict form requirements, however. Thus, formalism plays an important if not a central role within this extensive use of information technology in court proceedings.[15] This strict application of the formal requirements may however limit the parties in the presentation of their arguments as they will not be able to formulate their arguments as is the case in a writ of summons.[16] This limitation is not crucial, however, as written claims cannot be examined electronically. In this case, the parties should – once again – have the opportunity to have the decision re-examined by a human organ. Only at this stage of the procedure is a complete impression of the case is required.

---

11 Comp. H.W. FASCHING, 100 Jahre österreichische Zivilprozeßgesetze in: P.G. MAYR (ed.), 100 Jahre österreichische Zivilprozeßgesetze, 1998, S. 17, 29; R.H. VAN DEN HOOGEN, *E-Justice*, diss. Utrecht University 2007, p. 107, who speaks of '*clear cases*'.

12 Comp. H.W. FASCHING, 100 Jahre österreichische Zivilprozeßgesetze, p. 29 ff.; B. SUJECKI, Erste Überlegungen zum Europäischen elektronischen Mahnverfahren, *Multimedia und Recht (Multimedia and the Law)* 2005, 213, 214.

13 Vgl. R.H. VAN DEN HOOGEN, *E-Justice*, diss. Utrecht University 2007, p. 97.

14 An example is the German 'Mahnverfahren': the court software generates automatically generates an entitlement to enforcement and only if the defendant lodges a statement of defence, will a judge verify the claim. Comp. B. SUJECKI, *Mahnverfahren*, Müller Heidelberg 2007, nr. 161 f., 182.

15 Vgl. FASCHING, *100 Jahre österreichische Zivilprozeßgesetze*, p. 29.

16 Vgl. W. VIEFHUES/H. HOFFMANN, ERVG: Gesetz zur Verhinderung des elektronischen Rechtsverkehrs?, in: *Multimedia und Recht (Multimedia and the Law)* 2003, 71-76.

1.3. USE OF INFORMATION TECHNOLOGY AS A SOURCE OF KNOWLEDGE IN DUTCH CIVIL LITIGATION

Within the Dutch civil litigation, information technology is becoming increasingly more important as a source of knowledge. An example would be the website *www.rechtspraak.nl*. This website addresses the public and is visited daily by more than 100,000 people.[17] It contains all relevant information on court procedures (not only civil proceedings) as well as the different courts and their organization. Additionally, this website contains a databank with the pre-selected case law of the courts in the Netherlands. Finally, relevant provisions can be found on this Internet presentation. Exclusively for lawyers, a so-called *roljournaal* was introduced. With the *roljournaal* all registered lawyers can have access to the court registers or the cause list (the so-called *gerechtsrol*) and can see which procedures are pending in what court.[18] Whereas these websites are mainly addressed to the external parties in judicial proceedings, the judiciary uses its own internal information system, the so-called *Porta Iuris*. This internal information system contains 42 different databanks. Users have access to all the legal provisions of the Netherlands and the European Union. Additionally, *Porta Iuris* provides access to the databanks containing the case law as well as some legal publishers. Finally, the courts have the opportunity to create their own databank within the *Porta Iuris* system, where the case law of this court can be found. These databanks are not accessible to other courts or institutions.[19] Finally, a more general databank, the so-called *Intro*, has been introduced. This databank provides the members of the judiciary with daily news from the press as well as news form the judiciary. It also contains telephone books, programs to help supervise adjournments and to calculate the procedural costs as well as the interests.[20]

---

17 Vgl. R.H. van den Hoogen, E-rechtspraak, *Computerrecht* 2006, p. 249/250.

18 Comp. R.H. van den Hoogen, *E-Justice*, diss. Utrecht University 2007, p. 45.

19 See further on the *Porta Iuris*: R.H. van den Hoogen, E-rechtspraak, *Computerrecht* 2006, p. 249 ff.; R.H. van den Hoogen, Rechtspraak en informatietechnologie, in: *A. Oskamp/A.R. Lodder* (ed.), *Informatietechnologie voor juristen*, 2nd edition, Kluwer, Deventer 2002, p. 189, 192; A.D. Reiling, Rechtspraak in de digitale delta, *Nederlands Juristenblad* 2003, p. 2286, 2287.

20 Vgl. R.H. van den Hoogen, E-rechtspraak, *Computerrecht* 2006, p. 249, 252.

1.4. USE OF INFORMATION TECHNOLOGY TO IMPROVE THE COMMUNICATION WITHIN DUTCH CIVIL LITIGATION

Furthermore, information technology plays only a subsidiary role within civil litigation in the Netherlands. The Dutch Code of Civil Procedure does not contain any special regulations concerning e-justice. Article 33 of the Dutch Code of Civil Procedure is one exception, however. Before the introduction of the current version of Article 33 of the Dutch Code of Civil Procedure, documents could only be filed with a court during the opening hours of the court in question. Until ten years ago, there was no discussion on the question whether documents could also be filed with the court after or before the opening hours of the court as well. The Dutch Supreme Court decided in a judgment of 16th February 1996[21] that documents may also be filed with the court by means of a fax machine. In this case, the document may be submitted after opening hours. The registration of the time when the fax is submitted, which is usual in fax machines, is sufficient enough to determine whether, in the case of a time-limit, the document has reached the court on time. In this judgment, the Dutch Supreme Court additionally ruled that a document sent by fax to the court is on time if it was received before 12 p.m. on the last day of the set time limit.[22] This ruling was based on the fact that the parties to a judicial procedure should effectively be able to use the whole period of time that has been given to them. Therefore, the submission of the document after opening hours should be allowed. Furthermore, the Dutch Supreme Court ruled in a judgment of 20th March 1998[23] that whenever the court's fax machine does not register the time of the receipt of a fax, this can be achieved in a different way, such as a confirmation report by the addresser.

Additionally, the question was raised within the Dutch jurisdiction whether the signature on a petition transmitted by a fax fulfils all the formal requirements concerning a signature. According to the jurisdiction of the Dutch Supreme Court, a petition signed in an orderly manner containing a clearly visible signature and being transmitted to the court by means of a fax is considered to be a petition with an orderly signature.[24] However, if the petition sent by a fax does not contain an orderly signature by an attorney, it is defective. In this case, the party has the opportunity to remedy the defect

21 Hoge Raad 16th February 1996, *Nederlandse Jurisprudentie* (Dutch case law)1997, no. 55.

22 This ruling was re-affirmed by a later judgment of the Dutch Supreme Court, see Hoge Raad, 14th November 2003, *Nederlandse Jurisprudentie* (Dutch case law) 2004, no. 537.

23 Hoge Raad 20th March 1998 , *Nederlandse Jurisprudentie* (Dutch case law) 1998, no. 548.

24 Hoge Raad 27th November 1992, *Nederlandse Jurisprudentie* (Dutch case law) 1993, no. 569.

by submitting the original version of the petition which is signed in an orderly manner to the court within a short period of time.
Finally, case law had to determine the consequences of a defective fax transmission. Here one can think of situations where the transmission was defective, and the court in question was not responsible for this defect, for example a power failure. In these cases, the risk is borne by the addressor as he has chosen this method of transmission. Furthermore, the addressor has to take into consideration that there might be a possibility that, for example, the paper of the court's fax machine may have run out of paper and, therefore, the transmission might be impossible.[25]
This decision by the Dutch Supreme Court was laid down by law with the introduction of the current version of Article 33 of the Dutch Code of Civil Procedure on1st January 2002. This provision is applicable to transmission by means of a fax, but it does not specifically exclude other forms of electronic transmission, such as e-mail. However, it is not clear whether Article 33 of the Dutch Code of Civil Procedure actually has such a wide scope.[26] In order to remove all doubts an amendment to the law was desirable and this was introduced in 2006 and will enter into force on 1 September 2008.[27] According to the new Article 33 of the Dutch Code of Civil Procedure, all petitions and other documents may be filed electronically if this way of communication is allowed at the court in question, which has to be done by means of a separate decree. Additionally, the court may also send motions and other documents to the parties to the proceedings by using electronic means. According to the explanatory memorandum to the proposed Article 33 of the Dutch Code of Civil Procedure this new provision allows simple notifications as well as other more complex documents may be sent electronically. One exception, where electronic communication is not possible is the writ of summons. In this case, the original document has to be served on the defendant. Serving the writ of summons has to be done by a bailiff. Another example of a document that cannot be sent electronically from the court to

---

25 See further on this topic H.J. SNIJDERS, Het bereiken van een geadresseerde (per e-mail), *WPNR* 2001, p. 433 *seq.*, 457 *seq.*

26 See A.I.M. VAN MIERLO, in: A.I.M. VAN MIERLO/C.J.J.C. VAN NISPEN/M.V. POLAK (eds.), *Burgerlijke Rechtsvordering Tekst & Commentaar*, 3rd edition, 2008, Art. 33 Rv, section 2b, who is in favour of such a wide scope of Article 33 of the Dutch Code of Civil Procedure.

27 Wet van 20 maart 2008 tot wijziging van het Wetboek van Burgerlijke Rechtsvordering, de Advocatenwet en andere wetten in verband met het afschaffen van het procuraat in burgerlijke zaken en de invoering van elektronisch berichtenverkeer (Wet afschaffing procuraat en invoering elektronisch berichtenverkeer), Stb. 2008, 100 and Besluit van 3 juli 2008 tot vaststelling van het tijdstip van inwerkingtreding van de Wet afschaffing procuraat en invoering elektronisch berichtenverkeer, Stb. 2008, 274.

one of the parties is the judgment in an enforceable form.[28] This extensive use of electronic transmission will, however, not be introduced directly, but step by step. Additionally, the electronic transmission of documents from the court to the parties is only allowed if the receiving party has clearly indicated that it willing to receive court documents in this way. An exception to this will only be made in cases where a lawyer is to receive the document. As lawyers have to register their electronic mail address at the Chamber of Lawyers it will be assumed that the lawyers are reachable at this address as well.[29]

Besides the range of and the access to electronic transmission within civil litigation, the proposed Article 33 of the Dutch Code of Civil Procedure regulates the moment of the receipt of the electronic document as well. This is necessary in order to evaluate who is responsible for failures during the electronic transmission of the document. In the case of the transmission of a document from the parties to the court, the proposed Article 33 sec. 3 of the Dutch Code of Civil Procedure states that the document is received if it entered the data system of the court in question. If a time period has to be taken into consideration, the document is on time when it enters the computer system of the court before 12 p.m. of the last day of the time limit. This provision is identical to the current form of Article 33 of the Dutch Code of Civil Procedure applying solely to transmission via fax. In the case of an electronic transmission from the court to the parties, the transmission becomes effective when the electronic document has reached a computer system which the court does not control. This provision in the proposed Article 33 sec. 4 is reasonable, since it applies to the conventional transmission of documents. The receipt of a written document occurs not at the moment when the written document was actually read by the addressee, but at the moment when it enters the addressee's influence. When the document falls within the addressee's sphere of influence it is up to the addressee whether he opens and reads the document which he has received. At this moment, the court as the sending authority has done everything it can so that the addressee actually receives the document. Thus, here the responsibility for sending the document does not lie with the court.
Of course there are some requirements regarding the reliability and confidentiality of the electronic submission of applications and notices:

---

[28] Comp. Memorie van Toelichting, Kamerstukken II, 2006-2007, 30815, nr. 3, p. 14.
[29] Comp. Memorie van Toelichting, Kamerstukken II, 2006-2007, 30815, nr. 3, p. 14.

- a court should use a data processing system that is able to identify the sender and determine whether a message is authentic and actually emanates from the sender;
- a court should use a data processing system that is able to verify that the message is complete and not incompetent;
- a court should use a data system that is in accordance with national and international standards for furnishing information;
- a court should confirm electronically without delay the receipt of electronically transmitted requests and communications regarding the cause list.[30]

Finally, the proposed Article 33 sec. 2 of the Dutch Code of Civil Procedure empowers the Dutch Ministry of Justice to release detailed administrative rules on electronic transmission. Based on this provision, the Dutch Ministry of Justice can regulate which documents may be transmitted electronically. Since the electronic transmission has to provide at least the same guarantees in terms of security and especially party identification, the exact conditions of these guarantees may also be laid down in the administrative rules based on this provision. Within the explanatory memorandum, the question was raised how the parties should identify themselves in an electronically transmitted document. Since according to Article 3:15c of the Dutch Civil Code the substantive rules on electronic signature laid down in Article 3:15a and 3:15b of the Dutch Civil Code also apply outside property law, these substantive rules laid down in the Dutch Civil Code can be applicable here. Therefore, the electronically transmitted document must be signed with an electronic signature.[31] However, the explanatory memorandum does not further specify what kind of electronic signature will be required. This is left to the administrative rules that can be released on the basis of the proposed Article 33 sec. 2 of the Dutch Code of Civil Procedure. The administrative rules that can be released according to this provision may, furthermore, determine that certain documents can only be transmitted electronically. The communication between the court and the parties will then take place solely electronically. This extensive electronic communication requires however that the electronic communication functions properly in the judicial practice. Additionally, a sole electronic transmission of documents can only take place

30 Besluit van 3 juli 2008, houdende regels aangaande de betrouwbaarheid en vertrouwelijkheid van het elektronisch verzenden van verzoeken en mededelingen met betrekking tot de rol, Stb. 2008, 275.

31 Comp. Memorie van Toelichting, Kamerstukken II, 2006-2007, 30815, nr. 3, p. 14 ff.

in procedures where a statutory requirement to be represented by a lawyer is not prescribed. This ensures, as the explanatory memorandum points out, that the procedure is accessible not only via the electronic but also via conventional means.[32] Since, on the contrary, lawyers are obliged to give their e-mail address to the Chamber of Lawyers, it is assumed that they can submit their document electronically. In order to prevent a conventional admission by the lawyers and to stimulate the use of the electronic communication, the transmission of the documents can only take place electronically in cases where a statutory requirement to be represented by a lawyer is prescribed.

2. DIRECT USE OF INFORMATION TECHNOLOGY FOR THE PROCESSING OF JUDICIAL PROCEDURE WITHIN THE DUTCH CIVIL LITIGATION

2.1. MONETARY CLAIMS ONLINE

Next to these examples information technology does not have further reaching impact within the Dutch civil procedure. However, there are some pilot projects within the judiciary where the use of information technology is being tested within the civil procedure.[33] In these pilot projects information technology is being tested in all different forms within civil litigation.[34]

---

[32] Comp. Memorie van Toelichting, Kamerstukken II, 2006-2007, 30815, nr. 3, p. 15.

[33] See an overview of the current projects: R.H. VAN DEN HOOGEN, E-rechtspraak, *Computerrecht* 2006, p. 249 ff; R.H. VAN DEN HOOGEN, Rechtspraak en informatietechnologie, in: A. OSKAMP/A.R. LODDER (ed.), *Informatietechnologie voor juristen*, 2nd edition, Kluwer, Deventer 2002, p. 189 *seq.*; A.D. REILING, Rechtspraak in de digitale delta, *Nederlands Juristenblad* 2003, p. 2286 *et seq.*

[34] For this reason the Dutch judiciary established the so-called *ICT-Proeflokaal* at the regional court of Zutphen. The *ICT-Proeflokaal* is a courtroom in which the necessity of information technology for the judiciary is being tested under real conditions. This very interesting project was brought to an end, however. See further on the *ICT-Proeflokaal*: „Das *ICT–Proeflokaal* – Der elektronische Rechtsverkehr in den Niederlanden“, in: E. SCHWEIGHOFER ea. (ed.), Informationstechnik in der juristischen Realität, *Jahrbuch Rechtsinformatik*, Verlag Österreich, Vienna 2004, p. 323 ff..

One of the pilot projects is the so-called *Geldvordering (Monetary Claims) Online* procedure.[35] This procedure was set up under the supervision of the Dutch Council for the Judiciary (*Raad voor de Rechtspraak*) in cooperation with the Dutch Royal Professional Association of Judicial Officers. This procedure is basically based on the English *Money Claim Online*. Even though the Dutch Council for the Judiciary worked on the introduction of the *Geldvordering Online* procedure since 2003, at the end of 2006 this project was brought to an end. The reason for this is not entirely clear ('a result of unforeseen complexity').[36] The developments on the EU level with the introduction of such a procedure could have had an effect on the decision to end the project. As the *Geldvordering Online* procedure is the first and so far the only fully automated civil procedure developed in the Netherlands, it is surely of interest for this questionnaire and will be described. Another reason for halting this project could have been a financial one.

It has to be mentioned that some were rather sceptical concerning the project, such as the Royal Dutch Association of Bailiffs. They stated that regarding an order for payment, no matter how far it is automated, there would always be a phase when the alleged undisputed of the claim had to be verified. That would require a warning being issued to the opposite party. Without such verification the issuing of a writ of execution would be unfair and an order for payment, which the postal summons warning should replace, would not able to match an automated procedure regarding the writ of summons, neither as regards security, nor speed. It had to lead to the formal observance of longer periods. Illustrative is the difference between the deadline after which a party may be summoned - eight days in principle - and the time within which a court will order a European Enforcement Title that can be executed. In the European order for payment there are three distinct

---

35 R.H. VAN DEN HOOGEN, *E-Justice*, diss. Utrecht University 2007, p. 47, A.W. JONGBLOED, 'Ontwikkelingen in het burgerlijk proces ten gevolge van het toenemend gebruik van ICT', *Executief*, 2001, p. 56-64 and A.W. JONGBLOED, Judicial Case Management and Efficiency in The Netherlands, in: C.H. VAN RHEE (ed.), *Judicial case management and efficiency in civil litigation*, Intersentia Antwerpen-Oxford 2007, p. 103. *Jaarplan voor de Rechtspraak* 2006, p. 10 en *Jaarplan voor de Rechtspraak* 2005, p. 25, both to be found at <www.rechtspraak.nl/Gerechten/RvdR/>.

36 On page 24 of Jaarplan Rechtspraak 2007 (Annual Plan for the Judiciary) it is stated that the automation of that form is now imminent and the aim is that in the short term a limited pilot project with a limited circle of agents in one location will be executed. Later on the circle of users and the sites could be expanded. The results of the pilot project should have been made known in 2007. But by mid-2008, one can say this has been too optimistic thought, because as yet nothing has been learned from the project. A positive result of the project is that now there is a standard writ of summons which has been accepted by both subdistrict court judges as well as by bailiffs.

periods: the time - usually no longer than thirty days - for the issuing of a warrant that cannot not yet be executed, the time involved in the judicial service of that order and finally at least thirty days to oppose that order.

The introduction of the *Geldvordering Online* procedure aims to introduce a fully electronic civil procedure, which is based on the current legal basis contained in the Dutch Code of Civil Procedure. With this procedure creditors should obtain a legal instrument which enables them to execute their pecuniary claims in an expeditious, inexpensive and efficient way. Another aim of this procedure is to lessen the judiciary's so-called bulk cases. In these cases the judiciary does not fulfil a judging function as there is no real dispute, but rather an administrative role, since the courts make executorial titles. The introduction of the *Geldvordering Online* therefore results in a reduction of the number of judicial stuff. Finally, the Dutch Council for the Judiciary wants to increase the quality of Dutch civil litigation by introducing this electronic procedure. It is especially useful regarding debt collection cases as these cases are mostly standard. In the slightly longer term this leads to efficiency gains for the Judiciary.
In order first to test the practicability of the use of information technology within the judiciary the *Geldvordering Online* procedure shall only be applicable to pecuniary claims based on a contractual relationship where the amount of the claim does not exceed € 5,000. Therefore, this procedure is exclusively applicable in local court proceedings. This scope of application additionally guarantees that a statutory requirement to be represented by a lawyer is not prescribed and therefore the legal costs of this procedure are kept low. Before the *Geldvordering Online* can be started, the claimant is required to apply for a so-called *DigiD*.

2.2. DIGID: DIGITAL IDENTITY

The *DigiD* is a system which is shared between cooperating governmental agencies and which allows for the digital authentication of the identity of a person who applies for a transaction service via the internet, this can be used for identification at different Dutch authorities.[37] After the claimant has

---

[37] See for further details the website of this service: http://www.digid.nl/english/
The Social Insurance Bank (SVB, Sociale Verzekeringsbank), the Centre for Work and Income (CWI, Centrum voor Werk en Inkomen), the Employee Insurance Schemes Implementing Body (UWV, Uitvoeringsinstituut Werknemersverzekeringen), the Tax Authorities (Belastingdienst) and increasing numbers of local authorities are already connected up to DigiD, with many institutions following their example.

received his *DigiD*, he then has to access the central website of the judiciary, www.rechtspraak.nl, where he has to identify himself by using his *DigiD*. Afterwards he can fill out an electronic form which basically corresponds to the current form of a writ of summons. As one of the aims is to create an electronic judicial procedure which is also accessible to claimants without a judicial training, the language used in this form had to be kept simple. Regarding the form and language of the current form of the writ of summons, the design of the electronic writ of summons is one of the major problems within the *Geldvordering Online* procedure. Even if the detailed form and content of the electronic form is not finally regulated, the claimant has to provide the court with all general information on the parties and the court. Additionally, the claimant has to sufficiently describe the claim including all evidence as well as all known arguments brought forward by the defendant for not fulfilling his obligation. During the completion of the electronic form the claimant will be guided by a computer program which provides him with all necessary information and shows him all the mistakes he has made in filling out the form. This reduces the amount of default writs of summons being submitted to the courts. After filling out the form, the electronic writ of summons will be transferred to a bailiff with the request to serve it on the defendant. At this moment the claimant has to pay all the accruing legal costs. To stimulate the use of the *Geldvordering-Online* the introduction of a reduced tariff is taken into consideration by the Dutch authority. After serving the writ of summons the bailiff submits the writ of summons to the competent court and the procedure then follows its normal path.

The number of electronic services available through DigiD is continually increasing. It is already possible to submit online applications to the Social Insurance Bank (SVB) for child benefit allowances and statutory old age pensions as well as digitally signing a tax declaration at the Tax Authorities (Belastingdienst). One can also contact an increasing number of municipal authorities for internet-based services including:

- Requesting a copy of the municipal personal records database
- Applying for various permits
- Notifying of a change of address
- To discover the value of real estate
- Paying municipal taxes
- Paying parking fines

DigiD makes sure that the service it provides is as reliable as possible. After logging in, a secure connection is safeguarded using a Secure Socket Layer (SSL). This is a security technique protecting the flow of data between one's computer and DigiD, rendering it unreadable to any prospective third party. Indicating this, a closed lock icon is displayed in one's browser window. In addition to this, DigiD can rely on the system being tested regularly by an independent professional party.

Another impact on a more extensive introduction of the use of information technology within civil litigation in the Netherlands could be (EC) Regulation no. 1896/2006[38] introducing a European order for payment procedure. Since the European order for payment procedure, which will come into force on 12th December 2008, has a structure that basically allows an extensive use of information technology,[39] the Dutch legislator may use this opportunity to introduce information technology within this procedure.[40] As the European order for payment procedure is only applicable to claims relating to cross-border relationships, its scope is limited to a relatively small number of cases. Therefore, the use of information technology within civil litigation can be along the lines of the European order for payment procedure.

2.3. DAGVAARDING ONLINE (ONLINE SUMMONSES) AND DIGIDEUR

When the Dutch Council for the Judiciary took the decision in December 2006 to halt the above-mentioned project Geldvordering Online project, the Royal Organisation of Bailiffs (KBvG) had already put much time and energy into the project. Although they were somewhat sceptical, opportunities for the project were also seen, but this time in the form of Dagvaarding Online (Online Summonses). It is intended that everyone can fill in a model writ of summons to create one's own (draft) summons for a procedure before a subdistrict court. After payment (through direct debit) of a sum of several dozen euro's, the bailiff will commence the procedure before the competent court and he will return a copy of the summons to the client. Then the client can choose. Either he takes care of the procedure himself, because there is no mandatory legal representation in procedures before a subdistrict court or he will ask the bailiff to continue the proceedings. Of course it will be possible to give a bailiff via e-mail the information necessary so that the bailiff will prepare the summons. It is a service especially for the recovery of money by small and medium-sized enterprises. In many other cases it will soon become evident that it is too complex to create a writ of summons. This project is still in a (comprehensive) test phase.

---

38 Regulation (EC) no. 1896/2006 of the European Parliament and of the Council of 12 December 2006 creating a European order for payment procedure, OJ L 399, 30.12.2006, p. 1.

39 See further on this use B. SUJECKI, Initial Steps Towards an Electronic European Order for Payment Procedure, *Computer Law Review International* (CRi) 2006, p. 111 ff., 113.

40 See further on this topic B. SUJECKI, *Das elektronische Mahnverfahren*, Mohr Siebeck Tübingen 2008.

In line with this some bailiff offices have already received orders via e-mail. One example is DigiDeur.[41] Every year hundreds of thousands of official acts by bailiffs take place in the Netherlands. These instructions have been given in the vast majority of cases by ordinary mail. With the simple digital transmission of official acts between the client and the bailiff Digideur distinguishes itself from other providers in this market. Through the use of available modern communication facilities, including the means of transmission of digital official acts, Digideur would contribute to the promotion of efficient, safe, rapid and inexpensive communication between the client and the bailiff. The bailiffs selected by Digideur guarantee a prompt and thorough implementation of the given official acts throughout the Netherlands.

2.4. DIGITAL LITIGATION IN THE ADMINISTRATIVE COURTS

In the near future citizens will be able to digitally litigate in the administrative courts.[42] This means that pleadings and appeal can be transmitted electronically. The Ministerial Council approved such a bill on 11th July 2008. This provides a legal basis for rapid, reliable and confidential electronic communications between citizens and the administrative courts.
The proposed arrangement is consistent with the growing need in practice to adopt electronic capabilities during an administrative procedure. It stimulates the administrative courts to develop further digital litigation. This form of exercise has significant advantages. First it promotes the accessibility of administrative justice. In addition, the availability of digital pleadings will reduce the time it takes to reach a decision. Electronically sent documents can be stored easily and be consulted quickly by the treatment of new appeals. This is in contrast to paper documents, which need a great deal of storage space and cost money. Modern communication is efficient and over time it can lead to significant cost savings in the courts.
The citizen may start a procedure digitally, but this is not obligatory: there is no duty to engage in digital litigation. A person who, for whatever reason,

---

41 www.digideur.nl.

42 This is one of the consequences of the entry into force on June 1, 2004 of the Wet Elektronisch Bestuurlijk Verkeer (Executive Electronic Communications Act), 29 April 2004, Stb. 2004, 214. It added to the Algemene wet bestuursrecht (General Administrative Law Act) Articles 2:13-2:17. Now citizens and governing bodies can transmit an electronic message to each other, unless there is a special legal requirement that excludes this possibility.

does not make use of e-mail to start a procedure may in the future continue to pursue the paper route.

In 2007 the district courts in Rotterdam, Breda and Dordrecht started the project entitled "digital administrative procedure" which inter alia projects with electronic notices of appeal and the digital management of case files. In this way the courts wanted to see how the electronic traffic between parties and the administrative court could be shaped as efficiently as possible and what impact this might have on the management and the relationship between the different parties.
The Rotterdam district court started with the pilot digital file for competition and telecom cases and 50 cases are expected to be digitally processed. The pilot digital file was undertaken to gain experience with paperless work and it lasted for a year.
In the pilot project the following were examined:

- Electronic Data Interchange between the court and the litigants;
- The capture and consulting of all documents in an electronic file during all stages of proceedings, both by the court members and by the litigants;
- Electronically notifying the parties concerned and the stakeholders on changes in the file;
- The digital preparation of a case by the court members;
- Conducting a digital session.

After receiving a notice to start a procedure in a competition or telecom case a court member makes a digital file. The proceeding parties are authorized to access the digital file. From that moment, communication between the court and the litigants is done digitally, via a secure connection. This security is comparable to the security that banks use on the Internet.
The court puts all the documents in the digital file. This file can always be digitally consulted by anyone who is authorized to access this file. A meeting will take place in a special "digital courtroom" which is equipped with network connections. During the session the litigants and the court have access to the digital file.
A little bit earlier, from April 2007, it became possible for a number of administrative matters to lodge a procedure at the district court of Breda via the Internet. The Employee Insurance Schemes Implementing Body (UWV, Uitvoeringsinstituut Werknemersverzekeringen) in Breda designated its customers by issuing decisions on objections in social insurance on the ability to digitally appeal to the court. One can get a form at a special secure website, but the further procedure is not yet digital. It is also possible starting a procedure by simply sending a letter to the district court.

2.5. OTHER APPLICATIONS

The Almelo district court was the first court in the Netherlands to offer the opportunity to use the Internet to complain about the conduct aimed at "customers" of the court.
So far, only the text of the complaint procedure is published on the court's website. Complainants could previously only complain in writing to the administration. It is now possible via the Internet to make a complaint and to submit it. The program that the court Almelo has developed, leads the user in a few simple steps through the complaints procedure. Users can thus assess for themselves whether the court will deal with the allegations. In addition, the program helps them to incorporate all relevant information in the complaint. Working with this program promotes the smooth handling of a complaint.

In criminal cases digital case files have existed for more than five years. In November 2002 the Amsterdam district court started to use "digital dossiers" for the police court. The documents received are immediately scanned, so that everyone has access to an identical file. Documents and letters can be placed in the dossier more quickly. During the meeting the judge, the judge's clerk, the case officer and the lawyer can read from displays. To the accused and the public parts of the dossier can be shown through a projection screen. The system also offers the ability to include sound and video in the file. The paper file remains the source of the case and is made available to the legal profession inn the usual manner. The digital file does offer certain advantages. A better organization is possible and the search can be improved. The digital file can be consulted by different people at the same time and one no longer needs to wait for the paper file, which the paper decreases. This leads to more effective communication in the criminal procedure. Court staff and the public prosecutor's office prepare themselves with the digital file on the use of "intelligent agents", super-fast search engines, which can assist judges and district attorneys in their work.
Finally, it could be stated that the courts and the Council for the Judiciary digitally publish their annual reports through their website and www.rechtspraak.nl. Information regarding the court sessions is digitally available. Through image (plasma) screens in the central waiting room of the court that information can be given, including on the commencement of meetings and planning. This enables visitors, lawyers, witnesses, interpreters and journalists on arrival in the public waiting room to immediately see where the meeting is taking place and whether the sessions are on time. When a session runs out of time and the next session will have a later start,

this information can be relayed from the courtroom and will be immediately visible on the screens in the waiting room.

2.6. TOWARD A EUROPEAN STRATEGY ON E-JUSTICE

On 30th May 2008 the European Commission sent a Communication to the European Parliament, the Council and the EESC presenting ideas for the use of Information Society tools in the field of justice.[43] The Communication deals with current and future initiatives which will help to promote the European Justice Area. Vice-President Jacques Barrot, the Commissioner responsible for Justice Freedom and Security declared: "European citizens and businesses advocate better justice systems across Europe, which are capable of delivering better results in a more efficient way. The Commission believes that e-Justice can provide effective tools to make justice easier to access, speedier and less costly." "Judges, prosecutors and legal practitioners are also more and more vocal in demanding more effective judicial co-operation within the EU. This is also essential in order to provide adequate responses to cross-border crime. e-Justice can contribute to this aim too", he added.

For several years, initiatives in the field of e-Justice have been initiated at the national level or thanks to co-operation between some governments. With this Communication, the Commission draws up an inventory of the existing projects and proposes coordinated action at the EU level in the future in order to avoid risks of diverging technical solutions.

The objectives of e-Justice, which encompasses both criminal and civil justice, are broadly the following:

a. The creation of a *European portal* designed to facilitate *access to justice* by citizens and businesses across Europe. It will include relevant and updated information on the *rights of defendants and victims* in criminal proceedings and on the remedies available before the courts of another Member State in the event of cross-border disputes. To make it possible to exercise those rights in practice, the portal will also provide guidance to find the competent court or tribunal in the relevant country. Furthermore, the portal may allow access to certain on-line procedures, already foreseen in existing EU regulations, such as debt recovery action for small claims.

---

43 Communication from the Commission to the Council, the European Parliament and the European Economic and Social Committee, Towards a European e-Justice Strategy, SEC(2008)1947, SEC(2008)1944, and the Accompanying document to the Communication to the Council, the European Parliament and the European Economic and Social Committee "Towards a European strategy on e-Justice" COM(2008)329 final, SEC(2008)1947. Comp. Dutch Parliamentary documents 23 490, no. 509, p. 8/9.

b. The reinforcement of *judicial co-operation* on the basis of existing legal instruments. An area of major concern to the Commission will be the interconnection of Criminal Record Databases. This ongoing project allows judges and enforcement agencies across the EU to take account of defendants' past criminal convictions. The Commission also considers other actions, concerning exchanges of information between legal practitioners (for which a specially secured network will have to be devised), enhanced recourse to videoconference (so far, this possibility is little used in cross-border proceedings) and innovative translation tools, such as automatic translation, dynamic forms and a European database of legal translators and interpreters.
The e-Justice strategy, largely underpinned by the 2006-2010 e-Commission strategy, will represent a major challenge for the Commission in the coming years. Important human and financial resources will be mobilised in this exercise.

On page 3 of the Communication it is pointed out that the e-Justice approach uses ICT to improve citizens' access to justice and to make legal action more effective, the latter being understood as any type of activity involving the resolution of a dispute or the punishment of criminal behaviour. If judicial systems are to be modernised, the further development of E-Justice is crucial. The Commission, for its part, has long encouraged the use of ICT to promote judicial cooperation. Since 2003, the Commission has developed the portal of the European Judicial Network in civil and commercial matters,[44] and supported the creation of legal "atlases" for criminal and civil law, which enable professionals to identify competent legal authorities in the Member States. Similarly, the Commission has always encouraged the use of videoconferencing and the electronic transmission of acts between legal authorities and is actively involved in efforts to interconnect criminal records. E-Justice is a specific field under the more general umbrella of e-Government. E-Government refers to the application of ICT to all administrative procedures. Existing expertise in secure infrastructure and document authentication projects must be mobilised. The Commission intends to promote a European Interoperability Framework (EIF) within the IDABC programme.[45] European work on eSignature and e-Identity[46] is

44 http://ec.europa.eu/civiljustice/

45 http://ec.europa.eu/idabc/ Preliminary study on mutual recognition of e-Signatures for e-Governmentapplications (2007) and eID Interoperability for PEGS (2007).

46 Standardisation aspects of e-Signature (2007) http://ec.europa.eu/information_society/eeurope/i2010/docs/esignatures/e_signatures_standardisation.pdf.

particularly relevant in the legal field, where the authentication of acts is essential. E-Justice's potential scope is very wide-ranging and will have to evolve in tandem with the European judicial area and new technologies. Specific projects, however, should be initiated quickly. A perimeter for future action must be defined so that overextension does not handicap the effectiveness and credibility of EU action. Some projects pertain not to the legal sector, but rather to e-Government. And so, certain activities that sometimes involve legal institutions are themselves rather administrative in nature (e.g. land registers or the European Business Register).[47] Conversely, activities such as arbitration or alternative dispute resolution (ADR) mechanisms could be concerned with E-Justice, even when they are managed by non-legal bodies.
For the Commission, e-Justice's primary objective is to help justice to be administered more effectively throughout Europe, for the benefit of citizens. The first hallmark of priority projects should be that they help legal professionals work more effectively and citizens obtain justice more easily. They must also contribute to the implementation of existing European instruments in the field of justice and, potentially, involve all or a large majority of Member States.

47 COM(2007) 807, section 4.2.; www.ebr.org; www.briteprojet.net

CIVIL CASE MANAGEMENT: THE BELGIAN DEBATE AND REFORMS [1]

B. ALLEMEERSCH

1. INTRODUCTION

Case management has been a hot topic in civil procedural theory for more than two decades now. The concept behind case management is that the procedural treatment of a case should not be driven by the parties' strategies, but should be taken in hand and controlled by the court. It is the court that bears responsibility for the swift and efficient administration of justice, and therefore has to steer the case through the procedure – not just during hearings, but also during preparatory phases. To this end, courts have developed various approaches, which together we call 'case management'. The term suggests a new understanding of the judge's role in civil litigation, his mission being not only to decide the case as the parties present it to him, but also to manage the caseload that confronts his court in a way that every procedure is dealt with in the most efficient manner. It is clear that this implies a significant increase in the judge's powers; for that reason it may be surprising to continental lawyers that of all procedural systems, it is the American that put the idea of judicial case management on the research agenda of comparative proceduralists. Indeed, it was in the United States that the first case management pilot projects were conducted in the late 1970s, on the basis of which Professor Resnik published her standard-setting article, 'Managerial judges',[2] in the Harvard Law Journal. This does not mean, however, that American civil procedure was the first to give judges a larger role in the procedural treatment of cases. A number of European legal systems had already introduced and amended civil procedure rules, allowing judges of

---

1 The original text of this contribution, titled "The Belgian perspective on case management in civil litigation", was written in October 2006 (published in A. Pellegrini Grinover en P. Calmon (eds.), Direito Processual Comparado. XIIIth World Congress of Procedural Law, Rio de Janeiro, Editora Forense, 2007, 636-647; also in: C.H. VAN RHEE (ed.), Judicial Case Management and Efficiency in Civil Litigation, Antwerpen, Intersentia, 2007, 79 92). Meanwhile, important evolutions have taken place and the text was amended in May 2008 to reflect these.

2 RESNIK, J., 'Managerial judges', *Harvard Law Review*, 1982 (96), p. 374-448.

civil lawsuits to act more as a manager than as an umpire. France's early implementation of the *juge de la mise en état* was pioneering in this respect. In Germany the first steps towards an expansion of the judge's function to include what is called *Formelle Prozessleitung* were taken at the beginning of the twentieth century; those early attempts subsequently resulted in the implementation of the so-called 'Stuttgart-model'[3] in the 1970s. Finally, in England, under the inspiring leadership of Lord Woolf, a new set of procedural norms was drawn up in the form of the Civil Procedure Rules 1999, wherein judges were granted extensive powers 'to prevent unnecessary delay, expense and unfairness'.[4] The Council of Europe had previously advocated a more active role for judges in civil litigation. Recommendation No. 84/5 of the Committee of Ministers states that:

The court should, at least during the preliminary hearing but if possible throughout the proceedings, play an active role in ensuring the rapid progress of the proceedings, while respecting the rights of the parties, including the right to equal treatment. In particular, it should have proprio motu powers to order the parties to provide such clarifications as are necessary; to order the parties to appear in person; to raise questions of law; to call for evidence, at least in those cases where there are interests other than those of the parties at stake; to control the taking of evidence; to exclude witnesses whose possible testimony would be irrelevant to the case; to limit the number of witnesses on a particular fact where such a number would be excessive. These powers should be exercised without going beyond the object of the proceedings.[5]

The drafters of the 'Transnational Principles of Civil Procedure', who clearly also opt for an active role for civil judges, took a similar position,[6] as is apparent from the combined reading of the following principles in that document:

---

3 See OBERHAMMER, P. & DOMEJ, T., 'Germany, Switzerland and Austria', in: Van Rhee, C.H. (ed.), European Traditions in Civil Procedure, Ius Commune Europaeum 54, Antwerp: Intersentia, 2005, p. 215-221.

4 See, among many other articles, e.g. ANDREWS, N., 'A new Civil Procedural Code for England: Party Control "Going, Going, Gone"', Zeitschrift für Zivilprozeß International, 1999, p. 3-25.

5 Recommendation R (84)5, adopted 28 February 1984 by the Committee of Ministers of the Council of Europe, <http://www.coe.int> (last consulted in June 2007).

6 ALI/Unidroit, 'Transnational Principles of Civil Procedure', Uniform Law Review, 2004 (4), p. 758-808 (see also <http://www.unidroit.org>, last consulted in June 2007).

Commencing as early as practicable, the court should actively manage the proceeding, exercising discretion to achieve disposition of the dispute fairly, efficiently and with reasonable speed (Principle 14.1)
The court should determine the order in which issues are to be resolved, and fix a timetable for all stages of the proceeding, including dates and deadlines (Principle 14.3)

The court may, while affording the parties opportunity to respond: (...) Permit or invite a party to amend its contentions of law or fact and to offer additional legal argument and evidence accordingly; (...) Order the taking of evidence not previously suggested by a party; (...) Rely upon a legal theory or an interpretation of the facts or of the evidence that has not been advanced by a party (Principle 22.2).

These important changes went largely unnoticed in Belgium. This does not mean, however, that the role of the judge in civil litigation, and in the preparatory phase in particular, have not been a concern in this country. On the contrary, it has been the subject of heated debate, as both parliament and the government have discussed the introduction to the procedural system the concept of what is called 'the active judge'. Their motive will sound familiar: the criticism that civil litigation is too slow, too laborious, and too expensive. Sir Jack Jacob's 'three-headed hydra' (costs, vexation and delay)[7] exists in Belgium and fuels frequent social and professional debate on the future of the Belgian civil justice system.

The aim of the present paper is to provide a short outline of the Belgian evolutions in civil litigation case management.[8] To this end, I will concentrate primarily on Belgian judges' role in the preparatory phase of the case, which in French is called la *mise en état* and in Dutch *de ingereedheidbrenging.* This part of the lawsuit raises questions about the extent to which judges may determine time limits for the exchange of evidence and memorandums or decide ex officio when the oral hearing of the case before the court will take place. It should be noted that the concept of 'case management' often receives a broader interpretation in the Anglo-Saxon world, where it also determines the judge's ability to control the introduction of evidence or attempts to reach

7 JACOB, J., The Fabric of English Civil Justice, London: Stevens & Sons, 1987.
8 For further information about the role of the Belgian judge in general, consult Georges, F., 'Le pouvoir discrétionnaire du juge: rapport Belge', in: Storme, M. & Hess, B. (eds.), Discretionary power of the judge: limits and control, Mechelen: Kluwer, 2003, p. 377-393

an amicable settlement of a dispute. These issues rarely arise in the Belgian case management debate, perhaps because the Belgian judge's role to a great degree already includes these. We will examine these matters in less detail in the last chapters of this text.

2. CASE MANAGEMENT AND MISE EN ÉTAT: PRINCIPLES AND MAIN LEGAL DEVELOPMENTS UNTIL THE REFORM OF 2007

The rules that govern the preparatory stage of a civil case are inspired, historically, by the principle of party control over the proceedings. In French literature this is called *le principe accusatoire*; in Germany one speaks of the *Grundsatz der Parteiherrschaft*. It originates from the outspoken liberalism that existed in Europe at the time of the creation of the French *Code de procédure civile*, which was also introduced in Belgium.[9] It was effective in Belgium until 1970 and has greatly influenced Belgian views concerning the conduct of civil litigation. The old French code restricted the role of the judge predominantly to that of a sort of notary or umpire: the judge was there strictly to witness the procedural acts entered by the parties and for the rest to impose the formalities dictated by the law. There was not much room for the judge's own initiative or for interpretation: the procedure was to a large extent lead by the parties, who decided for themselves at what pace they wished to conduct their case. The doctrinal philosophy behind this style of procedure was one of an instinctive distrust of the judge, whose power had to be suppressed as far as possible in order to protect the rights of the parties. The norm was the judge's impartiality; it was thought that this could only be guaranteed by restricting the judge's role to a passive one. That explains why, initially, French legal literature primarily spoke of the principle of neutrality (*principe de neutralité*), instead of the principle of passivity of the judge.[10] As procedural theory developed, it became clear that neutrality and passivity are two different things and the use of the term neutrality in this context fell into

---

9 For more details and references for further reading, see WIJFFELS, A., 'French civil procedure (1806-1975)' & 'Powers of the judge – France', in: VAN RHEE, C.H. (ed.), *European Traditions in Civil Procedure*, Ius Commune Europaeum 54, Antwerp: Intersentia, 2005, p. 25-47 & p. 269-279.

10 E.g. in BARTIN, E., Aubry & Rau – Droit civil français, Vol. XII, p. 75, footnote 8ter; Planiol & Ripert 1954, Nr. 1416, p. 839 Paris: Librairies Techniques Juris-Classeurs, 1922.

abeyance.[11] In Belgium the basis for the allocation of tasks during litigation was instead found more and more frequently in the so-called dispositive principle (*principe dispositif*).[12] This principle probably arising first in Italian legal doctrine[13] but actively propagated by the French proceduralist Henri Motulsky,[14] states that it is the parties that decide if a particular dispute will be brought before the court and, especially, to what extent this is done. In other words, it gives the *materielle Processleitung*, the prerogative of identifying the subject matter of the dispute, to the parties. In Belgian legal doctrine, the formal (procedural) and substantive issues of the civil action are still often confounded. The justification for the approach is this: if the parties can decide if and to what extent they bring their dispute before a court, they can then also determine how long the procedure should take, what particular steps in the proceedings should be taken and when.

Until 2007, this view still prevailed in the Belgian debate on civil procedure. This did not mean, however, that the situation was exactly the same as it was two hundred years ago. Although the parties were still in charge of the conduct of the action, delicate changes had already been made to their relationship to the judge. The turning points in this evolution were the implementation of the Judicial Code of 1967 and the amendment of the rules of the *mise en état* (*ingereedheidbrenging*) in 1992 and 1995.

The Judicial Code was framed in the 1960s to replace the French Code of Civil Procedure. The Judicial Code was largely written by *bâtonnier* Charles Van Reepinghen, whose work was supported by thorough comparative legal research.[15] One of the most important intentions of the new Code was to push back legal formalism. The legislation was intended to simplify civil procedure, and to this end abolished a large number of old customary rules and formalities. The judge acquired some new powers to monitor the progress of a case, *inter alia* by the establishment of a so-called 'judicial case-file'. Van

---

11 Among many other authors, see for example Kohl, A., *Procès civil et sincérité*, Liège: Faculté de Droit de Liège, 1971, p. 172, footnote 1.

12 See in particular the contributions by Rigaux, F., *La nature du contrôle de la Cour de cassation*, Brussels: Bruylant, 1966, p. 46-65 and Rigaux, F., 'L'objet et la cause de la demande en droit judiciaire privé', case note under Court of Cassation 4 May 1972, *Revue Critique de Jurisprudence Belge*, 1973, p. 243-244, as well as the contribution by the late Attorney-General W.J. Ganshof van der Meersch 1970, p. 85.

13 In the publications of – amongst others – Calamandrei and Carnellutti.

14 See the collection of his most influential writings, published in his honour and memory: Motulsky, H., *Écrits – Études et notes de procédure civile*, Paris: Dalloz, 1973.

15 The results of this research can be found in Van Reepinghen, Ch., *Rapport concernant la réforme judiciaire*, Brussels: Moniteur Belge, 1964.

Reepinghen still relied heavily on the goodwill of lawyers and their willingness to apply the rules of civil procedure in a spirit of cooperation and good faith, as intended by legislation, to drive the pace of litigation. This is easily illustrated by the fact that the time limits set for the delivery of attorneys' statements of case to the court were not enforceable. Van Reepinghen's confidence was soon betrayed, however: despite the implementation of deontological rules that made dilatory behaviour unlawful, procedural manipulation and quibbling by lawyers, intent on stretching proceedings as long as possible in order to drive up costs, persisted.

To solve this problem once and for all, the procedural rules were thoroughly amended in 1992. Henceforth, 'loyal' parties confronted with undue delay might ask the judge to set a so-called 'procedural calendar' imposing strict time limits for the exchange of memorandums, written motions and evidence, and to appoint a date for the final hearing of the case.[16] If a party exceeds the time limits or fails to appear at the oral hearing, the judge can enforce his order ex officio by no longer accepting late statements of case or by disregarding the absence of the party in question. 'Last minute' manoeuvres are no longer accepted outside exceptional circumstances, wherein new information has surfaced which in the court's opinion warrants an additional round of briefs or motions.[17]

It was some time before the courts became familiar with the new rules and started to make full use of their newly acquired powers. The practice then became well established, however, and there was wide consensus that the cooperation between diligent parties and the judge in the fight against obstructive opponents had been successful.

Jurisprudence added significantly to the 1992 and 1995 rules. For example, as a request for a procedural calendar carries with it certain administrative burdens, courts encouraged parties to forego formalities and agree such a calendar amongst themselves, preferably at the time the action is initiated. Even though the Judicial Code did not provide for any sanction for breaching such an informal, private procedural arrangement, the Belgian Court of Cassation confirmed the court's right to disregard any brief or evidence presented beyond the time limits set by this mutual agreement.[18]

---

16 Article 747(2) Judicial Code. Similar provisions are to be found in Articles 751 and 753.

17 Article 748(2) Judicial Code.

18 Court of Cassation 1 June 2001, *Algemeen Juridisch Tijdschrift* 2001-02, 528, with case note by E. BREWAEYS; also published in *Tijdschrift voor Procesrecht en Bewijsrecht/Revue de Droit Judiciaire et de la Preuve* 2002, 42 with case note by P. TAELMAN & P. THION and in *Rechtskundig Weekblad* 2002-03, 134, with

Furthermore, occasional loopholes in the law were closed by case law based on the general principles of due process and fair play, and a ban on the abuse of rules of procedure. For instance, courts acquired the power to rule out legal briefs when these are presented at a time or in a way that disrupts what is called the 'good administration of justice', even if this was done within the time limits originally set by the court or by law.[19]

What is important is that one common thread ran throughout this approach: although the judge had received ample powers at his disposal to organise the preparation of the hearing and to impose sanctions at his own discretion, he could only exercise these powers at the request of one of the parties. If neither party made such a request, the judge had no choice but to watch and wait as the parties litigate at their own pace. Even if a party seeked a judge's intervention, the request could be withdrawn at any time and, in agreement with the opposing party, possible sanctions imposed by the judge could still be annulled. Consensualism thus continued to dominate Belgian civil procedural law and the rules of the *mise en état* in particular. The Belgian civil judge was considered active, but not authoritarian. His mission was to watch over the procedure and to intervene when a party asked him for help; he was not to impose his own vision when the parties were in absolute agreement on how to conduct the case.

3. CASE MANAGEMENT AND MISE EN ÉTAT: THE DEBATE (1992-2006)

Belgian judges were clearly evolving into procedural managers, while the parties largely maintained their legal monopoly over the organization of the procedure, assuming they could agree on the procedural path to be followed. A question that concerned Belgian judges was whether to promote a still more active role for the court. On a theoretical level there was nothing that could be held against this: it had gradually become accepted that the principle of party autonomy does not prevent courts from acquiring decision-making power over the purely procedural aspects of the case. While party autonomy

---

case note; *Tijdschrift voor Belgisch Burgerlijk Recht* 2002, 636, with case note by D. SCHEERS.

19 Court of Cassation 27 November 2003, *Journal des Tribunaux* 2005, 418, case note; Court of Cassation 14 March 2002, *Rechtskundig Weekblad* 2002-03, 138; Court of Cassation 22 March 2001, *Arresten van het Hof van Cassatie* 2001, 461, with opinion by Advocate-General De Riemaecker.

prevents courts from initiating procedures or passing judgment *ultra petita*, it does not impede a judicial decision defining the timeframe in which the case should be prepared. Consequently, case management of the formal aspects of the procedure does not constitute a breach of this fundamental principle of civil procedure.
This led some authors to argue that the parties should indeed lose their powers as regards the progress of the civil action. The French professor of civil procedure law, Albert Tissier, was one of the very first to defend this position, as early as the beginning of the twentieth century. He wrote:

'(C)'est (au juge) de diriger la marche du procès. L'État doit la justice; il la doit rapide et simple; il ne peut donc laisser les plaideurs (…) libres d'allonger, de compliquer le procès, et ainsi d'entraver et de retarder le cours de la justice à l'égard de tous les justiciables (...). Le juge dirigeant la procédure, c'est là, à notre avis, la clef de la réforme, le seul moyen de diminuer les lenteurs et les périls des procès, de ramener la procédure à sa fonction qui est le service du droit, du bien public, de la paix sociale'.[20]

This could be effected either by fixing time limits in the Judicial Code or by providing the judge with the power to enforce time limits ex officio. These proposals, now reclaimed and revived by the end of the twentieth and beginning of the twenty-first century, continued to provoke as much controversy as they had done when presented at the time when Tissier wrote his paper. Even within the magistracy. they were contested. Many were of the opinion that this type of innovation would not add any value, arguing that the present system already functioned adequately and that too much "dirigisme" would not necessarily be efficient. Moreover, some saw nothing wrong with the principle of consensualism that still governed Belgian civil procedure: why should the judge be able to fix time limits if the parties are in agreement about the pace of the procedure? Finally, judicially imposed time limits might increase the speed at which the case is prepared by the parties, but would judges be able pass their judgements at a similar speed? There was a fear that judicial case management simply shifts the delay, without eliminating it. Nevertheless, it some become clear that the trend was towards

---

20 Tissier, A., 'Le rôle social et économique des règles de la procédure civile', in: X (ed.), *Les méthodes juridiques: leçons faites au Collège libre des sciences sociales en 1910*, Paris: Giard et Brière, 1911, p. 105-122. See also TISSIER, A., 'Le centenaire du Code de procédure et les projets de réforme', *Revue Trimestriel de Droit Civil*, 1906, p. 625-652.

a more active role for judges, and there was widespread consensus among policymakers that the legislature could not ignore this. Among those influential voices to advocate further reform was the Belgian 'High Council of Justice', which in 2002 spoke out in favour of strengthening the judge's position in civil proceedings. This was done in an authoritative opinion on civil procedure reform proposals that were at that time before parliament.[21] The Council did not call for radical reform, but argued nevertheless that minor changes to the Judicial Code would sufficiently increase a judge's powers to improve procedural efficiency. To quote the Council's words:

'Le Conseil supérieur de la Justice estime, pour sa part, sous réserve qu'il soit satisfait à certaines conditions (dont il sera question ci-dessous), qu'il est souhaitable de renforcer le rôle du juge dans le déroulement de la procédure et de lui procurer les moyens d'en assurer le contrôle.

Cette position se fonde sur des constatations purement empiriques. Lorsque le juge utilise pleinement les possibilités qui lui sont offertes par les textes existants pour influencer la procédure, celle-ci se déroule avec davantage de diligence et d'efficacité. Une intervention active du juge dans la procédure permet un usage économique du procès civil. (...) [L]es textes existants offrent déjà tout un éventail de possibilités au juge pour accompagner activement le déroulement de la procédure. Il suffirait dès lors peut-être d'affiner certaines règles plutôt que d'introduire à la hâte une réforme complexe et peu réfléchie.

Cette prise de position est, en outre, basée sur la constatation que le besoin de donner au juge un rôle plus actif dans le déroulement de la procédure, se situe dans le prolongement des évolutions qui se manifestent dans la société, et plus particulièrement quant au rôle du judiciaire dans un état de droit démocratique. Un concours de circonstances fait que la pression sur les

---

[21] See, e.g.: the legislative proposal introduced by the members of parliament G. Bourgeois and K. Van Hoorebeke in 2000 and re-introduced in 2003 (published in the documentary series of the Belgian parliament, *Parlementaire Stukken Kamer* 2000-01, Nr. 969/1-4 and 2003-04, Nr. 574/1, also at <http://www.dekamer.be>, last consulted in June 2007); the draft bill to amend the rules of civil procedure in the Judicial Code, presented in 2001 – and, in a revised version, in 2002 – by former Minister of Justice M. VERWILGHEN; the 'Federal Government's Declaration', which served as formal announcement of the policy goals set by the current government coalition at the time of its creation (published in *Parlementaire Stukken Kamer* 2003-04, Nr. 51-20/1, 53).

institutions judiciaires est devenue intolérable ce qui se traduit par une arriéré judiciaire important dans certaines juridictions. La situation est telle que les institutions judiciaires risquent de ne plus être en mesure d'assurer le service public d'une bonne justice, ce qui est pourtant leur responsabilité. Dans ces circonstances, il n'est plus justifié de faire dépendre le déroulement du procès, dont le coût social est considérable, de la seule volonté des parties présentes au litige. L'intérêt particulier des parties doit s'effacer devant l'intérêt général qui exige une justice diligente et efficace. Il faut, dès lors, procurer au juge les moyens indispensables pour pouvoir intervenir dans le déroulement du procès dans l'intérêt d'une bonne justice, ceci bien sûr dans le respect des droits de la défense, du contradictoire et de l'égalité des armes'.[22]

4. CASE MANAGEMENT AND MISE EN ÉTAT: POLICIES AND SOFT LAW IN ANTICIPATION OF LEGAL REFORM

Despite enthusiasm among many academics, magistrates and attorneys for a debate on strengthening the role of the civil judge, the issue was not a priority for policymakers. While the debate among legal professionals was already intense at the end of the 1990's, it was at that time obvious that any legislative reform instituting the 'active judge' in civil matters would be a long time coming. In the wake of the mediatised child abduction cases that shook Belgian society's foundations in 1996, government and parliament gave all priority to a reform of the criminal justice system. The Belgian judges realised that a radical change to the balance of power between the parties and the judge was therefore probably not imminent but nevertheless, in practice, embraced their role as active supervisors of procedure. There was a trend among magistrates to make more use of their natural authority and to resort to creative measures with the aim of increasing procedural efficiency. This trend was amplified by the so-called 'Octopus-reforms' of 1998, by which the magistracy was released, to a significant extent, from the guardianship of the political government and gained considerable autonomy. A 'High Council of Justice' (*Hoge Raad voor de Justitie – Conseil Supérieur de la Justice*) was established and became responsible for appointing and evaluating magistrates, advising on proposals for legislation, and searching for possible dysfunctions

---

[22] Conseil Supérieur de la Justice/Hoge Raad voor de Justitie, *Avis relatif à l'avant-projet de loi modifiant le Code judiciaire en ce qui concerne la procédure*, <http://www.hrj.be/FR/download/avis0207cf.pdf> (last consulted in July 2007).

in the civil justice system.[23] This undoubtedly encouraged the courts to continue developing their own case management plans and policies.
The increased interest of the courts in case management was particularly evident in two areas. Firstly, various courts, when formulating their internal regulations, developed systems to guarantee a smooth judicial procedure. This was effected by, for example, entrusting the supervision over the procedural preparation of a case to one specific chamber of the court, which subsequently sent it on to another chamber when the case was ready for final hearing.[24] This system was similar to the French concept of the *juge de la mise en état*. Courts were paying more and closer attention to setting the most efficient hearings agenda possible to prevent too much wasted time. Also, agreements were reached among the courts about the manner in which particular rules of procedure were to be interpreted, so that all lawyers would know what they could expect, irrespective of which judge chairs the session.

A second way in which the courts devoted themselves to an active procedural policy was by drawing up special *protocols* with the bar. The purpose of these protocols was to make clear arrangements with the lawyers' representatives about the procedural preparation of cases. Arrangements were also made regarding aspects that were not explicitly regulated by law. For example, it was laid down in various protocols that when parties appeared at the introductory hearing they immediately had to agree among themselves the time limits within which they would submit their statements of case. Often, they also had to accept that failing to keep to these time limits would give the judge the authority to exclude late statements from the proceedings. Likewise, several protocols prescribed that the parties were to summarise their statements of case – thus saving the judge time-consuming reading – or that they were to notify not only each other of their means of proof in advance, but also the judge, and this at least two weeks before the hearing. In

---

23 Article 151 of the Belgian Constitution, as modified by constitutional amendment of 20 November 1998, *Belgian State Gazette (Moniteur belge, Belgische Staatsblad)* 24 November 1998, err. 24 February 1999. Fore more details and comments on this evolution, see DELPÉRÉE, F., 'Octopus, genèse et réalisations', in X (ed.), *Une justice en crise: premières réponses*, Brussels: Bruylant, 2002, p. 89-104; Matray, C., 'Le conseil supérieur de la justice: de quelques perplexités', in: X (ed.), *Une justice en crise: premières réponses*, Brussels: Bruylant, 2002, p. 153-190; VERDUSSEN, M., 'L'origine et la légitimité du Conseil supérieur de la justice', in: VERDUSSEN, M. (ed.), *Le Conseil supérieur de la justice*, Brussels: Bruylant, 1999, p. 15-26.

24 This is the system that was developed in the Dutch language section of the Court of Appeal in Brussels.

a certain sense one can therefore speak of a form of 'soft law', as there existed no legal foundation for such protocols.[25]

5. CASE MANAGEMENT AND *MISE EN ÉTAT*: THE ACT OF 26 APRIL 2007

By the year 2006, the Minister of Justice had understood the message: the professionals in the field had set course for a modernisation of civil case management and the Government was to follow. The Minister initiated a project called "Justice Dialogues" whereby magistrates and attorneys throughout the country were questioned about the state of civil justice and asked for concrete suggestions for reform. This resulted in a draft bill which was unusually swiftly pushed through the parliamentary process and became the Act of 26 April 2007 Amending the Judicial Code in View of Reducing the Judicial Backlog.[26]

The Act contains more than a dozen measures to increase the speed of civil justice. Some of the more notable are:

- promoting "fast track" proceedings which are now open to an increased number of claims and motions, such as requests for provisional and evidentiary measures, referral for lack of jurisdiction, etc.;
- strengthened duty for the parties to substantiate their claim and to submit their evidence to the court in advance of the oral hearing;
- obligation for the parties to submit summary statements at the end of the written phase of the trial;
- introduction of an "interactive debate" instead of the traditional oral pleadings;

---

[25] Court of Appeals Antwerp 5 June 2000, *Algemeen Juridisch Tijdschrift* 2001-02, 901. See also: REGOUT, M., 'La mise en état des causes', case note under Court of Cassation 13 February 2004, *Revue de Jurisprudence de Liège, Mons et Bruxelles*, 2004, p. 514 *in fine*.
For that reason, some authors have suggested legislative recognition of this practice, which would at least remove any doubt about the enforceability of these protocols: see for example ADRIAENSEN, P., 'De actieve rechter in het hof van beroep te Antwerpen', in: Hoge Raad voor de Justitie (ed.), *L'arriéré juridiciaire n'est pas une fatalité – Gerechtelijke achterstand: geen noodzakelijk kwaad*, Brussels: Bruylant, 2004, p. 283.

[26] For a commentary, see TAELMAN, P. and VAN ORSHOVEN, P. (ed.), *De wet van 27 april 2007 tot wijziging van het Gerechtelijk Wetboek met het oog op het bestrijden van de gerechtelijke achterstand doorgelicht*, Brugge, die Keure, 2007, 189 p.

- generalisation of the system of civil fines for abuse of process and unfair procedural behaviour by a party;
- mitigation of the rules of nullity sanctioning procedural formalities;
- enhanced supervision on judges to render judgment expeditiously.

The most fundamental innovation, however, is the new system for the "mise en état" of civil cases. In line with the tendency, observed in the local practice of many courts (cf. *supra*), to subject parties to binding time schedules and to demand more discipline in the preparation of the written phase of the trial, the Act has now formally introduced a strict regime. At the outset of every new action brought before a civil court, the parties are required to present their opinion with regard to the timing of the procedure and a schedule, called "calendar", must be set. Priority is given to a consensual solution: if the parties reach agreement amongst themselves on what the timing should be, the court must confirm and maintain it. If the parties do not reach an agreement within one month after the introductory hearing of the case, the court acquires the power to impose a calendar "*ex officio*" and at its own discretion. Postponing the trial for an undetermined delay, without setting out a fixed time schedule for the exchange of written pleadings, is no longer an option except if this is explicitly asked by all parties together. In the latter hypothesis, a binding calendar can still be reintroduced at any time during the procedure, by simple request of any of the parties.

In summary, the concept behind the reform is that insure a more speedy trial, the manoeuvre space for the parties (or better, for their attorneys) had to be reduced and the role of the judge had to be reinforced. However, consensualism remains the basic principle underlying the civil justice system: if all parties are in consensus about the way to proceed, the judge is bound by that agreement. This philosophy is also reflected in the sanctionary mechanism: any breach of the time schedule can be penalised by the court ex officio, but the parties may at all times agree to waive the sanction if they are all in agreement to do so.

6. CASE MANAGEMENT AND THE GATHERING OF EVIDENCE

Belgian civil judges also play an important role in the evidence collection process. The Judicial Code of 1967 invests judges with extensive powers to direct that process to the elements they considers most relevant. To that end, the judge can ex officio order a variety of measures, such as an expert investigation, a witness or party examination, or the production of documents. In addition, judges have the authority to verify the facts in situ, provided they inform the parties of their intention and invite them to attend.

Magistrates regularly make use of their powers to direct the process of gathering evidence and most attorneys do not object, as long as the rights of defence – including the right to be heard – are respected. Still, in the great majority of cases judges do not issue these kinds of orders on their own initiative but prefer rather to act upon a request by one of the parties. This is not problematic as long as the parties are sufficiently diligent and share the judge's understanding of which are the key issues.

Where evidence collection is conducted through expert investigations, delays are often incurred due to the untimely submission by the expert of the report containing his or her findings. To improve efficiency, new legislation was passed in 2007 whereby the procedure for expert investigations was thoroughly amended. In this Act of 15 May 2007, the Belgian legislator chose again to reinforce the role of the judge, which is now given more powers to adequately supervise the expert investigation and compel the expert to respect the court's timing.

7. CASE MANAGEMENT AND ALTERNATIVE DISPUTE RESOLUTION

An inherent part of judicial case management in civil litigation is the search for and promotion of settlements. It is generally accepted that parties have a minimal duty to give at least (reasonable) consideration to any invitation to discuss settlement.[27] The judge is expected to anticipate a potential settlement and motivate the parties to find common ground. Indeed, as long as one can remember, the Belgian civil judge has been vested with the mission of helping parties find an amicable solution prior to the imposition of such a solution through a court decision. This is done in the context of what is known in Belgian law as the procedure of 'conciliation', as described in Articles 731-734 of the Judicial Code. Although the (outdated) wording of

---

[27] Laenens, J., 'Règlement alternatif des litiges en Belgique', in: X (ed.), *The Belgian Reports at the Congress of Brisbane of the International Academy of International Law*, Brussels: Bruylant, 2002, p. 287-298. STORME, M.E., 'De goede trouw in het geding? De invloed van de goede trouw in het privaat proces- en bewijsrecht', *Tijdschrift voor Privaatrecht,* 1990, p. 404 *et seq.*, No. 24; STORME, M., 'Algemene beginselen van behoorlijke procesvoering', in: VAN HOECKE, M. (ed.), *Algemene rechtsbeginselen*, Antwerp, Kluwer, 1991, p. 159- 175. Storme, M., 'Pleidooi voor een procesnoodrecht – Syntheseverslag', in: STORME, M. (ed.), *Procesrecht vandaag*, Antwerp: Kluwer, 1980, p. 504-513. See also the recommendations of the Council of Europe, Rec(2002)10, § III.7 and R (86) 12, § I.c., and Guinchard *et al.* 2001, p. 714-715, No. 600.

Article 731 suggests that conciliation is a process that should precede the formal introduction of the claim, it is generally accepted that the court can also attempt conciliation during the hearing.[28] Nevertheless, most judges are, in practice, hesitant to do so. Commentators attribute this to the fact that judges lack the time to engage in lengthy discussions with the parties; that they think of themselves as unqualified to act as negotiator; and that they fear creating an appearance of bias if they push too hard for a settlement. The Belgian legislature has responded by introducing external mediators to civil proceedings. The judge now has the opportunity to suggest that parties submit their case to a mediation procedure and, if they accept his proposal, to suspend the proceedings and refer them to a qualified mediator of their choice.[29] Judges are expected to welcome this new possibility, and make a policy of referring parties to mediation as often as possible.

---

28 Brandon, I., 'L'office du juge dans la conciliation', *Journal des Tribunaux*, 1995, p. 508 & 515; Fettweis, A., 'L'usage de la conciliation pour le règlement des différends', in: Limpens, J. (ed.), *Rapports belges au Xe congrès international de droit comparé*, Brussels: Bruylant, 1978, p. 174; Ligot, F., 'Le pouvoir de conciliation du juge, la médiation et l'autorité des accords', *Annales de droit de Louvain*, 1996, p. 82 *et seq.*; Maingain, B., 'Le rôle de la conciliation et des accords dans le règlement des conflits familiaux: la montée de l'autonomie des volontés en matière familiale et le caractère accusatoire du procès', in: X (ed.), *L'évolution du droit judiciaire au travers des contentieux économique, social et familial. Approche comparative*, Brussels: Bruylant, 1984, p. 814; Rouard, P., 'Le préliminaire de conciliation dans le Code judiciaire', *Journal des Tribunaux*, 1970, p. 718; Van Compernolle, J., 'Le juge et la conciliation judiciaire', in: X (ed.), *Le contentieux interdisciplinaire – Het interdisciplinair geschil*, Diegem: Kluwer, 1996 p. 46; Van Houtte, H., 'Mediatie. Is het gras groener aan de andere kant van den heuvel?', in: X (ed.), *Liber Amicorum Jozef Van Den Heuvel*, Antwerp: Kluwer, 1999, p. 235.

29 Act of 21 February 2005 amending the Judicial Code with respect to mediation; Act of 19 February 2001 with regard to family mediation.

A MAJOR STEP IN THE HARMONIZATION OF PROCEDURAL LAW IN EUROPE: THE EUROPEAN SMALL CLAIMS PROCEDURE

Accomplishments, new features and some fundamental questions of European harmonization

X.E. Kramer

1. INTRODUCTION

European civil procedural law has been in a constant state of flux since the coming into force of the Treaty of Amsterdam in 1999. The Treaty of Amsterdam introduced Article 65 of the EC Treaty, which empowers the Community to adopt measures in the field of judicial cooperation in civil matters having cross-border implications. The introduction of Article 65 EC Treaty was followed by numerous Community instruments in the field of civil procedure, mostly regulations that have direct binding force in the Member States. These have changed the face of litigation in the European Union.

Most EU-regulations that have been established on the basis of Article 65 EC Treaty are "classical" private international law regulations.[1] Their primary aim is to coordinate national procedures in cross-border disputes, and not to introduce harmonized procedures. A well-known example is Regulation no 44/2001 on jurisdiction and the recognition and enforcement of judgments in civil and commercial matters (Brussels I), which replaced the Brussels Convention of 1968. Other examples are Regulation no 1348/2000 on the service of documents and Regulation no 1206/2001 on the taking of evidence. These Regulations do not fundamentally differ from traditional bilateral and unilateral conventions in the field of private international law

---

1 Private International Law in the broad sense, including questions of international jurisdiction, recognition and enforcement, other procedural issues (such as the service of documents, the taking of evidence and legal aid) and the conflict of laws.

and international procedural law,[2] except that they usually are a bit more progressive and systematic.

Two recent EU-regulations, however, take a different approach. These are Regulation no 1896/2006 creating a European Order for Payment Procedure, which was adopted on 12 December 2006[3], and Regulation no 861/2007 establishing a European Small Claims Procedure, adopted on 11 July 2007[4]. These are the first to create autonomous European procedures.[5] This is a major step in the development of European civil procedure, and in view of the initial political unwillingness to harmonize civil procedure it is also a remarkable step.[6] These new European procedures aim at simplifying, speeding up and reducing the costs of litigation.

This paper focuses on the recent developments in European procedural law, and more in particular the establishment of the first two European procedures. The emphasis will be put on the European Small Claims Procedure (abbreviated as ESCP), which as a full, adversarial procedure is more substantial than the primarily administrative European Order for Payment Procedure for uncontested claims (abbreviated as EOP). In section 2 attention will be paid to the harmonization of procedural law in Europe after the Treaty of Amsterdam and the current state of affairs. In section 3 the European Small Claims Procedure will be analyzed. Section 4 contains some thoughts on the harmonization of procedural law in Europe. First, the accomplishments and innovative features are discussed. Second, some difficulties and fundamental issues of the harmonization of procedural law in Europe are presented.

---

2 For example those concluded by the Hague Conference on Private International Law.

3 Regulation (EC) No 1896/2006 of the European Parliament and of the Council of 12 December 2006 creating a European order for payment procedure, O.J. 2006 L 399/1.

4 Regulation (EC) No 861/2007 of the European Parliament and of the Council of 11 July 2007 establishing a European Small Claims Procedure, O.J. 2007 L 199/1.

5 See for a comprehensive study on the regulations in the context of the harmonization of procedural law: XANDRA KRAMER, *Eenvormige Europese procedures voor de inning van vorderingen.* De Europese betalingsbevelprocedure en de Europese procedure voor geringe vorderingen, Kluwer 2007.

6 See also the initial political neglect of the proposals of the Storme working group, presented to the Commission in 1993: MARCEL STORME (ed.), *Rapprochement du Droit Judiciaire de L'Union européenne/Approximation of Judiciary Law in the European Union*, Martinus Nijhoff Publishers 1994. See further section 2.1 below.

2. HARMONIZATION OF CIVIL PROCEDURE IN EUROPE

Before the treaty of Amsterdam came into force, the competence in regard of civil procedure was limited. Except for the coming about of the successful Brussels Convention in 1968, civil procedural law was hardly touched upon. The attempt to promote harmonization by the extensive work of the Storme working group,[7] which presented its report to the Commission in 1993, undeservedly received relatively little attention in literature and was initially ignored in Brussels.[8] In 1998 the Commission did its first attempt to introduce a procedure for unchallenged claims and for small claims, in the Directive combating late payment in commercial transactions.[9] These proposals were rejected by the Council due to (the alleged) lack of competence to prescribe certain procedures, at least on the basis of Article 95 EC Treaty.

2.1. THE AMSTERDAM TREATY AND ONWARDS

The political climate regarding the harmonization of civil procedure changed shortly after. The Treaty of Amsterdam introduced Article 65 of the EC Treaty, which allows for measures in the field of judicial cooperation in civil matters having cross-border implications, needed for the proper functioning of the international market.[10] According to Article 65 sub a) and sub b) these

---

7 See previous footnote.

8 See on the harmonization of procedural law before the Treaty of Amsterdam *inter alia*: KONSTANTINOS KERAMEUS, Procedural Unification: The Need and the Limitations, in: IAN SCOTT (ed.), *International Perspectives on Civil Justice.* Essays in honour of Sir Jack I.H. Jacob, Q.C., 1990, p. 47 ff; WOLFGANG GRUNSKY, ROLF STÜRNER, GERHARD WALTER & MANFRED WOLF (eds.), Wege zu einem europäischen Zivilprozeßrecht, Tübinger Symposium, Zum 80. Geburtstag von Fritz Baur, 1992; MARCEL STORME, Rechtsvereinheitlichung in Europa. Ein Plädoyer für ein einheitliches europäisches Prozeßrecht, RabelsZ 1992, p. 291 ff; *idem*, Procedural Consequences of a Common Private Law for Europe, in: Arthur Hartkamp (ed.) Towards a European Civil Code, 1994, p. 87 ff; EBERHARD SCHILKEN, Die Vorschläge der Kommission für ein europaïsches Zivilprozeßgesetzbuch, Zeitschrift für Zivilprozess (ZZP) 1996, p. 315 ff. See for an analysis of the impact of the Storme proposals amongst others JAAP VAN RIJN VAN ALKEMADE, Een Europees procesrecht of een storme in een glas water?, in: EWOUD HONDIUS *et al.* (ed.), Liber Amicorum Paul Meijknecht, Van Nederlands Naar Europees procesrecht?!, 2000, p. ff.

9 Proposal for a European Parliament and Council Directive combating late payment in commercial transactions, 23 April 1998, COM(1998) 126 final, see in particular Article 5 and 6.

10 See BURKHARD HEß, Die „Europäisiering“ des internationalen Zivilprozessrechts durch den Amsterdamer Vertrag – Chancen und Gefahren, *Neue Juristische Wochenschrift (NJW)* 2000, p. 23 ff; THOMAS DRAPPATZ, *Die Überführung des internationalen Zivilverfahrensrechts in eine Gemeinschaftskompetenz* nach Article 65 EGV, 2002. See for a

measures include the cross-border service of documents, the taking of evidence, recognition and enforcement, the conflict of laws and jurisdiction. Sub c) includes measures eliminating obstacles to the good functioning of civil proceedings, if necessary by promoting the compatibility of the rules on civil procedure in the Member States. This Article 65 sub c provides the basis for both the EOP and ESCP.

The harmonization of European civil procedure has furthermore been boosted by the famous Conclusions of the European Council Tampere of October 1999.[11] These Conclusions emphasized the need to improve access to justice, the mutual recognition of judicial decisions and greater convergence in civil law, amongst others by preparing new procedural legislation in cross-border cases. The subsequent Programme of Mutual Recognition of 2000 is also relevant in this respect.[12] This singled out the abolition of exequatur for uncontested claims as one of the Community's priorities and furthermore referred to simplifying and speeding up the settlement of cross-border litigation in uncontested and small claims. At the end of 2002, the Commission adopted a Green Paper on a European order for payment procedure and on small claims.[13] In this Green Paper the Commission presented its two-tiered approach. The first was to abolish the *exequatur* for uncontested claims in the European Union. The second was the creation of a specific harmonized procedure for the recovery of uncontested claims. The Commission furthermore emphasized the disproportionate costs and duration of proceedings relating to small claims and launched a consultation on measures to simplify and to speed small claims litigation. In this Green Paper the Storme proposals finally got political recognition: the proposals regarding the payment order are appreciated as good reference and valuable source of inspiration for the creation of a European Order for payment. The Hague Programme of 2004 finally underlined the need to further enhance the creation of a Europe for citizens and the essential role of setting up a European Area for Justice in this regard.[14] Priorities for the coming years are furthering mutual recognition, approximation of law, including minimum

---

full overview of the development of European procedural law in this regard: KRAMER (fn. 5), p. 16 ff.

11 Tampere European Council, 15 and 16 October 1999, Presidency conclusions, no 28-39 (no 30).

12 Programme of measures for implementation of the principle of mutual recognition of decisions in civil and commercial matters, 30 November 2000, O.J. 2001 C 12/1.

13 Green Paper on a European order for payment procedure and on measures to simplify and speed up small claims litigation, 20 December 2002, COM(2002) 746 final.

14 The Hague Programme: strengthening freedom, security and justice in the European Union, 13 December 2004, O.J. 2005 C 53/1 (in particular point 3).

rules of procedural law, facilitating civil law procedure across borders and enhancing cooperation, amongst others through the European Judicial Network in civil matters.[15]

2.2. THE CURRENT STATE OF AFFAIRS IN EUROPEAN CIVIL PROCEDURE

The developments in private international law and international procedural law in the European Union have been stormy since the year 2000. One could say that the expansion of private international law has led to a new legal specialization: EU Private International Law.[16] The typical private international law regulations relating to procedural issues that are currently in force are: Regulation no 44/2001 on jurisdiction and the recognition and enforcement of judgments in civil and commercial matters (Brussels I); Regulation no 2201/2003 concerning jurisdiction and the recognition and enforcement of judgments in matrimonial matters and in matters of parental responsibility (Brussels IIA), which repealed Regulation no 1347/2000 (Brussels II); Regulation no 1346/2000 on insolvency proceedings (Insolvency Regulation); Regulation no 1348/2000 on the service in the Member States of judicial and extrajudicial documents in civil or commercial matters (Service Regulation), which will as of 13 November 2008 be replaced by Regulation no 1393/2007; and Regulation no 1206/2001 on cooperation between the courts of the Member States in the taking of evidence in civil or commercial matters (Evidence Regulation).

Furthermore, as the first layer of the two-tiered approach taken in the aforementioned Green Paper on a European order for payment procedure and on small claims[17], Regulation no 805/2004 creating a European Enforcement Order for uncontested claims (abbreviated as EEO) was established.[18] This Regulation marks the beginning of a new era for the recognition and enforcement of decisions as well as for European civil procedure. In the first place, it abolishes the *exequatur* for uncontested claims. Where a claim is uncontested within the meaning of Article 3 EEO Regulation, the court of origin may upon application certify its decision as European Enforcement

---

15 See also section 2.2 below.

16 See also the two recent handbooks on EU private international law: PETER STONE, *EU Private International Law. Harmonization of Laws*, Edward Elgar Publishing 2006; MICHAEL BOGDAN, *Concise Introduction to EU Private International Law*, Europa Law Publishing, 2006.

17 See section 3.1 below.

18 Applicable as of 21 October 2005, see Article 33 EEO Regulation.

Order when certain minimum procedural requirements are fulfilled. A judgment which has been certified as EEO shall be recognised and enforced in the other Member States without the need for a declaration of enforceability and without any possibility of opposing its recognition (see Article 5 EEO). Traditional grounds of refusal, such as the public policy exception, are therefore no longer allowed.[19] In the second place, it establishes minimum requirements for the service of documents, the provision of due information to the debtor about the claim and for review (see Articles 12-19 EEO). These minimum standards do not oblige the Member States to adapt their procedural rules, but are compulsory for the certification as EEO. Especially the introduction of certain minimum standards for the service of documents and the introduction of review of decisions, which is unknown in many Member States, are new elements in European procedural law.[20]

The second layer of the Green Paper approach consisted of the bringing about of a European Order for Payment Procedure (EOP), and later on the European Small Claims Procedure (ESCP). The EOP Regulation shall apply from 12 December 2008[21]; the ESCP will be available from 1 January 2009.[22] They will be applicable in all Member States, except for Denmark.[23] These regulations clearly take a different approach from traditional private international law rules. They do not merely coordinate national procedures, but introduce autonomous European procedures. The EOP and ESCP are available as an optional instrument, besides the existing national procedures.[24]

---

19 The EEO has been much criticized both for the abolishment of the public policy exception and its complicated rules. See on the EEO Regulation amongst others: THOMAS RAUSCHER, Der Europaïsche Vollstreckungstitel für unbestrittene Forderungen, Sellier/Verlag Recht und Wirtschaft 2004; ASTRID STADLER, Kritische Anmerkungen zum Europäischen Vollstreckungstitel, *Recht der Internationalen Wirtschaft (RIW)* 2004, p. 801 ff; STONE 2006 (fn. 16), p. 213, p. 250 ff; BOGDAN 2006 (fn. 16), p. 83 ff; CARLA BAKER, *Le titre exécutoire, Une avancée pour la libre circulation des décisions?*, Juris-Classeur Periodique (JCP) 2003, p. 985 ff; CARLA CRIFÒ, First Steps towards the Harmonisation of Civil Procedure: the Regulation Creating a European Enforcement Order for Uncontested Claims, Civil Justice Quarterly (CJQ) 2005, p. 200 ff.; XANDRA KRAMER, De Europese Executoriale Titel: een nieuw instrument ter verwezenlijking van het Europees procesterritoir, *Nederlands Tijdschrift voor Burgerlijk Recht (NTBR)* 2005, p. 375 ff.

20 See further section 4.1 below.

21 See Article 33(2) EOP.

22 See Article 29(2) ESCP.

23 See Articles 2(3) EOP and 2(3) ESCP. Denmark, as well as the United Kingdom and Ireland have a special position in regard of regulations based on Title IV EC Treaty. Denmark opted out, as it did in regard of all other regulations based on Article 61 in conjunction with Article 65 EC Treaty.

24 See Articles 1(2) EOP and 1(2) ESCP.

The claimant can therefore choose. Furthermore, the European procedures are only available in cross-border cases.[25] These limitations follow from the principles of subsidiarity and proportionality, as well as Article 65 EC Treaty. Especially the limitation to cross-border cases has been much debated. The first Commission EOP proposal of 2004 and the ESCP proposal also extended to purely national cases. As a result of the Council negotiations and the legislative resolutions of the European Parliament, the scope has been limited to cross-border cases.[26]

The EOP Regulation provides for a simple procedure for the collection of uncontested pecuniary claims for a specific amount recovery.[27] The creditor can apply for a European Payment Order by filling out a standard form and lodging it (directly, by postal mail or electronically[28]) at the competent court (Article 7 EOP). If the (formal) requirements are fulfilled and the claim appears to be founded, the court will usually issue the EOP within 30 days (Articles 8-12). The defendant has 30 days to lodge a statement of opposition, by filling out the standard form attached to the EOP served to him according to the rules of Articles 13-15 EOP (Article 16). If he does not lodge a statement of opposition, the EOP will be declared enforceable (Article 18) and will be recognized and enforced in the other Member States without the need of an *exequatur* and without the possibility of opposition in the state of enforcement (Article 19). Review of the EOP in the state of origin is possible in exceptional circumstances (Article 20). The ESCP is as a full, adversarial procedure more substantial than the EOP and will be analyzed more thoroughly below in section III. After the EOP and ESCP, a third European procedure might result from the Green Paper on the attachment of bank accounts that is currently under deliberation.[29]

Furthermore, worth mentioning are several instruments that have been established in support of European litigation. In 2003 Directive 2003/8 on Access to Justice and Legal Aid in Cross-Border Cases was established, which provides for minimum standards of legal aid in cross-border litigation. A directive on mediation in civil and commercial matters was proposed in

---

25 See Articles 1(1) EOP and 1(1) ESCP.

26 See further Section 3.2 and 4.2 below.

27 See on the EOP amongst others: KRAMER 2007 (fn. 5), p. 57 ff; XANDRA KRAMER & BARTOSZ SUJECKI, De Europese betalingsbevelprocedure. Een kritische beschouwing, *Nederlands Internationaal Privaatrecht (NIPR)* 2006, p. 365 ff; ANNE RÖTHEL & INGO SPARMANN, Das europäische Mahnverfahren, *Zeitschrift für Wirtschafts- und Bankrecht* (WM) 2007, p. 1101 ff.

28 If the competent court has electronic means available, see Article 7 EOP.

29 Green Paper on Improving the Efficiency of the Enforcement of Judgments in the European Union: the Attachment of Bank Accounts, 24 October 2006, COM(2006) 618 final.

2004, and is likely to be finally adopted in 2008.[30] Also important in this regard is the establishment of the European Judicial Network in civil and commercial matters (abbreviated as: EJN) in 2001.[31] The website of EJN includes practical information on procedural law of the Member States in the official languages of the European Union.[32]

3. THE EUROPEAN SMALL CLAIMS PROCEDURE

The Regulation establishing a European Small Claims Procedure introduces the second autonomous European procedure, after the European Order for Payment Procedure. The Commission proposal for the European Small Claims of 15 March 2005[33] has been intensively debated and many amendments have been proposed by the Council and the European Parliament,[34] but the core of the procedure remained intact. The ESCP is a simple procedure for claims not exceeding EUR 2000 to facilitate access to justice, by simplifying, speeding up and reducing costs of small claims litigation, while respecting the right to a fair trial.[35] Article 1 ESCP explicates its two folded aim. The Regulation is intended to simplify and speed up litigation concerning small claims, and to

---

30 Proposal for a Directive of the European Parliament and of the Council on certain aspects of mediation in civil and commercial matters, 22 October 2004, COM(2004) 718 final.

31 Council Decision of 28 May 2001 establishing a European Judicial Network in civil and commercial matters, O.J. 2001 L 174/25. See for the website <http://ec.europa.eu/civiljustice/index_en.htm>.

32 It also includes a link to the European Judicial Atlas that provides user-friendly access to information relevant for judicial cooperation in civil matters, such as the competent courts, competent authorities in regard of service of documents and taking of evidence and the filling out of the standard forms attached to the regulations. For direct access to the Judicial Atlas see <http://ec.europa.eu/justice_home/judicialatlascivil/html/index_en.htm>.

33 Proposal for a Regulation of the European Parliament and of the council establishing a European Small Claims Procedure, COM(2005) 87 final, 15 March 2005. See GEORG HAIBACH, The Commission Proposal for a Regulation Establishing a European Small Claims Procedure: An Analysis, *European Review of Private Law (ERPL)* 2005, p. 593 ff. See for a review of the text of the political agreement of 1 June 2006: XANDRA KRAMER, *The proposal for a European Small Claims Procedure*, Int'l Lis 2006, p. 109 ff.

34 European Parliament, Legislative resolution on the proposal for a regulation of the European Parliament and of the Council establishing a European Small Claims Procedure (COM(2005)0087), 14 June 2006.

35 Recitals nos. 7 and 8 ESCP. See on the European Small Claims Procedure amongst others: XANDRA KRAMER, The European Small Claims Procedure: Striking the Balance between Simplicity and Fairness in European Litigation, *Zeitschrift für Europäisches Recht (ZEuP)* 2008, p. 355 ff; KRAMER 2007 (fn. 5), p. 80 ff; PABLO CORTÉS, Does the Proposed European Procedure Enhance the Resolution of Small Claims?, 2007, section I.4, available at SSRN <http://ssrn.com/abstract=983527> (also published in CJQ 2008, p. 83 ff).

reduce costs. Furthermore, it eliminates intermediate measures necessary to enable recognition and enforcement in other Member States.

3.1. NEED FOR A EUROPEAN SMALL CLAIMS PROCEDURE

Most Member States have introduced simplified procedures for small claims. The requirements for these procedures, amongst others the quantitative threshold and the type of cases for which the procedure is available, as well as the procedure itself vary considerably. The Green Paper of 2002 provides some general features of existing small claims procedures in the (old 15) Member States, based upon a survey.[36] First of all, in all Member States there are quantitative thresholds, varying between EUR 600 (in Germany[37]) and £ 5000, currently around EUR 7.500 (in England/Wales[38]). The use of standard forms to initiate the procedure is quite common. Legal representation is not compulsory in any Member State. Several Member States have the possibility of a purely written procedure, without any oral hearing. In other countries, such as England, where a successful small claims procedure exists, an oral hearing is, however, essential.[39] In some Member States the small claims procedure is limited to pecuniary claims or other specific types of litigation. In all Member States several rules of procedure are relaxed, such as those concerning evidence. Several Member States have time limits for the delivery of the judgment. The rules concerning the recovery of costs differ considerably per Member State and the same goes for the possibility of appeal.

In the Green Paper the Commission explicated that costs, delays and vexation connected with judicial remedies do not necessarily decrease proportionally with the amount of the claim.[40] On the contrary, the weight of these obstacles increases in small claims litigation. At the same time, the number of cross-border disputes is rising, and the obstacles to obtaining a fast and inexpensive judgment in these cases are clearly intensified. The service of

---

36 Explanatory Memorandum Commission proposal (fn. 33), p. 4-5; Green Paper 2002 (fn. 13), p. 51-58.

37 See Article 495a Code of Civil Procedure (Zivilprozessordnung) that provides that the court can determine its procedure in its reasonable discretion ('nach billigem Ermessen') for claims with a maximum value of EUR 600.

38 Regulated in Part 27 of the Civil Procedure Rules (CPR). The judge has discretionary power to allocate a case to the small claims track; for some cases the small track is excluded or limited.

39 See CPR 27.8 and Practice Directive (PD) 27, rule 5.5 and 5.6. See also NEIL ANDREWS, *English Civil Procedure*. Fundamentals of the New Civil Justice System, 2003, 531.

40 Green Paper 2002 (fn. 13), p. 59.

documents, the taking of evidence and the enforcement of the judgment will inevitably take longer and cost more in cross-border cases. Practical implications of cross-border litigation are the extra need for legal aid due to unfamiliarity with foreign proceedings (even when representation by a lawyer is not obligatory), the costs of translations, and travelling expenses.[41]

The establishment of the ESCP, as the Recitals clarify, is justified by the requirement of the internal market,[42] which also Article 65 mentions as prerequisite for taking measures in the field of judicial cooperation. The substantial differences amongst the national small claims procedures cause a distortion in competition within the internal market. The ESCP will help to eliminate obstacles to the free movement of goods, persons, services and capital. The objective of the ESCP – to simplify and speed up litigation in small claims procedures – cannot be sufficiently accomplished by the individual Member States, since they cannot guarantee the equivalence of the rules. There is no level playing field if some operators have access to efficient and effective procedures while others do not.

The validity of the internal market argument is to some extent questionable. In relation to the harmonization of contract law it has been argued from an economical perspective that in case competitors in the same Member State are treated equally, there is a level playing field.[43] In this case only *between* Member States there is no level playing field, but that leads to healthy competition and is part of international trade. The validity of the internal market argument is undoubtedly weakened as a consequence of the limitation to cross-border cases, since this might very well lead to a different level of protection between operators from the same Member State on the national market and operators on the international EU-market.

Nonetheless, this leaves the fact unimpeded that international litigation is expensive and that this causes small claims to, in fact, be irrecoverable. Private international law rules can set some of the boundary conditions to simplify international litigation, but cannot solve the problems regarding the necessity of hiring two lawyers when litigating abroad, the inconveniences of unfamiliarity with foreign proceedings, translation costs etc. National small claims procedures are usually not designed for use in international cases. For

---

41 See on practical obstacles in international litigation amongst others PAULIEN VAN DER GRINTEN, PAUL MEIJKNECHT & FRANS VAN DER VELDEN (ed.), *Practical obstacles in cross border litigation: speeches and presidency conclusions of the international conference organised by the Dutch Presidency on 8 and 9 November 2004 in the Hague*, Kluwer 2005.

42 Recital no 7 ESCP. See also Explanatory Memorandum Commission proposal (fn. 33), p. 5.

43 GERHARD WAGNER, The Economics of Harmonization: The Case of Contract Law, *Common Market Law Review (CMLR)* 2002, p. 995 ff.

example in several Member States they mostly rely on physical presence of the parties at the court.[44] Many of these problems can be reduced by creating a simple, uniform procedure that contains effective provisions that contribute to reducing the costs and the duration of proceedings.

3.2. SCOPE OF APPLICATION

Pursuant to Article 2 the Regulation shall apply, in cross-border cases, to civil and commercial matters, whatever the nature of the court or tribunal,[45] where the value of a claim, excluding interest, expenses and outlays, does not exceed €2000.

3.2.1. Threshold of €2000

The ESCP is only available as an optional tool in case the value of the claim does not exceed €2000 at the time when the claim form is received by the court with jurisdiction, excluding all interest, expenses and disbursements. This threshold has been much debated during the negotiations on the proposal. Several Member States found it too low, and others – including many of the new EU Member States – found it too high.[46] The EESC expressed in its opinion on the proposal that the ceiling of €2000 is clearly insufficient given the current value of goods and services, and that it should be at least €5000 in order to contribute to a more-than-proportional

---

44 See also CORTÉS (fn. 35), section I.4.

45 The Regulation mentions "court or tribunal" in all relevant provisions. From hereon reference will only be made to the "court".

46 For example Germany, that has a threshold of EUR 600 for its national procedure, pleaded to lower the limit to a maximum of EUR 1000. See Deutscher Bundestag, Drucksache 16/1684, 31 May 2006, p. 4-5; Stellungnahme des Deutschen Anwaltvereins, Nr. 44/2005, August 2005, p. 8-9; Stellungnahme der Bundesrechtsanwaltskammer, June 2005, Nr. 15/2005, p. 3.
In the Netherlands, where the threshold is currently set at EUR 5000 (though this will be raised to EUR 10.000 shortly) it has been argued that the limit should be EUR 5000 in order for the ESCP to be effective. See Sociaal-Economische Raad, Commissie voor Consumentenaangelegenheden, Briefadvies small claims procedure, 13 January 2006, available at <http://www.ser.nl/nl/publicaties/adviezen.aspx>. A short English abstract of this advice is available at the same website.
For the United Kingdom the threshold was acceptable, though it should be allowed that parties should choose the ESCP should the value of the claim exceed EUR 2000. See House of Lords (European Union Committee), 15 February 2006, European Small Claims Procedure, Report with Evidence, p. 28-30. Also ideas to define minimum and maximum limits or to establish a maximum ceiling or minimum floor have been launched, see House of Lords Report, p. 28-30.

reduction in costs.[47] It remains to be seen whether this threshold will be enough to cover a substantial number of cases.[48]

In regard of this threshold, there has also been a discussion on dealing with counterclaims.[49] The Commission proposal provided that in case the value of the counterclaim exceeds €2000, the counterclaim shall only be considered if it arises from the same legal relationship and if the court considers it appropriate to proceed in the ESCP.[50] This did not meet the approval of the Council and Article 5(7) ESCP rules that if the counterclaim exceeds the limit of €2000, the claim and counterclaim shall not proceed in the ESCP, but be dealt with in accordance with national law.

3.2.2. Civil and Commercial Matters; Excluded Matters

According to Article 2, the ESCP is applicable in civil and commercial matters, whatever the nature of the court or tribunal. It shall not extend, in particular, to revenue, customs or administrative matters or to the liability of the State for acts and omissions in the exercise of State authority ("*acta jure imperii*"). This formulation is derived from Article 1 of the Brussels I Regulation and the case law of the European Court of Justice in relation to this provision.

In Article 2(2) the following matters are excluded: a) the status or legal capacity of natural persons, b) rights in property arising out of a matrimonial relationship, maintenance obligations, wills and succession, c) bankruptcy, d) social security, e) arbitration, f) employment law, g) tenancies of immovable property, with the exception of actions on monetary claims and h) violations of privacy and of rights relating to personality, including defamation. Sub a-e largely coincide with the exclusions in Article 1 Brussels I.[51] The other subject matters are excluded because some Member States have special procedures or even special courts for these cases.[52]

---

47 Opinion EESC, O.J. 2006 C 88/61, comment 6.1.

48 See also CORTÉS 2007 (fn. 35), section 2.2.

49 The concept of counterclaim should be interpreted within the meaning of Article 6(3) Brussels Regulation as arising from the same contract or facts on which the original claims was based, see Recital no. 16 ESCP.

50 See Article 4(2) of the Commission proposal.

51 Except that maintenance cases are included in the Brussels Regulation.

52 See also Council of the European Union Comments on the specific articles of the proposal, 21 March 2005, JUSTCIV 54, CODEC 177.

3.2.3. Cross-border Cases

The ESCP can only be opted in a cross-border case and is not applicable in a national case. The Commission proposal, as did the initial proposal for the European Order for Payment Procedure, also extended to purely national cases. According to the Commission, Article 65 EC Treaty – that provides that measures can be taken in civil matters 'having cross border implications' – should not be interpreted restrictively, since it would create new obstacles to access to justice.[53] It argued that procedural law, by nature, may have cross-border implications. However, 21 of the 25 Member States did not support the view of the Commission and neither did the European Parliament.[54] The scope of the ESCP is therefore limited to cross-border cases, as is the EOP.[55]According to Article 3 ESCP for the purposes of this Regulation, a cross-border case is one in which at least one of the parties is domiciled or habitually resident in a Member State other than the Member State of the court seized. This definition coincides with the one in Article 3 EOP Regulation.

3.3. KEY ELEMENTS OF THE PROCEDURE

The Regulation provides the most important procedural rules and some minimum requirements for the ESCP, but is not exhaustive. According to Article 19, subject to the provisions of this Regulation, the ESCP shall be governed by the procedural law of the Member State in which the procedure is conducted. The Regulation thus upholds the principle of *lex fori processus.* The Recitals express that the court should respect the right to a fair trial and the principle of an adversarial process, in particular when deciding on the necessity of an oral hearing and on the means of taking evidence and the extent to which evidence is to be taken.[56]

Special features and simplifications are that the procedure is in principle conducted in writing (Article 5), that on a necessary hearing the court may make use of video conferences or other communication technology if the

---

53 Explanatory Memorandum Commission proposal (fn. 33), p. 5-6.

54 See House of Lords Report (fn. 46), Minutes of Evidence, p. 2; European Parliament, Legislative resolution on the proposal for a regulation of the European Parliament and of the Council establishing a European Small Claims Procedure (COM(2005)87), 14 June 2006. The EESC, on the contrary, supported the view of the Commission, see Opinion EESC (fn. 47), comment 2.4.

55 See further on this issue section 4.2 below.

56 Recital no. 9 ESCP.

technical means are available (Article 8), that there are special rules for the taking of evidence (Article 9) and that representation by a lawyer or another legal professional is not mandatory (Article 10). There are time limits for conducting certain procedural acts and for giving judgment (Article 4, 5, 7 and 14). The Regulation is accompanied by four standard forms (Annexes I-IV). These are the claim form (A), a form to request completion or correction of the claim form (B), an answer form (C), and a certificate concerning a judgment in the ESCP (D).[57]

3.4. COMMENCEMENT, CONDUCT AND CONCLUSION OF THE PROCEDURE

3.4.1. Commencement

The ESCP is commenced by lodging the claim form A (Annex I) at the competent court, pursuant to Article 4(1). The claim form may be lodged directly, by post or by any other means of communication such as fax or e-mail, as long as this is acceptable to the Member State in which the procedure is commenced.[58] The claim form shall include a description of evidence supporting the claim and be accompanied, where appropriate, by any relevant supporting documents.

The claim form has been developed with special care, since the claimant should be able to fill it in without help of a lawyer. It contains closed fields and uses a tick-box system where possible, and provides a short explanation per item. The claimant is instructed that the form should be filled out in the language of the court.[59] The form is (electronically) available in all official languages of the EU, which facilitates the claimant when filling in the form in the language of the court.[60] According to Article 11 Member States shall ensure that the parties can receive practical assistance in filling in the forms. The Recitals clarify that the practical assistance should include technical information concerning the availability and the filling in of the forms.[61]

---

57 Some of these special features will be elaborated on in section 4, since they are common to both EOP and ESCP.

58 Member States shall inform the Commission which means are acceptable and this will be made publicly available (Article 4(2). In view of accessibility and costs electronic communication is preferable, but since not all Member States are sufficiently equipped yet, it is not is not possible to oblige them to receive electronic claim forms.

59 See also Article 6 ESCP on the language requirements.

60 These will be made available on the website of the European Judicial Atlas (fn. 32).

61 Recital no. 21 ESCP.

Information about procedural questions can also be given by the court staff in accordance with national law.[62]

One of the debates during the negotiations on the proposal focused on the question whether evidence should be lodged to the court together with the claim form. The Commission proposal stated that the claim should be lodged together with any relevant additional document. In order to avoid unnecessary translation costs, however, the Regulation provides that the claim form shall include a description of the evidence, and only where appropriate be accompanied by supporting documents. It goes without saying that, if necessary, the court may request submission of written evidence or other evidence during the proceedings.[63]

Where a claim is outside the scope of the Regulation, the court shall inform the claimant, and the court will proceed in accordance with national law, unless the claimant withdraws the claim (Article 4(3). Where the court considers the information provided inadequate or insufficiently clear, or the form is not filled in properly, it will give the opportunity to complete or rectify the form (using standard form B of Annex II), unless the claim appears to be clearly unfounded or the application inadmissible (Article 4(4). Where the claim appears to be clearly unfounded or the application inadmissible or where the claimant fails to complete or rectify the claim form within the time specified, the application shall be dismissed. The Recitals state that the concepts "clearly unfounded" and "inadmissible" should be determined in accordance with national law.[64]

3.4.2. International Jurisdiction

The ESCP does not contain jurisdiction rules, which means that the ordinary jurisdiction rules of Brussels I apply. The ESCP neither has an exclusive jurisdiction rule for consumers, contrary to Article 6(1) sub d of the European Enforcement Order Regulation (EEO) and Article 6(2) EOP, which contain a rule broader in scope than Article 15 Brussels I.[65] The background probably is that those Regulations concern uncontested claims while the ESCP, in principle, does not, so in this procedure it will be up to the consumer to contest jurisdiction. This, however, does not explain why the definition of "consumer" is broader under those regulations than under the ESCP.

---

62 Recital no. 22 ESCP.

63 See Article 9 ESCP on the taking of evidence.

64 Recital no. 13 ESCP.

65 These include all natural persons, and do not contain the restrictions of Article 15 Brussels I Regulation.

Furthermore, contrary to what is the case under Brussels I, the decision in the ESCP is enforceable throughout the EU, which means that the consumer does not get any protection in the stage of recognition and enforcement.[66] Since small claims litigation mostly involves consumer cases, a similar protective rule for the ESCP would in my opinion have been appropriate.

3.4.3. Conduct of the Procedure

Article 5(1) ESCP provides that the ESCP shall be a written procedure. During the negotiations the right to an oral hearing has been one of the debated issues.[67] The Commission proposal provided that an oral hearing may take place when the court deems it necessary, taking into account the demands of the parties. Article 5 ESCP, however, provides that the court shall hold an oral hearing if it considers this to be necessary or if a party so requests. This request may be refused if it considers that with regard to the circumstances of the case, an oral hearing is obviously not necessary for the fair conduct of the case. The reasons thereto shall be given in writing.

Within 14 days of receiving the properly filled in claim form, a copy of the claim form and possible supporting documents, together with standard answer form C (Annex III), shall be served on the defendant in accordance with Article 13 (Article 5(2). The defendant shall submit his response within 30 days of service by filling in standard answer form C, where appropriate accompanied by any relevant supporting documents, or in any other appropriate way, and returning it to the court (Article 5(3). Within 14 days of receipt of the response from the defendant, the court shall dispatch a copy thereof, together with any relevant supporting documents to the claimant (Article 5(4).[68] The claimant shall have 30 days from service to respond to any counterclaim (Article 5(6).

The language requirements are laid down in Article 6. These rules have received particular attention since the necessary translations may excessively increase the costs of proceedings.[69] The claim form, the response, the counterclaim and response thereto, and any description of relevant supporting documents shall be submitted in the language or one of the

---

66 See Article 35(1) Brussels I Regulation.

67 See also Council of the European Union, 29 November 2005, doc. no. 15054/05, JUSTCIV 221, CODEC 1107.

68 If the defendant claims that the value of a non-monetary claim exceeds EUR 2000, the court shall within 30 days of dispatching the response to the claimant decide whether the claim is within the scope of the ESCP (Article 5(5).

69 See also CORTÉS 2007 (fn. 35), section II.3.

languages of the court. The court may require a translation of documents received not in the language of the proceedings only if the translation appears to be necessary for giving the judgment. Furthermore, the rules of Article 8 of the (new) Service Regulation have been incorporated.[70] A party may refuse to accept a document when it is not in the official language of a) the country or place where service is to be effected or where the document is to be dispatched, or b) in a language which the addressee understands. The court shall inform the other party of a refusal with a view to that party providing a translation of the document.

Other procedural rules are laid down in Article 8-14 ESCP. An oral hearing may be held through video conference or other communication technology if the technical means are available (Article 8). The court shall determine the means of taking evidence and the extent of the evidence necessary for its judgment under the (national) rules applicable to the admissibility of evidence (Article 9). The court may admit the taking of evidence through written statements of witnesses, experts or parties. It may also admit the taking of evidence through video conference or other available technical means. In view of the costs, the court may take expert evidence or oral testimony only if it is necessary for giving the judgment. The court shall use the simplest and least burdensome method of taking evidence. The Recitals state that in the context of an oral hearing and the taking of evidence, the Member States should encourage the use of modern communication technology.[71] This is a fast and cheap way of hearing parties or witnesses, and will therefore promote the aims of the Regulation. As mentioned above, representation by a lawyer or another legal professional shall not be mandatory (Article 10), and practical assistance in filling in the forms should be made available (Article 11). Parties are not required to make any legal assessment of the claim, the court shall inform the parties about procedural questions, and whenever appropriate, the court shall seek to reach a settlement between the parties (Article 12). As to the time limits the court sets, the party concerned shall be informed of the consequences of not complying with these limits (Article 14). The fixed time limits provided for in Articles 4(4), 5(3), (5)6 and 7(1), may be extended in exceptional circumstances, if necessary to safeguard the rights of the parties. If in

---

70 Regulation (EC) No 1393/2007 of the European Parliament and of the Council of 13 November 2007 on the service in the Member States of judicial and extrajudicial documents in civil or commercial matters (service of documents), and repealing Council Regulation (EC) No 1348/2000, O.J. 2007 L 324/79. This Regulation will as of 13 November 2008 replace Service Regulation No 1448/2000.

71 Recital no. 20 ESCP.

exceptional circumstances the court cannot respect the time limits for the court, provided for in Articles 5(2-6) and 7, it shall take the steps required by those provisions as soon as possible.

3.4.4. Conclusion of the Procedure

According to Article 7, within 30 days of receipt of the timely response from the defendant or claimant to the counterclaim the court shall give judgment, or demand further details within a maximum period of 30 days, or take evidence in accordance with Article 9, or summon the parties to an oral hearing to be held within 30 days of the summons. The court shall give judgment either within 30 days of any oral hearing or after having received all information necessary for giving the judgment. If it has not received an answer from the relevant party within the set time limits, it shall give a judgment on the claim or the counterclaim. The Commission proposal provided for a 'final deadline' for the judgment of six months following the registration of the claim form. However, many delegations had doubts on a binding overall limit for the whole procedure besides the time limits for specific procedural phases, and it was therefore deleted.[72] In my opinion, this is regrettable. Though clear time limits per stage of the proceedings are more important, an additional overall limit of six months would have provided a good indication for the parties and guideline for the courts of the maximum duration of the proceedings.

3.5. SERVICE OF DOCUMENTS

In order to reduce costs, the ESCP has an autonomous rule which provides for a simple means of service of documents. Article 13(1) ESCP provides that documents shall be served by postal service attested by acknowledgement of receipt, including the date of receipt. Not all Member States include this simple means of service in their national law, and for these States the ESCP introduces a new way of serving documents in cross-border cases covered by the ESCP. If service in accordance with Article 13(1) is not possible, service may be effected by any of the methods provided for in Articles 13 or 14 EEO. These articles include ten different methods of service of documents, which are relevant in the context of the EEO Regulation as minimum requirements

---

[72] Council of the European Union, 29 November 2005, doc.no. 15054/05, JUSTCIV 221, CODEC 1107.

for the certification of a judgment as European title.[73] These methods are also prescribed under the EOP Regulation (Article 13 and 14 thereof).

3.6. APPEAL AND REVIEW

The ESCP Regulation does not include a uniform rule on appeal. In view of the substantial differences in the Member States on this issue, taking up a uniform rule was regarded undesirable.[74] According to Article 17, Member States shall inform the Commission whether an appeal is available under their procedural law against a judgment given in the ESCP and within what time limit. The Commission shall make that information publicly available. In my view a uniform rule for appeal would have been preferable, in order to promote a standardized procedure.

The Regulation, however, does provide for minimum standards for review of the judgment. Pursuant to Article 18 the defendant shall be entitled to apply for a review before the court with jurisdiction of the Member State where judgment was given where a) the claim form or summons to an oral hearing were served by a method without proof of receipt by him personally as provided for in Article 14 EEO, ánd service was not effected in sufficient time to enable him to arrange for his defence without any fault on his part, or b) the defendant was prevented from objecting to the claim by reason of *force majeure*, or due to extraordinary circumstances without any fault on his part. In both cases the defendant should act promptly. It is not clear what exactly is to be understood by 'extraordinary circumstances'. What is clear is that it is required that the defendant was not able to defend his case without his fault. This rule is intended to guarantee a possibility of review in situations where the defendant was not able to contest the claim.[75] This provision is derived from Article 19 EEO[76] and partly coincides with the provision laid down in Article 20 EOP.[77]

---

73 See for a comprehensive discussion of these methods RAUSCHER 2005 (fn. 19), p. 45 ff.

74 Commission staff working document, Comments on the specific articles of the proposal, COM(2005) 87 final, Article 15.

75 Recital no. 31 ESCP.

76 See on this provision RAUSCHER 2005 (fn. 19), p. 61 ff.

77 Article 19 EOP is broader since it also covers situations where the payment order was clearly wrongly issued (see Article 19(2) EOP. See further section 4.2.

3.7. RECOGNITION AND ENFORCEMENT

The judgment shall be enforceable notwithstanding any possible appeal, and without security required (Article 15). Enforcement in another Member State is regulated by Articles 20-23. These provisions for the most part duplicate the relevant rules of the EEO and EOP Regulations.[78] The judgment given in a Member State in the ESCP shall be recognized and enforced in another Member State without the need for a declaration of enforceability or the possibility of opposing its recognition (Article 20). At the request of one of the parties a certificate concerning a judgment in the ESCP, using standard form D (Annex IV), will be issued. The enforcement shall be governed by the law of the Member State of enforcement, and the judgment shall be enforced under the same conditions as a judgment given in the State of enforcement (Article 21). Other grounds of refusal, including the public policy exception, are excluded.[79] The party seeking enforcement shall produce an authentic copy of the judgment, and a copy of the certificate mentioned in Article 20(2), where necessary with a translation thereof in the language of the Member State or place of enforcement, or into another language that the Member State has indicated to accept. An authorized representative and a postal address in the Member State of enforcement are not necessary.

Enforcement can only be refused, upon application of the person against whom recognition is sought, if the judgment in the ESCP is irreconcilable with an earlier judgment of an EU Member State, or of a third country, provided that it involves the same cause of action and that it was between the same parties, and that it is given by the Member State of enforcement or enforceable in that Member State, provided that the irreconcilability could not have been raised as an objection in the Member State where the judgment in the ESCP was given (Article 22). Where a party has challenged the judgment in the ESCP or where such a challenge is still possible, enforcement proceedings may be limited to protective measures, or be made conditional on the provision of security, or under exceptional circumstances be stayed (Article 23).

---

[78] See Article 20, 21 and 23 EEO and Article 19, 21, 22 and 23 EOP. See on these rules of the EEO: RAUSCHER 2005 (fn. 19), p. 66 ff; on the EOP see KRAMER & SUJECKI (fn. 27), p. 372.

[79] See also the debate regarding the EEO in this context, section 2.2 and fn. 17.

3.8. COSTS

In view of the accessibility of the ESCP the rule on the costs has also been debated. The Commission proposal provided that the unsuccessful party shall bear the costs of the proceedings unless where this would be unfair or unreasonable, and that when the unsuccessful party is a natural person and is not represented by a lawyer, he shall not be obliged to reimburse the lawyer's fee of the other party. This was meant to encourage parties not to employ a lawyer.[80] However, several delegations preferred to apply the principle that the losing party has to pay irrespective of whether he is a natural or legal person.[81] Article 16 ESCP therefore provides that the unsuccessful party shall bear the costs of the proceedings. The court shall, however, not award costs that were unnecessarily incurred or disproportionate to the claim.

As to the costs of the proceedings, the Recitals state that it should be necessary to have regard to the principles of simplicity, speed and proportionality when setting the costs of dealing with a claim under the ESCP.[82] It is appropriate that details of the costs to be charged be made public, and that the means of setting any such costs are transparent.

3.9. EVALUATION

Some comments on specific rules of the ESCP have already been made in the foregoing. The question was raised whether the threshold of EUR 2000, which as a political compromise might be a good solution, will in view of the economic analysis by the EESC be enough to cover a substantial amount of cases, in order to outweigh the costs that are involved.[83] This shall be one of the issues to be taken into account when the operation of the Regulation is reviewed after five years pursuant to Article 28 ESCP, as this provision explicates. Another comment that has been made was that in my opinion a

---

80 See Article 14 Commission proposal; Comments on the specific articles of the proposal, Article 14.

81 Council of the European Union, 21 November 2005, doc.no. 14638/05, JUSTCIV 208, CODEC 1037, 6.

82 Recital no. 7 ESCP.

83 The Extended Impact Assessment made in relation to the proposal (see Commission Staff Working Document, 15 March 2005, SEC(2005)351) showed that the potential impact of the Regulation is considerable, since it might involve 7 million citizens per year and have a "turnover" of at least EUR 8.000.000.000. It was estimated that the abolition of the enforcement procedure will reduce the costs and duration by 20%. In these numbers, however, domestic claims are included. The limitation to cross-border cases limits the impact considerably.

special jurisdiction rule for consumers would have been in place. The consumer friendliness of the ESCP is further reduced by deleting the costs rule of the Commission proposal, stating that when the unsuccessful party is a consumer, he shall not be obliged to reimburse the lawyer's fee of the professional party, in case he was not represented by a lawyer himself. As for the time limits included in the Regulation, it would in my view have been preferable to include an additional time limit of six months for the whole procedure, as the Commission proposal provided.

Another weak point of the Regulation could be that many issues are left to be decided by national procedural law. The course of proceedings, the enforcement as well as the costs might therefore differ considerably per Member State. For example the possibility of appeal is to be determined by national law. This will cause already considerable differences in the level of protection and have an impact on the duration and costs of the procedure. The fact that many issues are to be decided by national law, necessitates a careful implementation of this Regulation by the Member States. The implementation is essential for the success of the ESCP. It is a pity that no explanatory report or practical guide is available in order to facilitate the implementation and operation in practice. The implementation laws and the operation in practice of the ESCP in the various Member States shall be thoroughly evaluated. Article 28 ESCP provides that by 1 January 2014 the Commission shall present a detailed report reviewing the operation of the ESCP. To that end, and in order to ensure that best practice in the EU is duly taken into account and reflects the principles of better legislation, Member States shall provide the Commission with information relating to the cross-border operation of the ESCP.[84]

A last general remark concerns the prospected effectiveness of the ESCP in view of the costs. In practice especially the costs of legal aid and translations appear to be the most important expenses. As to legal aid, it is to be hoped that filling in of the standard forms and the conduct of the proceedings are indeed simple and make support of a lawyer in normal cases unnecessary. Though the standard forms are carefully developed and contain clear instructions, it may still be difficult for the average consumer to fill in these forms.[85] It is important that practical assistance in the Member States is well arranged. Another aim of the ESCP is to reduce the need, and consequently costs, of translations. The claim form and answer form should

84 This shall cover court fees, speed of the procedure, efficiency, ease of use and the internal small claims procedures of the Member States.

85 For example to answer question 4 of the claim form on jurisdiction of the court.

be submitted in the language of the court. It is helpful that forms are available in all official languages of the Member States, so by reading the questions in his own language he knows what the question entails, and can find out which box to tick for the closed questions. But part of the forms consists of open questions. How many consumers will be able to answer these questions in another language? For most (educated) consumers English might, with a little help, still be possible, but how about Polish, Dutch or Greek? Of supporting documents the court may only require translation when this appears to be necessary for giving the judgment. The question is how many courts throughout the EU will be able to analyze for example a contract in other languages than their own language, except maybe for English, or German or French. It must be noted that in most cases a consumer will be able to litigate in his own country,[86] and therefore not encounter language problems, at least not in his communication to the court. A (counter) party may refuse to accept a document if it is not in his official language or a language he understands. It might be that in practice consumers will more often be involved in this procedure as defendant than as claimant and that it especially benefits companies active in the consumer business, such as mail order companies and phone companies.[87]

Nonetheless, the establishment of the ESCP is a step in the right direction to promote access to justice,[88] and to speed up, simplify and reduce costs of small claims litigation, while respecting the principles of a fair trial. It vouches for a careful balance between simple and relatively cheap proceedings on the one hand and the principles of a fair, adversarial procedure on the other hand.[89] Access to the court is facilitated by the use of simple standard forms, the possibility of electronic communication (if available at the court), the practical assistance that should be available at the courts, and the fact that representation by a lawyer is not compulsory. The time limits guarantee, as far as possible, a trial within a reasonable time, as required by Article 6 ECHR. Fairness of the procedure is promoted by the adversarial nature of the proceedings and several procedural checks and

---

86 Pursuant to Article 15-17 Brussels I Regulation.

87 The English small claims procedure is also criticized on this point. See recently LEWIS, The Consumer's Court? Revisiting the Theory of the Small Claims Procedure, *Civil Justice Quarterly (CJQ)* 2006, p. 52 ff.

88 As recognized in Article 6 European Convention on Human Rights. See also ECHR 21 February 1975, no 6289/73, Series A, No 18 (Golder v. United Kingdom). According to ECHR 9 October 1979, no 6289/73, Series A, No 32 (Airey v. Ireland) this also implies effective access to the court. This may entail the provision of legal aid or simplified procedures.

89 See for a more detailed analysis in this regard: KRAMER 2008 (fn. 35), p. 370-373.

balances. In my view the requirements for the service of documents guarantee sufficiently that the defendant has a possibility to defend himself, since in general service is attested by an acknowledgment of receipt. In case service has been effected without proof, and was not effected in sufficient time to enable him to arrange for his defence without his fault, he can request review of the decision.[90] The language requirements guarantee that a party is able to understand the relevant documents. Furthermore, a request for an oral hearing will be granted, unless an oral hearing is obviously not necessary. This is in conformity with the case law of European Court of Human Rights on Article 6 ECHR.[91] Lastly, review of the decision is possible in case the defendant was prevented from objecting the claim by reason of *force majeure*. In my view these elements sufficiently guarantee the right to a fair trial.

Whether the ESCP will become successful in practice of course remains to be seen and will be evaluated after five years. The optional nature of the ESCP leads to multiplicity of procedures, which might as such not be preferable, but it also implies that it will really have to prove its value in competition with the existing national procedures. This may well benefit both national small claims procedures[92] and the ESCP.

4. SOME THOUGHTS ON THE HARMONIZATION OF PROCEDURAL LAW IN EUROPE

4.1. ACCOMPLISHMENTS AND NEW FEATURES OF HARMONIZED EUROPEAN PROCEDURES

The bringing about of European procedures, and in particular the ESCP, is an accomplishment, especially in view of the scepticism that surrounded the harmonization of civil procedure until only recently.[93] Many (political) obstacles had to be removed, legal issues to be decided and practical problems inherent to international litigation to be solved. The text of the ESCP

---

90 According to Article 18 ESCP.

91 In Dory v. Sweden, the Court ruled that a court could, having regard to the demands of efficiency and economy, abstain from holding a hearing if the case could be adequately resolved on the basis of the case-file and the parties' written observations. See ECHR 12 November 2002, no. 28394/95 (Dory v. Sweden), available at <http://www.echr.coe.int/echr/>.

92 In the Netherlands the ESCP has given inspiration for the development of a national small claims procedure. See XANDRA KRAMER, Vereenvoudiging van de geschillenbeslechting in consumentenzaken: de Europese small claims procedure en nationale initiatieven, *Tijdschrift voor Consumentenrecht en Handelspraktijk (TvC)* 2007, p. 111 ff.

93 See also section 1 above.

Regulation is in general well-drafted, and the standard forms are carefully designed.[94] The European procedures are also progressive in the sense that they introduce several new procedural concepts and provide solutions that are not yet common in (all) the Member States and in the existing European instruments.

One of the new features is the use of standard forms to institute proceedings, for the answer of the defendant and for rendering the order or judgment. Most regulations in the field of European procedure also include standard forms, but these have a different nature and purpose.[95] The standard forms of the EOP and ESCP play a crucial – and sometimes exclusive – role in the procedures. Both procedures are (primarily) written procedures, and they are (mostly) to be used by the parties (businesses or consumers), who should be able to fill out the forms without help of a legal professional. The tick box system is implemented as far as possible, and – especially the forms of the ESCP[96] – are in general easy to use. Some Member States, such as the United Kingdom, also make use of standard forms to file (small) claims, but they are not as 'advanced' as the claim forms of the EOP and ESCP and are of course not (especially) equipped for cross-border cases.

Information technology also plays an important role in this regard. The use of information technology is promoted in both regulations.[97] ICT plays a role in the submission of the standard (claim and answer) forms in both the EOP and ESCP, in the examination of the application for a European order for payment (EOP), as well as in the context of oral hearings and the taking of evidence (ESCP).[98] Ideally the whole EOP should be conducted electronically. In the ESCP information technology is mostly supportive to the procedure. The use of ICT is not compulsory, since not all courts are yet sufficiently equipped, but its use should definitely be promoted and the exchange of technological and practical information between the (courts of)

---

94 The EOP contains several flaws, amongst others in the standard forms.

95 E.g. Brussels I has standard forms including a certificate of the judgment or authentic instrument, the EEO Regulation for the certification of the judgment or authentic instrument, the Service Regulation for, amongst others, the request, acknowledgment of receipt, notification and certification of service, and the Evidence Regulation for, amongst others, the request, acknowledgment of receipt, notification and information.

96 The standard forms of the EOP are in my view less well-developed and have several errors and omissions.

97 See amongst others Recitals nos. 11 and 16, as well as Articles 7, 8 and 16 EOP; Recital no. 20, as well as Articles 4, 8 and 9 ESCP.

98 See on the role of ICT in the EOP: BARTOSZ SUJECKI, Initial Steps Towards an Electronic European Order for Payment Procedure, *Computer law review international (Cri)* 2006, p. 111 ff; on the ESCP: CORTÉS 2007 (fn. 35), section II.4.

the Member States should be supported. The use of ICT will further access to justice, simplify proceedings and reduce costs. Furthermore, it reduces language problems inherent to international litigation. Both the EOP and ESCP are in principal conducted in the language of the court, and language therefore remains to be a practical obstacle to international litigation.[99]

Another feature of both the EOP and ESCP is that they are (primarily) conducted in writing. Especially in common law countries an oral hearing is essential in small claims proceedings, and also in several civil law countries oral hearings are of growing importance since it may help both the court and the parties to immediately get to the real issue of the dispute, and it may promote a settlement. In cross-border litigation oral hearings are, however, in general not efficient, since it increases costs and delays proceedings, due to the need for translations, legal aid and travelling. Though in view of the requirements of Article 6 ECHR in general an oral hearing is indicated if parties request so, the European Court also ruled by way of exception that a court could, having regard to the demands of efficiency and economy, abstain from holding a hearing if the case could be adequately resolved on the basis of the case-file and the parties' written observations.[100] The EOP is by definition a written procedure due to its uncontested nature. By simply lodging a statement of opposition, the procedure will be continued according to national law (see Article 17 EOP), including its rules on oral hearings. Under the ESCP a request for an oral hearing will usually be granted, unless an oral hearing is obviously not necessary (see Article 5 ESCP). In view of the low monetary value of the claim, in my view this rule is justified.

The introduction of time limits is another characteristic of the EOP and the ESCP. In most Member States such time limits are not common in civil procedure. In view of the aim to simplify, speed up and reduce costs of the recovery of uncontested debts and the resolution of small claims, these time limits are in my view an important asset. Many cases at the European Court of Human Rights have dealt with the requirement of a trial within a reasonable time, and many EU countries regularly violate this requirement in civil cases. The introduction of time limits in European litigation is therefore an important and daring step. The EOP and ESCP fixes a time limit of 30 days

---

99 See also on language problems ANDRZEJ RYNG, *How to deal with language problems in cross-border litigation in civil matters?*, in: PAULIEN VAN DER GRINTEN, PAUL MEIJKNECHT & FRANS VAN DER VELDEN (ed.) 2005 (fn. 41), p. 5 ff; ASTRID STADLER, *Sprachprobleme im Europäischen Zivilprozessrecht*, in: VAN DER GRINTEN, MEIJKNECHT & VAN DER VELDEN *(ed.)* 2005 (fn. 41), p. 11 ff.

100 ECHR 12 November 2002, no. 28394/95 (Dory v. Sweden), available at <http://www.echr.coe.int/echr/>.

for the completion of the procedure or for certain stages of the procedure. Though the 30 days-period seems to be randomly chosen and may in some cases be rather long, at least it seems to be acceptable as common ground to the Member States and it is consistently used in both the EOP and ESCP.

The last new feature to be discussed at this point is the review mechanism. With some variations this mechanism is to be found in the EEO Regulation, as well as the EOP and ESCP.[101] Several Member States, such as Germany and Austria, already had a similar system of review (in particular in the national order for payment procedure), but in most Member States a similar means of review at the same court that granted the order or judgment is not familiar. Though the review mechanism seems to rely on slightly different grounds in these three instruments, the overall justification seems to be the absence or – in case of the ESCP – possible absence of a possibility of appeal. Review serves as minimum guarantee that certain fundamental rules of procedure, especially. those relating to the right to be heard or the adversarial nature of the proceedings, are respected. In this regard it is important that Article 6 ECHR does not oblige states to create the possibility to lodge an appeal.[102] However, in general proceedings should be fair, and the defendant should be able to defend himself. The possibility of review relates to an ineffective service.[103] In the situations described in the relevant provisions, the defendant was not able to defend himself without any fault on his part or in case of *force majeure*. The EOP, however, is somewhat ambiguous since it also allows review where the order for payment was 'clearly wrongly issued' or in other 'exceptional circumstances'. The Recitals state that the possibility of review should not mean that the defendant is given a second opportunity to oppose the claim.[104] The exact nature and purpose of review is therefore not clear. A further explanation of what 'review' within the context of European procedural law entails, is desirable.

4.2. SOME DIFFICULTIES AND FUNDAMENTAL QUESTIONS

In spite of the accomplishments in the process of the codification and harmonization of European procedural law, the recent developments also

---

101 See Article 19 EEO, Article 20 EOP and Article 18 ESCP. See section 3.6 above on Article 18 ESCP.

102 See ECHR 17 January 1970, Series A, vol. 11 (Delcourt); this decision was repeated in several subsequent cases.

103 See section 3.6 for the ESCP; the EEO regulation is almost the same. See also Article 20, para 1 EOP.

104 Recital no. 25 EOP.

pose difficulties and raise some fundamental questions. Some of the difficulties have already been touched upon in the foregoing sections. These mainly relate to the explanation and implementation of the EOP and ESCP, due to the fact that certain procedural concepts, such as 'review' are not well-developed yet and that procedural law and practice differ substantially per Member State. As has been concluded before, it is a pity that there are no explanatory reports[105] or practical hand guides available (yet) for these new procedures.

Other difficulties follow from the limitations of European harmonization. These limitations primarily result from the principles of subsidiarity and proportionality, as laid down in Article 5 EC Treaty,[106] as well as the (interpretation of) Article 65 EC Treaty.[107] The three main limitations are 1) the limitation to cross-border cases, 2) the optional nature of the European procedures and 3) the 'minimum' harmonization. These limitations also affect future harmonization, such as the European Attachment of Bank Accounts that is currently being prepared.[108]

The limitation to cross-border cases of the European procedures is in conformity with traditional private international law rules in the field of international procedural law. International jurisdiction rules, taking of evidence abroad, service of documents where a defendant is domiciled in another country, and enforcement of a foreign judgment naturally imply a cross-border element. Private international law rules simply do not come into the picture in a purely national case. For the European procedures this limitation is, however, not so self-evident. Community directives that regulate substantive matters, and more recent also instruments that include procedural rules, which are based on Article 95 EC Treaty also apply to national cases. For example the – much criticized – Directive on the enforcement of intellectual property rights[109] contains rules on evidence,

---

105 Explanatory reports used to be provided for the EU-conventions (Brussels Convention and Rome Convention), as is the case for e.g. conventions of the HCCH, but for EU-regulations this is not possible.

106 These indicate that the European Union shall act only if and insofar as the objectives of the proposed action cannot be sufficiently achieved by the Member States and that the content or form of the action shall not exceed what is necessary to achieve the objectives of this treaty.

107 See also section 2.2 and 3.2.

108 See section 2.2 and fn. 29.

109 Directive 2004/48/EC on measures and procedures to ensure the enforcement of intellectual property rights, O.J. L 157/45. See the 'Professor's Letter' (supported by 36 IP Professors): WILLIAM CORNISH *et al.*, Procedures and Remedies for Enforcing IPRs: the European Commission's Proposed Directive, *European Intellectual Property Review (EIPR)* 2003, p. 447 ff.

measures to preserve evidence, provisional and precautionary measures, procedures on the merits and legal costs. This directive had a big impact on (national) procedural law and necessitated substantial amendments of the procedural codes.[110] Why should procedural rules concerning, for example, small claims be limited to cross-border cases? In my view the wording of Article 65 EC Treaty does not allow measures that also apply to purely national disputes, and in the case of the EOP and the ESCP most Member States were not in favour of extending the scope of these procedures.[111] That is a reality we have to deal with in Europe. But nevertheless this issue deserves a fundamental debate that is not limited to a particular instrument or procedure, but that includes all (future) European procedures.[112]

The optional nature of the EOP and ESCP also poses difficulties.[113] If one has a protectionist view regarding (one's own) procedural law, such as the United Kingdom and several other Member States, the optional nature, in combination with the limitation to cross-border cases, of the European procedure seems least 'harmless'.[114] But this so-called 28th regime – or without Denmark 27th regime – has as disadvantages that it makes procedural law scattered and that it leads to multiplicity of procedures. Also the European procedures may remain to be a "*Fremdkörper*", since they do not require incorporation in the national procedural law system.[115] This also results from the choice for a regulation, instead of a directive. A directive has to be implemented in the national procedural law, and will – dependant on what is regulated in the directive and how detailed it is – usually result in more coherent procedural system.

The third limitation related thereto, which (partly) follows from the principles of proportionality and subsidiarity, is the 'minimum' harmonization that characterises the EOP and ESCP. Both the EOP and ESCP

110 In the Netherlands this Directive resulted in the introduction of a whole new Title in the Code of Civil Procedure. See also for example the Green Paper on Damages actions for breach of the EC antitrust rules, COM(2005)672, which also includes important procedural issues.

111 See also section 2.2 and 3.2 above. See for a discussion of Article 65 EC Treaty section 2.1 above.

112 See amongst others on this issue PAUL MEIJKNECHT, Alleen voor grensoverschrijdende gevallen?, in: RENÉ FLACH, *Amice: Rutgers-bundel*, Kluwer 2005, p. 223 ff.

113 Under national law orders for payment and small claims procedures are usually optional as well, but in the case of the EOP and ESCP also national order for payment and small claims procedures remain available, and not only the ordinary procedures.

114 See also PAULIEN VAN DER GRINTEN, Vraagpunten in het Europees procesrecht, *Tijdschrift voor civiele rechtspleging (TCR)* 2007, p. 68.

115 Most Member States will not implement these procedures in their national procedural code, but through separate implementation laws.

are not exhaustive. National law still plays an important role. One example from the ESCP was already mentioned in the previous section; the question whether or not appeal is allowed is to be decided upon national law, provided that review should be possible under certain exceptional circumstances. The reason provided for the absence of a uniform rule on appeal is that the national rules differ too much in this regard. But at the same time, it undermines the uniform application and effectiveness of the ESCP. The regulation of the service of documents is another example of minimum harmonization, especially that of the EOP. A range of more than ten different ways of service of documents is included, which allows Member States to stick to their own (maybe inefficient) system of service of documents, as long as it is in conformity with one of the ways described. The Recitals of the EOP even explicate that harmonization as such is not the aim of this Regulation.[116] This approach is, however, somewhat ambiguous. On the one hand European procedures are established to overcome the problems inherent to cross-border litigation and to guarantee a level playing field, which – according to the Recitals – cannot be accomplished by the individual Member States.[117] But on the other hand these regulations leave so many issues to be decided by national law, that one may question whether they go far enough to indeed guarantee equal standards and how 'European' these procedures really are.

Of course one should keep in mind that the EOP and ESCP are the first European procedures, and a lot of difficulties had to be overcome and compromises had to be made. Nevertheless, the limitations and new concepts in European procedural law necessitate further debate.

5. CONCLUDING REMARKS

In the foregoing the stormy developments in European procedural law have been presented. Since 2000 many regulations in the field of private international law and international procedural law have been established, varying from international jurisdiction and recognition and enforcement, to cross-border service of documents, taking of evidence and insolvency. A landmark is the recent establishment of the first two European procedures, the European Order for Payment Procedure and the European Small Claims Procedure. The ESCP, that is contrary to the EOP an adversarial procedure, has been analyzed more in detail. Contrary to the EOP the ESCP is an adversarial procedure and is in that regard more remarkable and complex

116 Recital no. 10 EOP.
117 Recitals nos. 6-10 EOP and no. 7 ESCP.

than the EOP. Unlike several other regulations – some of which have already been or will be replaced –, both the EOP and ESCP Regulations have been carefully prepared and intensively negotiated. Many legal issues and practical problems have been tackled. A third European procedure, a European bank attachment that enables direct enforcement throughout the EU, is under consideration. Besides the accomplishments and several innovative features of these new European procedures, these also pose some difficulties and fundamental questions, amongst others those relating to the scope of these procedures.

The harmonization of procedural law is conducted in a 'piece meal' manner. This certainly has advantages and a step-by-step approach is probably the only (politically accepted) way to come to a further approximation of procedural laws in Europe. However, a disadvantage is that it endangers the coherence of (European) procedural law. To secure the coherence of European procedural law was also one of the priorities of the Hague Programme of 2004.[118] The ad hoc harmonization lacks coherent underlying concepts and it is not clear how and in what direction European procedural law should be further developed. In the Netherlands recently there have been calls for a more fundamental debate on where European procedural law should be heading.[119] I agree with this and suggest that this debate should be initiated and continued on a European, and when appropriate, on a world wide level.

---

118 See footnote 13.

119 See e.g. PAUL MEIJKNECHT, De moeizame geboorte van het Europees procesrecht, in: PAULIEN VAN DER GRINTEN & TON HEUKELS (ed.), *Crossing borders: essays in European and private international law, nationality law and islamic law in honour of Frans van der Velden*, Deventer 2006, p. 39 ff.; VAN DER GRINTEN 2007 (fn. 114).

PRESUMPTIONS IN DUTCH PRIVATE LAW (19TH AND 20TH CENTURIES) WITHIN A EUROPEAN CONTEXT

C.H. VAN RHEE

1. INTRODUCTION

The topic of presumptions has caused many difficulties and differences of opinion since its first comprehensive scholarly study by Jacopo Menochio (1532-1607) in the early-modern period.[1] The German author Hugo Burckhard (1838-1918), who wrote an interesting study on the subject in the Pandektist tradition of the 19th century, states that this is already the case when one consults 'die älteren, diesen Gegenstand behandelnden Schriftsteller, die ihr Werk beginnen oder endigen mit einem Klagelied über die Schwierigkeit der Materie, mit Anrufung des göttlichen Beistandes in Erkenntniss der menschlichen Schwäche gegenüber der Unermesslichkeit dieses Gebiets' ('the older authors dealing with this subject, who start or finish their work with a lamentation regarding the complicated nature of the matter, invoking God's assistance while recognizing human frailty in respect of the infinity of this matter'). According to Burckhard, some of the older authors were even of the opinion that a study of the topic should be qualified as 'ein unglückliches und nutzloses Unternehmen' ('an unfortunate and pointless enterprise').[2] Even though one may not agree with these authors, one will often think about these words during research into the topic in Dutch civil procedure. It appears that many of the problems that were discussed in earlier centuries still remained unresolved in later centuries. In fact, often the old problems continued to play a role. Even today, when presumptions are not mentioned as a separate, abstractly defined category any more in the Dutch Codes (they were removed as a separate category in 1988),[3] legal literature contains references to specific presumptions and the

---

1 J. MENOCHIUS, *De praesumptionibus, coniecturis, signis et indiciis commentaria* (first edition in two volumes, Venice 1587-1590).

2 H. BURCKHARD, *Die civilistischen Präsumtionen*, Weimar: Landes-Industrie-Comptoir, 1866, 1-2.

3 Law of 3 December 1987, Official Journal Nr. 590.

role they (should) play.[4] In addition, examples of specific presumptions can be found at various places in the Codes, for example in Article 7:610a of the present Dutch Civil Code (presumption as to the existence of a labour contract).

The central theme of my paper is the 19th and 20th century discussion on presumptions in the Netherlands. It will concentrate on two questions: (1) What is a presumption in Dutch private law?, and (2) What types of presumptions can be distinguished? In answering these questions, the Articles 1903, 1952-1953 and 1958-1959 of the former Dutch Civil Code of 1838 (abrogated in 1992) will be discussed. Article 1903 lists various means of proof that are recognized by this Code, including presumptions.[5] Article 1952 contains a definition of presumptions. It makes a distinction between presumptions that are specifically regulated by statute (these will also be called 'legal presumptions'), and presumptions where this is not the case (these will also be called 'judicial presumptions'). Article 1953 further defines presumptions regulated by statute and lists four examples.[6] Article 1958 continues with general rules on presumptions regulated by statute, whereas the final Article 1959 contains rules on presumptions that are not regulated by statute. Articles 1952-1953 and 1958-1959 are to a certain extent based on the French Civil Code of 1804 (Articles 1349, 1350, 1352 and 1353 respectively).

2. WHAT IS A PRESUMPTION IN DUTCH LAW?

As stated above, a definition of presumptions is provided by Article 1952 of the former, 1838 Dutch Civil Code. Translating this Article into English without at the same time interpreting the Article (at least slightly) is impossible. My translation of the first part of the Article runs as follows:

---

4 Some random examples: I. GIESEN, *Bewijs en aansprakelijkheid.* Een rechtsvergelijkend onderzoek naar de bewijslast, de bewijsvoeringslast, het bewijsrisico en de bewijsrisico-omkering in het aansprakelijkheidsrecht, Ph.D. thesis Tilburg, The Hague: BJu, 2001, 64ff; A.J. AKKERMANS, De 'omkeringsregel' bij het bewijs van causaal verband, inaugural lecture, The Hague: *BJu*, 2002, 9ff; C. BOSSE, *Bewijslastverdeling in het Nederlandse en Belgische arbeidsrecht*, Ph.D. thesis Tilburg, Deventer: Kluwer, 2003, 36ff.

5 Although Art. 1903 may give the impression that it contains an exhaustive list of all the available means of proof, most authors and case law recognized means of proof that were not included in this list. E.g. *R. VAN* BONEVAL FAURE, *Het Nederlandsche burgerlijk procesrecht*, Vol. IV.1, Leiden: Brill, 1896, 32.

6 Specific rules regarding one of these examples, i.e. the existence of a judgment having the force of *res iudicata*, are to be found in Arts. 1954-1957; see below, [18-19].

'Presumptions are conclusions of the legislature or the judge as regards an unknown 'matter' ('daadzaak') based on a known 'matter' ('daadzaak'). (...).[7]

Traditionally, presumptions are dealt with under the heading of evidence. The usual explanation is as follows. He who submits a claim to the court needs to prove the facts on which his claim is grounded, at least, as far as these facts are denied by his opponent.[8] In some cases, however, it is not necessary for the claimant to prove the very facts that are being denied. This occurs when the facts on which the claim is based can be presumed on the basis of other facts that can be established or proven by the claimant.[9] In this case presumptions are at work. Since, according to the traditional explanation, presumptions allow the claimant to prove other facts than the very facts on which his claim is based, they are often classified as mediate proof,[10] or artificial proof.[11]

Even though on the basis of the above one might think that presumptions do not pose many difficulties, it appears that this is not at all true: the subject has caused many problems. It has taken a long time to solve even the more obvious questions. This is due to the fact that the 1838 Civil Code is far from clear on this topic.

A first problematic issue is whether or not presumptions can be classified as a means of proof. The conclusion depends, of course, on how one defines means of proof. One definition is that the means of proof are *potentially* all those facts which are perceived by the judge during the legal action. However, due to the fact that in the greater part of the period discussed in

---

7 'Vermoedens zijn gevolgtrekkingen, welke de wet of de regter uit eene bekende tot eene onbekende daadzaak afleidt. (...).'

8 Of course, presumptions may also be at work where the defendant is required to prove certain matters.

9 E.g. *R. VAN* BONEVAL FAURE, *Het Nederlandsche burgerlijk procesrecht*, Vol. IV.2, Leiden: Brill, 1897, 186. *A.* GRÜNEBAUM, 'De verhouding tusschen wettelijke vermoedens en de verdeeling van den bewijslast', *Rechtsgeleerd Magazijn 1905*, 77-104 (89).

10 E.g. *A.* ANEMA, Mr C. Asser's Handleiding tot de beoefening van het Nederlandsch burgerlijk recht (Vol. 5: Van bewijs), 4th ed., Zwolle: Tjeenk Willink, 1940, 287: 'Voor de beoordeling of een bepaalde bewijsvoering tot de vermoedens behoort, stelle men zich enkel de vraag, of het bedoelde bewijs onmiddellijke zekerheid verschaft over *het gestelde feit zelf*, dan wel over *een feit, dat niet is gesteld*, maar alleen met de gestelde feiten in meer of minder eng verband staat.' See also J. EGGENS, Verklaring van het Burgerlijk Wetboek door Mr N.K.F. Land (Vol. 6: Boek IV, Titel I-VI), 2nd ed., Haarlem: De Erven F. Bohn N.V., 1933, 28.

11 E.g. J. EGGENS (n. 10), 202; A. ANEMA (n. 10), 284.

this paper - just as in the preceding period - the law contained many restrictions as regards the manner in which evidentiary facts could be perceived by the judge, these facts are only *potentially* means of proof. They become real means of proof when they are perceived in a certain manner, e.g. by way of witness depositions or specific documents.[12] It has become practice to identify the facts that are perceived in this certain manner with the manner of perceiving these facts. Consequently, the usual approach is to refer to the various authorized manners of perceiving facts as means of proof. As a result, witness depositions may, for example, be classified as a means of proof.

For modern observers, it seems clear that presumptions are not a means of proof. After all, presumptions may determine that a party is *exempted* from proving certain facts; they are not a means of perceiving these facts in a certain manner. This does, however, not mean that the burden of proof is shifted, because the party who wants to have certain facts established by way of presumptions needs to adduce and, when necessary, prove other facts.[13] As regards these other facts, the majority of authors held that these needed to be proven by way of the usual means of proof. The most that can be said about presumptions is that they may alleviate the burden of proof since they allow parties to prove facts other than the ones that are to be presumed. Consequently, the *onus probandi* is not shifted.

In some countries, such as Belgium, even in the 21st century it was still subject to debate whether (judicial) presumptions should or should not be classified as a means of proof.[14] In the Netherlands, the issue was only decisively solved by the legislature in 1988:[15] they could not be classified as such. One of the sources of confusion may have been Article 1316 of the 1804 French Civil Code, an Article that has remained in force in Belgium until today and that was replaced in the Netherlands by Article 1903 of the 1838 Dutch Civil Code. It reads as follows:

---

12 Cf. J. EGGENS (n.10), 26-27.

13 Consequently, Art. 1352 of the 1804 French *Code civil* is mistaken when it states that a (legal) presumption 'dispense de toute preuve celui au profit duquel elle existe'. See also *A. Anema* (n. 10), 296.

14 C. BOSSE (n. 4), 36. The question whether or not presumptions should be regarded as a means of proof was a point of debate in various European countries. For 19th century Germany, see H. BURCKHARD (n. 2), 3-4.

15 See however, before World War II, already A. ANEMA (n. 10), 285: 'De oude leer der vermoedens als afzonderlijk bewijsmiddel heeft vrijwel afgedaan.'

'Les règles qui concernent la preuve littérale, la preuve testimoniale, les présomptions, l'aveu de la partie et le serment, sont expliquées dans les sections suivantes.'

Although the French Article is superfluous since it is only an introduction to what follows, it may give the impression that it is more, i.e. that it contains a list of some or all of the means of proof that are allowed by the Code. The Dutch legislature of 1838 must have thought that in this respect an improvement could be introduced and, consequently, did not copy Article 1316. It introduced Article 1903 in the 1838 Code which makes it clear that what is meant is indeed a list of the means of proof.[16] Unfortunately, the Dutch legislature forgot to remove presumptions from this list, even though the definition of presumptions in Article 1952 indicates that they should not be classified as such. It is significant in this respect that the confusion regarding the classification of presumptions only ended in the Netherlands in 1988, since it was in this year that the Dutch law of civil evidence was modernised and transferred from the former 1838 Civil Code to the Code of Civil Procedure. As stated above, from 1988 presumptions are not mentioned as a separate, abstractly defined category any more in Dutch legislation; Article 1903 was struck from the statute book.

Let us have a closer look at the authors who, before 1988, positively held that presumptions should *not* be classified as a means of proof.[17] Authors who embraced this idea stated that Article 1952 of the 1838 Civil Code proved that

16 Art. 1903 Dutch Civil Code (1838): 'De bewijsmiddelen bestaan in: het schriftelijk bewijs, het bewijs door getuigen, de vermoedens, de bekentenis, den eed. Alles met inachtneming der regelen bij de volgende titels voorgeschreven.'

17 Examples of such authors are E. M. MEIJERS, '*Bijdrage tot de leer van het middellijk bewijs*', in: Verzamelde privaatrechtelijke opstellen, Vol. II, Leiden: Universitaire Pers, 1955, 223; J. EGGENS (n. 10), 28; A. ANEMA (n. 10), 287-288: 'Hieruit blijkt tevens, hoe onjuist de wet doet, door de vermoedens tot een afzonderlijk bewijsmiddel te maken. Vermoedens vloeien voort uit de gewone middelen, waarmee ook het onmiddellijk bewijs wordt geleverd (...).' Also A. ANEMA (n. 10), 285, where it is stated that presumptions are not classified as a means of proof in Germany and Austria. It is interesting to observe that in an early draft of the Dutch Civil Code from 1820, presumptions were not listed as a means of proof (Art. 3311 of the 1820 Draft; see Ontwerp van het Burgerlijk Wetboek voor het Koningrijk der Nederlanden aan de Staten-Generaal aangeboden den 22sten November 1820, 2nd edition, Leiden: J. W. van Leeuwen, 1864; see, however, R. VAN BONEVAL FAURE IV.2 (n. 9), 136). The Dutch Minister of Justice doubted whether presumptions should be classified as a means of proof, at least in 1824-25, when the draft Civil Code was discussed in Parliament (J. J. F. NOORDZIEK, Geschiedenis der beraadslagingen gevoerd in de Tweede Kamer der Staten-Generaal over het ontwerp van Burgerlijk Wetboek (zittingjaar 1824-1825, Vol. II, Bijlagen, bladz. I-XIV, 1-946), The Hague: Martinus Nijhoff, 1878, 636).

a *judicial* presumption was merely the *result* of a *mental activity* of the judge based on one of the 'real' means of proof, for example witness depositions. The fact that Article 1903 expressly classified presumptions themselves as means of proof could not change this situation. The authors emphasized the soundness of their approach by pointing out that the 1838 Dutch legislature had introduced restrictions to the ways in which parties could prove their case by listing the means of proof that were allowed and by laying down specific rules as regards these means of proof. These restrictions were based on the fact that the legislature did not want to leave it completely to the judge's 'intimate conviction' to decide whether or not a case was proven, but wanted him to reach his conclusion only on the basis of specific means of proof (here, the 1838 Dutch legislature was, of course, influenced by the system of legal proof of the *Ancien Régime*).[18] The authors held that if presumptions would have to be classified as separate means of proof, this would allow litigants to prove their case in a way that the legislature had most likely deemed to be unacceptable.[19] For instance, this would allow a party to prove his case by way of a single witness deposition, since this deposition might give rise to a presumption even though Article 1942 of the 1838 Dutch Civil Code specifically stated that a single witness deposition itself was insufficient.[20] If this approach was chosen, the only restriction that would apply could be found in Article 1959 of the 1838 Civil Code, i.e. that presumptions were forbidden in most cases where proof by witnesses was not allowed (for example, where a sum of money of more than 300 guilders was at stake). However, if presumptions would not be classified as a means of proof, but as conclusions based on the 'real' means of proof, to which certain restrictions applied, this problem would not exist.

A prominent Dutch legal author, J. Eggens (1891-1964), claimed that it would, nevertheless, not be a bad idea to classify judicial presumptions as a separate means of proof.[21] In his opinion, such presumptions should be viewed as a manner to escape from the strict rules on evidence regulating the other means of proof, allowing the judge to freely evaluate this evidence. Part of Eggens' explanation was that examples could be found, where presumptions were not based on facts proven by one of the 'real' (in his

---

18 On presumptions and the system of legal proof, see e.g. H. BURCKHARD (n. 2).

19 E.g. E. M. MEIJERS (n. 17), 221 ff. R. VAN BONEVAL FAURE IV.2 (n. 9), 190, who positively classified presumptions as a means of proof, did not see this as a problem where it concerned, e.g., the introduction of *de auditu* witness depositions by way of a presumption.

20 Art. 1942 of the 1838 Dutch Civil Code was abolished in 1988 with the modernization of the law of civil evidence.

21 J. EGGENS (n. 10), 34, 201.

opinion 'other') means of proof, for example, where a presumption was based on a party's refusal to follow the judge's orders. That such examples existed was, in Eggens' opinion, not a surprise since Article 1952 of the 1838 Code did not require that the facts on which presumptions were based should be facts proven by one of these means of proof. As has been noted, the Article only stated that a presumption is a conclusion based on a 'known' matter and not on a 'proven' matter. In Eggens' opinion, this was a possible explanation for the fact that presumptions were often regarded as a 'weak' type of proof.[22] This was not so because presumptions would always result in a situation where some doubt might exist regarding the veracity of what was established on their basis. The contrary could indeed be true, for example in the traditional textbook example of presumptions, where the absence of a person from the place where a deed was signed at the very moment this occurred would prove that this person's signature was false.[23] However, they could be regarded as a weak type of proof due to the fact that they were *in abstracto* 'distrusted' by the legislature because they were not necessarily based on a proven matter.[24] Consequently, according to Eggens, the legislature did not prescribe their probative value beforehand, but gave the judge freedom in what conclusion to reach on their basis.[25] This was different for the other means of proof. Originally, as regards these means of proof the 1838 legislature had strictly defined their probative value. Only as regards witness depositions this had been different. Eggens' conclusion, therefore, was that presumptions formed a separate category of means of proof, i.e. those means of proof which were not given a separate name by the legislature and whose probative value was left to the judge's discretion. This also led to the conclusion that witness depositions, whose probative value was not determined by the Code either, could, strictly speaking, also be considered as presumptions, but due to the fact that the legislature had regulated these means of proof separately and given them a separate name, they did, according to Eggens, not belong to presumptions in the strict sense (they did, however, belong to this category in the wider sense).[26]

Related to the classification of presumptions as a separate means of proof, was the question how judicial presumptions could be distinguished from the other means of proof. We have seen that Article 1952 defines judicial presumptions

---

22 J. EGGENS (n. 10), 33. For a different explanation, see A. ANEMA (n. 10), 286-287.

23 Also E. M. MEIJERS (n. 17), 211-212.

24 See also R. VAN BONEVAL FAURE IV.2 (n.9), 187.

25 J. EGGENS (n. 10), 33, 202. Also E. M. MEIJERS (n. 17), 229.

26 J. EGGENS (n. 10), 33-34.

as 'conclusions' of the judge as regards an unknown matter based on a known matter. According to some authors, this very definition did not set presumptions apart as a separate category, since the definition was also valid for means of proof other than the ones that would usually be classified as presumptions. In actual practice, proving a case always means bringing about conclusions of the judge on the basis of known matters resulting in knowledge about something that was not known before.[27] If witnesses, for example, state that at a certain moment in time they were present when the parties to an action uttered phrases which may be interpreted as the parties concluding a contract (and this is the only thing witnesses can declare; they cannot declare that they have seen the parties conclude a contract because they cannot be sure that the parties were *ad idem*), it is in the end the judge who, on the basis of a process of interpretation of these circumstances or matters, decides whether a contract has come into being and, consequently, whether the existence of a contract between the parties has been proven.[28] One could hold that also in this case an unknown matter (the existence of a contract) has been proven on the basis of the judge's conclusions based on a known or proven matter (the parties uttering certain phrases). However, this way of proving a case is not referred to as proving by way of presumptions. Nevertheless, this case does not differ at all from the standard textbook example of proving a case by way of presumptions, i.e. establishing that the signature at the bottom of a deed is false by way of proving the presence of the person whose signature is at stake at a place different from the one where the deed was signed at the very moment of signing this deed, for example on the basis of witness depositions.[29] Again, it is the judge's conclusion that counts. To phrase it differently, the judge is in both cases doing the same: he is giving 'legal significance' to the 'matters' that he bases his decision on, in both cases witness depositions. The legal significance the judge attaches to the presence of a certain person at a certain place is that the signature must be false, just as the legal significance the judge attaches to the parties uttering certain phrases is that a contract has come into existence. Of course, the usual explanation of the difference between the two cases is that what is proven in the former case is the absence of the person from the place where the deed was signed and only indirectly that the signature is false, whereas it is held that in the latter case the existence of a contract is directly proven. However, on second thoughts the difference is hard to see. In fact, if one approaches the

---

27 See, e.g., E. M. MEIJERS (n. 17), 226-228. Also *R. VAN BONEVAL FAURE* IV.2 (n. 9), 138.

28 J. EGGENS (n. 10), 30-31.

29 It should be noted that some authors questioned this standard textbook example. They felt that this was not a presumption at all. See, e.g., R. VAN BONEVAL FAURE IV.2 (n. 9), 139.

issue of proof from the perspective of giving legal significance to facts, the difference evaporates. In each case the question then is: what legal significance should be given to the facts in question? It can be said that in both cases, one is dealing with mediate proof by way of presumptions since in both cases the proof is based on deductions. A possible way to distinguish these situations is that presumptions are *in abstracto* ultimately (only) based on what usually happens in similar types of cases,[30] whereas the degree of certainty reached by way of the other means of proof may be higher, at least *in abstracto.*

Apart from these issues of classification, differences of opinion existed throughout the 19th and 20th centuries as regards the correct interpretation of Article 1952. According to the influential Leiden law professor R. van Boneval Faure (1826-1909), Article 1952 should be interpreted in the following manner:

'a presumption is the conclusion that a fact that cannot be proven immediately is true, on the basis of a deduction based on another, proven fact. This deduction should be justified by the circumstance that as a result of the existence of the proven fact, the fact that cannot be proven immediately can or must be considered to have taken place.'[31]

This definition has 'translated' the rather vague expression of 'matter' in Article 1952 of the 1838 Civil Code into 'fact', whereas it states positively that the 'known matter/fact' on which the presumption is based should be a proven matter/fact. Additionally, some information is given as regards the relationship between the 'known matter/fact' and the 'unknown matter/fact' ('can or must be considered to have taken place'). Consequently, information has been supplied that is missing in the Article. After all, neither in the Code nor in the Article is anything said on the meaning of 'matter' ('daadzaak') or

---

30 Cf. R. VAN BONEVAL FAURE IV.2 (n. 9), 138, who refers to R.-J. POTHIER, *Traité des obligations* (various editions), Nr. 840: 'Ces conséquences sont fondées sur ce qui arrive communément et ordinairement.' E. M. MEIJERS (n.17), 226-228, tried to save the distinction between presumptions and the 'real' or other means of proof by stating: 'Het eigenaardige van het directe bewijs is dan ook niet hierin gelegen, dat men zijn bewijs niet op een gegeven feit opbouwt, maar *dat dit gegeven feit een mondelinge of schriftelijke verklaring van een persoon is en men uit deze verklaring tot de juistheid van het verklaarde besluit.*'

31 R. VAN BONEVAL FAURE IV.2 (n. 9), 134: 'Een vermoeden is een besluit tot de waarheid van een niet onmiddellijk bewijsbaar feit, bij gevolgtrekking uit een bewezen feit, welke gevolgtrekking wordt gerechtvaardigd doordien, om het bestaan van het bewezen feit, het niet onmiddellijk bewijsbare kan of moet worden aangenomen te hebben plaatsgehad.'

on the necessity of proving the 'known matter', whereas information on the closeness of the relationship between the matter/fact that is known and the matter/fact that is to be presumed (in other words, the degree of certainty or probability that is needed as regards the truth of the knowledge acquired on the basis of the known matter/fact) is absent too (this is not changed by the very cryptic Article 1959 of the Code, which admonishes the judge only to take into consideration presumptions (*lege*: facts)[32] that are sufficiently grave, defined and in accordance with each other).[33]

The lack of clarity in Article 1952 was especially problematic as regards judicial presumptions, since these presumptions were left to the discretion of the judge, who, consequently, could not use statute as a guideline.

As regards the meaning of the word 'matter', the discussion focussed on the question whether the unknown matter that was to be presumed on the basis of a known matter could be a subjective right. This question was linked to the more general discussion on how the existence of a right could be established. Was it necessary to prove the facts which had given rise to the creation of this right – an approach that was popular in Germany at the end of the 19th century and the beginning of the 20th century - or could the existence of such a right also be proven in a different manner, for example by way of facts which could *not* have given rise to the creation of such a right but which could nevertheless give rise to the presumption that such a right existed? Only in the latter case could presumptions be used to directly establish the existence of a right and, in that case, the words 'unknown matter' in Article 1952 should not be interpreted as 'unknown fact' only, but should also include 'unknown right'.[34]

The authors who were of the opinion that rights could be established directly on the basis of presumptions, referred to Articles in the Code which in their opinion could be classified as legal presumptions and which directly resulted in the establishment of a right. An example was Article 681 of the 1838 Civil Code, in which the known matter that a wall separated two properties was taken as giving rise to the presumption of the joint ownership of the wall by

32 Ibid., 136-137.

33 The phrase 'in accordance with each other' in Art. 1959 of the 1838 Civil Code should *not* be understood in the sense that it requires several presumptions to coincide. See J. EGGENS (n. 10), 198-199; R. VAN BONEVAL FAURE IV.2 (n. 9), 136-137, 186, 189.

34 E. M. MEIJERS (n. 17), 213ff; J. EGGENS (n. 10), 31-33.

the owners of those two properties.[35] In addition, one author approached the issue by looking at the history of Article 1952.[36] Since the preparatory works of the 1838 Dutch Civil Code did not contain relevant information, he turned to Article 1349 of the 1804 French Civil Code, on which the Article in the Dutch Code was based. Article 1349 gave the following definition of presumptions:

'Les présomptions sont des conséquences que la loi ou le magistrat tire d'un fait connu à un fait inconnu.' (italics supplied, CHvR)

Evidently, this Article uses the word 'fact' ('fait') where the 1838 Dutch Civil Code uses the word 'matter' ('daadzaak') and, therefore, one could come to the conclusion that establishing the existence of a *right* by way of a presumption was not what the legislature had intended. However, according to this author, one should not attach too much significance to the use of the word 'fact'. He referred to a draft of Article 1349, which reads:

'La présomption est un jugement, que la loi ou le magistrate porte sur la vérité d'une chose, par une conséquence tirée de faits et circonstances et qui est fondée sur ce qui arrive communément et plus ordinairement.'

This draft is based on a definition of R.-J. Pothier (1699-1772), who stated that a presumption should be defined as 'un jugement que la loi ou l'homme porte sur la vérité d'une chose, par une conséquence tirée d'une autre chose', adding that '[c]es conséquences sont fondées sur ce qui arrive communément et ordinairement'.[37] Later, however, a definition was chosen for Article 1349, which to a certain extent followed J. Domat (1625-1696), who stated that presumptions are 'des conséquences qu'on tire d'un fait connu, pour servir à faire connoître la vérité d'un fait incertain, dont on cherche la preuve'.[38] The replacement of the word 'chose' by 'fait' in Article 1349 does not appear to have been a deliberate choice and, consequently, it was held that 'fait' could be read as 'chose'. Consequently, the wording of Article 1349 did not prevent the establishment of a right directly on the basis of a presumption.

---

35 Other authors, however, stated that in this case there was no presumption in the sense of Art. 1952. This case was, according to them, an example where the *onus probandi* was shifted, not where an unknown matter was proven on the basis of a known matter. E.g. R. VAN BONEVAL FAURE IV.2 (n. 9), 150.

36 J. EGGENS (n. 10), 178ff.

37 R.-J. POTHIER (n. 30), Nr. 840.

38 J. DOMAT, Les loix civiles dans leur ordre naturel (various editions), III.VI.IV.1.

The second problematic issue of the above interpretation of Article 1952 was whether indeed presumptions could only be based on *proven* matters. This question is tightly linked to the question whether or not presumptions are a separate means of proof. If the answer would be 'no', and if this would mean that in the case of presumptions only the means of proof that were specifically allowed by the Code could be used, situations could be avoided in which matters could be established by way of presumptions in a manner that most likely was considered to be unacceptable by the legislature. As was noted above, the question whether or not presumptions were a separate means of proof, and, consequently, the question whether or not they should be based on proven facts, was subject to debate.[39]

As we have seen, the interpretation of R. van Boneval Faure also contains some information on the relation between the known matter/fact, and the unknown matter/fact. This issue is especially relevant for judicial presumptions, since these are to a large extent left to the discretion of the judge. The author states that the deduction that is made in the case of presumptions 'should be justified by the circumstance that as a result of the existence of the proven fact, the fact that cannot be proven immediately can or must be considered to have taken place'. Of course, this interpretation does not offer much guidance. The author himself refers to Pothier to clarify his point of view.[40] As we have seen above, Pothier stated that the deduction should be based on what usually happens, or, in the terminology of Cujacius (1522-1590), to whom Pothier refers, 'id quod plerumque fit'. Again one may ask how much guidance is offered by this approach. The legislature must have realized that it was difficult (and maybe impossible) to abstractly describe the relation between the known and the unknown matter and, therefore, the Code only admonishes the judge to be careful where presumptions are at stake (Article 1959).

3. WHICH TYPES OF PRESUMPTION CAN BE DISTINGUISHED IN DUTCH LAW?

In Section 1, an attempt has been made to establish how presumptions were characterised in Dutch civil procedure in the 19th and 20th centuries. It has been shown that differences of opinion existed regarding various important

---

39 An author who held that presumptions were not necessarily based on proven facts is A. GRÜNEBAUM (n. 9), 90.

40 R. VAN BONEVAL FAURE IV.2 (n. 9), 138ff; R.-J. POTHIER (n. 30), Nr. 840.

issues. In the present section, the different types of presumptions that were distinguished will be discussed. Again, many differences of opinion as well as ambiguities may be observed.

In the introduction, it was stated that Article 1952 of the 1838 Civil Code makes a distinction between presumptions that are specifically regulated by statute, and presumptions where this is not the case.[41] In Article 1952, the former type of presumptions are referred to as 'legal presumptions' ('wettelijke vermoedens') and the latter type as 'non-legal presumptions' ('vermoedens welke niet op de wet zelve gegrond zijn'). In the present paper, the latter presumptions are referred to also as 'judicial presumptions'.

Judicial presumptions are not specifically defined in a separate Article in the Code. This was possibly not found to be necessary, since they are sufficiently covered by the general Article 1952 which makes it clear that these presumptions are to be defined as 'conclusions of the judge as regards an unknown matter on the basis of a known matter'. From Article 1959 it appears that these presumptions are left to the judge's discretion.[42] Nevertheless, certain restrictions apply. As we have seen, they could, for example, not be used in cases where proof by way of witnesses was forbidden.[43] In Section 1 of this paper, many of the issues concerning judicial presumptions have been discussed. What has not been discussed in this section are the different names under which judicial presumptions were known in legal literature. In fact, often authors used the terminology from the *ius commune* and referred to these presumptions as *praesumptiones hominis*[44] or *praesumptiones facti*.[45] The name *praesumptiones simplices* was not as popular in the Netherlands as in France, where Pothier had introduced

41 Art. 1952: '(...) Zij (i.e. presumptions) zijn van tweederlei aard: wettelijke, en de zoodanige welke niet op de wet zelve zijn gegrond.'

42 Art. 1959: 'Vermoedens welke niet op de wet zelve gegrond zijn worden overgelaten aan het oordeel en aan de voorzigtigheid van den regter, die echter op geene andere letten mag dan op die welke gewigtig, naauwkeurig, bepaald en met elkander in overeenstemming zijn. Zoodanige vermoedens kunnen alleenlijk in aanmerking komen in de gevallen waarin de wet het bewijs door getuigen toelaat, en ook bijaldien, uit hoofde van kwade trouw of bedrog, tegen eene handeling of akte wordt opgekomen.' Cf. Art. 1353 French *Code civil* (1804): 'Les présomptions qui ne sont point établies par la loi, sont abandonées aux lumière et à la prudence du magistrat, qui ne doit admettre que des présomptions graves, précises et concordantes, et dans les cas seulement où la loi admet les preuves testimoniales, à moins que l'acte ne soit attaqué pour cause de fraude ou de dol.'

43 Art. 1933 Dutch Civil Code (1838).

44 J. VOETIUS, Commentarius ad Pandectas, XXII.3.14.

45 H. BURCKHARD (n. 2), 4.

the French translation of the latter term ('présomptions simples').[46] Sometimes the traditional terminology was criticised. J. Eggens, for example, stated that the terminology *praesumptiones facti* was inadequate since it gave the impression that the unknown matter that was to be presumed could only be a fact and not a right. It is not a surprise that Eggens was critical as regards this terminology, since it was this author who claimed that rights could also be established by way of presumptions. Eggens was of the opinion that the name *praesumptiones facti* could only be justified if one focussed on the activity of the judge giving rise to a judicial presumption, the starting point of which was indeed a (known) fact.[47] However, as stated, the end-result could in his opinion be that a right was held to be established on the basis of this fact.

Let us now turn to legal presumptions. These presumptions were also referred to by their names from the period of the *ius commune*: either *praesumptiones iuris*,[48] or *praesumptiones legis*[49] or, in French, 'présomptions légales'.[50] Although Article 1952 of the 1838 Dutch Code contains a definition of both judicial and legal presumptions, a further definition of legal presumptions is given by Article 1953 of the Code. There we find that they are presumptions, 'which by virtue of a specific legal provision, are linked to certain acts or certain matters'.[51] This definition is not very clear, but from legal literature it appears that these presumptions could best be described as presumptions based on legal provisions that prescribe the particular conclusion the judge must reach when certain facts are established. The conclusion itself is not drawn by the judge, but has been drawn by the legislature.[52] Consequently, the judge does not have any discretion in this respect.[53] His only task is to determine whether the facts on which the presumption is based are sufficiently established. Therefore, legal presumptions can best be viewed as

---

46 R.-J. POTHIER (n. 30), Nr. 849. From Pothier's description of 'présomptions simples' it may, however, be deduced that only a particular type of judicial presumptions could be classified as 'présomptions simples'.

47 J. EGGENS (n. 10), 204-205.

48 J. VOETIUS, *Commentarius ad Pandectas*, XXII.3.15.

49 H. BURCKHARD (n. 2), 4.

50 E.g. Art. 1350 French *Code civil* (1804).

51 Art. 1953: 'Wettelijke vermoedens zijn de zoodanige welke, uit krachte eener bijzondere wetsbepaling, met zekere handelingen of met zekere daadzaken verbonden zijn. (...).' Cf. Art. 1350 French *Code civil* (1804): 'La présomption légale est celle qui est attachée par une loi spéciale à certains actes ou à certains faits. (...).'

52 J. EGGENS (n. 10), 196-197.

53 R. VAN BONEVAL FAURE IV.2 (n. 9), 174; *A. GRÜNEBAUM* (n. 9), 98-99.

legal rules regulating the probative force of a known matter.[54] Their result is that the person in whose favour the legal presumption exists is freed from the obligation to introduce further proof (*not* freed from introducing any proof, as the 1804 French *Code civil* states, since the facts giving rise to the legal presumption need to be established or proven).[55]

A legal presumption that is not mentioned in legislation does not exist. Therefore, it is important that it is clear when a particular legal provision contains a legal presumption. The 19th century legislature, however, did not choose a uniform way of making this clear. At times it seems that no effort at all was made to demonstrate that a legal presumption was at stake, as in the case of Article 1475 of the 1838 Civil Code. This Article states that where a creditor has voluntarily returned the document in which a debt is recorded to the debtor, this 'proves' that the debtor is liberated from the debt.[56] Nevertheless, most authors were of the opinion that this was an example of a legal presumption. As a result of this lack of clarity, part of the discussion of 19th and 20th century authors consisted of an evaluation of which provisions of the various codes dealt with presumptions and which did not. Some help was offered by Article 1953 of the 1838 Dutch Civil Code, which contains a list of examples where legal presumptions are at work.

The examples given in Article 1953 are:

a. Acts that are declared to be void by the law because on the basis of their character it must be presumed that they are performed in order to circumvent the law;
b. Cases in which the law states that (the right of) ownership or the liberation of a debt must be deduced from certain specific circumstances;
c. The significance the law attaches to a judgment having the force of *res iudicata*;
d. The force the law attaches to a confession or an oath of a party.[57]

---

54 J. EGGENS (n. 10), 194.

55 Art. 1958 Dutch Civil Code (1838): 'Een wettelijk vermoeden ontslaat dengenen, in wiens voordeel hetzelve bestaat, van alle verdere bewijzen.' Cf. Art. 1352 Cc: 'La présomption légale dispense de toute preuve celui au profit duquel elle existe.' See R. VAN BONEVAL FAURE IV.2 (n. 9), 170.

56 The Dutch word 'kwijtschelding' in Article 1475 of the 1838 Code should be interpreted as 'liberation' according to, e.g., R. VAN BONEVAL FAURE IV.2 (n. 9), 151-155.

57 Art. 1953: '(...) Van dien aard zijn onder andere:

Example one concerns wills and donations in which the apparent beneficiaries are presumed to be a front for persons who are not allowed to benefit. An example is where, for reasons of safeguarding the rights of children from an earlier marriage, a donation by the husband to a close relative of his wife or by the wife to a close relative of her husband was void because it was presumed to be a forbidden donation of a husband to his wife or vice versa.[58]

As regards the first type of cases mentioned under two, the authors found it difficult to give examples. They referred to Article 214 of the 1838 Civil Code concerning the purchase of immovables and stocks during the marriage of spouses who had opted for a specific marital property regime, the so-called 'gemeenschap van winst en verlies' ('community of profits and losses'); in that case there was a rebuttable legal presumption that the purchased immovables and stocks were to be classified as profits and therefore belonged to the community at the moment the community was terminated.[59] An example of the second type is where the creditor has voluntarily returned the document in which a debt is recorded mentioned above.[60] Examples three and four were deemed to be useless by most authors, since they were said to concern matters other than legal presumptions. According to these authors, example three is mentioned not because a presumption is at stake, but most likely because the drafters of the Code copied Pothier, who in his *Traité des obligations* discussed *res iudicata* directly after the presumptions and who

---

1. De handelingen welke de wet nietig verklaart, omdat zij, door haren aard en hare hoedanigheid alleen, vermoed worden gepleegd te zijn om eene wetsbepaling te ontduiken;
2. De gevallen waarin de wet verklaart dat de eigendom, of de bevrijding van schuld uit zekere bepaalde omstandigheden wordt afgeleid;
3. Het gezag hetwelk de wet aan een regterlijk gewijsde toekent;
4. De kracht welke de wet aan de bekentenis van eene der partijen of aan derzelver eed toekent.'

Art. 1350 French *Code civil* (1804): '(...) tels sont:

1. Les actes que la loi déclare nuls, comme présumés faits en fraude de ses dispositions, d'après leur seule qualité;
2. Les cas dans lesquels la loi déclare la propriété ou la libération résulter de certaines circonstances déterminées;
3. De l'autorité que la loi attribue à la chose jugée;
4. La force que la loi attache à l'aveu de la partie ou à son serment.'

58 Art. 239 Dutch Civil Code (1838); R. van Boneval Faure IV.2 (n. 9), 146-147.

59 Ibid., 148-151.

60 Art. 1475 Dutch Civil Code (1838); R. van Boneval Faure IV.2 (n. 9), 151-155.

needed some kind of introduction to his discussion of this topic.[61] Example four was generally held not to be concerned with presumptions, but with two separate means of proof that should not be classified as presumptions.[62]

Apart from the fact that the legislature was not very successful in giving examples of legal presumptions or referring to legal presumptions in a uniform way, further difficulties were caused by the fact that various provisions of the Code, due to the terminology used, gave the impression that they were dealing with legal presumptions where, on close inspection, this was not the case. A provision the authors referred to was Article 627 of the 1838 Civil Code, which provides that '(the right of) ownership is presumed to be unburdened'. However, this is not a presumption in the sense of Article 1952/1953. After all, the question could be asked from which known matter the legislature could have deduced the unknown matter of the right of ownership not being burdened. It is unlikely that the right of ownership itself could have functioned as such a known matter.[63]

Another example of a provision that gives the impression that it is dealing with legal presumptions in the sense of Articles 1952/1953, where on close inspection this appears not to be the case, is according to various authors Article 589 of the 1838 Civil Code. In this Article it is stated that 'the good faith of a possessor will always be presumed'.[64] In Article 2002 of the same Code, one reads that generally 'good faith is to be presumed'. In these two cases, again, we are not dealing with presumptions in the sense of Articles 1952 and 1953, since a known matter on which the unknown matter (good faith) can be presumed is absent. This known matter can definitely not be someone's possession, whereas other candidates for being the 'known matter' cannot be found.[65]

Generally speaking, the group of cases to which the above two examples belong concerns provisions shifting the *onus probandi* from the person stating

---

61 Ibid., 145-146. See also R. VAN BONEVAL FAURE, Het Nederlandsche burgerlijk procesrecht, Vol. II, Leiden: Brill, 1900, 309ff, and *A. Anema* (n. 10), 293.

62 R. VAN BONEVAL FAURE IV.2 (n. 9), 158-161, and *A. Anema* (n. 10), 295.

63 R. VAN BONEVAL FAURE IV.2 (n. 9), 140-141.

64 Cf. Art. 3:118(3) of the present Dutch Civil Code and I. GIESEN (n. 4), 67.

65 R. VAN BONEVAL FAURE IV.2 (n. 9), 141, 164-166.

a fact to the opposing party; not proving an unknown matter on the basis of a known matter.[66]

In addition to the problems that arose in the determination of the legal presumptions acknowledged in Dutch law, further problems were caused by the traditional distinction between rebuttable and irrebuttable legal presumptions in Article 1958 of the 1838 Civil Code[67] (in the terminology of the *ius commune*: 'praesumptiones iuris tantum' and 'praesumptiones iuris et de iure' respectively). Rebuttable legal presumptions allow the opposing party to prove that what is presumed on their basis is wrong. An example of a rebuttable legal presumption can be found in Article 1430 of the 1838 Dutch Civil Code: the payment of three consecutive instalments of a debt leads to the presumption that the previous instalments have also been paid, at least if the requirements of Article 1430 are met.[68]

Irrebuttable presumptions, on the other hand, do not allow the opposing party to prove that what is presumed on their basis is wrong. According to various authors, these presumptions should, nevertheless, be distinguished from fictions. The difference between fictions and irrebuttable legal presumptions is that in the case of fictions, certain facts are held to exist even though other, known facts do not necessarily make it likely that this is indeed the case. In the case of irrebuttable legal presumptions, however, the known facts make the existence of the unknown matter likely.[69]

---

[66] e.g. R. VAN BONEVAL FAURE IV.2 (n. 9), 141; J.H. POLENAAR, *Mr. B.J. Polenaar's Schets van het Nederlandsche Burgerlijk Procesrecht*, 6th ed., Haarlem: Tjeenk Willink & Zoon, 1925, 179.

[67] Art. 1958: '(..) Geen bewijs wordt tegen een wettelijk vermoeden toegelaten, in geval de wet, op grond van dit vermoeden, zekere bepaalde handelingen nietig verklaard [sic], of den regtsingang weigert; ten zij de wet zelve het tegenbewijs mogt hebben vrijgelaten, en onverminderd hetgeen omtrent den geregtelijken eed en de geregtelijke bekentenis vastgesteld is.' See also Art. 1352 French *Code civil* (1804): '(...) Nulle preuve n'est admise contre la présomption de la loi, lorsque, sur le fondement de cette présomption, elle annulle certains actes ou dénie l'action en justice, à moins qu'elle n'ait réservé la preuve contraire, et sauf ce qui sera dit sur le serment et l'aveu judiciaires.'

[68] A. ANEMA (n. 10), 296.

[69] A. GRÜNEBAUM (n. 9), 102: 'Noodig is echter, dat de *mogelijkheid* van de juistheid der gevolgtrekking bestaat, anders betreedt men het terrein van de *fictie*'; C. BOSSE (n. 4), 40, defines *fictions* as 'vaststellingen die menselijkerwijs niet waar kunnen zijn', whereas P. SCHOLTEN, *Mr. C. Asser's Handleiding tot de beoefening van het Nederlands burgerlijk recht* (Algemeen deel), Zwolle: Tjeenk Willink, 1974, 51, states that they result in 'iets bewust in strijd met de waarheid als feitelijke toestand [aannemen].' See also *A. ANEMA* (n.10), 290, and H. BURCKHARD (n. 2), 28, who states that according to Alciatus the 'Unterschied zwischen

According to Article 1958, a presumption should be classified as irrebuttable where, on the basis of this presumption, statute determines that a legal act is void[70] or where it 'refuses a legal action', unless counter proof is specifically allowed (if counter proof is allowed, the presumption should, accordingly, be classified as rebuttable).[71] The phrase 'where statute refuses a legal action' should, according to the authors, not be taken too literally, but referred to cases where a peremptory exception could successfully be introduced against the claim.[72] In actual practice, it appeared to be very difficult to establish whether or not a legal presumption could be classified as irrebuttable.[73]

Most authors held that irrebuttable presumptions are in actual fact mandatory statutory rules which have nothing to do with presumptions or proof.[74] An example of a legal presumption that was classified as irrebuttable was where statute declared - for reasons of safeguarding the rights of children from an earlier marriage - a donation by the husband to a close relative of his wife or by the wife to a close relative of her husband illegal because it was presumed to be a be a forbidden donation of a husband to his wife or vice versa.[75] In the opinion of most authors, the legislature had unjustly disguised this mandatory statutory rule as a presumption; in their opinion, the legislature should have stated positively that donations of a husband or of a wife to certain relatives of the wife or the husband respectively are illegal: exit presumptions.

4. CONCLUSION

The present contribution has shown that presumptions were a phenomenon in the law of civil procedure that posed considerable problems, both from the perspective of classification and conceptually. It was not clear how

Fiction und Präsumtion, [...] darin gefunden wird, dass diese in veritate fundatur, die Fiction aber legis adversus vertitatem dispositio ist.'

70 According to R. VAN BONEVAL FAURE IV.2 (n. 9), 176-177, Art. 1958 should be read in conjunction with Art. 1953(1): the act is void because it is presumed to be executed in order to evade the law.

71 According to most authors, examples where statute allowed counter proof in cases where, on the basis of a presumption, a legal act was held to be void or a legal action was refused could not be found in the original 1838 Civil Code. See R. VAN BONEVAL FAURE IV.2 (n. 9), 179.

72 Ibid., 177-178; A. ANEMA (n. 10), 296-297.

73 R. VAN BONEVAL FAURE IV.2 (n. 9), 176.

74 e.g. A. ANEMA (n. 10), 288-289; R. VAN BONEVAL FAURE IV.2 (n. 10), 142; A. GRÜNEBAUM (n. 9), 104; E. M. MEIJERS (n. 17), 209-210; J. H. POLENAAR (n. 66), 179: '*wettelijke vermoedens* (...), die echter zoo min vermoedens zijn als bewijsmiddelen, maar bepaalde wettelijke voorschriften van *materieel recht*, of wel regelen, omtrent de *verdeeling van den bewijslast*.'

75 Art. 239 Dutch Civil Code (1838). A. ANEMA, (n. 10), 294-295.

presumptions had to be classified, even if irrebuttable legal presumptions, which according to the majority of authors had nothing to do with presumptions proper, were left apart. Were presumptions to be classified as means of proof, or should they only be seen as conclusions based on means of proof? In addition, there was a conceptual problem since the Dutch Civil Code did not define presumptions very clearly. This became apparent where, for example, the question was asked whether or not a presumption should be based on a proven matter. Also, the meaning of 'matter' itself was subject to debate, especially where it concerned the 'unknown matter'. Did 'matter' mean fact, or could the unknown matter also be a right? In other words, was it possible to establish the existence of a right on the basis of a presumption? And, as regards legal presumptions: they could only exist if they were regulated as such by statute. However, it appeared not to be an easy task to determine whether indeed a legal provision aimed at creating a legal presumption. It was, therefore, not a bad idea of the Dutch legislature to remove presumptions as an abstract category from the statute book in 1988 since the legal rules were defective in many ways. This did, however, not mean that presumptions themselves disappeared from the Dutch legal landscape, as has been shown in this article. Nevertheless, it does not seem that in actual practice the disappearance of the abstract rules regulating presumptions has caused many difficulties in the Netherlands, even though this change in the law means that the judge is left without any statutory guidance in solving the questions that may arise as regards presumptions.

www.ingramcontent.com/pod-product-compliance
Ingram Content Group UK Ltd.
Pitfield, Milton Keynes, MK11 3LW, UK
UKHW051920100926
8556IPUK00021B/1291

9 789050 958608